'This book revolutionised my approach to leadership and cultural change.'
Wayne R. Hale, Chief Operating Officer, Century Aluminium

'I needed this book. I will use it, because I know the material works.'
Don Anderson, Executive Principal, Tagai State College, Queensland

'Don't read this book if you don't have the courage and perseverance to lead change.'
Mark Cutifani, Chief Operating Officer, CVRD-INCO

'I cannot recommend the practical importance of this work more highly to those serious about sustaining an effective executive career.'
Bruce Highfield, founding executive team member,
Virgin Blue Airlines Ltd

'This book guides you on how to develop yourself and others in your organisation to become great leaders.'
Alistair Ross, President, Platinum Operations, Lonmin

'I have seen the principals described in this book in action, I have used them myself and have seen the benefits show up in my own organization.'
Mark Daniel, retired Vice-President (Human Resources) CVRD-Inco

'This book is a must-read for those who want to attain sustainable competitive advantage as the world moves away from industrial relations systems to human relations models.'
David Murray, retired CEO of Commonwealth Bank and Chairman,
Australian Government Future Fund

For Ron Macdonald, a true role model

Systems Leadership

Creating Positive Organisations

IAN MACDONALD, CATHERINE BURKE
and KARL STEWART

GOWER

Published by
Gower Publishing Limited
Wey Court East
UnionRoad
Farnham
Surrey,GU97PT
England

Gower Publishing Company
110 Cherry Street
Suite3-1
Burlington
VT05401-3818
USA

Reprinted 2007, 2012, 2014

Ian Macdonald, Catherine Burke and Karl Stewart have asserted their moral right under the Copyright, Designs and Patents Act, 1988, to be identified as the authors of this work.

British Library Cataloguing in Publication Data
Burke, Catherine
  Systems leadership : creating positive organisations
  1. Leadership 2. Information resources management
  3. Information technology – Management
  I.Title II.Macdonald, Ian III. Stewart, Karl
  658.4'038011

  ISBN-13: 978-0-566-08700-4

Library of Congress Cataloging-in-Publication Data
Macdonald, Ian, 1950-
  Systems leadership : creating positive organizations / by Ian Macdonald, Catherine Burke, and Karl Stewart.
     p. cm.
  Includes bibliographical references and index.
  ISBN-13: 978-0-566-08700-4
  1. Organizational sociology. 2. Organizational effectiveness. 3. Leadership. I. Burke, Catherine G., 1939- II. Stewart, Karl. III. Title.

  HM791.M33 2006
  658.4'092--dc22

                                                                                    2006013671

Printed in the United Kingdom by Henry Ling Limited, at the Dorset Press, Dorchester, DT1 1HD

Contents

CD-Rom: Case Studies

1   The Century Story   *Joe Grimmond*

2   Organising Corporate Computing: A History of the Application of Theory
    Catherine G. Burke and Daniel L. Smith

3   Effective Leadership Programme, Commonwealth Bank of Australia (CBA)
    Geoff McGill

4   Inco Limited Divisional Shops   *Fred Stanford*

5   'A Journey to the Reality of Accountability' Western Cape College:
    The First Three Years   *Derek Hunter*

6   The Return to Work Process at Kaiser Aluminium: A Case Study in the
    Practical Application of System Leadership Modelling   *Phillip Bartlett*

7   The Leadership Programme at Kormilda College
    David Dadswell and Derek Hunter

8   New Zealand Aluminium Smelters Limited   *David Brewer*

9   Building New Mythologies: Countering Negative Views of 'The
    Management' – Organisational Development Strategy in Pacific Coal
    Phillip Bartlett

10 Parish life in the Anglican Diocese of Perth, Western Australia – the
    Bellevue– Darlington Story   *Michael Evers and Philip Biggs*

11 Working Together with Engineers   *Roy Feltham*

12 Weipa Kaolin: Tough Business ... Great Work   *Ken McDonald*

List of Figures

Acknowledgements

This book is the result not only of our own work and more than 30 years of experience; many others have contributed to our ideas. Just after World War II in England, a small group of theorists and managers, led by the late Dr Elliott Jaques, began a concerted effort to bring the discipline of science to the practice of management. They sought to develop explicit theories with hypotheses (predictions) and to test their validity. Wilfred (later Lord) Brown was the managing director of Glacier Metals who collaborated with Jaques in developing the ideas and putting them into practice (see Jaques, 1951; Brown, 1960; Brown and Jaques, 1965; Brown, 1971; Gray, 1976; Jaques, 1976). Together they produced one of the most original and far-reaching theories of organisational structure and design in the 20th century.

In the 1980s this body of knowledge became known as 'stratified systems theory'. In this book the chapters on structure draw on the early work of Jaques and Brown, especially the concepts of work, levels of work and organisational structure. We have, in the light of our experiences, modified their ideas, but their work was seminal to our efforts.

In 1966, Jaques was a founder and first director of the Brunel Institute for Organisational and Social Studies (BIOSS) at Brunel University near London. Dr. Ian Macdonald began working with Jaques at BIOSS in 1973. Dr. Gillian P. Stamp, who became director of BIOSS following Dr. Jaques, has done research on human capability and development that has informed our thinking. Other important research was conducted at Brunel by David Billis, R.O. Gibson, John Isaacs, Richard Joss, Lucy Lofting, B.M. O'Connor, Ralph Rowbottom and many others. A selection of their publications is listed in the Bibliography. This was a very creative time involving many staff at BIOSS contributing to stratified systems theory.

Dr. Jaques further developed his work in the 1980s in collaboration with Sir Roderick Carnegie who was then chairman and chief executive officer of CRA Ltd of Australia (now Rio Tinto). Sir Roderick, and later Jack Brady of CRA Ltd, led the implementation of these structural ideas in their organisation and provided major intellectual and material support as the work progressed. One of the authors, Karl Stewart, had the privilege of working for Sir Roderick and Jack Brady, first as an internal group consultant to CRA from 1983–1986 and later as managing director of Comalco Smelting. While at Comalco Smelting, he had the opportunity to extend the concepts and apply them in practice. It was during this time that many of the theories and models in this book were conceived, developed and implemented, especially those outlined in Parts 1 and 3.

As group consultant, Stewart was given the task of developing a plan to restructure Hamersley Iron (HI) Pty, a large mining complex in Western Australia. He was also to devise a set of theories that would allow the development of systems to underpin the restructuring. These systems were then to be used in other CRA business units. Members of the Hamersley Iron Organisation Development (OD) teams from 1984–1988 made significant contributions to this work. Terry Palmer took over from Stewart to lead the third and fourth HI OD teams. Later he became managing director of Hamersley Iron and then Chief Executive Officer (CEO) of Comalco Ltd. He was a long-time friend and colleague who made major contributions to the work of the authors. Before his untimely death he put these ideas into practice and provided clear evidence of their usefulness in helping a manager to predict behaviour and deliver outcomes.

Ian Macdonald worked with Stewart and Palmer at CRA where they created the 'values model', theories of leadership, behaviour, systems and symbols and the ideas concerning teams and teamwork. Catherine Burke began working with Stewart and Macdonald in 1985 and contributed to the development of these ideas in the United States. She has been able to test these ideas in an academic setting over many years and encourage her students to carry out further research.

John Fielder moved from general manager to department head, to vice president, to senior vice president and then president of Southern California Edison (SCE) during the course of our mutual association. He had the courage and foresight to adopt many of these ideas, bringing them into his organisation, allowing further testing in the US culture that demonstrated the validity and the value of the models. He was especially instrumental in demonstrating by application the value of the theories in a rapidly changing high technology environment of computing and communications. The book that follows began as a training manual for his managers. All the authors, especially Burke, are very grateful for his support.

The original, and crucial, support at SCE came through the efforts of Dr Dan Smith, Manager of Quality and Training in the Information Services Department who brought Burke in as a consultant. They enjoyed a close collaboration for nearly ten years. Other managers at SCE also made important contributions – Lynn Adkins, Bill Bentley, Roxanne Cox-Drake, Don Fellows, Jan Halliwell, Jim Kelly, Robert Ramirez, David Tommela (both at SCE and later at Earthlink.net) and many others who worked on various OD teams over the years at Edison.

Brigadier General Roderick Macdonald of the British Army (and brother to Ian) spent a year on a Defence Fellowship with Burke at the University of Southern California studying leadership processes (Macdonald, R., 1991). While still in the army, he spent significant parts of his leave time working with his brother and Stewart to develop the values model and theories of leadership. Brigadier Macdonald was able to bring the personal experience of combat leadership as a test of the concepts of leadership. Since leaving the British Army he has moved to the US, where he continues to work with us and to apply the theories within an American corporation where he is executive vice president.

In recent years, Ian Macdonald has formed an international association of consultants, Macdonald Associates Consultancy Ltd. All the consultants have contributed to our work. These include the Rev. David Dadswell, Dr Richard Joss, Tony Dunlop, Phillip Bartlett and the Revs Michael Evers and Philip Biggs.

Steve Burke has worked as a consultant with Dr Burke since the early 1990s. He has made significant contributions to our thinking and especially to the systems of performance management. His experience in business beginning as a labourer then a tradesman through the leadership of a large business enterprise has provided us with much practical advice.

Over the years, managers and scholars in Argentina, Australia, Canada, Denmark, Singapore, Sweden and the United States contributed to the development of both theory and practice. We are deeply indebted to all of these people, many of whom we have worked with closely up to the present time. Dr Neils Busch-Jensen, Les Cupper, Kathy Gould, the late Colonel (and Dr) Larry Ingraham, Dr Harry Levinson, Geoff McGill, David Brewer, Dr Carlos Rigby, Mark Woffenden and many other managers and theorists have contributed, perhaps more than they realise. They and other members of the Social Analytic Learning Society, which was active from 1985 through the early 1990s, took time to listen, to argue and to illuminate ideas which would be far less well developed were it not for their hard edged analyses and criticisms.

In addition, we are indebted to the managers and employees of the organisations we have been associated with. The organisations include mines, smelters, city governments, voluntary organisations, churches, indigenous communities, housing associations, colleges, schools, banks, health authorities, the US and British Armies, rolling mills, computing organisations, utilities, an internet service provider, an airline and even a manufacturer of vitamins. They used and commented upon earlier versions of this book. They also gave their time to test, argue, criticise, develop and anguish over the application of the theories in practice. Without their perseverance, often in the face of real anger and frustration, this work would not have been possible.

There are many doctoral students who contributed by testing these ideas through their dissertation research with Dr Burke. Drs Wilsey Bishop, David Boals, Loren Goldman, Donald Gould and Mu Dan Ping have used these theories to study nursing, public libraries, police agencies, university libraries and cross-cultural relationships.[1]

We thank them all. This book represents their thinking as well as our own, though their interpretations and thinking may differ from ours. We hope we have not abused their ideas, and we accept full accountability for any errors, misinterpretations and omissions.

Finally we are especially grateful to David Dadswell and Duncan Harvey, both of Macdonald Associates. They have been invaluable in the preparation and editing of the manuscript. No chapter has been to the publishers without first being 'Dadswelled': quality checked for content and grammar. This has been so helpful because David has been involved in both the development and implementation of these ideas in many companies and countries. Without their help and encouragement this book would have been much more difficult and taken even longer to finish.

---

1   These dissertations are all listed in the Bibliography.

Preface

Today's organisations provide for most of our needs as individuals and as a society. It is largely through our organisations that we take actions today that will influence and shape our future. In the industrialised democracies, the majority of citizens are employed in such organisations. The quality of our lives is dependent on the quality of work that we carry out in organisations, which in turn depends upon the quality of the workforce and its leadership.

The degree and rate of change in technology; global competition; process innovations that tightly link relationships among suppliers, producers and customers; and changing social and political relationships make leadership more complex and difficult.

However, many leaders and commentators see those changes as being driven by technology, or 'markets'. While a great deal of money is poured into new technical processes and their development, the understanding of their impact and dependence upon social processes is underrated. The critical work of people can easily be underestimated.

It is as if we do not see the need to develop such a deep understanding of social process as we do of technical process. We assume that somehow people will cope and that if help is needed in this area there are plenty of short cuts; ideas that in retrospect are fads – a few principles, steps or rules that seem to simplify the most complex problem. When they fail, there are plenty more available.

This book does not offer fads, short cuts or magic. It recognises that leadership is difficult and hard work; that people are complex and have opinions. It recognises that, if an organisation is to be successful, then understanding the social processes is just as important as understanding the technical or commercial processes. People should not be taken for granted; goodwill is not inexhaustible.

If leaders *do not* understand people and how they view the world, they will fail. If they *do* understand people, they have a chance to engage the knowledge and creativity embodied in everyone. Technology can be bought or sold. Two organisations can have the same technology. No two organisations have the same workforce or the same leaders. Having the right people in the right place at the right time is difficult but immensely rewarding for both the organisation and the people in it or doing the right work associated with it.

Many leaders will say 'people are our most important asset'. Yet their behaviour contradicts this every day. Even describing people as an 'asset' or as 'human capital' shows a lack of understanding that people are living beings with a will of their own. This will can be directed to the benefit or detriment of the organisation.

Creating a positive organisation is not easy; even for the more serious leader or student of organisations there are difficulties. What theory, method or model is relevant? One problem is that often concepts are disconnected. There is one theory for structure and another for systems,

---

There are three areas in life where people seem particularly vulnerable to fads and short cuts: dieting, parenting and leadership. We seem to want to hear about a magic, quick and easy solution. If that is your view about leadership, this book is not for you.

yet another for team-building and more for leadership, management, capability, succession planning, building trust, change processes, transformation, process re-engineering and so on.

Leaders have found that too many management 'theories' are not really theories at all. They are presented as magic. They tell you what goes in and what comes out, but you don't know what happens in the 'black box' in the middle.

They make assertions, followed by stories of a few exemplars who have had success. There is no context, no linking of cause and effect – no linking of action to outcome. There is no statement as to how and why it works, nor is there a statement regarding conditions where it will succeed or where it is likely to fail. Too often managers find themselves in the position of the old Indian Chief in the movie *Little Big Man*: when his prediction did not come true, he said, 'Sometimes the magic works and sometimes it doesn't.'

As a consequence members of the organisation just wait for each wave to pass. Contradictions in the 'theories' lead to contradictions in behaviour. The workforce becomes more cynical and Dilbert becomes an international hero.

Micklethwait and Wooldridge (1996: 60) perhaps say it best: '… from the management industry's viewpoint, the beauty of the system [where one management theory rapidly follows on from another] is that none of the formulas work – or at least they do not work completely as the anguished and greedy buyers hope. The result is enormous profits for the gurus but confusion for their clients.' In one organisation that had pursued fad after managerial fad, the managing director said, 'We put a lot of planes in the air; we are very good at take offs, but not very good at landings.'

Such fads also leave behind real fear and anxiety, as well as considerable human wreckage. At the most basic level, managers and workers fear losing their jobs. Managers also find contradictory advice not only frightening, but disorienting. As one recently promoted senior executive, with a highly successful 30-year career, put it, 'I don't know what my job is, and I'm afraid someone will find out.'

Our work suggests he is not alone. The ways we perceive the world, absorb information and turn it into useful knowledge still have much in common with our ancestors. We need safety and security, recognition and esteem. We hope to succeed, but we must live with the fear and insecurity of our imperfections. Working in today's social, political and economic environment takes great courage. It would be helpful to have some sound advice.

Purpose

The purpose of this book is to present a coherent conceptual framework that explains why people behave as they do in organisations. This in turn can guide leaders of such organisations along the path of creating the conditions that encourage genuinely constructive and productive behaviour. In short, this book is about how to build a positive organisation.

To achieve this purpose we present a set of concepts and models that predict what will and will not be effective in organisations regarding leadership, systems, staffing and structures. Rather than providing a set of prefabricated solutions or recipes for success, our purpose is to provide you with tools that help to create more effective leaders and build a positive organisation. Using these tools, managers and leaders have found they can greatly, simultaneously, improve the working lives of people in their organisations and the performance of the organisation as they gain greater understanding of the underlying values and social processes in the world around them and in turn more effectively achieve their purpose.

Overview of the book's content

First, we should point out that this book is not intended to be a complete primer on management. We focus on human social processes and relationships. We do not present a complete picture that would include financial, technical or legal elements of leadership and organisations. These are available in other publications. We do, however, try to show the links to these other important areas of organisational practice.

This book is written to help leaders create conditions that actively encourage people to use their capabilities in achieving constructive goals.

We argue that this is not a matter of applying a few simple rules. It is not easy because elements of an organisation are connected. The structure is influenced by systems and in turn influenced by the capability of people. The quality of leadership, clarity of work and role and the underlying nature of relationships all help to determine how an organisation runs. This is why understanding these relationships requires a coherent, overall, conceptual framework from which a set of tools can be fashioned to help understand and manage these relationships. There is no short cut, no silver bullet. We have found, that for many leaders of organisations understanding this material gives a structure and meaning to experience. It gives 'common sense' a rationale. We have had many good, leaders say to us how these ideas gave form to what they do intuitively and filled in the gaps; helping them understand why some actions worked and others didn't.

This book is about how to build and run a positive and successful organisation. Success is defined as:

* achieving the organisation's purpose;
* providing work to match and challenge the capabilities of employees/members;
* providing appropriate recognition and reward for that work;
* making a positive contribution to the society within which the organisation operates (or a range of societies in the case of multinational and international organisations).

Running a successful organisation over time cannot be done by charismatic leadership alone. There need to be structures and systems that can survive individuals. Therefore this book is organised and written to build from very general statements and propositions about human behaviour to very specific examples of implementation in particular contexts.

Each part of the book builds on the previous part and will not make full sense without understanding the basic propositions made earlier.

In summary

Part 1 explains the basic principles of human behaviour which are relevant to social organisation. It is about how we make sense of the world and how we influence, and are influenced by, others.

Part 2 sets these principles in the context of particular types of organisation and shows how constructive behaviour can be encouraged or distorted. It lays the foundation for effectively organising work and it examines the nature of work and organisations. Students of Jaques will recognise the linkages to his work and the work of his colleagues. We also highlight some significant differences. This part concentrates on the basic purpose and structure of organisations, what is meant by a meritocracy and how that reflects the nature of human capability. These are the basic building blocks, and the foundations.

Part 3, Systems Leadership, builds on this foundation to explain the elements of systems leadership that help the organisation run and live. It puts the flesh and blood on the skeleton of the structure. It is the human component: how leaders build culture, use their authority, build teams and create a living organisation which can act as a positive force within society.

Part 4 turns to the very practical lessons of how to implement and sustain positive changes using the concepts dealt with previously. It clearly states the necessary conditions for success and how they are underpinned by the design and implementation of effective systems. It also highlights the traps and dangers of change programmes and warns against the exploitation of goodwill and the need for consistency of purpose and leadership.

Finally, we have included a range of case studies, real practical examples of the use of the concepts by leaders and some of the expected and unexpected benefits of applying systems leadership. These can be found on the CD-ROM attached to the book.

The theory and managerial practices presented provide analytic tools, a methodology, and logic for good management and leadership practice. They can never, however, take the place of the managerial judgment that is the lifeblood of the organisation.

It is vital that this distinction be understood, as it is the common thread throughout the book. We emphasise the difference between *necessary* and *sufficient* conditions. Too often organisational texts suggest we can create systems that provide *both* the necessary *and* sufficient conditions for success. We believe this is a misguided quest that ends in the creation of organisations and systems that function as straitjackets. When such systems are implemented they lead to frustration and failure. Eventually, if the organisation is to survive, people will simply get round them.

Once again: theories and systems can only provide the *necessary* conditions; the *sufficient* conditions must be provided by human judgment. We will discuss the elements that properly set the limits on managerial judgment while at the same time allowing (and requiring) managers to exercise their judgment. We respect the right and necessity of each manager to make such judgments, and none of our propositions should be seen to conflict with that right and necessity.

Systems Leadership: What Use is Theory?

Relating theory to practice

Each of the authors has heard managers argue that theory is worthless; experience is what counts. Some managers seem to pride themselves on their disdain of theory. These same managers then go on to quote their own views of management, for example, 'it is just common sense', But what is 'common sense' other than an implicit theory?

All capable managers use such implicit theories every day, often with success. When this is done exceptionally well, we refer to the person as a 'charismatic leader'. This always carries a hint of mystery and magic.

On the other hand, some scholars articulate theories, but never put them to the test of practice. These are the 'academic theories' often scorned by many managers. Even where such articulated theories are put to the test, the methods too often reflect a distorted view of science that eliminates human intentions and values, or are so 'experimental' they are unrealistic. See the many journal articles on social organisation that have no impact on real managers. 'It may sound good in theory, but it won't work in practice.' 'We tried that (name your least favourite theory). It was just a waste of time.'

To get things right requires an understanding of the elements and relationships illustrated in Figure I.1.

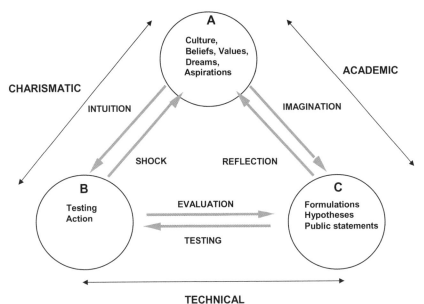

Figure I.1   Human Decision-Making Model

We argue that all human beings have beliefs, values, dreams and aspirations. Any valid theory of human behaviour must take these into account. All managers operate on the left side of the diagram, using cells A and B, some of the time. Their actions are guided by their intuition ('gut feel'). When the result they intended does not occur, the shock forces them back into their beliefs to consider what happened and how they might change their actions to reach their intended goal. Unfortunately, if their theories are implicit and unformulated, they are largely untestable. Therefore it is more difficult to replicate success and to avoid future failures.

Sometimes, it is impossible to articulate to others what we have actually learned. This can become quite serious as one of the authors observed in a meeting with Hewlett-Packard executives in the early 1980s. Both Bill Hewlett and David Packard were long retired, but in this meeting to deal with several difficult issues, the question came up more than once, 'What would Bill and Dave have done?'. Executives recognised these two founders had insights that others were struggling to grasp, but they had not been able (or perhaps even aware of the need) to pass their insights on to their successors.

Academics often get locked into A and C, caught in a loop that never makes contact with the real world. If people are locked into the relationship between B and C, the formulations and the tests are devoid of human meaning and intention. Some of this research may be useful, but it is difficult to apply when the human dimension is omitted, often on the claim of being 'value free'. This leads to tragedy, as when scientists become so disconnected from their human values they are capable of inhuman experiments like those conducted at Auschwitz.

What is required, of course, is that all three elements be used together. This may be better done by a number of people working together. It is not that managers cannot articulate their hypotheses; it is that they are often too busy and time-pressured to take the time to define terms clearly and formulate clear hypotheses. In our experience, such formulations do not come easily or quickly. They require much hard work, and once articulated, they often have to be modified as they are tested in practice.

That is why the authors have found their joint working relationship so productive. We were continuously in touch with all three elements of the model. As you reflect on your work, keep in mind that *all* the elements, A, B and C, are essential.

Language – social and scientific

One difficulty that all writers and practitioners involved in organisational theory and behaviour confront is that unlike physics, chemistry, biology or engineering, there are no terms or concepts with universally accepted definitions. In the sciences, key concepts such as mass, volume, acceleration, DNA, cell, tensile strength and stress are agreed upon, even where there are competing theories. Thus, it is possible to share meaning quite precisely. This is a difficulty that Elliott Jaques[1] was highly aware of and described as a major problem in the field.

To study social processes such as management, two types of meaning need to be introduced. The first is 'scientific' meaning, where an entity or term has an agreed meaning by which we can determine whether an entity is 'one of those' or not. The second type we term 'social' meaning. In our everyday lives we approximate and assume an overlap in understanding without worrying too much if we mean precisely the same thing.

1   We will refer to and discuss Dr Jaques' work with regard to 'organisational behaviour' at various points in this book.

Throughout our life we gradually learn increasingly sophisticated and more abstract discriminating (in the literal sense) categories. Thus, for a small child, all animals might be 'dog', but gradually the set of 'animal' becomes superordinate to dog, cat, cow, kangaroo and so on (see Box I.1).

One of the problems in the field of organisational theory is that language to describe the concepts is often in the domain of social meaning. That is, we have a general understanding of terms such as manager, leader, authority, power, team or organisation, but there may be and often are significant differences. Is a manager also a leader? Is a leader a manager? Can one be a manager if one has no direct reports? Do you have a team if a manager appoints the leader or must a team select its own leader?

In everyday conversations such details usually do not matter. To emphasise such details would appear at best pedantic, at worst bizarre. For example, if friends get together for lunch and one asks another, 'What do you do?', a typical reply might be, 'I am a supervisor at the local plant'. It would be odd, indeed, if the first person then asked, 'So what exactly is the extent of your authority; how does it differ from that of a manager?' (although Karl Stewart, one of the authors, might do so).

In the workplace, however, such issues of authority are of utmost importance, especially to the worker who may be asked to carry out a task. He or she needs to know if this person has the authority to tell him or her what to do, and within what limits. These are significant issues for both the worker and the supervisor, issues that may change the response of the worker to the supervisor's direction. When trying to implement a new way of working, social meaning can cause considerable confusion.

The practical value of good theory

A good theory uses defined terms and specifies the relationships between and among them so that clear formulations can be made and tested. So often in books and journals we see terms undefined. Jaques often asked people to write down the definition of a manager. It is an interesting task. Critical terms such as 'leader', 'culture', 'authority', even 'work' are just not defined but simply used, assuming a shared definition. Like Humpty Dumpty in *Alice in Wonderland*, words can mean what we want them to mean and so misunderstanding is 'your fault'. Terms then get recycled to sell 'new' ideas: 'change' becomes 'transformation', 'detail' becomes 'granular', 'redundancy' becomes 'down-sizing' or 'right-sizing'. For an excellent treatise on this point see Don Watson's *Weasel Words* (2004).

We have confusing terms such as 'self-directed teams' and 'team pay'. Do such teams have no manager or leader? Do they all get the same pay? We have found that asking these questions is often regarded as pedantic.

Michael Armstrong, in *Rewarding Teams* (2000), asserts 'There is no secret to success. It is never wise, it is never fair, it is never safe to generalise about team based pay.' If this is the

---

Box I.1   Social and Scientific Meanings

Social meaning: A term which is assumed to have similarity for the purpose of social interaction: 'you know what I mean?'.

Scientific meaning: A precisely defined term with deliberately clear boundaries for the purpose of testing hypotheses: 'this is what I mean'.

case, then it raises questions about the quality of the underlying theory, or the lack thereof. To be valid, a theory must explain all the activity in the field it covers and allow users of the theory to predict outcomes under varying conditions. Clearly the current theories about team pay fail this test.

Professionals in other fields are not so reluctant to be specific about, for example, the effect of smoking on the lungs, stress on a bridge, aerodynamic properties required to keep a plane in the sky, or the temperature in a reduction cell needed to produce aluminium. It is important to note, however, that all these propositions depend absolutely upon a base of shared definitions of entities and the clear description of properties, relationships and constraints. In turn such definitions and descriptions allow clear understanding of the relationships (or processes) that apply in given circumstances and allow prediction of the effects of changing the parameters or constraints of those processes.

Without clear concepts, generalisations are largely meaningless. For example, what can we say about 'flatter organisations' or 'performance-based pay?' Many argue that organisations need to be more 'flexible', able to 'respond more quickly', or should be 'constantly re-organizing', 'organic', 'fostering chaos', 'changing the culture' and so on. What do these phrases mean in the social context, never mind the scientific context? They may generate the illusion of both meaning and significance but have little substance in reality.

While there is no argument in technical fields regarding the need for theory, definition and clear articulation of process, organisational behaviour and design fields remain theory deficient. Indeed, in these fields ideas and concepts are widely criticised for being too academic if they are specific. Worse, ideas and concepts are considered 'out of date' or 'at the end of their shelf life', as new fads replace the old. The implication is that an organisational theory is allowed only a specific amount of time, regardless of its content. While this constant turnover of ideas is lucrative for consultants and opens the field for publication by academics, it does not further our understanding of organisations and management. Such turnover is a positive hindrance to the advancement of knowledge.

In the absence of real knowledge and testable theory, there seems to be a tacit assumption held by many that in leadership and management we cannot do a lot better than we are doing now, though many would like to. Better or worse leadership remains somewhat mysterious, even though recognised examples of both abound. We believe and argue in this book that leadership and management *can* be understood, that significant improvement is possible, and that the methods of implementation and the outcome can be predicted accurately from theory. As you can undoubtedly recognise, even with a good theory, good management is often not easy to put into practice; positive organisations do not grow by default.

Buckminster Fuller (1969) noted that if we find ourselves on a sinking ocean liner and a piano lid floats by, we can use it as a lifeboat. On the other hand, were we to design a lifeboat, we would not create a piano lid. Too often in organisations we are operating with piano lids; what we need is better understanding of leadership processes, systems and organisational design so we can create more effective organisations to meet human, organisational and societal needs.

People and science

There is a long, traditional argument about whether or what scientific method is valid for studying people. Science deals with things we can observe, either directly or with the aid of various instruments. People, on the other hand, have intentions: purposes that cannot be observed but can only be revealed in the course of dialogue with others. We may never see them and we may not even be aware of them. People may or may not choose to reveal their actual intentions to an outside observer. Further, people have opinions about being observed, and this may influence their behaviour.

When we observe human behaviour, we interpret what we see in order to provide meaning for ourselves. This may or may not accurately reflect the meaning or intent of the person being observed. As we will discuss in later chapters, we make such interpretations all the time. Those who become good at observing social processes often make what appear to be quite accurate interpretations. Nonetheless, developing a scientific base for interpreting social phenomena remains difficult.

We grow up learning how to predict behaviour and our environment. We learn to read our mother's behaviour first, and over time we evolve internal 'theories' that we may term rules of thumb, hypotheses or prejudices concerning why people behave as they do. We use these theories to order our own behaviour so it, in turn, produces the outcome we desire. Sometimes we are right, thus confirming our theories; sometimes we are wrong. When we are wrong, we must decide whether our failure to predict is because our theory is wrong or, if it is accurate, the event was a special case.

Thus, we develop our own ideas about human behaviour. Consequently, propositions such as are made about organisations, which are essentially about human behaviour, compete with our own – usually implicit – theories. This is very different from theoretical propositions in the natural sciences.

We don't have to grow up developing theories about aeronautical engineering, physics or chemistry. We can get by in life without having theories about smelting, open-heart surgery or nuclear physics. We *cannot* get by without theories (or at least working models) about human behaviour. We must have these predictive theories even if implicit, internalised and built on experience. If we didn't we would not be able to predict either how others will react to us, or how we might respond to others. This is why autism is so debilitating. People with autism find it very difficult to create accurate models and theories about others.

Developing a common language

The scientist Antoine-Laurent de Lavoisier developed the language of chemistry in the early 18th century, and it was only after his publication of a standard vocabulary that the science of chemistry began its rapid development. His statement of the importance of language to the development of knowledge applies as much today as in his own time:

> We cannot improve the language of any science without at the same time improving the science itself; neither can we, on the other hand, improve a science, without improving the language or nomenclature which belongs to it. However certain the facts of any science may be, and, however just the ideas we may have formed of these facts, we can only communicate false impressions to others, while we want words by which these may be properly expressed. (Lavoisier, 1789 in Bolles, 1997: 380)

In this book we provide a language for developing, discussing, thinking and working with propositions about organisations and management. Of necessity we use words that have a common social meaning, but we have defined them carefully for our purpose so that those who use them can have shared definitions. This does not mean that other definitions are wrong; they are simply less useful for our purpose, which is to advance knowledge in the fields of leadership and organisation. This will continue to be a contentious area until there is an acceptance that we need universal definitions in this field.

In part because there are alternative definitions, the specific language requires mental discipline to understand and apply. Initially, neither the shared definitions nor the methods are easy to learn, and as instructors we have found in using this material that the insistence on 'correct' language is at first regarded as being pedantic. As they apply these ideas in the work setting, however, most people come to understand the value of a clear language to communicate organisational issues. This language allows you to ask questions and to think through answers, all with the discipline of shared definitions upon which the formation of testable propositions is dependent.

A number of the concepts we use were developed by Elliott Jaques and colleagues as the basis for stratified systems theory (Jaques, 1976; 1989). These concepts led him to a theory of organisational structure. Using (and in some cases modifying) the concepts as well as expanding on this theory, managers and researchers have developed a number of definitions of organisation and management terms that are far more precise than everyday social language.

These precise definitions are emphasised to facilitate communication within an organisation and among students of management and organisational theory. Their precision also allows managers to make fine discriminations among phenomena that are often viewed as similar. Such fine discriminations make it far easier to detect error and correct problems early, as well as spotting and seizing opportunities. Peter Senge (1990) noted, 'The ability to learn faster than your competitors may be the only sustainable competitive advantage.' As we have argued and as Lavoisier demonstrated, it is impossible to learn in the absence of clear, shared terms and concepts.

We provide such terms and concepts, but members of the organisation will need to learn this language, or create a language of equal or greater precision, if they are to gain the advantages of clarity and accuracy in communication and analysis.

Caveat: The theories presented may appear to be simple, even simplistic, on first encounter. This apparent simplicity is, however, deceptive. As one gains experience with these ideas, the surface simplicity gives way to a deeper complexity. We believe, and many managers have confirmed, that this makes the theories more powerful for practising managers who must deal with complexity in human relations, new technologies and rapidly changing organisational environments. It also makes it more difficult to learn the concepts and become proficient in their use, but we will not insult your intelligence by pretending things are simple when they are not. As one of our clients remarked during a workshop, 'This is hardly rocket science', a comment came back, 'no, it's much more difficult'.

None of what we say replaces one critical factor: the decision making of leaders. With all the advice in the world, a decision must still be made by someone with appropriate authority. It is not helpful to blame advisers for decisions. They are accountable for the quality of their advice. Any advice, including military intelligence, is just that. It does not absolve the person with executive authority for their poor judgment.

As such, the authors respect executive authority. We do not tell you what decision to make but rather present some tools to help you consider, analyse and predict the consequences of your decisions. We offer guidance in the form of principles, concepts and tools that will improve the systems and leadership of any organisation.

> **Box I.2   A Note on Managers and Leaders**
>
> There is considerable confusion in the literature regarding the concepts of 'manager' and 'leader'. Often 'leader' is used as a positive term suggesting vision and charisma, while 'manager' is used in a slightly denigrating way indicating someone who is concerned only with efficiency or the stewarding of material resources.
>
> We believe, with Drucker (1954: 9), that 'management is the specific and distinguishing organ of any and all organisations'. We define a manager as a person who is 'accountable for their own work and the work performance of people reporting to them over time' (see Chapter 12). Using this definition, all managers are leaders of people; they have no choice. Their only choice is whether to be a good or bad *leader*. In this we again agree with Drucker, 'one does not "manage" people. The task is to lead people. And the goal is to make productive the specific strengths and knowledge of each individual' (1954: 21, 22).

There is no magic here and we use very few metaphors or analogies such as 'Who moved my cheese' (Johnson, J., 1998). Used correctly, metaphor and analogy can be helpful. For example, there is a famous story of the scientist Kekule who in 1865 dreamt of a snake whirling in space biting its tail. This led him to the discovery of the cyclic formula of the benzene ring, a linchpin in the study of carbon chemistry. Used badly, metaphor and analogy can become an impediment to the development of knowledge. They become a justification for poorly formulated, half-baked ideas – in short, for stories masquerading as science (Church, 1999).

Our intent is to move beyond magic, metaphor and analogy. We seek to take the next step in the growth of knowledge – to define terms clearly, to state organisational relationships as hypotheses to be tested, to predict outcomes, and explain why particular outcomes do or do not occur. In other words, we are trying to move toward the sort of science described by Karl Popper (Munz, 1985).

Effective leaders must have clear statements of relationships that link action to outcome so they may test and learn from their actions. Without this it is difficult to know how to replicate success or avoid repeating failure.

Leaders also need a language that allows them to discuss their management and leadership process with accuracy and precision. As we have argued, we take this language facility for granted in the hard sciences. A legal or commercial document begins with a glossary of terms, yet the field of management is a linguistic free-for-all. It is impossible to pass on what one has learned if it cannot be articulated clearly. We may also communicate false impressions to others if we do not have a common language to express our observations and ideas. However as a leader it is not enough to know it, or say it. You must be able to *do* it, consistently and in real time.

Human beings are not machines. Each of the authors has had the satisfaction of seeing people prosper when provided with the right leadership, organisational role, authorities and systems. Some members of Karl Stewart's workforce even testified in court about the improved quality of their working lives. (See Parts 3 and 4 and the Comalco/Rio Tinto case studies.)

We also recognise the high value people place on organisations, not only in order to accomplish personal goals and earn a living, but also to provide a means to use their capabilities to achieve larger social purposes. Ian Macdonald (1990) has shown how we develop our very identity through our work. Work is our connection to the world and reality. David Whyte (2001: 5) states, '... the consummation of work lies not only in what we have done, but who we have become while accomplishing the task.' On the cover of his book, Whyte notes, 'Work is an opportunity for discovering and shaping the place where the self meets the world.' 'Work is difficulty and drama, a high-stakes game in which our identity, our esteem, and our ability to provide are mixed inside of us in volatile, sometimes explosive ways' (Whyte, 2001: 11).

The Gallup Organization recently conducted a poll of 1000 workers in the US. They found 19 per cent of them 'actively disengaged' from their work. Active disengagement meant they did not know what is expected of them; they did not have the materials to do their jobs; and they could not get the attention of their bosses. Gallup said 'actively disengaged workers, based on their numbers, salaries and productivity cost anywhere from $292 billion to $355 billion a year', and that 'Disengagement varied from unit to unit within the companies, suggesting individual managers are a big variable' (*Wall Street Journal*, 2001: A1).

While the business outcomes are essential if the organisation is to survive, we agree with Elliott Jaques who wrote, '... the efficiency of one or other form of organisation cannot be assessed merely in terms of economic or material outcomes; it must be considered in the fullness of its impact on human feelings, on community, and on social relationships and the quality of life in society' (Jaques, 1976: 15). The concepts we set forth in this book, we believe, fully take into account both the needs of the organisation and the needs of the human beings associated with it.

We have used these ideas ourselves in business and consulting practices. The results have been satisfying indeed and have been sustained over a number of years. One manager in a large utility referred to this material as 'the stuff that really works'.

This book is about leadership that can liberate people and organisations from stultifying systems and structures. It is about eliminating the waste caused by unclear objectives and arbitrary use of power, and reducing the wasteful levels of activity and effort found in the 'disorganised' organisation. The human and material costs of bad organisation are a disgrace to an enlightened society.

1 *Principles of Behaviour*

1 *Principles of Behaviour*

Systems leadership is essentially about how to create, improve and sustain successful organisations. This is a social process. While we do not underestimate the critical issues in creating commercial and technically viable organisations, even these are built on the social process of human relationships.

There are qualities and principles in human relationships that are not limited to work organisations but are relevant to all relationships. Although human beings are adaptable, they are not chameleons. We do not completely transform as we move from one relationship, say work; to another, say family. Of course there are important and significant differences but there are also similarities. Indeed, the ability to transform totally and be a completely different person in different situations is regarded as socio- or psychopathic.

Part 1 of this book proposes a set of general principles about human behaviour relevant to all relationships including work organisations. Like the outer layers of an onion, these principles form the context that surrounds the more specific relationships we have found in organisations. If we do not understand these general principles, then the deeper meaning of specific relationships will be hidden. Behaviour will seem either more mystical or technical than it should, and the ability to change our own behaviour and to influence others' behaviour will be diminished.

In this section we look at how we try to order our social environment, make sense of it, and make decisions about whom we can or want to associate with. We look at how and why we try to change our own and/or other peoples' behaviour. All of these principles apply in an organisation, but we explain in Part 1 how they apply more generally as well. As we move into the book, we gradually move the focus from the general to the specific. If we started with the detail, we would lose the sense and depth of structure underlying these relations and end up with a more shallow and probably descriptive account rather than a set of propositions that allow us to understand and predict more effectively.

We have outlined this first in the form of nine core principles. Some might think this is sufficient for a book, but this is not a simple book and the nine core principles are merely the foundation on which systems leadership is built.

Principle 1: People are not machines

This 'common sense' statement is nevertheless central to understanding change processes. It is one that, despite its appearing obvious, is easily forgotten.

Change processes are often described as 'organisational change', 'culture change', 're-engineering'. We look for 'efficiency improvement', 'performance enhancement' and 'productivity gains'. What all of these have in common is that people have to change their behaviour. Without behavioural change there can be no improvement. Thus all change processes, whether technically or commercially driven, depend upon people doing things differently. Therefore any discussion of organisational change needs to address how behaviour is influenced. Anyone who wants to bring about organisational change therefore needs to consider their assumptions about behaviour and how and why it changes.

This does not mean that everyone or even those leading an organisation has to be a professional psychologist. What follows are some core principles about behaviour that may well have significant impact on the success or otherwise of any social process.

Many change processes are initially driven by technological change, the availability of equipment, resources and materials that can potentially lead to improvement in effectiveness and efficiency. This should not obscure the essential social process (see Box 1.1).

PERSON–OBJECT

In the relationship shown in Figure 1.1, we do not have to worry about the object's will or intent. What matters is the person's will. The object will react to any action on it in a predictable way, according to the laws of physics. Thus if I throw a cup on the floor and it breaks, it will break according to the force applied to it, the hardness of the floor, the angle that it hits the floor, and so on, and will depend on what the cup is made of. In this process I do not have to worry about what the cup 'thinks' about being thrown to the floor. It will not 'try' to break neither will it 'try not' to break. It will not consider my intent as cruel or unjustified or reasonable. Neither does it have any notion of its own value or the value I attribute to it. Thus I can experiment quite freely on physical objects and entities.

Figure 1.1   Person–Object Relationship

PERSON–PERSON

Look at Figure 1.2. You can see that when it comes to my action on people there are (at least) two wills operating. If I try to throw a person, say, Mary, on the floor, she will certainly have a view about it. The context as well as intent will influence behaviour. For example, is Mary a wrestling partner or a complete stranger? Mary will presumably 'try not to break'. She will try to make sense of my behaviour. Why did I do that? Was it accidental? Was it typical? If I announce my intent, that will also influence the event, unlike the relationship with the cup, which will behave no differently whatever 'warning' I give it. Further, this event will not end at impact. Mary will try to make sense of what happened after the event, which in turn will

---

Box 1.1   Different Types of Relationships

In our relationship with the world there are basically two fundamentally different types of relationship. The first is our relationship with other people; the second is our relationship with objects.

For an in-depth analysis and discussion of these relationships and their differences, see D.J. Isaac and B.M. O'Connor, 'A Discontinuity Theory of Psychological Development' in *Levels of Abstraction in Logic and Human Action* (1978), ed. E. Jaques, Heinemann Educational Books.

Figure 1.2   Person–Person Relationship

influence future relationships. Mary, just like any other person, also has a sense of both her own personal value and a judgment about how I value her.

The distinction between people and object relations may seem very simple and obvious. However, despite this simplicity we all sometimes muddle them up. The authors have heard leaders describe people as 'units' (of labour) or numbers. In one organisation workers had their employment number instead of their names on their overalls 'so as to make their laundry easier'! We hear about 'cost reduction' and 'efficiency improvement', meaning that people will lose their employment. The phrases used to describe change often do not mention people specifically, for example, 'cultural change'. We have all heard discussions that assume that people have no will or that their will is a nuisance. All the while the leadership extols 'vision' and 'mission' statements about the apparent value of people, customers and being the 'chosen supplier, employer'. Planning the change process can reduce people to statistical events. Treating people in this way may not even be deliberate but it has the effect of objectification. It can be comforting for the leadership to assume the people–object relationship because it gives the illusion that people can be controlled. We can control objects; we can only influence people. Treating people as objects breeds cynicism and malicious compliance. If your workforce is cynical, examine how high-level discussions, the current language used and the systems reduce people to objects.

Of course we can also get confused the other way round. We sometimes behave towards objects as if they did have will and intent. We plead with a car to start, curse a computer for crashing. We try to persuade machines to keep going, encourage them to work faster or stop. What do we think we are doing at such times? We have projected the qualities of people (at least will) onto the object. If we can do this, we have a chance of persuading the printer to work. Every now and then such 'persuasion' coincides with a 'restart' of the machine. This only encourages us to continue with the illusion that objects are temperamental and have human qualities.

While it may be amusing to reflect on our own or others' attempts to persuade objects to act reasonably, it is less amusing to reflect on people being treated as objects. In extreme form this constitutes oppression and abuse. The irony is that attempts to control people completely are essentially self-defeating. Not only is there a question of morality but the energy required to maintain such a controlling regime will not, over time, produce an efficient outcome since by definition it stifles initiative, creativity and enthusiasm. The energy put into control will exceed the energy produced from the 'controlled' person or group (this occurred, for example, in pre-1989 Eastern European economies). Confusion between people and objects often occurs without deliberate intent, for example, when introducing a new IT business-wide system, or during technological production process improvement. The discussion often focuses on the benefits of the new 'objects' while the role of people who must implement, run and improve these systems are effectively ignored or discounted. The case for the change may be judged to be obvious, in terms of rational, economic argument, so we expect people to comply. If people based all their behaviour on purely objective logic why would anyone smoke, not wear safety equipment or drive too fast?

Certainly many projects are started or relationships entered into without due consideration to people's views or without articulating the hypothesised answers to these three questions.

If we really can be disciplined about not treating people as machines or objects then we can try to understand how people view the world. We need to understand not only what 'the organisation' needs, but what people need and what they value. Only then can we be really effective in introducing change and begin building a positive organisation (see Box 1.2).

Principle 2: People need to be able to predict their environments

Most of the time all of us are in environments that are relatively familiar, and at such times we are not aware of how we are scanning the environment and testing it against our expectations. We often only become aware of this process when there is an exception or surprise. We can underestimate how important it is to predict and monitor precisely because we are not fully conscious of doing so. Indeed, if we were fully conscious of the process all the time, we could not easily concentrate on the task at hand. Whenever we see or experience an unusual event or failure of prediction, we cannot ignore it. We cannot simply note an exception; we must explain it, so that we do not get surprised again.

For example, a work colleague who is usually friendly and courteous cuts us short. Why? We must have an explanation and if we can't find one we will invent one. We are very inventive. So our colleague may be (a) very busy, (b) upset, (c) angry at a work related task or (d) some other reason. Most people are primarily concerned to discover 'is it anything I have said or done?'. We need to know what reactions we provoke by our own behaviour or the world becomes a relatively chaotic and potentially threatening place. Some explanations may mean that we do not have to change our predictive model: 'His mother has recently died'. Others may imply that we do: 'He is fed up with you constantly asking how he is'.

From virtually the moment we are born, we embark on the quest of observing and classifying behaviour so that we may understand it and learn how to predict it. This heuristic process helps us figure out from our experience what makes someone come to feed me, what makes someone laugh, what makes someone angry. We learn to predict what encourages generosity, what encourages love, what causes indifference, what leads to friendship, what to bullying and so on. We learn from our immediate family and friends, then from school, the community, the media and the organisations in which we work.

We do not have to be taught to do this. It is an essential, natural, human process. This heuristic methodology results in a set of principles and rules for predicting behaviour of people

---

Box 1.2   Consider Relationships

Thus, if we are serious in accepting that people are not machines then each relationship needs to be considered in the following terms:

*   What is the other person's view of an event?
*   How does the other person view you?
*   How is the other person likely to react now and over time?

and the physical world around us. In doing so we are all developing our own theory of human behaviour as well as of the material world. It is not only important to us, it is essential to our sense of well-being and even survival. In certain circumstances, if we 'read' the situation wrongly, it may put us in serious danger.

Think for a moment about what makes you nervous or anxious. It is most often caused when you are about to go into a situation where prediction is difficult, but the outcome is critical. For example, many people become anxious before having a job interview, a final exam, a public presentation, a negotiation or, at the extreme, combat. What eases that anxiety is the reassurance of preparation – the work of anticipating and rehearsing the 'what ifs'. What if I am asked this? What if she gets angry? What if they find the presentation boring?

If we are to avoid constant stress and are to feel comfortable, we must be in an environment where, in general terms, the situation and people's behaviour are predictable. Now, of course, this does not mean we need or want to predict exactly what someone is about to do or say. This would certainly be boring and eventually stressful in itself. As in, for example, the movie *Groundhog Day*.

Nonetheless, to avoid anxiety we do want people to behave in a way that stays within predictable boundaries. This means we can operate in a stable environment and consequently focus our attention on what we have to do – operate the machine, discuss a business deal, write a report.

When one of the authors, Macdonald, first started working in a large psychiatric hospital in 1975, he made his first visit to a locked ward. On entering, some of the residents immediately rushed up to him. One put his face a few centimetres from his; another touched his arm; another circled him, staring. In ordinary life such behaviour would have been extremely threatening. It is not benign for strangers to behave in such a way unless there is a threat or intention of sex or violence, or both. Macdonald very quickly had to learn a different set of predictive rules, to ascertain in this context what was a real threat and what was simply a different normality.

In a less dramatic way we all have to learn these new rules or norms when we visit countries overseas, move to a different community, move to a new organisation or simply visit someone's home for the first time. Most people can remember instances from childhood when such visits led to surprises. 'This family does/does not eat together.' 'They argue a lot.' 'They don't talk to each other.' 'They let/don't let their children watch certain TV programmes.' 'They do/do not take off their shoes in the living room.' We learn not to blurt out our surprise, but to observe, learn and increase the scope of our predictive models. Some we find can be comfortably accommodated, others not so.

Similarly, in the workplace, think about visiting or starting work in a new company. Induction is not simply about work and safety processes. You must learn how to address people. Do you use first names? Where do you find facilities, for example, the canteen or toilets? What is a reasonable break time? And so on. It is at times like this our heuristic process becomes more conscious and so we are more aware of the process we have used and continue to use all our lives.

It is important to state here that predictability gives a sense of stability and reassurance even if the situation appears to be counter-productive. Again, Macdonald has worked with families that may be described as dysfunctional but are in another sense stable. Children learn to see the patterns of behaviour and avoid at least the worst excesses. They learn what triggers violence, how differently an adult behaves when drunk or high. These may be very unhappy relationships, but they endure because the participants have learned the dance of survival by predicting behaviour.

If we look at industry, certain companies are characterised by dreadful industrial relations, but they are predictable. The workers 'know' the management are bastards and out to 'get' them. The management 'knows' the workers are lazy, out for what they can take with the least amount of work. Each side plays its predictable role, keeps to the script and enters a regular ritual of protracted, tough negotiations trying to win points from each other. It may be economically wasteful, even disastrous, but it is predictable. Everyone knows their place and hangs on to their 'correct' view of the world. 'We all know where we stand.'

Thus predictability is critical. The most extreme public example of this happened on September 11, 2001. Worldwide, many people have that date imprinted in their minds forever. The loss of life was appalling. However, the deeper shock was the unpredictability of the event. Worse, unlike an earthquake, it was a deliberate, indeed meticulously planned, human act that was not foreseen.

In the media interviews, people used revealing comments. 'It was not a "normal" hijacking.' Now hijackings are not normal in one sense, but we had come to expect that hijackers don't want to die. They make demands: they threaten; they do not deliberately fly planeloads of innocent people into buildings. Why? For what purpose? What on earth had we done to deserve this? What sort of people are the hijackers?

Enormous amounts of energy have necessarily been expended trying to answer these questions. Until we can answer them, we cannot feel safe. When we board a plane or work in a skyscraper, we cannot help wondering and considering what we would do if .... What could we do? Why do some people hate us? Why do some love us? It is intolerable to leave these questions unanswered, or we would live in a random universe, a world of uncertainty where we have little or no sense of influencing our own destiny.

Now, sadly we are much more familiar with suicide bombings and they no longer produce the level of shock to the outside world although their victims are no less damaged or killed.

So we must learn to predict; to have an effective model that does not result in constant surprises, especially shocks. People who have great difficulty heuristically constructing such models, for example, people with autism or obsessive compulsive behaviour, suffer great anxiety and express a great need for control.

However, it is not simply a matter of having predictive models. We also imbue these models with value and morality. They are infused with a sense of right and wrong, good or bad, and all the shades of grey in between.

This brings us to the next principle.

Principle 3: People's behaviour is value based

We have explained that we need to predict our environment, both in terms of how others behave and how others react to us. This stems from a very basic need not only for security and survival, but for association. We are social, and our survival depends upon others. So who can we depend upon? Who is on 'our side', who is friend, who is foe? Our fundamental proposition is that we answer these questions by judging, or evaluating, behaviour against a set of universal, core values (see Box 1.3).

Part of the problem with the word *value* is that it can be used as an abstract or concrete noun, an adjective in terms of a quality and a verb in terms of an activity.

Box 1.3   Common Language and Definitions

Before we examine this in more depth it is important to define our terms. As mentioned earlier we have to use language that is in common usage and has social meaning. We are not saying these other meanings are invalid, only that we need to be precise about what they mean in this context. Here we define and discuss the way some terms are used.

VALUE

Defined as 'that which has worth to a person or members of a social group'.

CORE, UNIVERSAL VALUES

This is a set of six 'values' which are essential *properties* of constructive social relationships. They can be adjectives describing behaviour: loving, trustworthy, dignifying, courageous, honest, fair; or they can be abstract nouns: love, honesty, trust, respect for human dignity, courage, fairness.

HEURISTICS

Defined as 'a method or process of discovery from experience'.

Our use refers to how we find out and learn from a range of experiences what is valuable and what is not. It is how we generate the rules of thumb by which we can judge situations.

MYTHOLOGY

Defined as 'the underlying assumption and current belief as to what is positive and valued behaviour and what behaviour is negatively valued'.

These *are* the 'rules of thumb' we have learnt heuristically, for example, 'don't trust strangers', 'salesmen are not honest', 'managers are bastards'. These statements are the top of the iceberg; again heuristically formed. We build mythologies unconsciously and consciously, for example, tales of morality, films, lessons from family, friends, and so on; the media; observation of others. Figure 1.3 visually shows how some mythologies, like icebergs, are bigger and stronger than others.

Clearly some mythologies can be stronger than others; the ones that have been built from early childhood or a traumatic experience, mean that C is very large.

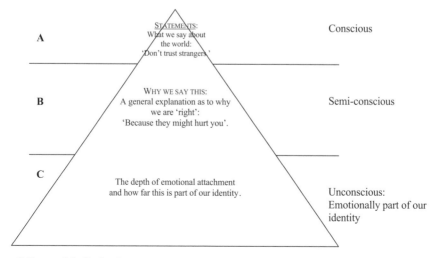

Figure 1.3   Mythologies

We call these assumptions or opinions mythologies because:

1. They are linked to the core values.
2. They are a mixture of mythos (stories with emotional content) and logos (rationality).
3. Myths are stories that contain a fundamental truth, even if the 'facts' are not true, for example, the story of Daedalus and his son Icarus: Icarus ignored his father's warning not to fly too close to the sun or the wax holding his wings would melt and he would fall and die. Icarus ignored his father's warning and did fall into the sea and die. Thus the fundamental truths – don't ignore your father's warning, and know your limits and don't try to exceed them.

As people we do not operate either entirely rationally or entirely emotionally.

In our experience people use the term 'value' in many different ways to describe very different concepts. Many people mix the concepts of value, heuristics, mythology and behaviour and call them all 'values'. For example; someone might say, 'People don't value the old values anymore'.

*   As far as we are concerned values, in terms of the core, universal values do not change. Neither are they a matter of choice.
*   The way we learn what behaviour is valued is a heuristic process.
*   Our current assumptions concerning what behaviour is of value is described by our mythologies; stories of explanation. These can and do develop as we learn and gain more experience. This is what people often call 'changing, new or different values'.

Finally, we also acknowledge that people 'value' material objects, goods and services. Whilst we recognise this as an emotional and important part of society it refers to the 'person→object' relationship. I may value a house but it has no mythology about me. What we are discussing here is the content of social relationships, that is, 'person(s)↔person(s)' relationships where values and valuing occur from both parties.

Thus, I may find that behaviour valuable (adjective) because it is supportive. I, therefore, value it (verb) and that behaviour may be part of a set that forms part of my values (abstract noun).

This confusion of language can be seen in many settings. For example, when talking to workers and their managers about difficulties in their working relationships, we often hear, 'The problem is they have different values from us.' When we talk to these same people in the context of their communities, churches and sports teams and ask why they can work together there so constructively there, they say, 'Here we have the same values.' Often these are the same people. We do not believe people change their values with their work shirts. It is clear that something is different, but we do not believe it is their values.

It is our argument that core values form the deep bonds that connect human beings one to another. When we examine our evolutionary history, it is obvious that humans would not have survived as a species had they not been able to form and maintain social groups. The other species which co-existed with our earliest ancestors all had sharper teeth, longer claws, were faster, could jump higher and in general physically outmatch the earliest humans. Newborn human babies are extraordinarily vulnerable and dependent. They require a social group – a family or clan – to support them for years, or they will die. If this had happened too often, we would have become extinct and our present discussion would not be occurring. Therefore, we believe, that to survive humans had to evolve as social animals.

As social animals we needed (and still need today) a methodology to allow us to function as productive members of a social group. This is true of all social species. For example, the social insects have specific, complex chemicals that allow individual insects to function as productive members of a very coherent social group, for example, a beehive or an ant colony. These chemicals are their operating methodology and function as their heuristics and mythologies.

CENTRAL PROPOSITION

We propose that all people, societies and organisations actually share the same set of core values. We have articulated these in various publications and articles, and they have been tested in commercial, public and not-for-profit organisations, and in a wide variety of communities and countries around the world by the authors and their associates.

Working with both the Hamersley Iron Organisational Development teams and Roderick Macdonald, we have identified six values which we believe make up the set of shared core values which are necessary for the continuing existence of human social groups. Each of these can be thought of as being on a continuum from positive to negative. Behaviour at the positive end of the continuum strengthens the social group; behaviour at the negative end weakens and will eventually destroy it.

Most of a member's behaviour must be at the positive end of the scale in order for him or her to be accepted and relied upon by others. Without such positive, reliable behaviour social groups must fail. Simply predicting behaviour is not enough. It is possible to predict that an individual will behave in a cowardly way, but such behaviour will weaken the group.

Figure 1.4 shows the core values upon which we propose that all societies are based. These are the fundamental social qualities that underpin relationships.

The basic propositions are:

1. If a group of people is to maintain a productive relationship that lasts, then the members of that group must demonstrate behaviour that will be rated at the positive end of the continua of the core values by the other group members.

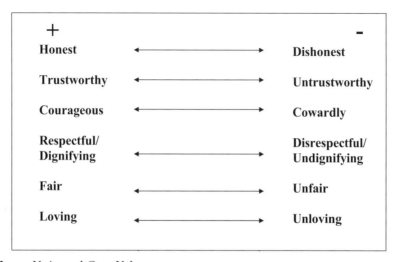

Figure 1.4   Universal Core Values

2. If a member of that group demonstrates behaviour that is judged by the other group members to be at the negative end of one or more of the continua of core values, the person will eventually be excluded (although attempts to change the behaviour may be made prior to exclusion).
3. If several people exhibit behaviours that are similar, but judged by the rest of the group to be at the negative end of one or more of the continua of core values, then the group will break into separate groups. This often happens with political organisations and religious organisations whose members break into 'factions' or 'sects'.

Values, per se, cannot be observed. We can and do observe what people say and how they behave. All of us interpret behaviour and draw conclusions about the values that an individual's behaviour demonstrates. Sometimes we have to wait for confirmation that our conclusions are correct, and sometimes we may be left in doubt. In some cases we may disagree with others as to how particular behaviour should be interpreted. In general, however, within a coherent social group, agreement is gained in time, often very quickly.

In essence, values are the criteria against which we assess our own worth and the worth of others. We argue that all people use these values as the basis for judging their own and others worth as they observe and interpret behaviour.

Consider a situation that might happen in any group. Imagine a group of people of which you are a member. You believe one of the other members has behaved in at least one of the following ways: told lies, stolen something, made fun of a less capable member, been indifferent to another's serious misfortune, regularly failed to keep promises, demanded more than his or her share, or consistently avoided difficult situations. Is it possible for this person to maintain membership of the group if he or she fails to change their behaviour?

We cannot maintain a productive relationship with someone we cannot trust, or who is dishonest, cowardly, does not respect others' dignity, is indifferent to our feelings or unfair. It is likely that we and other members of the group will point out the negative behaviour, but if it persists, the person will be actively excluded from the group. This reflects the basic need of any group or society.

However, specific rating of behaviour cannot be set in stone if the group is going to exist over time. We not only judge but also ask; if Joe has taken the last cake, why? For example, why would Joe think that his behaviour was fair? In other words the leader of the group and the members must demonstrate their ability to understand 'the other', that is, be able to see the world from another's point of view. This differentiates the mature adult world from the egocentric world of infancy and early childhood where the other's needs are not seriously considered except to satisfy the self. It differentiates the fundamentalist position from that of reflective consideration. Not being concerned for the 'Other' is a classic condition of psychopathy. Others are manipulated for personal gain with no regard for well-being. It is the antithesis of productive co-existence, and destroys working relationships.

WHY THE SIX VALUES?

It is, of course, relevant to ask why these six? Over the years we have had many debates on this topic, both among ourselves and with others. First, the authors do not posit these as immutable and unquestionable. They are, however, related to two criteria. First, if there are other, similar words, are they already covered by the existing six? For example, integrity is a similar term but already covered by honesty and trust. Fairness and justice are very similar, but we prefer fairness because of the possible legalistic implication of the term justice. We have tested these core values in different societies including with indigenous groups, in different continents and in very different types of organisations – multi-nationals, churches, schools, voluntary organisations, local authorities, manufacturing, services, finance – and they have survived so far.

The second criterion is that a person's behaviour may be judged to be positive in terms of one value but at the same time be judged negative in another. A manager may admonish a team member publicly for his or her poor work performance. The manager may be at the same time being honest, but showing lack of respect for human dignity. A soldier may admit fear and run away in the battle. The soldier is again honest, but may be cowardly and not to be trusted in combat. Another person may insist on the exact distribution of resources as authorised, believing they are acting fairly, but at the same time be indifferent to the greater or special needs of some individual or group. Thus, no two values ever (or should ever) correlate perfectly. If they did, they could be combined.

Thus we are saying that positive values are the defining properties of a cohesive social group. If members behave in a way that is perceived to demonstrate those positive values, then the group will remain cohesive. If members do not demonstrate such behaviour, that is, the other members regard their behaviour as a negative expression of values, the group will fragment and fracture. It is all but impossible to achieve any productive purpose over time if the group is not socially cohesive.

Love is chosen because it is different from care. It is love that causes parents to sacrifice themselves for a child or a soldier to go out under enemy fire to bring back a wounded mate. As a corporate organisational development team member once said, 'the difference between love and care is passion, good leadership is always passionate'.

Sometimes we attribute these values directly to people, for example, 'He is a loving person.' 'She is trustworthy.' 'He is fair.' 'She is courageous.' What we are really doing is making a judgment about the likely behaviour of an individual. This may be based on direct experience, another's report or reputation. What we are essentially saying is, 'I expect that person to behave honestly.' 'I expect that person to behave courageously.' 'I expect that person to treat other people with dignity', and so on. It is actually dangerous to infer that values are inherent properties of people, or that people inherently lack values. This false assumption leads us then to either idealise or objectify people; as is the case with racism and sexism. The only way of reducing these six values is merely to replace them with 'good' or 'bad', 'right' or 'wrong'. That, we have found, is just too simplistic.

The values continua forms part of our predictive model. It therefore helps to categorise behaviour and make judgments very quickly.

At the heart of these propositions, and any society, is the need to understand how others perceive the world and, hence, will judge behaviour. We do not *choose* to have these values. We argue that they are properties of relationships whether we like it or not. We *cannot* pick or choose. We cannot say 'I will adopt these as our new corporate values'. You are already being judged by them! This also implies you could say, adopt four. Honesty and courage are too difficult, so we will leave them out. Tough luck! We might want to leave them out but others will not let us. These core values are as oxygen to social groups. We cannot choose to function without them.

The next principle looks at how these judgments are made in more depth.

Principle 4: People form cultures based upon mythologies

There is a wealth of literature today around culture. 'Cross-cultural', 'multicultural', 'culturally sensitive'. Culture is defined in terms of geography, religion, ethnicity, food, traditional dress, language, institutions, currency or behaviours (often called tradition), all of which can be both interesting and confusing at the same time (see Box 1.4).

As with other concepts such differences can make discussion difficult unless terms are defined. We have a simple definition of culture that is not limited by any of the usual boundaries.

A very obvious quality in people is the speed at which we make judgments, especially judgments about behaviour. For example, a manager has very clearly explained to her department that absenteeism and lateness are unacceptable and that in future people taking days off sick without proper cause will be disciplined. A week later one of her team is late and then takes an unauthorised sick day. On return to work she reprimands him but after a one-to-one discussion, she does not take any disciplinary action. What do we make of this? Is it fair to the rest of the team? Is it loving toward the individual? Is it cowardly? Is she likely to increase or decrease trust? We might like to know more. Was there a special reason?

Although we often say that we would like more evidence, a common characteristic is that we often form an opinion on the basis of very little evidence. Two classic examples of this are (1) the remarkable ability of sports fans to be able to judge the accuracy of a referee or umpire's decisions instantly, even from remote positions in the stadium and (2) the speed at which we make decisions about people at first meeting, the well-known 'first impression.' (Gladwell, 2005)

Although these examples stand out, think how quickly we all form views about the behaviour of politicians, celebrities or the police. There is now a huge business built around this in the form of TV 'reality' shows where people are voted out of the house or off the island by 'the public'. Why and how do we do this? A basic survival mechanism suggests that from the earliest times we had to quickly decide who was and who was not a threat. We had to judge whether the behaviour of a person makes them 'one of us' or 'one of them', friend or foe.

This is not to argue that all judgments are made this quickly or that, once made, they are irreversible. We merely make the point that human beings not only have the capacity but also the tendency to make judgments about behaviour very quickly, even if they are later reconsidered.

How do we do this? The terminology that we use here is that we judge through our 'mythological lens'. We all effectively wear a pair of perceptual glasses. We see the world through a lens that refracts what we see onto the continua of shared values. That is, we observe behaviour and the lens directs that behaviour to be seen as fair or unfair, honest or dishonest, loving or indifferent, and so on. Clearly this is not a simple bi-polar rating, but the behaviour is placed somewhere along the continuum of one or more of the core values. If it is not, then it has no value and we are literally disinterested in it.

Box 1.4   Definition of Culture

A *culture* is a group of people who share mythologies. That is, they share assumptions about behaviours demonstrating positive or negative values. Essentially the more mythologies people share, the stronger the culture.

How is this lens made? Our experience and research is consistent with other psychological research and common sense that suggests this lens through which we view the world is made by our experience. It is formed as we are growing up and changes as we change. We learn from every experience, that is, heuristically: first from our immediate and extended family experiences; from our school, fellow students and teachers; from our community; from our workmates and bosses; from the media.

It is interesting to note that in biology there are very similar theories used to explain perception and hearing. This is now seen as a very active process based on heuristically learned patterns. Essentially, mythologies are based upon perceived patterns. For example, a boss assigns a task. It is completed but he gives no feedback, thanks or recognition. This happens again. A pattern has started, it happens a third time and it is virtually a law. 'This person *never* gives any thanks'. The mythology now is building that this manager's behaviour is indifferent, undignifying and maybe even unfair. Now we have established a mythology, we have an unconscious tendency to do two things:

1.   reinforce the mythology and
2.   form a culture.

We will now be sensitive to this manager's behaviour and note every instance that confirms the pattern. We are also likely to discuss it with other colleagues and be most at ease with people who have the same view. There is great comfort in the phrase 'yes, you're right, I agree with you'. If we find someone who has received praise or recognition we can put this aside as 'a special case' or 'the boss's favourite'.

This specific relationship and associated mythology can now, with reinforcement from others (the embryonic culture), become generalised. Now we build a mythology about managers at this company. This can grow to managers as a class and all sorts of evidence from history can be used to strengthen the culture and build mythologies.

Although some people have argued that the term 'mythology' implies the assumption or belief is 'untrue', this is a limited view of mythology. We have pointed to the combination of mythos and logos. We should also recognise that historically myths are stories that have a fundamental truth embedded in them (Campbell, 1949). Stories and myths have been told throughout the centuries to inspire people and to tell us how 'good' people behave and how

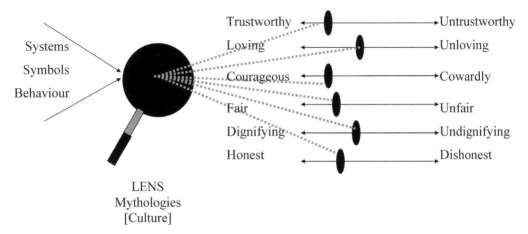

Figure 1.5   Making Sense of the World Through the Mythological Lens

'bad' people behave. They help to set and reinforce behavioural norms. It is not a question of true or false that would be used as evidence in a court of law, which is pure logos.

Children love stories; they demand that their favourite stories be read or told over and over again. In adulthood, the film industry and a large amount of television and entertainment are based on telling stories. Some of the most popular films, such as the *Star Wars* series, and books, such as *Harry Potter* and *Lord of the Rings*, are based on ancient myths that have been retold for generations. Even computer games have story lines with heroes and villains. All the major religions are based on books that essentially tell stories about what is acceptable and unacceptable behaviour.

Our mythologies give us a framework within which we can begin to organise our world and behaviour. They combine the story with its essential emotional component together with the logical, rational, scientific element. Thus our lenses are a combination of the two, neither wholly one nor the other.

This is of particular relevance in relationships when some behaviour or opinion is dismissed as 'illogical' or 'emotional', as if rationality is the only, or, at least, the superior element. Underneath this dismissal is actually an admission of the failure to empathise with the other or to understand how they view the world. We ignore other people's mythologies at our peril.

Thus we all have a unique pair of mental glasses with mythological lenses. One wonderful quality of such lenses is that we each have a pair which apparently, accurately sees the world, while, sadly, everyone else's lenses are slightly or significantly distorted. While all lenses are unique to the individual, they do have similarities with other people's lenses. We all have experiences both of sharing opinions and of coming into conflict with others with different opinions. No one exactly matches our world.

Thus over time people seek out and form relationships most easily with people who share their mythologies, that is, share a view about how to interpret behaviour as positive or negative on the values continua. That is, they form *cultures*.

This definition of culture is quite liberating since it is free from many assumptions of what constitutes a culture.

The strength of the culture will depend upon:

1. the extent of shared mythologies – how much overlap there is among individuals;
2. the relative importance of these mythologies to those concerned, and
3. the context and significance of the issue/behaviour being judged.

Thus 'cultures', in this definition may well cross geographical boundaries, ethnic association, organisational or professional boundaries. We would argue that not being precise as to the definition of culture leads to dangerous, even racist assumptions. For example, is there an African-American culture? Do all African-Americans share mythologies and to what extent? Do some African-Americans have more in common with people outside this category than inside it, and how do we express that?

Many groups of people do have common stories, especially if they have experienced oppression. Mythologies created from oppression are rich in heroes and villains, and they have great strength and depth. It may be a false assumption, however, that later generations will necessarily internalise such mythologies in the same way as their earlier relatives. In fact, history is constantly being rewritten and re-evaluated based on contemporary issues and concerns (Becker, 1958).

There may be many different cultures within an organisation or ethnic group. It is important to ask the same basic question, 'What is similar about the ways in which these people rate behaviour?' We must be careful about assuming there will be significant similarities just because a person is 'working class' or 'male' or 'first generation' or 'Italian' or 'in sales' or whatever general and perhaps too-convenient label can be stuck to them. This is simple stereotyping that is a crude and often inaccurate grouping of people on the basis of one or two variables that may have nothing to do with mythologies.

Culture is more subtle than that. Cultures may or may not be long lasting. Recently single-issue politics have produced an apparently diverse group of people who join together to resist an urban development or campaign for animal rights or against genetically modified foods and so on. At the other end of the spectrum there is a current anxiety with regard to what is termed globalisation, that international capitalism is creating a dominant culture that rides roughshod over less powerful and localised cultures.

Such concerns have been expressed, for example, in *The McDonaldization of Society*, by George Ritzer (1993). It is interesting to note that Ritzer explains some of the attraction for this process in terms of expanding predictability, for example, McDonald's, Holiday Inn and other similar organisations that are almost identical wherever in the world they are located, including controlled internal climates, furnishings and services. This appeal is understandable in terms of the need for predictability discussed earlier.

We have stressed the importance of mythologies in creating culture. Indeed, we would argue they are essential. We continue to argue for the need for clear definition, hence the choice and explanation of the term 'mythology'. Essentially we are influenced from birth not just by what we observe but by the way we make sense and categorise these observations. This sense is a combination of the stories we are told and the rational, logical application of reason.

From this we are able to categorise and rate behaviour along the values continua. We are naturally attracted to people who rate behaviour similarly. Another part of the entertainment industry is based on this. *Oprah, Ricki Lake, Question Time* and other TV shows where opinions are sought and commented upon are highly popular (even in the extreme, *Jerry Springer*). What you may notice is that such shows rarely produce any change in view. Their main function appears to be to reinforce views and assumptions and draw even clearer boundaries around cultures.

Cultures do not usually consist of people whose mythologies exactly overlap in every sphere of life and behaviour. Other cultures may form in apparently disparate groups concerned with a single issue or small range of issues.

So far we have looked generally at these concepts. The next step is to look more specifically at how such cultures are shaped and changed.

Principle 5: Change is a result of dissonance

Through the development of our mythological lenses we learn to predict and how to interact with people and the world around us. Gradually, for most people a relatively stable worldview develops that is, for the most part, accurate in its predictions of how people and objects are likely to behave.

This does not mean that a stable or predictable world is necessarily pleasant or productive. Children in abusive families learn to discern with necessary accuracy the patterns of abusive behaviour so that they might avoid them. For most people a predictable, stable environment, even a relatively unhappy one, is actually preferable to an unpredictable one. It may seem odd to an outsider that a violent relationship continues, that adversarial industrial relations continue, that people repeat dysfunctional relationships. However, that is to underestimate the strength of the need for predictability, summed up in such phrases as 'better the devil you know', 'out of the frying pan into the fire'. Habitual patterns of behaviour are hard to break, especially if they appear to be underpinned by economic necessity. So does this mean we are therefore captives of our mythologies caught in a repetitive cycle of behaviour where change is an almost hopeless uphill struggle? No.

There is, however, an essential ingredient that is necessary for change to occur and that is *dissonance*. Dissonance, a term which we use in the same way as Festinger (1957), is an experience where our expectations or predictions are challenged. To put it simply, the data does not fit. This could be a minor experience. For example, a recipe, apparently followed as before produces a sponge cake like a brick. More seriously, it could be when a trusted friend is deceitful. This is a challenge, major or minor, to our worldview. We have several ways of dealing with this depending upon the strength of our attachment to the worldview:

1. *Denial.* In this case we simply ignore the data. It is cast aside. It may be described by others that we are 'blind to his faults'. Essentially we try to pretend it hasn't happened. Denial is never completely successful and requires more and more energy to sustain, becoming more and more dysfunctional over time.
2. *The exception that proves the rule.* Here we move from denial but wish to maintain the original view. Therefore we need to explain it in terms of a 'one-off'. There were unusual circumstances. The person didn't realise what they were doing, didn't mean it, didn't see the consequences. If the person is a member of a group, for example, in an instance of police corruption, we might say that they are 'bad apples', or an 'unrepresentative minority'. In the example of the manager we may say: 'he couldn't help but say thanks for that', or 'he was probably told to say that by his boss'.

If instances persist, these methods of defending our mythologies become ever more difficult and more disturbing. We reach a point where the difference between what we predicted and reality simply cannot be reconciled. This is the state of dissonance and we cannot tolerate dissonance for long. If the strategies of denial and exception fail we need a new explanation, a new predictive model. The manager 'really has changed' and consequently we behave differently towards them. Paradoxically, once the balance has shifted, a new mythology established, we may well then reconstruct the past to justify the shift. We remember other instances, which viewed with hindsight or more commonly with the new lens, did give us a clue. We now listen to others who tell us 'I never thought he was that bad'. Thus the new mythology is established and nurtured as carefully as the previous mythology.

Sometimes this experience is shocking and upsetting as, in the case of shifting from positive to negative, for example, where a work colleague has betrayed your trust. Other times it is less emotionally dramatic as in realising that due to a normal process the machinery is wearing out, or that person is no longer interested in the job and has become careless.

There is a common assumption that people (especially in organisations) are resistant to change. Further, that this resistance is inherent. In fact, we have found people are remarkably interested in change. From an early age we are experimenting, trying new approaches, learning, testing. However we are doing this in order to build a predictive model of the world. Apparent resistance to change is characterised by three factors:

1. There is no dissonance. Our predictive models still appear to work.
2. There is no association between the change and benefit to the individual. Why should I adopt this new approach when it appears more difficult and does not appear to result in any improvement for me?
3. There is a sense of helplessness. 'Although I do not like the situation, I feel that there is nothing I can do about it.' For example, the demise of a business through market changes or a pattern of delinquent behaviour or addiction (see Box 1.5).

CHANGING BEHAVIOUR: SYSTEMS, SYMBOLS, BEHAVIOUR

From our experience some years ago we concluded that building a new culture and changing behaviour is the essential task of a leader. It is a key part of the work of management. Although many discussions of organisation assert the need to change an organisation's culture, very little is said about how this is to be done.

We identified that to bring about such change, the leader has three tools.
1. Their own behaviour – leading by personal example.
2. The systems of the organisation – aligning systems with a constructive, productive purpose that are seen to be so by others.
3. Symbols – described as the currency of leadership including badges, insignia, clothing, voice tone and so on to signify change or consistency.

We note that this trilogy has become popular and has been developed by others (Taylor, 2005).

In this section we deal primarily with the leader's behaviour. Systems and symbols will be discussed later.

From the discussion above, the work of the leader is to:

1. *Identify the mythology and the associated behaviour:* 'You, (the manager) are unfair and unloving because you never give us feedback'.
2. *Create dissonance:* Face up to the mythology and associated behaviour as if it is true (this can be painful). Don't try to argue. 'Well, I know I do sometimes.' Then create dissonance by behaving differently, that is, clearly and without ambiguity give some feedback.
3. *Continue with consistency:* Do not expect to build a new mythology on the basis of one new behaviour. Keep at it, and then keep at it again, and again.
4. *Don't expect behaviour change for some time:* There will be a lag between the manager's new behaviour and the building of a new mythology and new behaviours. Don't be discouraged.

Dissonance is at the heart of all behaviour change. There is an old saying that 'insanity is continuing to do the same thing whilst expecting a different result'. The work of anyone

---

Box 1.5   Factors Influencing Change

In order for change to occur, a person:
- must experience dissonance;
- must have a sense that the new behaviour will improve the situation (for the individual or social group);
- must have a sense that he or she is an active player in the process, that he or she can influence the process.

involved in changing behaviour is to demonstrate actual contradictions between expectation and reality.

Until a new myth is established, even a single instance of behaviour that reinforces the old myth may destroy your efforts at change. Once a new myth is established, occasional deviations will be interpreted as that, deviations, not as instances of the old myth.

During the process others may not perceive the situation as you do. This too can cause them to interpret your behaviour in a way that is different from your own interpretation. You may believe you are demonstrating respect for dignity by your behaviour but your team may perceive your behaviour as demonstrating their dignity is only important when it is convenient for you, not when the chips are down. Therefore they perceive you as dishonest, lacking courage and not to be trusted.

We emphasise the importance of understanding other mythological lenses so that your behaviour will be seen at the positive ends of the continua of core values through *their* eyes, not simply your own. One of the best ways to learn this is to come up through the ranks, to have experience at the lower levels of organisation and have learned how your friends and peers at those levels see the world. Another way to learn this is to spend time with your employees, get to know them and talk about their views. A third way is used by the military, where sergeant majors have the role of interpreting the needs and beliefs of the troops to the officers. Whatever the method used, such understanding is essential for effective leadership that is able to build new mythologies and organisational cultures and behaviour.

We argue that a further element of the work of leadership is to turn mythologies into hypotheses, creating questions where there were certainties. Be aware, however, that the attempt to build mythologies carries significant risk. In fact, we do not believe mythologies really change; the old mythologies may recede into the background, may even be apparently forgotten, but they are likely to be present for many years. If behaviour slips to the negative side of the scales of shared values, the old negative mythologies will be stirred up and be more powerful than ever, since the newer mythology proved to be false: 'We have been let down, it was a trick'.

Some have suggested to us that knowledge of this model of leadership processes could make it easier for dishonest managers to fool their direct reports. Any manager, who believes they could do this, might like to try it. The process is subtle and unforgiving, requires constancy and consistency, people will spot a dishonest manipulator every time.

Behaviour alone, however, will not change the culture of the organisation as a whole. It can change the relationships between leaders and team members, but for overall change, the other tools of leadership – systems and symbols – must be engaged. These tools will be explained in more detail in later chapters.

It is both a behavioural example and a symbol if a leader does not pick up litter, or, worse still, causes it, while at the same time extolling the virtues of 'good housekeeping'. The leader may or may not be in a position of authority to change systems, but he or she can certainly try to improve them, if only by suggestion. Finally words of praise, a small gift/presentation/ award, contacting or visiting a sick worker may be symbolic examples which, if rated positively on the values continua, can support more substantive change.

Obviously some changes are more difficult to bring about than others. Years of industrial conflict may have undermined trust between workers and leaders to such an extent that a great deal of hard and consistent work may be needed to rebuild it. The extent and emotional depth of the mythologies, including the reinforced and refined stories of events past, will influence the process. If people have already seen the contradiction (for example waste, poor practice, poor behaviour) but have not been in a position to do much about it, change may well be applauded. It is more difficult where habitual behaviour has become entrenched – 'we've always done it like this', 'it is running to its full capacity', 'bosses are just like that'. Nonetheless, change is always possible if there is both an understanding of how to bring it about and the will to do it.

Finally, there is no point in change if it can't be maintained. Regaining trust only to be let down again results in an even worse situation than we started with. The negative mythologies will be reinforced.

In summary if we want to change our own or others' behaviour, there are several key steps:

1. Understand the mythology: why do people think that behaving as they do now is justified in terms of the values continua?
2. Understand the strength of the culture: how well reinforced is the mythology in terms of stories and past events.
3. How can dissonance be created? What behaviour, systems and symbols would be useful to demonstrate a contradiction between expectation (prediction) and actual events now? It is important to state that this cannot be based on trickery. There really has to be a demonstrable contradiction, say, between an old method of working and safety; smoking and good health; a mythology about leaders not telling the truth (dishonesty) and a genuine change that makes real information available.
4. Sustain the change with consistency. If the process has been successful, if changing behaviour has succeeded, it needs to be constantly and consistently reinforced or the old, habitual behaviour will return. It is crucial to remember that while in the change process new mythologies can be created, the old ones never die; they lie like silt on a riverbed ready to be stirred up again.

Dissonance is not always negative. The positive aspect of a shift of balance can be summed up in the phrase 'the penny dropped', or 'the light went on'. Change of behaviour occurs when our expectation changes as a result of changing our internal predictive model, but this is often not an easy task.

Principle 6: It is as important to understand social process in detail as it is to understand the detail of technical process

If someone wanted to build a road bridge across a river, make aeroplane engines, prescribe drugs for the sick, run a railway or drill for oil, there would be no doubt that the person would be required to demonstrate a detailed knowledge of the technical process to be used. Considerable alarm would be generated if, when discussing the safety of a nuclear power plant, a group of people with little experience and less technical knowledge claimed that they would decide what was safe by using 'common sense'. 'Oh', says one 'I think we should put the waste in big, secure containers'. 'Yes', says another 'and I think those containers should be metal, perhaps steel with some good locks'. 'Yes', says a third 'my experience is that some good steel should be fine'. After a while a member of the group who has been silent says, 'Perhaps we should be more specific? What sort of waste will this create? Will steel be protective enough?' Then the person has the temerity to start discussing isotopes and half-life; contamination.

He is told not to be so pedantic and so theoretical. This is, we hope, an absurd scenario but, when translated into a discussion about social process, it is not quite so unrealistic.

'We need someone to head up the new marketing division for the UK.' 'Yes, we need someone with experience, and good leadership qualities.' 'Yes, someone who can get real results. Those marketing types can be difficult. There are some real prima-donnas in the marketing department.' 'What about Johnson from head office?' 'Not a bad idea, she's really bright and has had some experience in Japan.' 'Yes, but she's a bit young. Will she be able to impose herself?' And so the discussion goes on. Terms are used with little definition. There is an assumption about shared meaning, but it is not tested in any rigorous way. Critical decisions are often made on the basis of such 'common sense' and pragmatism, which is so highly prised over theory. Why is this so, especially when compared with the value of theory and detail in technical areas? There are three main reasons for this:

1. *People–people relations are actually more complex.*
    Although there are references to people–people relationships as the 'soft' areas and technical issues as 'hard', this is misleading. These 'soft' areas are often highly complex and difficult to explain. Unlike objects, we cannot effectively ignore people's purpose, will, mythologies and culture. These are all less easy to observe and manage than objects.
2. *There is a lack of a shared language.*
    While there are universally accepted definitions in many of the so-called hard sciences, this is not the case in social science. There are no generally accepted theories in the sense of clear expositions of principles with predictive validity.
    Instead of a rigorous and agreed set of terms and definitions, social science and perhaps, particularly organisational theory, is subject to fads and jargon. All disciplines have scientific language, which may not be easily understandable from outside. However, in the area of organisational literature there is a suspicion that jargon is used in a deliberate attempt to make something simple appear more complex and technical than it is. Another suspicion is that jargon is used to make something that is unpleasant more palatable or acceptable. In the military killing your own troops is 'friendly fire'; killing civilians is 'collateral damage'.
3. *We already have our own theories about social processes.*
    As discussed, we all have our own theories about people. We do not start with a blank sheet when considering social processes. Thus, any outside theory of social process will be judged against our own theory, any predictive statement is compared with our own. As explained in the discussion of values these 'theories' may be deeply embedded and very emotionally charged. To propose an alternative is not an innocent or even purely rational process.

If a change process is to be managed, it is critical that there is a shared understanding of how to analyse social process and how it can be influenced effectively.

Many of the criticisms of business process re-engineering can be seen as pointing to a failure to take into account the need for a detailed understanding of social process.

In an issue of *People Management* (2 May 1996), in an article entitled 'Business Process Re-engineering RIP', Enid Mumford and Rick Hendricks argue that 'the corporate panacea of the early 1990s is widely seen as a disastrous experiment'. Yet earlier, the books 'Process Innovation' by Tom Davenport (1993) and Hammer and Champy's *Reengineering the Corporation* (1995) had become obligatory additions to managers' bookshelves superseding *In Search of Excellence*

(Peters and Waterman, 1982), *The One Minute Manager* (Blanchard and Johnson, 1982) and others.

Mumford and Hendricks argue that the concept allowed managers to cut numbers of workers because of re-engineering requirements rather than take direct responsibility for the layoffs. They say that 'in the early 1990's companies were keen to become part of the new game'. In the Nov/Dec 1993 edition of *The Harvard Business Review* Hall, Rosenthal and Wade (1993) examined why process improvements had not resulted in bottom-line improvement and argued it was because the difficulty of planning and implementing a redesign was underestimated.

Hammer and Champy's response was to explain that 'reengineering' had been interpreted to mean 'downsizing' (dysfunctional issues) and that 'management isn't aligned behind the change' (process issues). Results showed only '16% of senior executives were fully satisfied with their re-engineering programmes'.

Tom Davenport (one of the original reengineering gurus) stated, 'The rock that re-engineering foundered on is simple: people'. As in the cases quoted in books such as *In Search of Excellence*, the success stories of re-engineering are no longer such success stories (Capital Holding, Hallmark and Mutual Benefit Life).

In their article, Mumford and Hendircks identify one of the main reasons for failure as the absence of theory. In fact both Davenport and Hammer put this absence forward as a positive aspect. As Mumford says, 'This was a message that attracted the macho-manager who had never believed all that soft, look after the people stuff.... This may be a viable strategy for a company on the verge of bankruptcy where fast action is essential. It is not a safe strategy for a company that is doing quite well but wants to do better' (see Box 1.6).

In recent years the term 'emotional intelligence' has become popular. This has some similarities with what we have always referred to as social process in that both concepts refer to people–people relationships. However, we prefer 'social process' as it focuses on the relationship whereas a term such as emotional intelligence can imply a quality of an individual with all the problems of nature/nurture, and direct comparisons with other 'types' of intelligence.

We analyse social process by applying a general set of tools such as understanding mythologies, values and culture. However, social process is also impacted by elements other than individual behaviour. It includes understanding the effect of systems, symbols and behaviour. How the organisation is structured is also a vital part of social process. We do recognise the importance of the individual's ability to understand and influence social process and that is discussed in subsequent chapters (see Chapter 3, Human Capability and Chapter 9, The Work of Leadership).

We simply argue here that, until leaders devote significant time and resources to improving their detailed understanding of social processes, they will remain confused as to why some apparently excellent technical and commercial processes fail. Quality is a leadership issue, as is safety, waste reduction and improved effectiveness. This cannot simply be left to 'common sense'.

Box 1.6   Social Processes

We are saying that:

1. Social processes have as significant an impact on the output of human endeavours as do commercial and technical processes.
2. Social process is, however, treated differently, partly because we all have our own 'theories' and partly because we lack a universal theory and hence language to discuss it.
3. It is often underestimated because it is 'soft' whereas we say *this is the hard part*!

Principle 7: Understand the difference between prediction of a population's behaviour and the prediction of an individual's behaviour

Understanding social processes involves not just explaining why someone behaved as they did but also predicting likely behaviour. It involves understanding mythologies and culture and being aware that people do not like to be manipulated or treated like objects. Consequently, it is important to distinguish between predicting behaviour in general and predicting an individual response. For example, if a person is working and producing an output, it is a general principle to say that, if that person receives valid feedback and due recognition, he or she is more likely to continue to work hard, giving care and attention to the quality and quantity of what is produced compared with someone who receives little or no feedback or recognition. This will not, however, be true in every single case. Some individuals will work hard despite poor leadership. Others will find it difficult to work hard even with good leadership. Thus, we can work from general principles about people in general but we need to consider the individual case and exceptions, bearing in mind that an exception does not necessarily invalidate the principle. If we confuse the general and the particular we can make some serious mistakes. For example, a person who smokes may well cite an elderly relative 'who smoked all their life and never got cancer' as a means of denying the dangers of smoking. In effect, this technique is a way of avoiding dissonance.

It is impossible to predict in minute detail any individual's behaviour (including our own). This does not, however, differentiate natural science from social science. No theory can predict exactly the behaviour of a single entity, be it a person or atomic particle. Paradoxically we can make a general prediction (in social science) that people will actually resist prediction if it is felt to be manipulation. People *in general* do not like to be labelled, categorised or put in boxes because it appears to deny our unique individuality. This general prediction will not account for every person's behaviour. We are unique but we also know that we are extraordinarily similar in terms of biological makeup and our need for food, shelter and companionship. We respond similarly to perceived threat, cold, lack of sleep and so on. In our everyday lives we depend on the general predictability of behaviour of those around us in the street, on trains and in our workplace or home, but we resist the notion that therefore we are totally predictable as individuals.

A culture, defined as a group of people who share mythologies, is in some ways similar to the statistical definition of a population. Whilst there are always differences, there are also common characteristics. The problem with using statistical models and probability statements lies with the reality that probabilities are about populations while personal experience is by definition singular. Therefore, whereas it may be both true and accurate to predict a company will reduce the workforce by 10 per cent over the next year, at the end of the workforce reduction employees do not experience a 90 per cent role. Either I keep my job or I do not, zero or one. When we look at safety statistics by plane, train or car, we may know the statistical safety figures. However, for each of us we either have an accident or we don't, again zero or one. Many of us choose to behave unsafely at work because 'we will get away with it', gambling on the zero not the one. Thus, experientially, we are not overly impressed or influenced by statistical evidence even when it is true because the basic gamble is win or lose. Even when we lose, we may fool ourselves that we 'nearly' won because our raffle ticket was the number above or below the winning ticket.

Leaders seeking to influence behaviour will not be very successful if the main or only argument is quoting statistics. The example must be taken through to personal experience, so that the person links the statement to personal experience. We do not particularly like to be normal, average, or accept the implication that we are effectively indistinguishable from others. This lack of individual difference reduces us again to apparent objects. In understanding the detail of social process we must work from general principles about people to specific hypotheses about particular groups of cultures and then to individual need. It is important to work at all three levels at once and not exclusively at any one or two. That is, we must move carefully from the general to the particular, shaping our explanation and behaviour as we do. For example, at work I may start with a general assumption that people require feedback and recognition. I, then, may make a specific statement about a particular group, say a crew of underground miners, a team of young indigenous Australians, a troupe of actors in a theatre company. This will involve *how* that recognition and feedback is most appropriately given. Do not single out miners or a particular 'racial' group publicly, or slap them on the back. Give such recognition quietly and with little fanfare. An actor, however, may require public individual praise, applause and so on. One final important step, however, is to take into account individual differences. Not all miners, indigenous Australians or actors are the same (see Box 1.7).

We are very keen on exceptions, because it appeals to our individuality and a sense that we are not victims of predetermined fate. There are huge industries that exploit our need to do this: smoking, drinking and gambling. The gambling industry and particularly lotteries are dependent upon our belief that we might beat the odds. Some of the most dangerous behaviour at work and socially is founded on the notion that 'it won't happen to me', exactly the opposite of the gambler who hopes, against the odds, 'it could be me'. Thus we have the contradictory behaviour of someone running across a busy street to buy a lottery ticket.

Box 1.7   Individuals – Statistics

In a mining company in Australia the leadership were about to offer staff conditions including a salary structure to supervisors who were at the time on hourly rates of pay with overtime. As part of the consideration an analysis was done to see what percentage of supervisors' pay was due to overtime. The overall figure came out as just over 15 per cent. Therefore it seemed logical to think about 'buying out the overtime' by adding a figure around 15 per cent to the salary.

On closer analysis, however, a very small proportion of supervisors covered a significant amount of overtime (some up to 40 per cent of base pay). Further, we found that those supervisors who earned these large amounts were disliked by their crews and fellow supervisors. Their crews' mythologies saw them as dishonest, since they fixed the system so that they came in on weekends, outside of the normal shift, for the slightest of reasons. They also saw this as unfair. Very few were even moderately trusted. Taking this small group out of the equation reduced the overtime loading to below 10 per cent. Therefore, the leadership built in a loading to the salary of 10 per cent which was seen as fair and honest by the productive supervisors and highly punitive by the poor supervisors, most of whom left. Thus, by using an analysis at all three levels – general, group and individual, the organisation retained effective workers; lost people who were exploiting it and reduced cost from the first analysis. This example also works if it is seen as using the trio of leadership tools: systems, symbols and behaviour: the systems being the employment and overtime systems, the behaviour being the leadership's efforts to carry out a detailed analysis (perceived as fair and honest) and the symbolism of rewarding effective supervisors and not rewarding poor performers.

Building general, predictive models with attached statistical probabilities is not demeaning to individuals. We do it throughout our lives. However, a leader must not impose this model on either a specific group of people or an individual since it objectifies the person. Instead, it is a starting point to be able to identify groups and, within groups, specific individuals.

Principle 8: It is better to build relationships on the basis of authority rather than power

There are many different definitions of authority and power in the literature. Some overlap. The way that the terms are used here is as follows. They are both concerned with influencing behaviour. A person can exercise authority or power in order to direct another person's behaviour towards a particular purpose. If a person uses authority then he or she will be acting within limits known and agreed by the other person. The use of power will breach one or more of these limits.

For example, if I come to work and start an activity without the proper safety equipment, say hard hat and glasses, and I am seen by a supervisor, then I know there may be some disciplinary procedure to follow. Let us assume that I know both the policy and the consequence of non-compliance. The supervisor has been *authorised* to carry out this procedure. Let us say that he offers to 'turn a blind eye' for a favour in return (say covering for his absence). This is classic *power*.

This may be obvious but sometimes it is difficult to tell the difference between authority and power due to:

1. Lack of Knowledge. In particular circumstances the person may be using authority but I experience it as power because I am unaware of his or her rights and my own.
2. Lack of Recognition. Although I know the person has been 'authorised' by his or her organisation I do not accept it, for example, being arrested by a soldier of an occupying country, the soldier may see it as authority, I see it as power.
3. Lack of Clarity. A situation occurs where neither side has clear knowledge of their boundaries of authority. There the problem may lie in the fact that there is actually no policy or role description. This is not unusual in organisations.

The basis of healthy and productive relationships is authorisation, where influence is exerted within mutually agreed and understood boundaries. The use of power is the main source of negative mythologies. Organisations are rife with stories of people and situations where power has been used. We discuss this in more depth later (particularly in Part 3, Systems Leadership). However, it is important to point out that it is not simply a matter of authority being 'good' and power being 'bad'.

It takes a great deal of work to construct and operate effective, authorised relationships. Our work and Jaques' work among others do not claim this is easy but that over time it is much more effective. Other approaches and some current fads around argue that 'authorising' relationships is 'hierarchical and bureaucratic' and by implication old-fashioned. Metaphors and analogies abound about organic, flexible, liberated organisations that are unrestricted by rules and therefore more creative; leaderless teams and unclear authority abound. Anyone who has worked in such organisations is aware of how quickly they degenerate into power and politics with dominant so-called charismatic individuals manipulating the organisation and people overtly or covertly taking advantage of the confusion.

COHERENCE

An insightful analysis of order has been made by Mike Church. In his paper *Organizing Simply for Complexity: Beyond Metaphor Towards Theory* he refers to a most important continuum of control and order.

Table 1.1   Order and Chaos

Description of control	No control	Strange attractors	Control without controlling	Command/ control	Total control
System type	Random	Chaotic	Coherent	Top-down command	Mechanistic or rigid
Relationships	Independent random relationships	Randomness within underlying regularities	Highly ordered interdependent relationships in which the costs of achieving order are minimised, that is, 'order for free'	Predominantly dependent relationships; order is controlled from above with significant added costs	Fully dependent, fixed and immutable relationships. Very high cost to sustain

The information in Table 1.1 forms the core of his argument. *Coherence* is what is being sought. At any time, because it is in a changing environment and made up of people, an organisation is moving towards more order or disorder (to the right or left on the continuum). It is the work of the leader to try to achieve and maintain coherence.

In our view, consistent with Church, the leadership of an organisation should maintain the organisation so that it achieves its purpose with the minimum number of rules (structure and systems). Higher order thinking is consistent with generating a simple set of interrelated rules (epigenetic) which can help the organisation cohere without, so called, bureaucracy and red tape (see levels of complexity and system design).

Principle 9: Clarity of boundaries is the basis of freedom

From the argument above we can see that if the 'rules' are designed at the appropriate level of complexity (that is, they are simple but interrelated), they do not produce complicated and wasteful systems and procedures. Indeed bureaucracy, in the negative sense, is produced precisely because systems and procedures have been designed at too low a level (see also Chapter 17, How to Design Systems). The result is an obstructive, clumsy process that wastes time and energy, causes frustration and invites people to cut corners and work out ways to get round the system. Thus, an overcomplication invites the use of power.

There is another way of inviting power and that is to be unclear as where the boundaries lie. Thus power is associated with too many or too few boundaries with people left wondering where the boundaries are or why they are set in such a way.

Power is inevitable where there is a lack of clarity. It is a classic methodology manipulative people use to blur boundaries. In organisations people will intimidate or sexually harass others and claim it was only a joke, an accident, unintentional, and so on. Racism, too, falls into this category and is most effective when boundaries are unclear. In child development the lack of boundaries causes extreme distress, lack of control and abusive behaviour. The lack of boundaries or rules does not lead to creativity; it leads to power. It causes anxiety because behaviour cannot be predicted and there is severe doubt as to who is justified to do what.

However, when boundaries are clear, we can work creatively and safely. Creativity occurs most effectively when a person is not under immediate threat. Despite the romantic notion of the creative artist living in a garret producing works of genius, the reality is quite different. Many great works have been produced under patronage (Michelangelo, DaVinci, Tchaikovsky, and so on.) The creator is left to grapple with their creation (work) without constant anxiety about their environment.

Similarly, a good leader or manager should work to reduce anxiety and uncertainty in their team so that the team members can concentrate on their work. This is done by establishing clarity in roles, expectations, goals, tasks, resources, and so on. If the team members are constantly concerned about lay-offs or a plant closure, it is difficult for them to concentrate on their work.

We believe that these are the conditions that build trust and will result in behaviours which are likely to be experienced positively and valued. It is hard work but worth it. Finally Church in his paper discussed above argues a similar point when he criticises pseudo-science. He quotes from Sokal and Bricmont (1997) the accusation that many people in this field are, 'displaying a superficial erudition by shamelessly throwing around technical terms in a context where they are completely irrelevant. The goal is, no doubt, to impress and above all, intimidate the non-scientist reader' (see Box 1.8).

Church refers to an excellent example of the use of power, accompanied by mysticism and magic. It is the antithesis of this book, which attempts a more difficult path of clarity, openness and dialogue.

Box 1.8   Clarity

It is a constant theme in this book to strive for clarity:

1.   clarity in the definition of terms and meanings;
2.   clarity in relationships and authority;
3.   clarity in purpose.

An essential element in a positive organisation is clarity.

---

2 *The Nature of Work and Organisations*

Turning intention into reality

Our survival and development is dependent upon social organisation. We must produce goods and services to support our families, our communities and the wider society. Such goods and services are not realised by wishes and intentions alone. We need to *work*. Our definition of work is '*turning intention into reality*'.

We need to organise ourselves as individuals and in social groups so that we can turn these intentions into reality. We need to be clear about our purpose and determine a plan to achieve that purpose. This involves gathering resources, setting goals and times to completion, understanding the constraints within which we all live and work and understanding needs and markets.

In this part we examine how, in complex societies, groups of people associate in order to achieve their purpose, attract resources and create plans. The original association may not have the capabilities or skills to do this work themselves. In such cases the association is likely to employ people to carry out much of the work needed to achieve the purpose. Such people are not brought together randomly but need to be selected and organised in such a way that they know what they are supposed to be doing, have the capabilities to do the work, and understand the nature of their relationship with others.

The most common and potentially effective method of organising to achieve the purpose is an employment hierarchy where people report to others and where the hierarchy is organised in terms of relative authority. Such organisations typically are headed up by a chief executive officer (or equivalent) who reports directly to the board, which, in turn, is appointed or elected by members of the association. It is the work of the leadership of the organisation to develop a strategy or method of successfully achieving the overall purpose.

Of course, a plan is not created in a vacuum. There are constraints that set a context. Some of these constraints are social, imposed by society – the laws of the land, local regulations and even geographical or demographical factors. Each organisation will develop its own policies to achieve its strategic objective. These policies may be related to external and internal relations. They may include a policy with regard to relationships with the local and wider community.

Managing relations within the organisation also needs a wide range of policies, for example, with regard to recruitment, appointment, promotion, equal opportunity, travel, subsistence, the nature of the employment arrangements, labour relations, use of vehicles, health and safety (beyond legal requirements), discipline, appeals, remuneration and so on. Such policies may be generally stated but for their implementation the leadership must design and operate actual systems and procedures, which in their detail may enact, or if badly designed and operated, contradict or obstruct the intended policy.

This part of the book has connections with the work of Elliot Jaques. This is hardly surprising since all the authors worked with him for many years. Jaques and his colleagues at Brunel Institute of Organisation and Social Studies have produced many books and papers; the best listing of these is on www.globalro.org/main.html. There are some subtle and some more obvious differences between our material, Jaques', and others'. There are, for example, many different ways of describing the 'level of work'; for example in Jaques (*Requisite Organization*, 1989), Stamp ('Listening to My Story', 1986), Jaques, Gibson and Isaac (*Levels of Abstraction*, 1978), Rowbottom and Billis ('Stratification of Work and Organisational Design', 1977) and ourselves.

What follows is our construction that acknowledges, draws upon and departs from these formulations. We have written our material in the light of our experience and to be integrated with the further development of ideas in the form of systems leadership, which forms the core of Part 3.

2 *What is Work?*

It is interesting to note that, although many books are written about work and organisations, it is rare to find a clear definition. The word 'work' is used often and in many different ways. The *Oxford English Dictionary* affords the term considerable space referring to expenditure of effort, striving, exertion of force in overcoming resistance, tasks to be undertaken, achievement, employment, earning money and to have influence or effect – to mention only a few.

Despite the many social meanings of the term 'work', we have found it useful to define human work as follows:

Box 2.1   Definition of Work

Work: Turning intention into reality.

Work is the process by which an idea becomes evident in the external world and open to recognition. While this undoubtedly requires effort, it is not simply the expenditure of effort. This definition is closely related to Jaques' definition and can be seen as such by reference to Jaques' explanation in his book *A General Theory of Bureaucracy* (1976: 100, 113), in which he says 'The term work refers to activity, to behaviour, to that human activity in which people exercise discretion, make decisions and act so as to transform the external physical and social world in accord with some predetermined goal in order to fulfil some need', in short, turning intention into reality (Jaques, 1976: 101).

Schutz (1972) also emphasises this transformation when he describes a person as working when that person is trying '... to produce an objective output which is the realisation of a subjective project'. One of the authors, Macdonald (1990), wrote about the concept and emphasises the need for recognition of that process particularly in his doctoral thesis: 'Identity Development of People with Learning Difficulties through the Recognition of Work'. The link with recognition is crucial.

As Macdonald wrote, 'The whole process allows the person to identify themselves as an active agent in the world' (Macdonald, 1990). Kegan (1982) in *The Evolving Self* also emphasises this by saying '(work) directs us to that most human of regions between an event and a reaction to it ... to this zone of mediation where meaning is made'. Sigmund Freud also stressed the importance of work when he stated, 'no other technique attaches the individual so firmly to reality as laying emphasis on work; for work at least gives a secure place in a portion of reality'.

Like Jaques, Schutz, Kegan and Freud, the authors regard work and recognition as essential to mental health and wellbeing; it is a fundamental part of our identity. This is in contrast to views of work as labour or toil. For example, Dahrendorf (1985), says that 'work in the simple everyday sense of the world, has never been regarded as a particularly agreeable dimension of life'. Marx in *Das Kapital* even argues that freedom begins where work ends; to paraphrase, 'instead of working, people are free to fish or write poetry as they please'.

This perspective of work as a burden has grown up, in our view, because of a separation of the process of articulating intention from the process of transforming reality. There is a qualitatively different experience in realising someone else's intention than realising one's own. This is seen, for example, when completing a task assigned by someone else for someone else. Similarly, if the intention is mistakenly or deliberately attributed to someone else, then alienation also results. This is why it is so important for a leader to engage with team members so that all genuinely share the purpose (intention). They, therefore, identify with the transformation and gain recognition for their contribution to the result.

To put it very simply, if in performing:

1. we are prevented from realising our intentions (either by others or ourselves), and/or
2. we do not get recognition for our contribution to the process and result, then
3. we will not only be alienated from our work but our identity will suffer.

Macdonald (1990) used this understanding to explain both violence in institutions and attention-seeking in general. It is better to gain personal recognition, even punishment for a (destructive) act than to have one's work ignored and treated with indifference; however negative the attention, at least we know we exist.

Thus work is essential to our wellbeing. It is potentially a creative expression of ourselves, especially when recognition is given accurately and appropriately. This definition, 'turning intention into reality', clearly extends beyond the realm of employment work. We see small children working extremely hard (at play), applying intense concentration and effort, experiencing immense frustration – a process we continue throughout our lives if we are to enjoy a positive identity and some creativity.

While the definition of work goes beyond employment work it is also very relevant to it. Jaques in *General Theory of Bureaucracy* uses a most helpful diagram, reproduced here as Figure 2.1, to highlight the process of work.

Thus in employment work we see that activity is directed toward achieving a goal which can be specified in advance. This activity will always be bounded by constraints or limits (see Figure 2.2). These can be variously described in terms of the laws of society, policies of the company and more particularly the resources available – materials, money, people and so on.

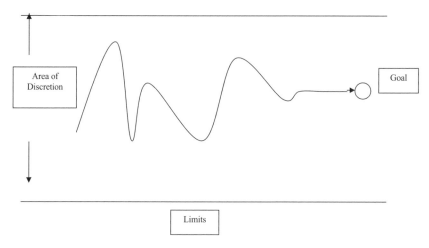

Figure 2.1   The Process of Work (Jaques)

The goal is set in a time context. It is never open ended; there is always a maximum completion time, which if not achieved devalues the goal. The person carrying out the work must devise a way to achieve the goal within all these constraints.

Human work and identity

The construction of a pathway towards the goal is at the heart of work. The person must make decisions and choices, overcoming obstacles while staying within the constraints. It is this decision making that is essentially human. No two people will ever construct exactly the same pathway or method. Also the same person will rarely, if ever, construct the same pathway twice, even if the goal and the constraints remain the same.

The pathway is, thus, unique to the individual; it is like a signature and part of our identity. It may appear to be the same either between individuals or an individual 'repeating' an activity, but close observation will always reveal some difference, even if very small.

Herein lies the opportunity for improvement. Human beings have a natural drive to improve methods. Think of an occasion when you have attempted a task for the first time. It is almost impossible to prevent reflection on how to do it better next time. Sometimes in the way that we organise work or design and implement systems in organisations, we inhibit this process or even actively try to prevent it. Nonetheless, most people will at least think about improvement even if they cannot act on those ideas. Inhibiting a person's ideas for improvement not only frustrates the individual, it destroys an opportunity to advance the organisation's goals.

If we look at work as a constructive and productive process that contributes to individual wellbeing, then it is important that the person carrying out the work can identify with the goal. This is not to say that the person would carry out this work whether employed or not, but rather to say the person should see the goal as a worthwhile objective that he or she actively wants to achieve.

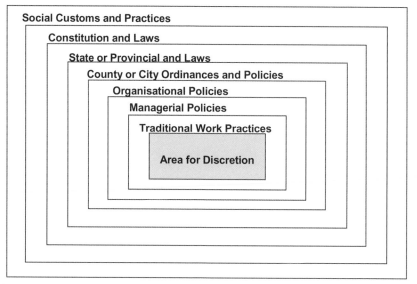

Figure 2.2   Constraints or Limits Bounding Activities

The person should also understand the nature of and reason for the constraints. It is not good enough merely to be informed of them and instructed to achieve the goal. If the person is not aware of why the constraints are there, it may lead to dangerous or illegal behaviour as the person sees no need for the constraint and therefore breaches it in an attempt to reach the goal. It will also lead to the sort of alienated situation that Marx and Dahrendorf describe. We can find this situation in extreme form in forced labour camps and less extremely in poorly led organisations that use the rationale, 'Just do as I say.' That statement effectively replaces a person–person relationship with a person–object relationship.

Thus, when tasks are assigned, the leader should be clear about the context of the work (for example, the overall state of the market or business or the political or societal situation for government agencies or non-profit associations), the purpose (to satisfy an important potential customer), and the quality requirements of the output (goal) as well as the quantity requirements. In addition, the person needs to know what resources are available and what limits are operating. Last, but not least, the time to completion must be clear. None of this interferes with the work of determining how the work should be done (as will be discussed in more depth in Part 3).

Thus our definition that work is about how we turn an intention (goal) into reality. Now, clearly, some work is more difficult than other work. Some tasks take more time to complete than others. The pathway needed to achieve the goal may be more or less complex and involve more or fewer abstract variables, in other words, elements that cannot be seen or touched. For example, designing a remuneration system is probably more complex than photocopying a letter; constructing an effective strategic plan is probably more complex than cleaning an office. These differences in complexity of work will be explored in more depth in Chapter 8.

Whatever the complexity, however, all these activities require work. They are all about turning intention into reality and they all require the person to work out the best way (the how) of achieving the goal. All of these types of work, in their own way, can be satisfying and creative.

The person in the process of working has to determine the relationship between what he or she is doing and the output. Each one of us has to recognise how our current behaviour impacts on, or is more or less likely to produce, the desired result. It is the understanding of this relationship between process and product that is critical to achieving our intention.

As such, work may involve understanding a primarily technical process such as aluminium smelting, electrical transmission, photographic development, dressing a wound or servicing a car. Work may also require understanding a primarily social process – leading a team, interviewing or recruiting a potential new employee, providing customer service or communicating information. In employment work there is usually some interaction between the technical and social processes.

Work fundamentally is about understanding cause and effect; bringing about a deliberate change by managing an intervention in the world. As mentioned, these processes may differ in complexity. Causal chains may be long and complex. There may not even be an obvious chain but a pattern or even a more abstract connection.

Throughout our lives, we continue to learn and refine our understanding of how process relates to outcome. As discussed in Part 1, we need to predict our environment. We also like to feel that we have an influence and effect on the world. It is essential for our sense of identity and mental health. Depression is essentially a state of mind where we feel we do not or cannot have any positive and productive effect, and it leads to a withdrawal from work.

The affirmation of our contribution to the process and outcome, especially when positive, has the effect of encouraging us to use and develop our capabilities. This is why recognition of work is so important. It is very significant if the leader can accurately recognise the different contributions of team members.

We have all had the experience of our work being wrongly attributed to, or even claimed by, others. We have also had the experience of our work being ignored. These are very demoralising experiences, causing perhaps anger and resentment, or a feeling of 'why bother?'.

We use the term 'recognition' because it is a neutral term and does not presuppose a successful outcome, unlike 'reward'. It is essential to understand why a process failed to produce the desired result so that we can improve in the future. Recognition of apparent failure does not necessarily imply blame as the person may have done everything she or he could or was supposed to do. Without proper recognition there can be very little learning.

We have argued that, while there are many, varied definitions of work, the authors have found it useful to define work as 'turning intention into reality'. This is not an idiosyncratic definition as it is consistent with others' definitions, notably those of Jaques and Schutz. Like Jaques we see work as essential to a sense of identity and productive relationship in the world.

Work is essentially about the 'how'. It is concerned with the construction of a method, or pathway, in order to achieve a desired result. Work may differ in complexity but has the common feature of requiring human judgment and decision making. Work (especially employment or paid work) inevitably involves constructing this pathway within limits. We cannot do whatever we wish. We do not have unlimited resources.

The final essential component of work is the accurate recognition by another, or others (for example, team leader, fellow team members), of our contribution. Such recognition encourages us to use our capabilities to our full potential.

3 *Human Capability*

Elements of individual capability

In any organisation there is work to do. That work differs in kind: from designing a new product, to articulating a long-term strategic plan, to stacking shelves or maintaining equipment. Some of this work requires significant leadership work with people; other work requires more technical knowledge and skill. It is fairly obvious that not everyone can carry out all of the tasks equally successfully. This is not just a question of volume of work but the nature of the work itself. People's skills and ability differ. A positive organisation is one where each person's skills and ability matches the work they are required to do. In order to consider assigning work appropriately it is necessary to have a concept of human capability. Elements of capability can become muddled. What we mean by a term can be confused, for example, what elements can be learned and influenced – and how? Our concept of human capability has been developed and refined by experience and practice. In this chapter we will explain it and then raise some questions of comparison and why we have not included some more popular concepts.

When selecting a person for a role or considering a person for a particular project or task, the following elements are critical. We will define and discuss each in turn. All of these elements should be examined, although some are more open to influence than others (see Box 3.1).

KNOWLEDGE

Knowledge here consists of two types: first, part or all of an accepted body of knowledge, and second knowledge that has been produced as a largely self-generated body (see the discussion of heuristics in Part 1).

Knowing all or part of a body of knowledge is what we have referred to before as scientific meaning. It is concerned with knowledge of currently agreed-upon definitions, theories or facts, for example, nuclear physics, the periodic table, algebra, calculus and/or other scientific disciplines with current but not necessarily uncontested definitions. In the arts there are also bodies of knowledge covering facts ('Who wrote *Great Expectations* and who are the main characters?') and knowledge about opinions ('Do you know Christopher Hill's analysis of the English Civil War? How does he critique this conflict?'). Essentially this element is about what we learn in schools, colleges and universities and from our own researches. Employers and educationalists may differ as to what is important to learn but it is about learning subjects from an established curriculum. We make assumptions about knowledge from the shorthand of qualifications, even though there are debates about the 'value' of degrees from certain universities or institutions.

Another type of knowledge is self-generated – heuristics. Thus a person may have 'knowledge' of people with mental illness, living in a large family or travelling internationally.

> **Box 3.1   Elements of Individual Capability**
>
> - knowledge
> - technical skills
> - social process skills
> - mental processing ability
> - application.

The point about this knowledge is it may not be organised into disciplines or accepted structures. It is more difficult to test, but can be elicited by careful questioning and listening.

All roles and all tasks require some prior knowledge and it is important to be clear what that is and to what extent the person has such knowledge.

TECHNICAL SKILLS

This element refers to a proficiency in the *use* of knowledge. It includes learned routines that reduce the complexity of work required to complete a task.

It has been recognised that having a skill makes a task easier. It essentially reduces the complexity of a task because you do not have to think through or work out the process. This emphasises the difference between knowledge and skill. I may have a significant amount of knowledge about the internal combustion engine, but can I change a piston? I may know all the letters on a keyboard, but can I type?

The need for skill and the difference between knowledge and skill is most apparent when we learn a new skill: driving, playing tennis, golf, skiing and so on. At first it is very difficult to steer, change gear and keep an eye on the road at the same time. Gradually the processes become less conscious until it is internalised and 'second nature'. This allows us to concentrate on what is really important. In the case of driving, not having 'to think' about steering, breaking or changing gear allows us to concentrate on the road, other traffic and pedestrians. This is most apparent when we suddenly have to re-awake to the process because of a flat tyre, poor brakes or loss of steering.

In effect, technical skills once acquired do not require much cortical brain activity. This effectively allows more room for the cortical activity to be applied to real and current problem solving (see Mental Processing Ability, below). The more pressing the immediate problem, the more important the embedding of the skill. So a firefighter does not want to be working out how breathing apparatus works whilst in a burning building. A combat soldier does not want to try and remember how to load a rifle in the middle of a battle.

We recognise that certain skills appear to be learned or acquired more easily by some people than others. We recognise that some people have what is usually referred to as a 'natural aptitude'. Others appear to have no aptitude at all: they are 'all fingers and thumbs', or more technically, they suffer from 'dyspraxia'. We do not intend to discuss this in depth here as our experience is that technical skills in organisations can be taught to most people if they are sufficiently interested. Those organisations where the key staff are there first and foremost for their extraordinary technical skills are not usually traditional employment hierarchies, for example, professional athletes and artists.

Whatever the work, just as we have said about knowledge, it is critical to identify what skills are required and make an assessment of whether and to what extent a person has or could quickly acquire such skills.

SOCIAL PROCESS SKILLS

For many years we have given significant attention to understanding relationships. Work is a social activity. Survival requires social cohesion. Values are embedded in the process of all relationships. Their significance is obvious throughout this book. Therefore understanding and managing social processes is critical (see Box 3.2).

This element is at the heart of leadership. Too often in organisations we have seen leadership roles given to people who are very technically skilled and/or intellectually very able but who have poor social process skills. The result is usually disastrous and at times tragic if the person involved is lost as to why they are failing.

By social process skills we do not mean the ability to 'be nice' or 'get on with people'. Social processes may involve handling confrontations, disciplinary issues or poor performance. In the Church and many voluntary organisations people equate good relations and social process with being friendly or not upsetting people, whereas we are referring to the wider spectrum.

As mentioned in Part 1 of the book, relationships with people is not 'soft science'. This area can be highly complex and sensitive. Brute force, oppression or intimidation will not only fail over time but will not release capability. If we are not to objectify people we must understand how they see the world. We must understand their mythologies how they view us and each other. In addition we must work out ways of influencing these relationships so that they are directed to a productive purpose not simply to building the harmony of the group. In short, if we put too much emphasis on output and thereby ignore social process, that output will not be sustained over time. If we put too much emphasis on social processes in the sense of harmony, we may forget the need for output.

This highlights a fundamental difference between work relationships and friendships. Work relationships exist to produce a good or service that is valued by others. Friendships exist for the sake of the relationship. A friendship does not have to be productive or even particularly valued by others outside the friendship. Friends can just be with one other. Confusing these different types of relationship can lead to problems. It is not necessary for people at work to be friends as long as they behave towards each other positively according to the values continua. It is not necessary for friends to engage in highly productive work. This does not mean that work colleagues cannot be friends, or that friends cannot be actively engaged in making or doing things merely that the social processes are different. You may have experience or know friends who have embarked on a business venture or turned a hobby into a business who have become disillusioned. You may have experience or know of colleagues who have been 'let down' by people at work: 'I thought you were my friend – why did you apply for that job?'.

The authors have long been wary of companies that promote a lot of social events, 'bonding', inviting spouses and partners to events and talking about work being like a family. It is not that these are inherently bad but they can cause confusion and cynicism when my 'invitation' is really a requirement and the 'social, bonding event' is really a covert assessment centre.

Here we are referring to a person's ability to establish good, productive working relationships both directly and indirectly through teamwork and delegation. It requires an interest in and

---

Box 3.2   Definition of Social Process Skills

Social process skills are those skills that give the ability to read social situations, understand the underlying social processes and to influence those processes productively.

genuine regard for people, an appreciation of people not as 'production units' but as creative and curious individuals who have their own unique way of seeing and being in the world.

This element, that for many years we have termed social process skills, has similarities with the more recent term *emotional intelligence* (Goleman, 1996). While we have detailed differences and concerns with that concept in Part 1, we do agree that this element has been underestimated by many organisations as an essential part of successful working relationships.

MENTAL PROCESSING ABILITY

Perhaps the least familiar of these components of human capability is mental processing ability (often referred to as MPA). We begin with Elliott Jaques' definition of cognitive processes: '... the mental processes by which a person takes information; picks it over; plays with it; analyses it; puts it together; reorganises it; judges and reasons with it; and makes conclusions, plans and decisions, and takes action.' (Jaques, 1989: 33). These mental processes are the way an individual organises thinking when working (attempting to turn intention into reality) (see Box 3.3).

The richness and diversity of the world that each person creates is indicative of the complexity of the mental process that a person can apply to make sense out of their experience of the world. Because our environment is constantly changing this effort to make sense of it is a continuous process. It requires constant work – turning intention into reality.

From our own experience we know that people are more able or less able to comprehend a situation, to formulate cause and effect relationships between events they experience in the world. People show differences in their ability to generate and test hypotheses about relationships and to predict the outcome of a course of action. All of us have differing abilities to do work. The specifics of these differences will be discussed later (see Chapter 8).

Each of us perceives the world in our own way. Some people will see the world as it presents itself in front of them; they are most comfortable with what they can directly see and even touch. They like direct links between the action they take and the result they get. Their solution will deal with what is immediately present. Other people will see that the results they

---

Box 3.3   Definition of Mental Processing Ability (MPA)

Mental processing ability: The ability to make order out of the chaotic environment in which humans live out their lives. It is the ability to pattern and construe the world in terms of scale and time. The level of our MPA will determine the amount and complexity of information that we can process in doing so. (This definition draws in part from I. Macdonald (1984: 2) and also from Jaques (1989: 33). Also see his definition of cognitive power, above).[1]

1   By 'chaos', we refer not to random disorder, but to the patterns of complexity and the multiple scales of complexity that are now being studied as part of a general theory of chaos (see Gleick, 1987, if you wish to pursue this topic). Classical science and much theory of organisation has searched for ordered linear patterns that allow prediction: if this, then that.

Chaos theory studies non-linear patterns where prediction becomes more and more difficult the further you move out into the future, a situation which covers virtually all significant organisational and policy problems today (see Zimm, 2002). A minute change in one tiny variable may cause profound changes out into the future. Chaos theorists refer to this as the 'butterfly effect'. The idea that a butterfly fluttering its wings in Beijing in January disturbs the air and this perturbation may be one of the causal links for a thunderstorm in New Jersey in June.

Chaos theory forces us to confront the fact that no matter how much experience we have and how well we understand the present, the predictions we make about the future will become progressively less accurate as they extend forward in time. Our mental processing ability is the facility to make order of this chaos, to perceive the universe and to 'discover' or 'create' the patterns (order) which we can then use as we take action.

want cannot be achieved directly, that many different systems and outside influences will have to be changed, if there is to be a successful outcome. The difference is in the way different individuals take in and organise information, how broadly they see the interrelationships of what is going on, and how much they can encompass in their vision of the world.

For example, a mechanic is given a truck with a broken gearbox. To one person that is the problem and can be fixed today. Another person thinks that maybe this is caused by poor driving and considers how it might be rectified. Another considers the design of the gearbox. Another questions whether we need to use trucks at all for this work.

Like Jaques, Gibson and Isaac (1978) and Stamp (1978), we agree that these different ways of seeing the world are divided into distinct groupings. Rather than MPA being seen as a gradual, continuous line along which the whole population is spread, what Jaques originally found was a series of types of processing. Because each approach to the world and problem solving is discrete, someone with Type II MPA will see a problem and its potential solutions in a completely different way from someone with Type IV MPA. The person with Type II MPA will simply not see the problem with the same range of variables, relationships and consequences. These differing approaches are neither right nor wrong, but their appropriateness depends upon the context and particular task to be accomplished.

There have been many attempts to describe this intellectual or cognitive element of capability. This ranges from the classic IQ to new and different forms of 'intelligence' such as crystallised and fluid (Belsky, 1990). What is common about all of these attempts, including ours and Jaques', is that all are concerned with problem solving and all are concerned with moving from the concrete to the abstract as part of the higher complexity problem solving.

We discuss this in more depth in Chapter 8 and by comparison with Jaques' concept below.

APPLICATION

Application is defined here as 'the effort and energy that a person puts into applying the other elements of capability to their work'.

People may be very able in terms of mental processing, very skilled in managing social processes. They may have great general knowledge and technical skill, but unless they actually apply it in the workplace it is of only latent value. Practising managers value this attribute for its obvious practical relevance.

When one of the authors (Macdonald) worked for the British Civil Service Selection Board, this element was divided into 'drive' and 'determination'. Kolbe (1991) refers to it as 'conation', a term we like and which has a similar concept. Essentially this is the element that affects not whether a problem can be solved (by someone) but whether it will be solved. A person with high application sees a task through to completion.

So why not include experience, competencies or personality/temperament?

Many models of capability include experience as an element; we do not. In fact, we include what is usually meant by 'experience' in our concepts of knowledge (especially self-generated knowledge) and technical and social process skills. We deliberately do not use it as a separate element because we have found it often leads to a trap. This trap is to ask for 'experience' which translates to years or time doing something rather than what has been *learned* from doing something. For example, 'Oh good, she has three years' experience in sales' or 'Oh dear, he has no experience of working in another culture'. A well-known saying raises the question 'Does he have five years' experience or one year's experience repeated five times?'.

We do not use the extremely popular term *competency*. This is for two reasons. First, at a more general level, 'competency' is not specific enough. Competency fits well when unpacking other elements. For example, in technical skills, we need to ask in what process should a person be competent for this role? We regard competencies as related more to specific skills in the technical, commercial and social areas. One danger with competencies is that they can be poorly defined in terms of complexity and level of work. So, for example, is a person competent in terms of leadership? Well, does this mean at any level of work? Is it better to be described as social process skills? *Planning* is another word that floats from level to level but, as with other competencies, can be evident at one level and absent at another. Drawing up a strategic plan for a multi-national corporation is quite different from a departmental plan or shift plan.

With regard to personality or temperament, like Jaques we see this as possible negative distraction. We agree with Jaques that a role can be filled and successfully operated by people of very different personality. Only at the extremes, virtual mental illness or psychopathy, does this have a significant bearing. We again can fall into traps of assuming that sales people should be extroverts, and that leaders should be charismatic. One of the most effective leaders in the British Army in recent times, Sir Peter de la Billier (commander of the British Forces in the first Gulf War and head of the SAS), is a quiet, relatively small, introverted man who certainly does not fit the stereotypical, macho leader but is most highly regarded and decorated for his capability as a leader.

We have seen Myers-Briggs type indicators used creatively to understand existing team dynamics better but are very wary of associating any specific personality type with a role type.

Nature or nurture?

When discussing any human attribute, there is usually a debate about what is inherited, what is constitutional, innate, learned, acquired and so on. Many people have devoted a great deal of time and effort to such questions, which cannot be resolved here in a few paragraphs. For practical purposes we need to address the nature/nurture debate because it is important to determine where it is worth putting in effort to improve. In doing so we are cautious about any proposition that makes absolute statements, especially about human attributes that are supposed to be unalterable. In this we have been influenced by the work of Stephen Jay Gould, *The Mismeasure of Man* (1996) and Stephan Chorover, *From Genesis to Genocide* (1979). Here Gould quotes the early 20th century psychologist Goddard from his book *Psychology of the Normal and Subnormal* (1919) to demonstrate the kind of statement that must be avoided:

> We must next learn that there are great groups of men, laborers, who are but little above the child, who must be told what to do and shown how to do it; and if we would avoid disaster, must not be put into positions where they will have to act upon their own initiative or their own judgement.

(pp. 243–244)

MENTAL PROCESSING ABILITY

Despite these caveats, we cannot ignore the reality of difference, especially with regard to mental processing ability. Further, like Jaques, we do see this as a maturational process and one which may not be much influenced by external factors. Further, we see the way in which a person makes sense of the world (complexity of their processing) as set by the time a person reaches early adulthood. We have not seen successful examples of adults learning entirely new mental processes, although people can learn techniques and methods that enhance their current abilities or help realise potential. These are in fact much closer to learned skills.

TECHNICAL SKILLS

On the other hand there is plenty of evidence for the acquisition of skills, even late in life. While, as we stated, some people appear to have more aptitude than others (hand/eye co-ordination, for example, or balance or dexterity), most skills are teachable to the level of organisational requirement. Some aspects of very fine craftwork or sporting prowess may be more difficult to learn and are either due to aptitude or life-long learning (child apprenticeships). For the purposes of this book and the range of activities covered by most organisations, the technical, mechanical and other skills required to work effectively are, from our observation, possible to teach to the great majority of people.

SOCIAL PROCESS SKILLS

Again, we believe these can be taught. We do not subscribe to the simple 'born leader' theory. It is inevitable that early experiences and opportunities can strongly affect this area. A person brought up and encouraged to engage in social processes is more likely to be adept and skilful than someone brought up either in a more isolated milieu or someone who has been encouraged to develop relationships with objects rather than people.

It is interesting to note here the general, but not exclusive, nature of socialisation for boys and girls. Girls are more often encouraged to engage in social process (talking, discussing, analysing relationships) and playing social games (including families, dolls and so on) than boys. Boys are likely to be socialised into interest with mechanics, technical, electronic games and simplify or ignore the 'gossip' of feelings and motivation with any depth.

Even so, we find empathy is necessary for even the most ordinary relationships and, as such, even an ordinary 'male' life cannot avoid the development of mythologies. All human relationships are still founded on values. There are very few lost causes.

The analogy for social process would be more like learning a language. If it happens early in life, it is easy, natural and the facility is both acquired and used with apparently little effort. Learning a language later in life is not only physically more difficult; it requires more determination, effort and desire. It is not, however, impossible.

KNOWLEDGE

Clearly, like skills or even more so than skills, knowledge can be acquired throughout life unless there is a biological reason preventing this, such as Alzheimer's. It is, by definition, learned. Even self-generated knowledge acquisition continues. People, however apparently 'fixed in their ways', will not be able to prevent learning even if it is uncomfortable. However the *rate* of learning and hence the amount that can be learned will vary, and will also vary according to mental processing ability. A person who can handle high levels of complexity and construe and understand complex patterns and reduce them to more simple structures will acquire knowledge at a faster rate. This is generally described as learning from first principles (see Box 3.4).

Thus while we can continue to acquire knowledge the rate of acquisition and use of it depends upon our mental processing ability.

APPLICATION

Together with Kolbe's concept of conation, we again recognise that some people appear to have more energy, drive and determination than others. Whether this is innate or strongly influenced by early experience, we do not know. What we do know is that application in the workplace is very strongly influenced by the context. This includes in order of influence:

- The quality (that is, behaviour) of the person's immediate leader including how well or not the leader clarifies expectations and gives feedback.
- The structure and systems of the organisation: Is the work of the role clear? Does it have proper authority? Are the work systems helpful in achieving goals or are they a bureaucratic hindrance of 'red tape'?
- The general quality of relationships. This includes other leaders, the manager one removed and work colleagues.
- Symbols: the quality of the equipment, plant, housekeeping and so on.

So while some people may give up before others, and few of us have the drive and determination of the explorer Ernest Shackleton, this element, for most people, is influenced by their environment. In Gallup and other work surveys there is a consistent message that the main reason for people leaving an organisation (for negative reasons) is poor leadership in the form of the person's immediate manager.

One of the authors (Macdonald and Couchman, 1980 and Macdonald, 1990) observed and documented significant changes in behaviour, especially 'application', when the context changed for people with learning difficulties (see Box 3.5).

Caveats

We have already warned of the dangers of labelling so clearly stated in Gould's work *The Mismeasure of Man* (1996). There are other dangers:

It is very easy to fall into one of two main traps:

1. *Assess the person not the role.* Here we look at ranking people against each other rather than being clear about *what the work is that needs to be done*. Before we look at capability we must be clear about capability for what? Too often people are assigned to poorly designed roles, given poorly defined tasks in the hope, sometimes realised, that they will work out what to do. Apart from leading to poor accountability, power and chance achievement this is simply passing the buck or asking someone else to do your work. They should at least get a percentage of your salary for doing your work.
2. *Be careful not to elevate one element above others.* Certain roles or tasks will appropriately emphasise one or more of the elements. For example, a leadership role may require more

Box 3.4   Working – Under Pressure by Roderick Macdonald

In 1982 I was commanding 59 Independent Commando Squadron Royal Engineers as a young (34-year-old) major in the Royal Engineers. We had just sailed 8000 miles from the United Kingdom and audaciously landed a force of 3000 Royal Marine and Army Commandos and Parachute troops on the Falkland Islands. The Falkland Islands, close to the Antarctic continent and the coastline of Argentina, had recently been invaded by 11 000 Argentine troops covered by combat air patrols flying from Argentina. They had plenty of time to establish strong defensive positions.

The history of amphibious landings is not glorious. Many thousands of soldiers died at failed landings in World War I, such as Gallipoli, and in World War II on the beaches of Calais. Even when landings were successful, such as during the American war in the Pacific against the Japanese or Allied landings in Sicily and Normandy, they all had one thing in common; yet again thousands of soldiers died. Another defining issue in all successful landings was overwhelming air superiority in support of the amphibious forces. For the first time an amphibious landing was to be undertaken by Western forces without air superiority. The British paid heavily. Warships, logistic ships and civilian ships taken up from trade were sunk by the Argentine air force with impunity. I was part of the small British force that landed in San Carlos, 75 miles away from the capital Stanley. We were without supply of ammunition, food, clothing or helicopters. This occurred in the midst of an Antarctic winter where temperatures regularly dropped well below zero and wind, snow and rain blew in excess of 30 miles an hour. There was no shelter because there are no trees. In order to regain air superiority from the Argentines it was essential that a landing and re-fuelling strip was built on the island, and this was one of my tasks.

The combat and commando Royal Engineers supporting 3 Commando Brigade had some experience of doing this work; however, there was need for technical expertise to give guidance on the intricacies of both the design and construction process. Design started quickly but ran into trouble when we discovered that most of the equipment for the task was sitting at the bottom of the South Atlantic Ocean. The stores had been loaded on a supply ship, *The Atlantic Conveyor*, which had been sunk by Argentine aircraft. We did manage to unload some equipment that had been transported on another ship specifically for repairing the airfield at Stanley when it was eventually taken by British forces. Even the fuel supply, pumping and rafting equipment was not fully intact. This posed considerable problems for the young troop commander who had been given this task. He turned to the technical expert who had been given to him to do this design work and the answer was swiftly given.

'We can't do it, this is not possible. We don't have enough equipment to build this installation!'

The technical expert was correct. According to the book, which he knew in detail, the work could not be done. However, this was not the answer I needed to hear. Soldiers and sailors were dying because we did not have air superiority and we needed to build this installation regardless of what the book said. The technical expert did not have the mental processing ability to adopt a different strategy. It was now up to the troop commander. This young officer did have engineering knowledge. This was a combination of theoretical engineering knowledge from his degree course at Cambridge University and down-to-earth practical training from Army engineering school and training exercises. His higher level of mental processing ability allowed him to come up with a unique design to complete and build this installation with the equipment available. This was accomplished in very difficult circumstances. As a result the British achieved air superiority with their Harrier aircraft. It was a small but important step in helping achieve overall victory in the campaign. The young troop commander was mentioned in dispatches (bronze oak leaf medal) for this and, later, for bravery under fire.

So what do we learn from this? We certainly do not learn that technical knowledge is not important. It is. It is equally dangerous to come up with a theoretical design that does not work because there is a lack of understanding of basic engineering principles as it is to fail to come up with a design because resources are not exactly as stated in a learned procedure. We learn that it is important to have both. We need to have mental processing ability to be able to apply an apposite level of complexity to solve a problem at the appropriate level. Equally we need knowledge, experience and skills, both technical and social, to be able to come up with a practical design and more importantly to implement the solution with other people. There is no golden key here. To succeed under these circumstances we need it all.

Box 3.5   A Comparison with Jaques' Theory of Human Capability

Those familiar with Jaques' theory of capability, most completely summarised in his book *Human Capability* (Jaques and Cason, 1994), will note similarities between his conclusions and ours. This is hardly surprising as all of the authors worked directly with Jaques for many years, discussing and refining these ideas. Jaques' concept of 'applied capability' distinguishes the mental processing component from others such as 'values' and 'skilled knowledge'. What Jaques means by 'valuing' the work, we refer to as 'application': the underlying active interest and drive to do the work. We distinguish 'skills' from 'knowledge' and further separate out technical skills and social process skills, which is consistent with our general differentiation between the ability to work with objects and the ability to work with people.

Jaques was also concerned with terminology, and in *Human Capability* (1994: 19) he states 'we have decided to switch from the language of cognition and cognitive processes to the language of mental processing'. Indeed the authors found this switch to be helpful and have used the term 'mental processing ability' to describe this element for many years.

The difference here is in the nature of maturation. Whilst we agree with Jaques that while the *capability* to do work (that is, the ability to apply all the necessary components) does mature, the *type* of mental processing does not. We agree there are different types (see Chapter 8) and that they can be described as Jaques and Stamp, a long-term colleague who worked extensively in this area – see Stamp in Jaques et al., *Levels of Abstraction*, (1978) – describe 'mode', but that these different types are evident from an early adult age (certainly by the early 20s).

Indeed, Jaques himself says 'If this multi-track maturation hypothesis is valid, then it ought to be the case that [this] should be observable at young ages.' He then cites Cason's and Jacobs' reliability to do this but says 'no one has as yet been able to articulate precisely what that is'. Our experience is like Cason's and Jacob's (long-term colleagues of Jaques in the USA – See Jaques and Cason, 1994) but even more so because their explanation of complexity in mental processing is the most obviously identifiable feature. The mental processing ability is identified by listening to argument or analysing writing to examine the complexity of that argument. This is also the way that others associated with Jaques' work identify mental processing ability.

What is changing is the ability to carry out sustained work over time, that is, in the context of uncertainty using all elements of capability. Thus increasing social and technical skills, knowledge and having a clear sense of direction or purpose all help to sustain activity. This is what we believe to be at the heart of Jaques' insight into time-span, that is the ability to continue an endeavour (work) further into the future. This is clearly dependent upon the nature of mental processing ability but not dependent *only* upon this. Thus mental processing ability is a necessary but not sufficient condition.

Why is this so important? If someone uses Jaques' maturational developmental curves (see

Human Capability, 1994: 85 and 86) then a problem becomes apparent. If I identify a mental processing of, say, type IV complexity (Jaques' second order: B4) in a person of 25 years, do I then decide this is a current view and likely to change (Jaques' mode VII or VIII) or, if it does not change, this will place the person in maturation mode IV – a very significantly different analysis and prediction of future ability.

To take a slightly different approach, Macdonald worked with young adults in their 20s and 30s with mental health problems, many of whom were diagnosed as schizophrenic. It was clear from discussions with them that many were of relatively high mental processing ability (Jaques' mode III, IV, V) but they were unable to apply this ability for any length of time in work projects either in employed or voluntary work. This gave them a further serious problem since they were only able to engage in work which was far below their intellectual level, for example, cleaning, manual work due to anxiety and stress if they engaged in work of higher complexity. This is an extreme form of the interruption of the maturation of the *capability* to engage in work (over time) as opposed to the evidence of their mental processing ability.

social process skills than a technical maintenance role, which in turn may require more specific knowledge and technical skills. However, it is dangerous to emphasise one element at the expense of another. For example, while mental processing ability is necessary, it is not sufficient and will not entirely compensate for poor application or social process skills.

If we assume that the knowledge and technical skills are slightly easier to specify (as in criteria for selection, for example, must have clean driving licence, degree in Chemistry, keyboard skills or computer literacy) we are left with three dimensions: mental processing ability; social process skills and application, we can see those in comparison using the example of three people A, B and C (see Figure 3.1).

This representation is not strictly accurate since MPA should actually be discontinuous. However, we can see that person A may be very impressive in terms of drive and energy but may well fail to address or even understand the work really required. With luck they may not cause too much damage as poor social process skills may cause them to be isolated. However in a leadership role this could be catastrophic. Person B is certainly bright enough and relates fairly well to people but does not have the energy to get much done. The saving grace may be that the person is bright enough to find the short cuts! Person C is heading for a heart attack or breakdown since they are highly committed (as evidenced by the high application score), and relate really well but just cannot do the work (solve problems) required. They will put in more and more hours and be at a loss to know why efforts are failing.

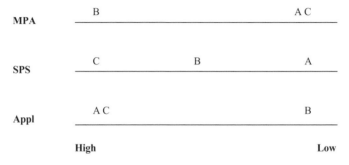

Figure 3.1   Comparison of Mental Processing Ability, Social Process Skills and Application in Persons A, B and C

The point here is that we must be wary of believing that a high ranking of one element will compensate for another; that a high degree of energy will make up for a lack of MPA or really good MPA will compensate for poor social process skills. As has been mentioned, application and social process skills can be improved but not to the extent that they make another element irrelevant. In determining what is required in each of these five elements it must be borne in mind that each is a *necessary but not sufficient condition*.

Perhaps the most important caveat is not to confuse capability and the worth of a *person*. These elements refer to the capability to do work. A major problem is that a hierarchy of capability to do work of certain types can become confused with a hierarchy of personal worth. That is to fall into the trap of assuming that 'if I have a higher MPA than you, I am a better person', that somehow operators are less worthy as people than managers. This has echoes of feudalism and aristocracy and is still evident in many industrialised societies especially in Europe. It also reflects a confusion between a meritocracy and other types of social organisation, the subject of the next chapter.

We have seen many of these ideas, especially complexity and level of work, become substitutes for old status symbols. They must be monitored and addressed as they can become destructive.

This model of capability, with its five elements, can be used not only to consider an individual's suitability for a role or task but also to review an entire organisation or part of it. The leadership can review the organisation's capability in more general terms: How do we score in mental processing ability? Do we have enough technical skills and/or knowledge? Do we have people who are committed and have the drive and determination? Is it a high or low energy organisation?

The issue of capability is highly significant in organisations that are producing goods and services because the most effective way of delivering them is through a meritocracy, as we shall discuss in the next chapter.

Summary

We have outlined a model of human capability to work in terms of five elements: knowledge, technical skills, social process skills, mental processing ability and application. We have described these elements and considered how far each can be influenced especially by external factors.

We have also drawn attention to the dangers of labelling (as discussed by Stephen Jay Gould), and the misuse of these concepts. Despite claims over the years by many writers, these are only *hypotheses* and not absolute facts. We offer this model as a way for people, especially managers, to consider the capability and suitability for people to carry out tasks and/or fill roles. The decision is still a matter of managerial judgment.

Even more important is being clear about *what the work is*. One of Jaques' favourite and best questions when confronted with organisational puzzles was 'what is the work to be done?' We regard this as one of the best organisational questions anyone can ask. This must be addressed before considering who might do it. Far too often we find, despite the fact that the first question has not been answered, selection or task allocation still occurs.

Finally, we have also found that most people have a very good sense of their own capability. They are neither passive nor waiting to be told by their superiors. We do have a saying, 'Beware anyone whose ego is bigger than their intellect – no matter how big the intellect'. However, by and large, if a person has a real understanding of what is required (the work to be done), they have a good sense of whether they can do it, even if it involves acknowledging it will be challenging, or will involve learning skills.

This assessment of capability should not be something that is done *to* someone but should entail mature, adult discussion. We hope the elements described above will help to make that discussion more realistic and constructive.

4 *Meritocracy*

We, like others, observe that now most goods and services are provided through organisations, and more so than at any other time. Prior to the industrial revolution agriculture was dominant over manufacturing and people worked and lived in the same communities, primarily in family groups or collections of family groups.

Organisations beget bureaucracy, but the phenomenon of bureaucracy is not new in itself – in pre-industrial times bureaucracies were more limited to government or religious spheres (see, for example, Shafritz and Ott,, 1996). Although there was some writing on this subject in the 18th and 19th century, for example, by Adam Smith and Max Weber, most of the writings on organisation, Taylor (1972), Weber (Gerth and Mills, 1946), Fayol (1930), Gulick (1937), Barnard (1938), Roethlisberger and Dickson (1939), Burns and Stalker (1966), Blau (1956), Emery and Trist (1960), Jaques (1976), Drucker (1954, 1969), Mintzberg (1989) and so on are products of the 20th century. Bureaucracies and organisations on this scale are a recent development. As a widespread social phenomenon, they have come to dominate in most developed human societies.

We argue throughout this book that a meritocracy is the most efficient way of producing goods and services. We do not say that a meritocracy has to be large, international or publicly owned. We are not confusing it with a bureaucracy, which may or may not have some of the characteristics of a meritocracy (see Box 4.1).

People are rewarded on the basis of merit and people can ask, without irony, 'what have I done to deserve this?'. We describe this simply as:

- the right people
- in the right roles
- doing the right work.

This may seem obvious, but true meritocracies are quite rare. Most organisations are hybrids involving other systems that are not based on merit.

Organisational principles alternative to merit

SENIORITY

Another, and still quite common, form of organisation is based on seniority. That is, people get rewarded and/or promoted on the basis of either age or length of time in role or employment. This has been popular for two reasons. First, it appears to be more objective and 'fairer' than using a system of judgment or measurement of performance. However, it is essentially a statement that either the organisation cannot differentiate between the performance of

---

Box 4.1   Definition of a Meritocratic Organisation

Meritocratic organisation: A social organisation where those selected and appointed to work to produce goods and services are chosen on the basis of their capability to do the work required.

The reward, promotion and disciplinary systems are operated on the basis of work performance and behaviour that has been or could be specified.

---

individuals or that the method of judgment is inaccurate or unfair. Second, it more obviously relates to family life or agriculture where rewards and celebrations are based upon the passing of time (birthdays and anniversaries) or seasons passing in a cyclical way. This system also presumes that people are unable to use judgment but are, instead, essentially extensions to machines and effectively indistinguishable from them.

NEPOTISM

Here position and reward are based upon kinship. This is still clearly evident in large global organisations such as Fox (which is owned by the Murdoch family) or the 2005, Glazer take-over of the UK football club Manchester United where the three Glazer sons are appointed to significant roles by their father, the owner. This is not to say that these people are automatically incapable of the work, rather that their appointment is primarily based on family relationships. This is a system of favouritism where family relationship is a significant factor.

Societies have historically used such systems in governance. The concept of a royal family, and an aristocracy with inherited wealth, governing a country well relies on what we believe to be chance factors that a son or daughter will have the capability to carry out the work of the role. History has seen the consequences of such systems in the form of the English Civil War and the French and Russian Revolutions. This system of authority is compounded when other sources of authority are assumed, such as God's will. The theory of the divine right of kings in Europe and Japan not only perpetuated a family dynasty but underpinned that authority by claiming a divine authority to the system.

DEMOCRACY

Here the appointment to positions of authority is by vote. As a system of governance this is now put forward as the most effective and assumed to be a 'good thing' for everyone especially by the current Western governments. The passion with which democracy as a form of authority is defended can be compared with the missionary zeal and governmental support for Christianity and missionary work during British colonial rule.

In fact, we can see that publicly owned businesses do include a democratic process. Here the right to vote is obtained by owning a share. This, in turn, gives the authority to elect board members who in turn appoint an executive. The difference in democratic societies is that, by being a member of society (a 'social shareholder'), an adult has the right to vote for a government, which then appoints an executive which in turn is supported by an appointed civil/public service. This is discussed in more depth in the next chapter.

The important issue with any appointed executive is that appointments are made and rewards distributed on the basis of merit.

Authoritarian versus democratic organisations

There is considerable confusion concerning democracy in organisations. Some argue that organisations should be 'more democratic and less authoritarian' and assume this is an inherently 'good thing', like universal democratic government (Pateman, 1970). What exactly does this mean? Our view is that hierarchies are not inherently authoritarian. Being clear about authority does not necessarily lead to oppression. Usually this 'democracy' take the form of increased participation or consultation, both essential but discretionary processes available to a leader. Listening to people before making a decision is often a very wise practice. It does not, however, mean the team members have the right to vote, and, by implication, the authority to overrule the leader.

Tony Dunlop, a psychologist who has contributed to these ideas and was a principal of Macdonald Associates, clearly expressed the significance of a meritocracy and the difficulty in creating and sustaining it when he wrote:

> For a meritocracy to function effectively the key requirements are quite specific. Meeting these requirements is more difficult, in that it requires good system design and implementation, and consistent and effective leadership behaviour.
>
> (Dunlop, 1999)

See Table 4.1 for a clear explanation of Dunlop's theory of meritocracy.

Table 4.1   Towards Meritocracy: Aligning System and Leadership

Basic Requirements	Implications for People Systems (Systems, Structure, Staff, Style)	Implications for Leadership (Staff, Style, Skills, Shared Values)
Organisation viewed positively by staff. Cultural alignment.	Comprehensive set of systems backed up by Fair Treatment System to promote appropriate behaviour.	All leadership behaviour, systems and symbols aligned with organisational goals.
Competency in role. Capability matches work complexity.	Recruitment based on capability. Clear role descriptions. Requisite structure.	Assessment of capability in current roles. Judgments on role requirements.
Clear expectations. ('What is expected of me?')	Standard task assignment approach.	Providing context and purpose. Accepting accountability and exercising appropriate authority. Team process management.
Performance review and feedback. ('How am I doing?')	Work performance review system.	Monitoring, coaching and counselling skills.
Merit-based reward.	Performance pay system.	Making and delivering judgments of work performance
Development of potential ('What is my future?')	Career assessment system.	Capability for assessing potential. Mentoring.
Managing unacceptable performance.	Due process exit system.	Confronting and counselling skills.

When people are employed by a meritocracy, they must understand the commercial realities of the business and how their work fits into the overall purpose of the business. They must buy into the business goals and believe that the organisation is worth working for. They must be clear about what they need to do in order to be judged to be performing work successfully, and must trust that the processes in place to determine merit will actually reflect the contribution they are making, taking into account their ability to make a difference from where they are placed in the organisation.

They must be given work that is within their capability, while remaining challenging and providing an opportunity for them to add value by contributing. They must be clear about what is specifically expected of them, get feedback on how they are doing, in a timely manner, so that problems can be addressed, and receive recognition and reward that is related to their contribution to success. Over the longer term they must see that the organisation is willing to support and develop the potential they have, in order for them to make an even greater contribution in the future.

In cases where the person is not performing, where they are not meeting the reasonable expectation of the role, the organisation must address this in an effective way. Avenues must be available to resolve issues of ongoing unacceptable performance efficiently and fairly; because in a meritocracy it is apparent to all that such poor performance should not be carried by the other staff if the business is going to thrive or even survive.

Leadership in itself will not achieve a meritocracy because no matter how well intentioned a leader may be, they all make mistakes. Leadership relies on individuals. Good performance may vanish when people change roles unless leadership is underpinned by systems. Each factor that contributes to a credible meritocracy places specific requirement on leaders, and these requirements should be supported and reinforced by effective systems. The appropriate systems need to be in place to drive and support the appropriate leadership behaviour. The system designs need to include control and audit processes, which provide a flow of data on the behaviour of leaders, and on the effectiveness of systems in achieving the business goals (Dunlop, 1999).

Dunlop goes on to explain the critical nature of specific systems and structure, including the need for a fair treatment system (to appeal against felt poor judgment), good task assignment and review, clear performance measures, differential reward, potential assessment and development and unacceptable performance (all of which are discussed in Parts 3 and 4 of this book). Perhaps most importantly Dunlop emphasises the role of leadership in a meritocracy. He writes:

The implications of a meritocracy for leadership capability and performance are enormous. As most outcomes for individuals in a meritocracy depend on leadership judgement, all employees need to have leaders whose judgement they can trust. This means that all leaders must be capable of their role, and must be appropriate in their behaviour. They must be able to understand their manager's work and their own context, so as to add value and provide the context for their teams work. They must have a good understanding of their individual team members' capability, effective task assignment skills, and pay appropriate attention to monitoring and coaching. They must demonstrate the standards themselves, that they wish others to meet, so must be effective schedulers, and meet the reasonable expectations of all team members.

All leaders need to have adequate coaching, counselling and confronting skills in order to deal with issues that arise. They also need to be able to manage social processes within the team, so that the teams' capabilities are harnessed effectively, for problem solving and in taking action to achieve objectives.

(Dunlop, 1999)

Summary

We argue that a meritocracy, if built properly, is the most effective way to deliver goods and services. In order to do this we must distinguish appointment and reward and recognition based on merit from other approaches such as seniority or nepotism. We must also be clear about the differences between a meritocracy, a democracy, and other sorts of human organisation like a gerontocracy or even a theocracy.

This is not to say there is no room in a meritocracy for acknowledging birthdays, religious holidays or years of service; merely that these are distinguished from the work of the role and recognition for that work. Meritocracies are difficult to build and maintain since they require robust structure and systems and, perhaps most importantly, good judgment by the leadership. Output measures are not sufficient; the measures must be related to how people achieved the output: their work performance (see Box 4.2).

Box 4.2   Why Is Meritocratic Hierarchy Potentially So Effective?

In producing goods and services in the context of competition then the three most significant attributes that give advantage are:

1. The relative quality of the good or service – how does it compare with your competitors?
2. The speed at which decisions can be made.
3. The speed at which resources can be distributed.

While some people will complain of hierarchy as 'bureaucratic and slow', in fact, if capable people are in the right roles and they have clear and accepted authority, such an organisation can, because of the vested authority, make decisions without long processes of discussion, voting, consensus and so on. Similarly, authority can be given in a moment to redistribute resources to where they are needed. Clearly the quality of the decisions will depend upon the capability of the people in every role. In an organisation with incapable people in incorrect roles it can very quickly implode, especially in a highly competitive environment.

Capability is important because an organisation can so quickly either advance or go backwards. An obvious example of the need for fast distribution of resources and decision making is an army in combat (a very rigorous form of direct competition). The huge territorial gains made initially by the German army in World War II were based upon clear authority at every level, which allowed for fast decision making whilst the context was changing. It took the Allies several years to match this.

One frequent mistake in organisational theory is to confuse authority and decision making with information. The explosion of information technology and systems has seduced some people to think it is enough just to give people information. However, without clear purpose, authority and capability this method may overload people or simply allow poor decisions to be made by the wrong people.

Information systems (including technology) can be a major help to a meritocracy but only if the information is used at the right level and in a form that is relevant, in other words, by providing real information and not just data.

Finally, a further danger lies in the very strength of meritocracies when they compete with other forms of organisations. If a multi-national corporation is a meritocracy and does not have to worry about specified terms of office, the leadership can potentially plan further into the future and commit sometimes huge resources, they may come into conflict with governments and other forms of civil structure. Often these same civil systems, by their nature, appropriately take significant amounts of time understanding opinion, canvassing, discussing, voting, reviewing and so on – and they may take even longer to deploy resources. Indigenous groups that Macdonald and Stewart worked with needed to combine a system of family relationship with consensus decision making which could take weeks, months or even years. It is a current concern that organisations of very different types need to develop and improve ways of interrelating with each other (see Chapter 7).

5 Associations and Employment Hierarchies

It is sometimes difficult to discriminate meaningfully between different types of organisations. For example, a Scout troop, the Anglican Church, General Motors, the City of Pasadena, the Red Cross, a Law Partnership and the Army can all be accurately described as organisations, yet their purposes, structures, financial sources, systems, leadership, members and employees (if any) all differ.

One common classification separates organisations into public, private and voluntary, but that is of little help in understanding how they operate. More importantly, the terms public and voluntary have social but not scientific meaning. We have only a general understanding when we use such categories. Consequently, people are likely to have different views as to which category a particular organisation belongs. For example, the US Army is made up of volunteers, not draftees, but is it a voluntary organisation? Are the paid employees of the Red Cross volunteers? Where in this three-fold classification does a publicly regulated, shareholder-owned utility fit?

Although the tri-partite classification serves some useful societal, political and even tax purposes, it does not help to inform us regarding leadership, organisational structure, internal and external processes or their design. What does help is to separate out two concepts, those of *association* and *employment hierarchy*. These concepts have been identified by Brown (1971) and Jaques (1976). We agree with this differentiation and describe the qualities of each, including critical issues that need to be considered if organisations are to be effective.

Associations

Almost all of us are members of associations. As a shareholder, you are a member of a business corporation. Many workers are members of a union. You may be a member of the Red Cross, which is a voluntary association. In the United States, as a citizen you are a member of several governments – a city, a county, a state and a federal government. A partnership is a form of association as is a university. Associations may be religious, involved in sport, medical, legal or scientific endeavours (see Box 5.1).

The written document may be a constitution, a charter, articles of incorporation or authorising legislation. Some associations such as neighbourhood groups may not have a written document or formal rules, but they will have at least verbal agreement about who they are and their purpose for associating.

Membership in these associations has a different meaning for the members according to their commitment. Shareholders may be less likely to feel they are members of a corporation than are the employees of the corporation who depend upon it for their livelihood. Of course, this depends upon the extent of their shareholding. Nonetheless, most shareholders can exit

---

Box 5.1   Wilfred Brown's Definition of Association

Associations are people coming together for a purpose. The purpose is either agreed tacitly or expressed in a written document. (Brown, 1971: 48)

---

quickly, often with little emotional attachment, simply by selling the shares. This different sense of membership causes concern when it is asserted that the primary purpose of the corporation is to increase shareholder value, which sometimes is done at considerable cost to employees. The debate about whether corporations should consider multiple stakeholders revolves around this issue.

Individuals can have dual roles, being both members (perhaps through owning shares), and employees of the corporation. There has been considerable discussion of how the ownership of shares may change the behaviour of the employee. Often higher-level managers are expected to be shareholders, as well as employees, based on the belief that they are more likely to increase shareholder value if they themselves are shareowners.

In the case of democratically governed societies, it is not so easy to exit the association, and the emotional ties may be significant. Governments are associations of place, so that if you live in that place, you are a member of the association, whether you are an active or passive member. This is true, of course, only in democracies where citizens have rights and responsibilities. In authoritarian systems, people are subjects and usually do not have the same sense of association membership. To exit membership, you must move to a different governmental jurisdiction. The employees of governments are almost all citizens of that government as well – something which can create a serious dilemma for civil servants if they are asked to carry out policies that offend their concerns as citizens.

Unionised workers are members of one organisation, the union, and employees of another organisation, the business or public agency. Union members' commitments to their unions may vary depending upon the felt need for protection from perceived management abuses and the competence of the leadership.

Members of voluntary associations may have greater or lesser degrees of attachment to their association. Some members may simply write a cheque to a cause they support. Others may take a more active role as a paid or volunteer worker. One of the interesting dilemmas in voluntary associations is to manage the work of both employees and volunteers, often a highly sensitive issue (see case study 'Parish Life in the Anglican Diocese of Perth, Western Australia – the Bellevue–Darlington Story').

Whatever the feelings and ties of membership, members of associations are, in principle, equal. One share gives one vote, one citizen has one vote, or one union member has one vote. In a corporate association additional shares command additional votes.

Associations operate through consensus, voting, debate and persuasion. Except in the case of very small associations, members usually elect a few of their number to be their representatives in a governing body that is authorised, usually through articles of incorporation, a charter, or authorising legislation to act on behalf of the members. These representatives set overall association policy within the limits allowed by their charters, and when necessary, ask the membership to vote on changes that go beyond the charter or seek to amend the charter. When the workload of the association becomes too large to be handled by the board and its members, the board can be authorised to employ staff (employees) to carry out the association's purpose.

Figure 5.1 illustrates generic patterns of member, representative, 'governing board' and employee relationships.

In a business, the articles of incorporation set the authorities of the board and indicate the requirements for election to the board. Once the board is set up, shareholders must vote to accept the board members and annual elections are held where the shareholders must reaffirm all or part of the board. If an original entrepreneur controls the majority of shares, then he may also, in effect, control the board.

As businesses grow, we have found it is much more effective to have the entire board made up of outside members except for the chief executive. If subordinate employees of the company sit on the board, their employment relationship with the company and the chief executive may come into conflict with their board responsibilities. We also believe that it is better to have an outside chair of the board rather than the CEO acting as chair. Again, there is a potential conflict of interest if the CEO holds both roles. In fact, these practices are now proposed legal requirements in the US after recent abuses and scandals.

The authority of the board is a collective authority. Members of the board are authorised to act as a body, not as individuals. Where individual board members attempt to influence the CEO or other employees as individuals, not as someone speaking for the board as a whole, difficulties occur. The board member who does this is exercising power, not authority (see Chapter 7) and the employee is likely to be confused about what should be done. This is especially true if the board member is asking the employee to do something that is outside the employee's authority.

In addition, there are many other association structures we do not discuss, such as partnerships, unions, universities and churches. In all these cases such associations may employ people to carry out the purpose of the association. These employment hierarchies have much in common with each other and are most effectively structured in a similar pattern that we will describe more fully in later chapters.

EMPLOYMENT HIERARCHIES

Employment hierarchies begin, in the simplest case, when a governing board is authorised to employ an executive director to work to achieve the association's objectives. This director is authorised (when the workload becomes too large for one person to handle) to hire additional

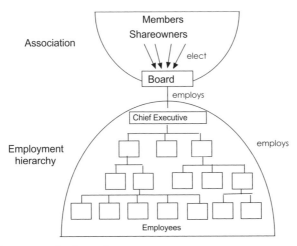

Figure 5.1   Corporate Business Structure

employees within constraints of the association's objectives, budget, personnel and policies as set by the board, a legislature or the membership (see Box 5.2).

An employment hierarchy is a form of organisation that is subordinate to an association. In such a hierarchy people are employed for a wage or salary to carry out the purposes articulated for the association by its governing body. Authority is hierarchical in that the chief executive is authorised by the governing body, while the roles subordinate to the chief executive and their subordinate roles are authorised either by the governing body or by their superior manager.

The discussion of authority as we are using the term extends back to the work of Max Weber (1922; 1947) where he discussed various types of authority regimes – patriarchal, paternal and legal–rational. Legal–rational authority is the dominant form found in modern democratic societies. Weber argued that the best organisational form in a legal–rational society was 'bureaucracy'. The term 'bureau' is French for office, or literally desk, and Weber found that organisations where authorities were distributed to offices rather than individuals were the most effective where law is the source of all authority.

Although 'bureaucracy' has justifiably earned itself a very bad reputation due to the lack of understanding as to how to lead, structure and operate such an organisation, in our own work we have also found that authority is the underlying principle of employment hierarchies. It is the primary set of relationships that distributes work and marshals resources, whether in businesses, governments or voluntary associations. Authorities are allocated to various roles, which in turn, allow them to develop accountability relationships between manager and subordinate such that the subordinate accepts the manager's criteria for review of the subordinate's work. For accountability relationships to function effectively, they must derive from the authorities conferred to roles by the organisation and accepted by the employees of the organisation.

The chief executive officer is provided with certain authorities and this allows the board to establish an accountability relationship with the CEO. This relationship outlines the basis upon which the board will judge the CEO's work. The CEO agrees to be held accountable by the governing body for their own work and for the work performance of their direct reports. The CEO's reports, in turn, are authorised to develop accountability relationships with their reports such that they accept accountability for their work and its review by their manager.

Thus hierarchy is created, not only out of the requirements of a changing environment and the different capabilities of humans, but also from the necessity to have authority regimes that allow the employees of the association to know and understand what it is they are being asked to accept accountability for, that is, carrying out the work of the association and not doing something else. An employment hierarchy is not, and by its very nature cannot be, a democracy.

If you employ someone to paint your house, it would be ludicrous for them instead to build an additional room since that is what they would prefer to do. The same is true when associations employ people to do their work. This does not mean that employees cannot or should not provide their governing boards with ideas on how to achieve the purposes of the association more effectively. You would hope that your chosen house painter would advise you of a more effective and efficient way to paint your house should they know of one.

Box 5.2   Wilfred Brown's Definition of Employment Hierarchy

Employment hierarchy: 'that network of employment roles set up by an association of people to carry out work required to achieve the objectives of the association.' (Brown, 1971: 49)

Employees' ideas and contributions to the setting of policies and direction are essential for success over time. What employment does mean is that the authority to act comes from the association and that employees can use those authorities as a resource to develop accountability relationships with their manager whereby they accept the basis for review of their work, that is, they are held accountable for their actions by their managers while the chief executive is held accountable for their actions by the board.

Employment hierarchies are both secondary and dependent institutions. They are secondary in that they cannot be formed in their own right; there must first be an employing body that decides to establish an organisation and provide the authorities within which employees carry out their work. They are dependent in that their continuity depends upon the continued existence of the employing body.

A variation is the entrepreneur who sets up a business and initially embodies both the association and the employment hierarchy. The entrepreneur decides the purpose of the business, the strategy, whom to hire, whom to fire, how to structure the organisation and what systems will be used – albeit within the law of the land. Once the business moves beyond the sole proprietor stage and must seek articles of incorporation, then the association of shareholders is brought into being. The entrepreneur may still control the association through majority share holdings, but there is now both an association and an employment hierarchy though the entrepreneur controls both.

The differences in the roles and relationships within associations and within employment hierarchies are illustrated in Table 5.1. The failure to make such distinctions leads to endless difficulties and confusion, both theoretical and practical. These two institutional forms differ and the roles of individuals within them differ fundamentally. To be an elected representative of an association is profoundly different from being an employee of that association. Even where terms like 'leader' or 'accountability' are applied to both roles, the ideas and the lived reality behind these terms are significantly different.

The elected union leader is in a very different relationship to the workers who elect him or her than is the CEO of the corporation who employs those same workers. In the case of the union leader, the workers are members who can, through the election process, throw the union leader out of office. The CEO is in a position to hire the workers and to fire them within the limits of law, organisation policies and the union contract if such exists. They, in turn, are not in a position to remove the CEO (though very bad CEOs may find their subordinates undermining them, which results in dismissal by the board).

Unions also hire staff who are employees of the union and therefore part of an employment hierarchy. They too may have their own union. The executive director of a union and the employed staff are in the same relation to the union leadership as is the CEO and staff of a corporation to the corporate board. Much to the embarrassment of employing unions, their staff union may, and have, called strikes and have walked out over pay or working conditions.

Voluntary associations may become even more confusing since they too may hire an executive director and staff who are employees, while at the same time using volunteers who are members of the association to carry out some of the work. Employees and volunteers of such organisations can testify to the difficulties that occur in this situation. As members, the volunteers are the ultimate 'bosses' who elect the governing board. As workers, they may be subordinate to a full-time employee – a tricky relationship unless authorities and accountabilities are fully articulated and understood.

Table 5.1   Characteristics of Associations and Employment Hierarchies

Associations	Employment Hierarchies (Bureaucracies)
Primary	Secondary
Independent	Dependent
Authority relationships based on the charter and social customs and practice.	Authority relationships based on the charter and the policies of the board of governors. Social customs and practice set limits on authority.
Members	Employees
Members are equals.	Employees are in superior/subordinate relationships.
Act through representatives who are held accountable by members.	Act through employees who are held accountable by higher-level managers. Top manager held accountable by elected board of the association.
Leaders held accountable by members.	Leaders hold direct reports/employees accountable.
Operate through consensus, debate, persuasion, voting.	Operate through executive decision processes.
Set objectives and policies of the association within the authority of the charter. Where necessary seek vote of members.	Receive initial objectives and policies from the association. Formulate policies for board decision/vote.
Take instructions from members and advise.	Listen to suggestions from subordinates, decide, give instructions.
Representatives relationships collegial.	Manager/subordinate relationships hierarchical.
Representatives have term of office.	Employees have open-ended employment contract.
Members need not perform in order to remain a member; only obey rules of the association.	Employees must perform or lose job.

Wilfred Brown (1971: 48–59) has discussed some of these relationships extensively, particularly for those working in government and voluntary associations where the association/employment hierarchy relationship is more complex. The theories and models presented in this book apply to all types of employment hierarchies, though the primary model we are using is the simplest model, that of a corporation. This, we believe, will allow us to make the general principles clear, and these in turn can be applied in other organisational settings.

While many of the theories and models we present apply in a variety of human interactions, the theory of a stratified structure, as developed by Jaques, applies primarily to the employment hierarchy. The structural concepts have relevance in other settings such as partnerships, but that requires some alternative ways of applying them in practice. The theories of human capability apply to all humans, but their significance is different in the association and the employment hierarchy. Just because the association governs the employment hierarchy does not imply the members or their representatives are of higher mental processing ability. The knowledge and skills required to be a representative are significantly different from the knowledge and skills required of an employee. Although it is very helpful to have at least one member of a governing board who is equal to or preferably one step above the chief executive of the employment hierarchy, it is not a necessary condition.

In employment hierarchies, employees are expected to work within the laws of the land and abide by the social customs and practices (the unwritten laws) of their society. They are also expected to work within association policies. Employment work is further constrained by objectives, resources, and deadlines (targeted completion times) that are given by the organisation. Within these constraints, however, the employee is expected to exercise discretion, to find a way that will accomplish the given objectives, using the given resources and complete the task in the time set by their manager. (For further discussion of parameters of a task see Chapter 11).

Although both corporations and governments are associations, at the federal level of government in the US, for example, Congress is not a board of directors nor is the president a CEO. Together with the Supreme Court, Congress and the president form a government with powers that are both separated and shared. Governments are associations of place and that gives them some non-voluntary characteristics. Their objectives are subject to dispute, and they have special powers over the lives of citizens. Yet despite these significant differences between governments and other types of associations, in democratic societies governments can still be usefully depicted as associations (Jaques, 1976; Tussman, 1960; MacIver and Page, 1960; Dewey, 1927).

We should also note that there are other forms of organisation that exist in both developed industrial societies and the developing world. Partnerships, independent proprietors, collegiums (of university faculty), doctors in the British National Health Service, priests in the Anglican church, to name a few examples, work under differing conditions which are not employment hierarchies. Movie stars and most professional athletes are, in fact, independent entrepreneurs who can negotiate for whatever the market will bear in terms of salary and other perquisites. Though sometimes termed 'employees', their relationship to their 'employer' is quite different from our use of the term employee. If you wish to pursue the nature of these differences see Jaques, 1976 and Jaques, 1982.

6 *The Work of the Board with the Executive Team*

Determining purpose, policy, systems and strategy

We have discussed how employment organisations develop from associations and have discussed organisations large and small which provide goods and services locally, nationally and internationally. These organisations are critical social institutions. In order to continue they not only need to be viable commercially but like other social institutions need to be trusted. Are they what they say they are? Are they offering a fair and reasonable exchange of value? Who regulates them?

There is considerable debate about 'global capitalism' and its potential for exploitation or benefit. Most international companies are based on meritocratic principles, at least in intent. A meritocracy which is also organised in terms of clear decision-making authority in role, for example, a managerial hierarchy, has great advantages. Potentially the speed at which decisions can be made and resources redeployed means that such organisations can be highly effective. If however, the authority is abused, that is, exercised as power, then significant harm can be done in a short period of time. For example, the power exercised by people in companies like Enron or Parmalat, who do not abide by their own rules or decide that their rules transcend their actual legal requirement. So called smart, clever accountancy practices are not so smart in the long run. The collapse of such organisations not only destroys huge amounts of value commercially but also destroys the value of other large organisations by undermining trust in such institutions.

How can we be sure that such organisations can be trusted not to behave in such clearly exploitative ways? One way is to increase regulation: laws, inspections, audit, reporting and so on. Supporters of this approach could claim it would help to ensure fair and proper practice. However, it would also undermine the inherent advantages of such organisations in terms of speed of decision making and deployment of resources. The question is then whose work is it to keep such organisations effective and ethical?

This surely is the work and purpose of the board. This chapter outlines what board members should be doing on behalf of the association which has put them there. We do not examine in detail the nature of different types of shareholding and representation. Here we are concerned with what board members do once elected or appointed.

PURPOSE

Many people would argue that the purpose of any commercial organisation is 'to make money'. In most countries only one organisation is allowed to do that – the Mint. Therefore, when establishing a company it must be stated what its purpose is: to provide goods and/or services. Of course, any commercial venture must create wealth. If it is a public company, it must compete for capital and so provide a return to shareholders. However, investments are not made simply on the single criterion of 'maximum return'. People make decisions in terms of the nature of the risk and hence return, the nature of the company and ethical concerns.

It is the work of the board to articulate and review the purpose of the company and seek to ensure there are policies and strategies in place to maintain that purpose so that the company continues over time. This is highly significant work, even though the board requires others to enact the policies (this is the work of the CEO and other executives). The board is not there simply to endeavour to ensure that the company complies with the law. It is much more active. However, all activity can be traced back to the fundamental work of clarifying the purpose of the company and determining how it can be realised. In this way the work of the board is consistent with our definition of work: 'turning intention into reality'. The board's work is turning the intention of the members of the association into a functioning social reality in the world.

MORALITY AND ETHICS

We have argued and will argue that higher-level work and complexity must go beyond the concrete and deal with the abstract. The intangible variables are as critical if not more so than the tangible. It is not just a question of having cash in the bank but also whether the company is trusted. Only a company that sustains the trust of the society in which it is embedded will be allowed to exist over time. It is part of the work of the board to ensure the company and the behaviour of its employees are acceptable to society at large. It is for the board, working with the CEO and executive team, to establish a general ethical framework, which in turn will inform policy. This ethical framework does not have to be detailed, since it gains its expression through policy. It is the overall sense of 'what we stand for and how we do business'. The ethical framework is experienced by stakeholders whether they be employees, customers or members of the community. It is what the advertisers try to express in their campaigns, usually implicitly, and may vary according to the business or sector. While superficially it may be referred to as 'image' or 'brand', it is in fact much deeper. It is the reputation of the organisation based on the reality and experience of *how* it seeks to achieve its purpose.

POLICIES

The formal expression of this ethical framework lies in the policies of the organisation. Policies are statements of intent. They are aspirational and act as clear direction for behaviour. While an overarching policy could be 'do not break the law', again this is not sufficient. Policies reflect dilemmas. For example, what is the policy with regard to equal opportunity if you are a UK-based firm with a subsidiary in Saudi Arabia? What is your policy with regard to minimum wages? Is it purely determined by the country you operate in? Similarly, with age of employment, benefits and all terms and conditions? What about environmental issues, land usage, relations with indigenous people and local communities? The formulation of policies in these areas will determine the nature of the organisation and how it is perceived. This is core work for the board with advice and recommendations from the CEO and the executive team.

SYSTEMS

Policies are statements of intent but rarely contain full descriptions of how that intent is to be realised. That is where the systems (or processes) take the enactment of intent one stage further. *Systems are policies in action.* The board need not be concerned with all the systems and processes as they operate within the organisation. However, board members should know and understand how the corporate systems work; what behaviour they are likely to drive and whether, in reality, they are helping both to enact policy and achieve the purpose of the organisation.

This is where reporting to the board is critical, and the board must be confident in the accuracy and relevance of the reporting systems. It is now being increasingly recognised, that this applies not only in the financial area, where the concept of audit has long been accepted, but also in technical and social areas. How does the board find out what the various stakeholders think of the company? How does the board find out about the capability of the leadership? Some board members may regard looking at the corporate systems as 'too much detail'. However, if they are not aware of at least the system design, then they may not realise that well-intentioned policy is not in fact honoured in the systems and how poor system design and implementation can actually reverse policy (in Part IV we look in depth at system design and implementation).

Relationship with the CEO

It may seem as if the board is doing all the work. In reality the board should be working very closely with the CEO and the CEO's team. Central to this is the relationship between the chair and the CEO. This relationship is vital. There must be mutual confidence in each other's ability and a deep mutual trust. This is true of all boards and CEOs, and not only in business. Consider, for example, the chair of a school or college governing board and a principal or head teacher, the leader of a local council or a chief executive. This is why the appointment of a CEO is so important and why, when the incumbent of either position changes, the other cannot assume 'business as usual'. A new relationship must be built or serious problems in this relationship will echo throughout the organisation, the stakeholders and the market.

If we assume that the relationship is a good working one, then the design work of policies and corporate systems (including deciding which systems should be corporate wide) is sometimes shared, often based on proposals from the CEO and members of the executive. It is critical that, wherever such proposals come from, the board:

1. critically analyse them;
2. authorise them (if they are accepted) and
3. have relevant information from reporting systems to identify problems and non-compliance with all policies and corporate systems.

Most boards have committees for subject areas, such as compensation, environment, financial and tax (audit committee) and appointments/staffing (governance and nominating committee). This is a sensible distribution of work but should not encourage over-specialisation such that the board does not see how it all fits together.

While many books are written on the nature of organisations, few discuss the nature of the association or the board. There are many mythologies about being a board member. Many people see it as a 'job for the boys', ideal for retiring CEOs and executives. How many companies have a clear description of the work of board members, apart from the necessity to ensure good legal governance? This is indeed their work – but how are they to go about this? We propose that all board members should be able to understand and articulate why policies and systems should achieve positive results. This is not simply a matter of insisting on proper accounting and monitoring financial policies and systems. Board members should also understand why and how 'people systems' work. For example, what is the purpose of a bonus system and what behaviour does it drive? Should the company be encouraging or discouraging third-party involvement? What is the effect of the current structure?

In technical areas, should the company introduce '6 Sigma' or 'lean manufacturing'? Why and how should a change in technology or the introduction of, for example, an enterprise computing system, benefit the association?

Of course, we are not saying that board members do not do this now, merely that in our experience their capability is quite variable but often assumed to be sufficient solely on the basis of 'experience'. This experience may not cover changes needed to meet changing environments or the development of approaches or systems that are either critical or absent.

CEO and chair – one role?

There has been considerable debate about whether these two roles can be combined. In the 1980s and 1990s it was quite common, but since the mid 1990s less so. Our view is that there is an inherent contradiction in combining them. It is the role of the chair to represent the view(s) of the shareholders or association in determining the purpose and nature of the organisation. The CEO is the executor of policy and the leader of the employed workforce. Whilst these two groups may not necessarily have competing views or ambitions, if they do, it is difficult to resolve them if the role is combined. The authors worked with a particular chair and CEO (Sir Roderick Carnegie) who dealt with this problem in a unique way. He actually had two physical chairs and carried out dialogue between the two roles he occupied by sitting in one chair, and then to another in his other role. Although this may be unusual, it clearly articulates the different perspectives and authorities of the roles. The blurring of these roles can lead to decisions that are not really in the interests of the association. Take an example: an energetic CEO is determined to grow and develop the company. She works to acquire some businesses which will not only double the size of the company but change its shape and nature. Examples could be a manufacturer moving to buy businesses further up or down the supply chain; a service-providing company moving from hotels to travel companies or an airline; an insurance company acquiring a bank and so on. In example one the CEO is convinced and *is* also the chair. In example two the CEO is convinced and *not* the chairperson. Consider how these two scenarios might play out. It will depend upon other board members, the CEO's team and so on, but at the heart, if the roles are separated, then it requires the full articulation and presentation of a case which is then open to scrutiny.

Executive and non-executive directors

Like the argument concerning the chair/CEO role(s) there is an argument as to whether directors should or should not be executives in the relevant organisation. Whilst there may be a definite advantage in terms of potential knowledge and ability, there is again a possible conflict of interest in that it is close to the concept of being accountable to yourself. There is also a question of differentiation. Why should some executives be directors and not others?

Executives including the CEO are and should be accountable to the board. Dual membership confuses this relationship. We do not recommend it. The expertise of the CEO's team is available to the board in terms of board papers and presentations. Board members/directors do not have to be experts but do have to understand strategy and policy sufficiently to determine whether they will produce the desired result. As such their work is to question and comment on the executive proposals. The directors must act primarily in the interests of the members of the association. They must shape and determine the organisation such that the organisation can thrive and prosper. Blurring roles and authority does not help this process. The further conflict of interest arises in that an executive who is a board member is, at the same time, a subordinate of the CEO who assigns his or her tasks. How comfortably does an executive express, as a board member, a disagreement with their CEO on a board issue?

STRATEGY

Next determine the required strategy. Strategy is one of the most used and yet vague words in the business language. It seems to substitute for goals as well as plans. In our experience there is often a confusion between strategy in the sense of a plan and strategy as an expression of a goal. A CEO might say 'our strategy is to double in size', 'gain a 50 per cent share of the market' or 'reduce costs by 40 per cent'. All of these are goals but, stated as such, there is no explanation of *how* these might be achieved. *In our view a strategy is a high-level plan with a clear purpose.* For us the difference between a strategic plan and a 'tactical' or other type of plan is simply the level at which it is pitched (see Chapter 8, Levels of Work).

   If we accept that strategy is a high-level plan to achieve a purpose, then both the purpose and the means to achieve it must be clear. It must relate to all other aspects of the business. For example, how will the acquisition of a new company affect our other policies and systems? How will it affect how we are structured, remunerated, carry out employee relations, benefits, equal opportunity and so on? Too often, in our experience, strategy means vague or general statements of intent: the 'big picture is what matters, not the detail'. In our experience the devil is in the detail. It is in the detail that the earliest signs of variance appear. It is not a particularly high-level or complex task to outline a general 'vision' for the future; it is however a complex and different task to articulate how that 'vision' is to be realised.

   The board must rely on the CEO and the CEO's team to fully articulate strategic plans. Board papers and presentations are a necessary part of this process and the board members must read them and be able to spot how and if:

1.   the strategic plan impacts on the purpose of the organisation;
2.   the strategic plan takes fully into account new or existing policies, strategies and systems.

Summary

The executive team, reporting to the CEO, must work closely with and for the board. While some board members may specialise in certain subjects (useful in committees), their primary role is to work on behalf of the association to determine the purpose, policy and nature of the organisation. The CEO's actions must be with board approval. This is most symbolically demonstrated in the direct relationship between chair and CEO, and why those roles are better separated.

   The board must go beyond mere legal compliance. Along with the CEO and executive team, they will either deliberately or by default create an ethos and context that encourages certain behaviours, condones some and discourages others. Our view is that it is better if this is a managed process.

There is rightly a deep concern about corporate governance. Many multinational companies affect millions of people worldwide. Their collapse can ruin communities and destroy lives as well as reputations. Out of control they can be exploitative and dangerous. However, increased external regulation is not a guaranteed solution. The basic questions regulators might ask of board members could be:

1. Do you really understand the work of your role?
2. Can you really carry out the work of your role?
3. What mechanisms/systems do you have to ensure that the answers to 1 and 2 are yes?

Board membership and CEO team membership is not so much about making money as making institutions. The quality of our societies is dependent upon this being done well.

7 Leadership, Power and Authority

Leadership

Leadership theory has been dominated by models that stress characteristics or traits such as charisma, extroversion, aggression or even size. Sometimes it is defined by personal competencies – vision, courage, determination, drive or maturity. Other models have stressed the situational approach. What is important to some are the characteristics of the situation, whether it is structured or unstructured, whether the leader is in a powerful or weak position, whether the climate for agreement is friendly or hostile which determine whether or not a leader is effective or ineffective, or how he or she should behave.

Some have said that we 'lead people' and 'manage things'. Leaders are often characterised as visionary: 'doing the right things'; while managers are characterised as rule-following (in the pejorative sense of that term): they 'do things right'. Leaders are concerned with effectiveness; managers with efficiency. One gets the sense from these authors that leaders are great, while managers are pedestrian. We believe this dichotomy is both insulting and misleading.

Too often, the concept of leadership is portrayed as almost magical – the implication is that one is either born a leader or not. Certainly some people are far more able as leaders than others, and some may be more effective in some situations than others. The difficulty is that the current theories of leadership produce too many exceptions which go far beyond 'proving the rule', making it hard to know what to do when one finds oneself in a leadership role.

We believe all managers are, by definition, leaders (though not all leaders are managers). Managers have people who report to them and for whose work performance they are accountable; therefore the manager must lead them.

We believe there are two essential elements in understanding effective leadership:

1. the capability of the individual as defined by our five elements (see Chapter 3) and
2. the ability of a person to create a productive culture through social process.

What is not often discussed in any real depth is the *work* of leadership. While effective leaders are described and 'rules' extrapolated from assumed common features we are left with the question of what exactly a leader is meant to do. We can describe outputs, willing followers, goals achieved against 'odds' or demonstrated loyalty. We can describe consequences in terms of praise, accolades or medals but how does a leader achieve these milestones?

This part of the book will address this in general terms but the very specific tools of systems, symbols and behaviour, together with teamwork and its associated elements will be discussed in detail in Part 3.

It is important to bear in mind that while leadership is deeply rooted in social process it also relates to other elements of capability. For leaders to build trust they must have:

*   the necessary technical skills and knowledge;

- good application and
- the required mental processing ability.

Without these elements leadership based only on social process is an illusion that will not last.

The work of a leader is to create, maintain and improve a culture so that people will achieve objectives (purpose) and continue to do so over time. How? If we accept that the heart of this is the requirement to create a genuine willingness to work then we must look at social processes.

Some people will follow technical leaders because of the lure of knowledge; this is central to the traditional university system but it will not suffice for large organisations creating goods and services, administering a country or fighting battles.

We emphasise here the person–person relationship over the person–object relationship. The core quality here is that: *leaders must actually like people.*

One of the author's children (as a seven year old) remarked that the reason for her poor relationship with her class teacher was, 'well she doesn't like children'. It may be an obvious quality but it can be overlooked. We have seen people in leadership roles who just find other people irritating, a nuisance or a chore. They appear to see their team members as an encumbrance not a resource. Good leaders are fascinated by people, wonder why they behave as they do and what might influence their behaviour. This does not mean they have to like each and every individual but in general terms have a positive curiosity that leads to an enjoyment of trying to understand and influence social process.

This requires understanding the current mythologies of the team and those more generally in the organisation. It involves understanding the systems and how they actually operate and how people perceive them on the values continua. It requires exemplary behaviour, consistency of that behaviour and a willingness to accept accountability and exercise authority.

Leadership is concerned with influence; in fact human life is concerned with influence since we are both social and goal directed beings. A lack of desire to either influence or achieve is a strong characteristic of depression. Leadership in organisations is a more specific process of influence since it involves achieving goals that have been specified and can be measured or at least evaluated (that is, the quality and quantity of the goods and services).

There are three main ways in which people influence each other: *force, manipulation* and *persuasion.*

1. *Force*: This is simple in concept and powerful in experience. Here the 'leader' uses the threat and/or actual exertion of physical force to require a person to act in a certain way. This ranges from personal relationships like bullying and intimidation to societal relationships, including war or the arrest and imprisonment of people. Whatever the context, force occurs when one person's will (or one group's will) is imposed upon another's. It usually requires the shift from person–person relationships to person–object relationships since 'the other's' will has to be invalidated. This is often referred to as *coercion.*

2. *Manipulation*: Here there is a distortion of the social process, to create an illusion designed to achieve willing compliance. We will not go into the techniques and details of the process, but they are those of the con-man, snake-oil salesman and demagogue. Essentially what people are being sold is an emotionally appealing simple solution to a complex problem. The emotional appeal usually involves the idea that whatever the problem is it is certainly (a) not my fault and (b) the leader will fix it, if only I do what I am told – think George Orwell's *Animal Farm* (1945).

   Using manipulation, the complex problems facing Germany in the 1930s could be distorted to create an illusion that they were simply caused by Jews and those of 'impure' race and would be solved by obedience to Hitler. Blaming the outsider, minority or elite is always an element in manipulation. The difference between manipulation and force is that (when it works), people are not being obviously coerced; instead they are convinced that they are now doing the right thing. The clue to when manipulation is the technique being used is that you are not allowed to ask questions. This is not the same as religious orders where people take on a vow of obedience, if the vow has been a decision without deliberate external manipulation and a free decision of the person concerned.

There are many books and studies on the 'art' of manipulation, from extreme cases such as the Nazi party, to advertising and political spin-doctoring. The point being made here is that the process relies on the dominance of emotion over rationality (as explained in Chapter 1 when discussing 'charismatic' leadership). It is leadership of sheep or lemmings, and the cliff awaits.

3. *Persuasion*: Here one person (or persons) attempts to influence another (or others) to act in a particular way without using force or manipulation. This is what requires real social process skill since it is necessary to engage *both* emotionally *and* rationally. It assumes the other has a will and seeks to engage that will positively and willingly. The process is based on mutual trust and the other positive elements of the values continua and is only likely to occur if the relationship is open and clear about the purpose and outcome (much of Parts 3 and 4 of the book are dedicated to explaining this process in practical terms). This persuasive process requires leaders to understand how to use systems, symbols and behaviour in a way that demonstrates:

- They understand how others perceive the world.
- They understand how others perceive them.
- They understand how others perceive each other.

The leader must also understand how to manage that social process to achieve the goal.

This does not imply that a leader may never resort to force. If attacked, or if people are stealing or bullying, the leader may well call the police with the consequence of someone being imprisoned or at least arrested. Using persuasion does not imply that force can never be justified. What it does argue is that the main process used by good leaders is persuasion in terms of managing social process through the understanding of mythologies, values, systems, symbols and behaviour.

Power and authority

All of the above approaches may be authorised or not. It is rare that manipulation is authorised, but it does happen in the form of propaganda (during war) or via illusion and magic in entertainment. In democratic societies we authorise armies and the police to 'enforce' the law. As Rousseau noted in his *Social Contract* (1762), there is an implicit agreement between people and the government (or employees and employers) which assumes that:

- Manipulation is not the main process of information delivery ('spin').
- The majority will still listen and take account of minority concerns.

Thus we do not expect an elected dictatorship (see Box 7.1).

Box 7.1   The Invasion of Iraq

If we take these concepts and apply them to the 2003 invasion of Iraq we see serious concerns from people in the countries that supported the war.

1. *It was clearly the use of force*, but was it justified? Who should have authorised it? Was it legitimate without explicit United Nations approval (authorisation)? We note the clear contrast between the US government, who showed little active concern as to the need for further UN resolution, and the British government. Surely it is no coincidence that the US has no history of needing alliances to defend its territory from invasion, whilst Britain and the European nations have centuries of history of war and alliances?
2. *Was it manipulation?* To what extent were people misled by claims of 'weapons of mass destruction' (WMD) and links to international terrorism? This is of significant concern to many as the facts of the matter after the event (that no WMD were found) are not as relevant as the intent. Was it an honest mistake based on poor intelligence? Or was it a deliberate manipulation to build a strong case on what were known to be weak foundations?
3. *Persuasion*: Another view is that despite flaws and poor intelligence many people were genuinely persuaded that in the long term this was a reasonable use of force.

    For those whose perception was that it was not justified force, that they were manipulated and not listened to, we could hardly expect the leadership to rate positively on the values with regard to love, dignity, fairness and honesty even if the actual soldiers involved were regarded as courageous.

- We define *influence* as 'the ability to exert one's will in social context' (people–people).
- We define *authority* is 'the mutual acceptance of agreed limits in exerting one's will'.
- We define *power* as 'the exertion of will while breaking one or more limits of authority'.

Therefore our definition of influence is probably more akin to the way power is defined in some literature. Bertrand Russell (in Russell, 1938: 35) said 'Power may be defined as the production of intended effects.' Max Weber (1947: 152) defined power as 'the probability that an actor within a social relationship will be in a position to carry out his own will despite resistance, regardless of the basis on which this probability rests'.

Kenneth Boulding (1989) saw 'three faces of power' – destructive, productive and integrative. He added there were three methods of power – threat, exchange and love (respect). He also noted there could be active power – to produce wanted change and defensive power – to prevent unwanted change.

Max Weber (1947) has written most extensively on authority which he defined as the right, accepted by others, that a person could legitimately exercise power. He found three sources of authority: (1) personal charisma, (2) tradition and (3) law. Excepting charisma, authority always operates within accepted limits.

We define the terms as we do because we want to separate out the common desire to act purposefully *with others' involvement* that is influence, from the way in which this influence is exerted, that is by force, manipulation or persuasion. Further, we do it to be clear whether such action is authorised or not.

Let us take a few examples, some more obvious than others. In each case we must be specific about whose view (or lens) we are looking through.

Example 1   The 2003 invasion of Iraq from:

A. a George Bush Supporter
B. an Iraqi oppressed by Saddam Hussein
C. an Iraqi opposed to 'Western democratic imperialism'.

All three would see 'influence' by *force*. A and B may also see this as 'authorised' and be persuaded by its necessity; C would see force but through *manipulation* not persuasion, and thus experience the exercise of *power* as the parties have not agreed mutual limits.

Example 2   A manager asks one of his team to countersign a false environmental report to cover up a chemical leak at a refinery. He says if the person does not do it he will make her life hell and get rid of her.

A. manager
B. team member
C. local environmental officer.

A and B clearly acknowledge the use of *force* in influencing behaviour, albeit not physical. B also experiences this as unauthorised (we hope) by the company, breaking policy and the law, and therefore as *power*. C, if and when she finds out, identifies the use of *power* and *force* and will prosecute. This is also force but is authorised. Whether A accepts this legal process as authorised may well depend upon why he felt the need (influence) to falsify a report.

The boundaries around authority can be numerous. They include:

1. the operating limits of the role and role relationships;
2. the policies and procedures of the organisation;
3. the law (local, national and international) and
4. the ethical framework of the company, often expressed as 'custom and practice' or 'the way we treat people' providing it does not breach 1, 2 or 3 above.

The point about leadership as persuasive, authorised influence or managing social process within boundaries is that all leadership depends on mutuality. The people being led should feel treated as adults with a will, who willingly enter into known arrangements (employment, policies, role-relationships) freely. If the initial relationship is not free (as in master-slave relationships), leadership is already set in the context of power.

Our view is that, to be effective, leaders must work so that organisations can run without needing to resort to force or manipulation, that is, power. It is a more difficult route to put aside such techniques but we have seen the toll they take on members of organisations. Whilst the people at the top of the power pecking order may enjoy it, and it may appear more exciting and dramatic, it causes significant harm to people – not least a sense of cynicism and mistrust in a failed authority. Most people find these 'power' organisations demoralising and debilitating. 'Office politics', unclear accountabilities, shifting blame and making decisions on the basis of who will gain power rather than their effects on the long-term viability of the enterprise are all evident in such organisations. Power struggles may also lead to good people being dismissed because they are part of a group where the leader has lost the political power struggle, and all the supporters must go too.

The models and concepts we propose in this book can provide conditions where clear systems of authority and accountability can be created. Such systems of authority and accountability show respect for human dignity, drive out power networks and thus release tremendous energy for productive purposes.

Managers and other employees are empowered – in that they can work more effectively – but they act through authorised systems, within limits that are subject to review. Their ability to act derives from a clear grant of authority from the organisation, which holds role incumbents accountable for the proper exercise of that authority.

We have found that people who operate and depend upon power intensely dislike the concepts we present. They claim they are 'restrictive', 'pedantic', 'bureaucratic' or worst of all 'too theoretical'. What these concepts actually do is expose the power networks, demystify the manipulators and question capability, none of which are at all popular with a bully. Power, like seniority or nepotism, undermines a meritocracy.

Summary

In a positive organisation good leaders lead and influence people primarily on the basis of persuasion through excellent social process skills. They use their own behaviour as an example and demonstrate they can see the world (and opinions) through other's eyes. This does not mean they will or have to agree with such views.

Such leaders then need effective structures and systems to work with and authorised means to achieve their goals. In doing so they not only refrain from the use of power but actively confront it.

Even with such skills set in the context of well designed and implemented systems leaders also need to meet the other criteria of capability, appropriate to the role. Clarity of purpose and open information systems then give the possibility of long-term and sustained success with far fewer casualties along the way.

8 *Levels of Work*

Organising work

Large organisations are characterised by layers or levels. We refer in general terms to 'shop floor', 'operators', even 'workers'. We talk about supervisors and first-line managers, then middle managers, executives, managing directors, vice presidents, presidents, chief operating officers and chief executive officers. In the civil and public service and the armed services there are ranks and grades forming a quite deliberate hierarchy. Even in smaller organisations there are managers and reporting structures. People over the years have criticised or attacked hierarchy but it is surprisingly robust and can be traced back for hundreds, even thousands of years (Jaques, 1990). Notable writers such as Weber, Blair and Scott, Burns and Stalker and Mintzberg have all described and analysed this organisational feature.

Like Jaques, we regard this form not as coincidental, but as indicating a deeper human quality and a potentially effective and constructive way of organising work. Also, like Jaques, we see many current fads, criticisms and alternatives as misleading, sometimes vacuous attempts to 'cash in' on the fact that many hierarchies are not nearly as efficient or effective as they could be, often because several different concepts are muddled together to form a tangle which is not easily unravelled. To quote Jaques: 'The problem is not to find an alternative to a system that once worked well … the problem is to make it work efficiently for the first time in 3000 years' (Jaques, 1990).

What is muddled?

When people design, operate or criticise organisations, they can confuse several quite different, albeit related, elements:

1. *Level of management*: The underlying structure of an organisation is actually a structure of management, as such it is an *authority structure*. It defines or clarifies who has the authority to:
   a. Require someone else to carry out some work (assign tasks).
   b. Review that work and apply consequences (positive or negative) in the form of recognition and reward.
   c. Depending upon performance or a changing context, begin processes to remove a person from a role. (The corollary being the manager also authorises the person into the role.) This is what Jaques so clearly identified and with colleagues, including the authors, researched in many organisations. They found similarities across organisations in many fields of endeavour.
2. *Grades*: Many organisations (perhaps most obviously in the public sector) also have grading structures; these do not automatically confer authority over others but are primarily

concerned with career development, which recognises differences in skills or qualification. These operate within management levels. For example:

In Figure 8.1 there are actually three levels of management. Manager A manages B1, B2, B3 and B4, but note that B1, B2 and B3 are differently *graded*. There are severe repercussions if B1 thinks and behaves as if actually the manager of B2 and/or B3 by assessing their performance, issuing instructions and so on. B1 is however the manager of C1, C2 and C3 (who are also graded differently). Note that C1 and C2 are not actually managers at all (perhaps stand-alone technical specialists) while C3 manages D1 and D2.

There is, most perilously, a dangerously implied hierarchy of authority in grading structures which causes significant distress, anger and resentment: 'pulling rank', 'overbearing', the exercise of power: these are multiplied when movement through grades is purely based on seniority or time served and has no relation to ability or achievement.

3. *Complexity of tasks*: All tasks have an inherent complexity. We all recognise this in terms of how difficult we find a task. The critical factor here is to separate out skill and knowledge from the underlying complexity of pathway or method of achieving a goal, as described earlier in Chapter 3, Human Capability.

If we imagine that there are literally thousands of tasks that need to be done in an organisation, it makes sense to order these in some coherent way. This is often done by gathering or bundling tasks of similar complexity together and calling that a 'role'.

4. *Mental processing ability*: This refers to the actual ability of an individual to complete tasks (or solve problems) of a specific complexity. This too varies. Some people will be much more comfortable with tasks of a particular complexity than others.

There is great potential to muddle these different concepts. For example, looking again at Figure 8.1, let us put a person, Ben, into role B1 on the basis of seniority. After years of hard work and loyalty Ben has 'risen through the ranks' based on years served. In actuality, Ben cannot do the work (complete tasks of relevant complexity), but does like to behave as if he manages not only C1, C2 and C3 but also B2 and B3. Now let us suppose that the person in role C2, Claire has a much higher mental processing ability than Ben and indeed could quite

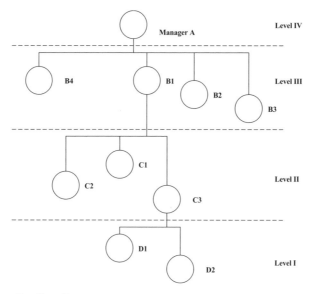

Figure 8.1   Grading Structures

easily do the real work of Ben's role much better than Ben can. Further, the people in roles B2 and B3 have very specialised jobs and are experts in their knowledge. It does not take a genius to work out the possible scenarios and working relationships; few can be productive.

Now let us imagine that Manager A, Anne, notes not only that work is not being done but also that work relationships are being strained and are at times openly hostile. What does she do? If she has read the latest anti-hierarchy pro-personality literature, she may well hire consultants who will endeavour to 'improve the working relationships' by a combination of psychological therapy and/or restructuring that moves either people or roles to avoid the immediate problem. For the organisation, nothing lasting will be achieved, but considerable money will have been spent on consultants. People may have wrongly diagnosed the problem as another one associated with hierarchy, whereas, in fact, it is precisely the result of *not* applying the principles of building a meritocratic, managerial hierarchy. The actual solution for Anne is:

1. If Ben really cannot handle the work of the role (complexity of tasks rather than a lack of knowledge and so on), he must be moved, either to a role he can handle or out of the organisation.
2. The new incumbent must be made aware that this role does *not* manage B2 and B3 (who report directly to Anne).
3. Claire should be interviewed by Anne to see what real potential (mental processing ability) she has and some testing, using higher complexity tasks, should be assigned which if achieved well might lead to promotion.

No need for therapy, no need to attack hierarchy, no need for consultants. Rather, a need for a sound understanding of principles, clear thinking, courage and good social process skills.

Untangling these elements is easier if we distinguish between these concepts of managerial level, grade, complexity of task and mental processing ability. However there is a fundamental and critical relationship between them.

How are they related?

To answer this question, we must ask why this form of organisation, despite its many detractors, is, and has been, so prevalent. The purpose of an organisation is to provide the goods and/or services intended by the association or board. It is not primarily to provide careers or even employment, although these are socially important secondary gains. Over time, many forms of organisation have been tested and the managerial hierarchy is extraordinarily resilient. Our experience and work supports Jaques' basic propositions that this is for two main reasons: first, that tasks can be categorised into qualitatively different types according to their complexity and second, that this reflects the way people construct their worlds, that is, the way they process information. In other words, work itself is a construct of the human mind and people see the world (in terms of work in qualitatively different ways). In Chapter 3, Human Capability, we described how for one person a malfunctioning piston is technical hands-on repair; for another it is a reflection of how the vehicle is driven and for a third it is a design problem or transport issue. Each perception is relatively more abstract.

Thus we see that *mental processing ability*, an individual quality, gives rise to an analysis and solution of a particular *complexity*. These tasks can be bundled together to form a role that can be placed at an appropriate *level* in the organisation (level of work).

In this way each level upwards reflects a qualitatively more complex, and abstract way of perceiving and acting in the world of work. More importantly we have a specific rationale for the generally vague term of 'adding value'. Each level, potentially, adds value to the work of the level below by setting it in a broader, more complex context.

This is what employees intuitively refer to when they comment as to whether the person in their manager's role 'adds value'. Most critically, in terms of power and authority, if the manager does add value it is more likely that the team members will accept the manager's authority. This is in contrast to the power exerted by the more senior, higher graded colleague which is resented.

We have mentioned these 'levels of work': qualitatively different types of complexity of tasks and mental processing ability. How to describe and recognise them is, however, not easy. Jaques, with the authors and many others, especially Cason, has described these levels and mental process in slightly different ways (see the general theory of bureaucracy, requisite organisation, human capability theory and others). We have laboured also with the help and input of many others with our own versions, which are described in published and unpublished work, often for specific organisations. There are two issues here. The first is what we mean by qualitative differences, or discontinuities in both the complexity required to complete tasks and the mental processing ability of people. The second issue is how to describe such discontinuities in a way that is useful.

With regard to the first issue there is ample evidence of discontinuity, in addition to ordering, discernable through the day-to-day observation of people. In the book *Levels of Abstraction in Logic and Human Action* (Jaques, Gibson and Isaac, 1978), Chapter 2 describes a range of theories of discontinuity and compares them. Chapter 17 (by Stamp) compares a further range of theories including Bennett (1956–1966) on mathematics, Bloom (1956) on education and Kohlberg (1971) on moral development. Further theories even more well known such as Piaget (1971) and associated researchers have hypothesised and experimentally demonstrated such discontinuities in the way people perceive and act in their worlds. Stamp (in subsequent work) clearly describes similarities between the discontinuities found in her own work and that of Jaques, Macdonald and others. The summary of the descriptions are shown in Table 8.1.

Whilst these are general descriptors, there is a need for those trying to design and run real organisations for more precise, behavioural descriptors.

After some 30 years of effort, including years of work with Jaques, Stamp, Rowbottom and Billis, the authors believe that the perfect set of descriptors is somewhat like the search for the Holy Grail. The difficulty in coming up with perfect descriptors will fail for two reasons. First, any description in words will be ambiguous because of the inherent ambiguity of words, and their change in meaning over time. Second, we have found that useful descriptors are best written in the context of a particular organisation, describing work in terms of that organisation. Thus, we see a comprehensive set of descriptors for the work of social services in the UK by Rowbottom and Billis (1977).

Despite these reservations, the following is an attempt to provide a general set of descriptors. Again, like Jaques, we note the importance of time to completion. Jaques' (1976, 1989) very specific arguments about timespan are well documented and we will not discuss them in depth here. We do note that complexity and time are related. However, this relationship is not as simple as it might appear. Whilst we note that a task which will take more than three months to complete will be more complex than a task of type one complexity there can be tasks of high complexity which have to be completed relatively quickly, for example, the saving of Apollo 13. Also we regard the only way unambiguously to describe the complexity of these relationships is using geometry and/or maths. As such the best descriptors of all are that of Isaac and O'Connor (1978: 95). This is probably the definitive work with regard to the explanation of discontinuity theory.

We have used a combination of descriptions of tasks *and* the application of mental processing ability. These descriptions assume that the complexity of the task and the mental processing ability of the individual match. Of course in reality this will not always be the case.

LEVEL I

Box 8.1   Level I Focus

Hands on – completing concrete procedural tasks correctly

At Level I there is direct action on immediately available material, customers or clients. There is a clear understanding of the work to be done, the procedural steps to be followed and how they are linked. Direct physical feedback indicates whether the work is being performed correctly. The work is often immensely skilful, with significant use of judgment, discretion and adjustment by 'touch and feel' or 'trial and error' if previously known solutions or learnt trouble-shooting methods do not work. A known pathway is followed until an obstacle is encountered and then practical judgment is used to overcome the problem.

Useful input to improving working methods can be expected from the day-to-day experience built up, sometimes over many years, by using the procedures and from trial and error. The patterns observed and described are all physical events.

LEVEL II

Box 8.2   Level II Focus

Monitoring and diagnosis of operational processes

At Level II, the key work is diagnosis whilst observing people working in established, known systems and processes. Significant data collected in the form of suggestions from those operating the process and from the flow of concrete events observed in the process are compared with a known model or system. Improvements and modifying actions may be taken on the basis of this information. Diagnostic patterns may be learned through training and education, for example, in engineering, social work, financial analysis or nursing, or through years of experience. Indicators of learned patterns (algorithms and systems) are sought to recognise significant data and so to formulate alternative methods of performing tasks, to decide whether the diagnosis is correct or that the case is from another pattern.

This and the general work of task assignment demand the mental construction of how tasks might be envisaged and solved without direct physical, hands on feedback. 'Trial and

Table 8.1   Levels of Abstraction

Level	Gibson & Isaac Logical Analysis and Dualities	Jaques Levels of Organization and of Abstraction	Rowbottom & Billis Work Levels	Gillian Stamp Assessment of Managerial Capacity	Ian Macdonald Assessment of Mental Handicap	Summary Generalization
Level One	T and F refer to unambiguous behavioural entities, T being used concretely in that it is strictly behavioural, that is associated with an object actually discriminated by a subject: if P (a 'statement' in the sense of an actual response) then $\sim P$ is T (accepted) and vice versa. This sample behavioural acceptance-rejection (go-no go) pattern, however, is seen as expressing the mutual exclusion and exhaustive alternation in the ambiguity of the and/or connectives.	Perceptual-concrete relation with prescribed task. Working relationship that of a person working in a concrete manner to transform a thing or to produce an effect on another person. No manager-subordinate relationship. May be collateral working together, but not with one person accountable for the work of another. P → thing / person-thing	Prescribed output: working towards objectives which can be completely specified (as far as is significant) beforehand, according to defined circumstances which may present themselves.	Concrete rule-obeying: rules are immediately obeyed. Prime focus of behaviour is to relate abstract shapes to concrete objects. No ambiguity is perceived and uncertainty is strictly limited by translating the abstract into the concrete. Frequent use of the exclusive 'either/or' when discussing solutions.	Externally fixed goal and plan: person very concretely tied to a particular goal and plan as completely prescribed by someone else. Dominated by uncertainty without external help.	Emphasis is upon concreteness, intuition, and uncertainty. The goals of activities are given in concretely prescribed form. Strict rules and procedures are either provided or assumed. The relationship with the object of activity is direct and concrete. Work is by the immediate process of operation upon the object, usually referred to as skill. This skill is based upon the 'touch and feel' of the situation, that is to say, it operates by intuition, by induction, within an externally given context. Based upon intuition, the situation is one of considerable uncertainty.
Level Two	The basic truth tables are introduced: the duality between the 'and ($\wedge$)' and 'or ($\vee$)' conjunctions is taken as having become explicit, and is joined by the at this level implicit duality between the 'if-then ($\rightarrow$)' and the 'if-and-only-if ($\leftrightarrow$)' conjunctions. Level 2 thus introduces explicit ambiguity.	Imaginal-concrete, with specific tasks and solutions imaginally (ambiguously) dealt with. Manager gets work done through subordinates; or professional works with clients within a general objective. Relationship in which one person experiences uncertainty of being accountable for another person (a subordinate) achieving a transformation in a thing or client. P → thing / person-thing	Situational response: carrying out work where the precise objectives to be pursued are ambiguous and have to be judged according to the needs of each specific concrete situation which presents itself.	Judgement and action within rules: Rules seen as limiting the context within which judgement and action will be taken. Awareness of ambiguity emerges but the capacity to tolerate uncertainty is limited and ambiguity is handled by separating situations one from another.	Externally fixed goal and flexible plans: if a fixed goal is externally set, person can deal with ambiguities in flexibility of his own plan for reaching that goal.	Ambiguity enters into the situation in the form of incompletely specified goals or means. The ambiguity is handled by a flexible use of rules (deductive context) within which intuitive inductive process can be used to fill out the objectives and needs of each concrete situation. Each activity is handled in its own right. The flexible use of rules, and the elimination of complete dependence upon intuitive inductive processes, gives greater certainty than at level 1.
Level Three	Truth tables are extended in the usual way, now making it possible to make a qualitative jump to the use of truth tables as such. The conjunctions or relational statements between the items in the truth table columns. The ($\rightarrow$ and $\leftrightarrow$) duality is now shown to be explicit, but at a higher level of denotation and connotation in dealing with relations between truth table columns and not just with items from each column. The operations on the extended truth tables are shown to be irreversible, so that level 3 takes on the quality of a system of items occurring in uni-directional series from which extrapolations can now be made.	Conceptual-scanning operating through serial scanning. Manager in control of a unit in which he works through two rows of individuals; or professional working without externally set objectives; the situation is sufficiently concrete for them to know all the members or clients, and all that is going on, by serial scanning and extrapolation. person or person-thing	Systematic service provision: making systematic provision of services of some given kinds shaped to the needs of a continuous series or sequences of concrete situations which present themselves.	Extrapolation from a given rule as a starting point for the development of systems of solution for a serialist approach to the problem. Assumption that the solution will emerge in time. Uncertainty not seen as a potential resource for action but as defining the limits of the system for solution. 'If-then' statements often used as a basis for a serialist approach to solution.	Goal and plan self-established; person now able to set own goals and plans, but can cope only by establishing rigidly fixed system in which he proceeds serially through each successively fixed step towards that goal.	Emphasis in all the data is now upon activities occurring seriatim. The work remains concrete in the sense that each task is specifically given, or in the use of the logical analysis each specific truth table item can still be used. But system is introduced, giving a feeling of maximum certainty and allowing for extrapolation from the trend of specific instances taken serially.

Table 8.1   Continued

Level					
Level Four	The new implicit duality arises out of the use of truth table columns as sets, and the relations are now between the truth table columns themselves. Individual T and F items are absorbed into these columnar sets. With the disappearance of individual items, generalized principle must now be intuitively employed, the implicit duality being that between the concept of relationship itself and the terms or poles of that relationship. Thus, at level 4, intuitive generalization emerges and behaviour becomes intuitively abstract in the innovative sense of detachment from specific items.	Abstract modelling, with genuine innovation. A manager can no longer know all his subordinate staff, nor a professional all his clients, nor can they serially scan all that is going on. Anonymity begins, and genuine innovation. Similar to the fact that in the columnar sets of level 4 not all the terms of the sets can be known: imaginative innovation from general principle becomes essential.	Comprehensive service provision: making comprehensive provision of services of some given kinds according to the total and continuing needs for them throughout some given territorial organizational society (rather than concrete extrapolation). Application of intuitive judgment to detect gaps in service.	Search for and maintenance of a pattern for a rule structure. Hypotheses explicitly stated in general form and tested. Negative information can be used after a hypothesis has been built. Phrases like 'as well as, not instead of' are used as a means of acknowledging both sides of an issue or two possible strategies.	Own fixed goal but flexible plan: behaviour now sufficiently generalized to be able to set own goal but to keep it fixed, while adapting flexibility to unanticipated obstacles (i.e. the unknown). / A distinct and important change in the focus of activity. All the concrete items of activity can no longer be known. The individual is thrown back upon the use of inductive generalizations related only to particular examples of the concrete case. Recourse must be made to hypotheses about the unknown (identification of gaps), and the testing of hypotheses. The level of true abstraction and innovation has emerged, with increase in uncertainty as compared with level three.
Level Five	The analysis moves to the most general universe of discourse. The truth table analysis becomes that of relations between the columns combined into classes of that columnar sets. The shift is now to a predicate calculus, the implicit duality introduced being that between the universal quantifier ($\forall$) and the existential quantifier ($\exists$), giving an underlying intuitive foundation of implicit theory – the relationship between the universal and the particular – in a specified domain. At level 5, the analysis thus returns to level 1 but in a general and encompassing form in that at level 1 T and F are implicitly or intuitively used, whereas level 5 states and defines in principle how T and F are to be used.	Work by use of theory and theory construction, including concern for overall nature of enterprise. A manager has and is two levels removed from the level-3 manager who is still able to be in direct contact with the shop and office floor. The level-5 manager must be capable of working with universal principles, or theories, within which he can contain the general principles used by his subordinates in their work.	Comprehensive field coverage: making comprehensive provision of services within some general field of need throughout some given territorial or organizational society, i.e. the domain is now universalized.	Rule-making: Individuals will define the situation for themselves. Disorder may be deliberately induced and uncertainty welcomed as a possible source of further information. The importance of the not known as a possible source of information is often stressed and the necessity of being sensitive to things which do not happen. Negative information is readily formulated and used.	Own flexible goal and plan: person now able to function towards tasks as generalizable domains, i.e. to shift either or both the goal or the paths, depending on the particular circumstances which may obtain. / Emphasis changes to intuitive relationships with the universal – with theory construction or general rule-making – to be applied in relation to particular cases in a comprehensive domain. Uncertainty again dominates, as in level 1, because of the inductive intuitive relationship with the universal. This level completes the total system, for it exhausts the particular universe of discourse within which the five levels may be applied.

error' solving of problems will not be sufficient. Problems are treated as a particular case fitting a known type rather than a new trend or pattern needing identification of a system.

There is still direct access to the area of work and often-physical contact with the work. Leadership roles characterised by work at this level will be managing those who are operating the production process and applying the systems and so will have regular direct contact with them. They will be accountable for ensuring their work is not constantly interrupted so that they achieve their outputs reliably.

LEVEL III

Box 8.3   Level III Focus

Discerns trends to develop and refine existing systems

Work of III complexity requires the ability to recognise the interconnections of significant data from a flow of events within a single knowledge field, or discipline, and to discern the linkages between them. Trends are developed and systems are derived to mesh the interlinked activities in a way that will achieve the desired end result. The process is one of conceptualising alternative means to achieve the goal by forming 'if this, then that' chains of hypothetical systems that are tested through to completion. The system which best addresses the current situation and links it to projected desired objectives is selected, taking into account local conditions, cost, risk, time and the need to conserve human and material resources.

Because the work of hypothesis generation and test remains within one knowledge field, Level III capability will not recognise the often confounding effect on the proposed system caused by variation in another field generated simultaneously by the activity of that proposed system. Information that arises from what is not there (negative information) is not recognised as significant. The inability to comprehend the simultaneous effect of planned activity in other fields causes many system failures, thus 'The Law of Unintended Consequences'.

Work of III complexity can create high efficiency productive systems or optimise existing systems through the application, for example, of rigourous cost analysis, work method development and risk analysis. III complexity work is well suited for the leadership of a department of up to 300 people in a typical enterprise with geographic spread, technology variation and work type all having a bearing on the number of people and resources being managed. It is also well suited for highly specialised stand-alone roles requiring great depth of knowledge in a particular discipline.

LEVEL IV

Box 8.4   Level IV Focus

Parallel processing – integrating and managing the interactions among multiple systems

---

Work at Level IV requires working in several disparate knowledge fields simultaneously, while carrying out two distinct activities. One is to use theory to understand simultaneously the abstract linkages between several systems of Level III complexity in and thus mesh the Level III activities so they work in concert and achieve the greatest overall effectiveness. The second is to compare existing methods and processes with potential methods and processes that may not yet exist and to bring the potential into existence to improve organisational functioning. Alternatives are seen as both/and, rather than either/or.

Level IV is concerned with interacting trends while continuously linking III systems and adjusting them in relation to each other. This may require consciously sacrificing resources in order to achieve the overall good of the organisation. At IV is the first level where the individual looks for what is missing. Negative information is significant. It is also where awareness things may not be as they appear emerges, e.g., although production may be up, the facility may be in trouble and vice versa.

LEVEL V

Box 8.5   Level V Focus

Shaping and managing an organisation within its environment – maintaining the organisation's systems and processes so that it is self-sustaining within that environment.

At this level, entire theories and not just principles are used to link multiple knowledge fields or disciplines. As a result of understanding and predicting the environment, the organisation is modified to address and minimise any potential negative impact (social, political or economic) from the environment, for example, by deciding in what line of business the organisation should be in five years' time and managing the effects that change of direction will have on internal systems and capability, ensuring the organisation is still achieving its purpose. Whilst not only being able to construct the relationships between systems, the second-order consequences of those relationships will also be foreseen. This includes understanding what impacts changes in another part of the organisation of which this entity may be part may have on its productivity and viability over time. Understanding what impacts systems may have on people, the use and management by example and symbol are crucial tools.

At this level, the entity constitutes an accepted whole with a complete boundary within the external environment. Consequently, work at this level is associated with boundary conditions and the interactions between the environment and the entity.

The work will involve complex organisational projects such as major information management systems and new technological or people systems. The data on which the work is based is both abstract and concrete; observable and unobservable, with a need to recognise remote, second or third-order consequences and multiple linkages between cause and effect. The absence of data becomes much more important and is used extensively.

LEVEL VI

Box 8.6   Level VI Focus

Shaping the organisation of the future – creating the ethic on a national and international basis that allows entities to function and manages the relationships between entities of a significantly different character.

The work at this level demands direct interaction with the external social, political and economic environment in order to influence and mitigate any possible negative impacts on the organisation/businesses. Essential to this is constructing an overall framework in which the relationships between fundamentally different types of organisations can be handled. This may involve managing the relationships between two organisations built on very different organisational assumptions, principles and purposes, such as the relationships between a commercial company and government or a mining company and an indigenous community. It also involves the ability to form relationships by understanding sometimes very different perspectives and how they might be addressed productively. The management of this framework of relationships results in the construction of policies that influence and, if done well, enhance the organisation's reputation, often internationally.

Compliance to the legal framework is insufficient at this level; ethical frameworks for behaviour need to be created which will make the organisation acceptable within its environment. The organisation does not simply comply with local laws, such as those involving child labour or safety but sets its own (higher) standards.

Long-term goals are set and policies and corporate systems are shaped and audited to achieve them. If this work is not done well, organisations are constantly exposed to unexpected, major, destabilising problems which distract attention and drain energy from the business. If done well, this work will add significant national and international value to a brand or reputation.

The work at this level is often seen as 'political' and involves building constructive external relationships with relevant leaders and opinion formers. Within the organisation leadership will be demonstrated primarily by symbolism and example.

LEVEL VII

> **Box 8.7   Level VII Focus**
>
> Sustaining a successful long-term future by understanding, predicting and influencing worldwide trends that will affect the viability of the organisation.

The work at this level entails comprehending the fundamental forces driving changes in the environment (national and international). This involves worldwide trends that may affect economic, social, political, technological, environmental and intellectual forces far into the future. On the basis of that understanding, predictive hypotheses are developed to position the multinational or major organisation or corporation, taking account of the fundamental forces, building long-term plans for the organisation's growth and viability. This involves the creation of new Level V entities and the winding down of existing Level V entities on the basis of the invention of new forms of institutions, relationships and interactions. Being able to handle the 'unknowability' of future worldwide contexts, the work envisages realisable possibilities for their own organisation and for potential, entirely new markets, needs, products and services.

Leadership of an organisation at this level entails the creation of an ethical framework that will allow the organisation to thrive in its various social environments: 'We have to do what is right.' There is a concern for the whole of society and not just narrow self-interest. The setting of the ethical framework may be for a whole sector (non-governmental agencies, banks, manufacturing), and not just for their own corporation.

All levels of work are essential

While we can recognise the extraordinarily high MPA of certain individuals, and it may be interesting to speculate as to who they might be, the vast majority of us work at less exalted levels. This does not mean we have less value as human beings; it simply means we pattern and construe the world differently and that we have differing abilities to carry out work.

The environment presents us with problems that require the application of all levels of work discussed and, perhaps, more. All these levels of work are essential if a society is to survive and thrive over time. If a problem requires Level IV complexity in its solution but MPA of II complexity is applied to solve it, the result is failure.

A person or a society does learn from trial and error, but at a cost. With effort, time and the correct environment, a useful solution to a problem can be delivered, and providing the effect of error is not too damaging to the person or the society, such a process of problem solving can be tolerated. If there is not time to learn from this process or if the results of the inadvertent experiment are too disastrous, there may be no person, business, or society left to take advantage of the result. If the environment presents a problem and there is no one who has the mental processing ability to deal with it, the society will be damaged or fail.

As businesses, government agencies and non-profit organisations are all work societies, and if they are to meet their goals and survive, they must have people within their organisations who can work at the levels required to achieve their goals in their respective environments. The quality of work carried out at all levels of the organisation will determine the quality of results obtained. Thus as human beings we should delight in all levels of work. We all have something to contribute to the whole.

Role and person

Although work roles have minimum mental processing requirements, individuals who fill those roles may or may not have an ability to match those minimum requirements. There are people in roles with requirements that exceed their mental processing abilities; others are in roles that require less than their full mental processing abilities.

The issues that surround the match or lack of match between the capability of the person and the complexity of the work of a role are of vital importance to the organisation, which must set up and operate systems to deal with them, for example, what does the future CEO look like in a Level II role just after they have joined the organisation at age 24? These are not issues, however, which bear upon the concepts embedded in the levels of work complexity save that overriding concept of work being a construct of the human mind as it seeks to build order from the chaos of the surrounding environment.

The level of work of a role does not tell you much about the MPA of the role incumbent. If the person is successful in role, it is safe to assume they have the required knowledge, skills, application and MPA. Beyond this minimum, the role the person currently fills tells you little about the person's MPA. This is a very good thing because it makes it clear we cannot pigeonhole people based on their current job. Because the question is always open, the intrinsic humanity of the individual is easier for all to respect.

As we describe the levels in an organisation, the term we use is 'stratum', as in an organisational layer. The definition of an organisational stratum and its relation to levels of work follows, but for now it is important that the terminology must always be 'a person in a Stratum II role' and never a 'Level II person'; even though the level number will match the stratum number, they do not mean the same thing (see Box 8.8).

Box 8.8   Appropriate Terminology

The appropriate terminology is to refer to 'a person in a Stratum II (or III, or IV, and so on) role'. *Never* a 'Level II person' or a 'Level V person'. This is both insulting and demonstrates ignorance of the theory.

Summary

Thus, in summary, what we are saying is that as people work, each pathway developed to a goal is, in reality, unique. There are, however, common patterns which sort the pathways into discrete groups, or levels of work. The levels of work are discrete because the problem-solving methodologies created through an individual's mental processing ability are discrete. Because we need to make goods or services, we formulate tasks. Each task will have a complexity for its resolution based on the level of chaos needed to to be resolved. The mental processing ability of the person who identifies and performs the work of the task will determine the complexity of the work. If this complexity is equal to or greater than the inherent complexity of the task, the resolution will be successful.

At higher levels of the hierarchy, the pathways needed to formulate or to accomplish a task will be constructed in less certain conditions relative to tasks at lower levels. In general, as one moves from one level of work to the next, complexity increases in that:

- there are more variables to take into account;
- more of the variables are intangible;
- there is an increasing interaction of variables;
- results are further into the future;
- the links between cause and effect are extended in time, space and logic;
- apparently negative information (what is absent or does not occur) assumes more importance;
- the achievement of the objective requires the *simultaneous* ordering of more than one knowledge field.

We must recognise that the patterns we have described are incomplete. Although it is tempting to want precise descriptions that would allow us to place everyone in their specific box, such an ability would be disastrous for human freedom and the ability to control one's destiny. Instead the patterns we describe are, we believe, chaotic patterns, rather like clouds. Although no two clouds are alike, we can recognise the patterns of cumulus, cirrus, stratus or cumulo-nimbus clouds. The same is true of levels of work. No two people are alike, but with practise we can learn to recognise the patterns of complexity resolution they demonstrate. We can never be certain of our judgment, but we can do this well enough to select people for organisational roles more effectively than we can without this knowledge.

Essentially what we are providing is a language to describe differences probably already familiar. This is made easier when there is a language to describe the differences in complexity. The levels of work described are only a summary. These levels of work have been identified in several different research studies, and they have been tested in practice in business, governmental and voluntary associations. There are also descriptions of the types of tasks found in organisations which can be completed by people using the mental processing abilities associated with that level of work complexity (see Box 8.9).

Box 8.9   The Importance of a Person's Worth

We cannot overemphasise the danger of equating MPA with the worth of a person. A person's worth, in our view, is not calculated just by how 'clever' they are, and we must not confuse an organisational hierarchy of work with hierarchy of worth. People contribute much, much more than intellectual ability to life and society.

We also stress that we have talked about a meritocratic, managerial hierarchy based upon a hierarchy of complexity of work. Not all work has to be done in a managerial hierarchy; not all organisations are appropriately managerial hierarchies. Churches, universities and law firms/partnerships, for example, are properly organised in different ways, but all will need to understand the complexity of work to be done and who is able to do it.

3 *Systems Leadership*

In this part we describe the systems leadership approach. It is essentially a social process based on the core values and requires the understanding of mythologies and how to create a culture. Leaders need to use the tools of their own behaviour, systems and symbols to create their culture. These are not just general statements but involve very specific understanding of the role of systems; how they bind and separate people; how they influence people's behaviour. We have underlined the need for clear and appropriate authority if there is to be accountability. This includes, or has at its centre, the need for clarity in formulating, assigning and reviewing tasks. Finally, we describe a very specific process that integrates the roles of team leader and member to form a model of teamwork essential for productive work in any organisation.

9 The Work of Leadership: Creating a Culture

The work of leadership

This is probably the most written-about topic of all. It ranges from the more descriptive biographies and autobiographies of people who have been in significant leadership roles, for example, Mandela and Churchill, to theories of leadership such as Hargreave's *Sustainable Leadership* (2006). Arguments abound as to whether leaders are 'born, not made' and to what extent leadership can be taught or learned.

In order even to discuss these ideas, it is first of all important to determine what leadership is and how it might be recognised. It is interesting to note what current definitions of leadership come to mind, if any. Could you write down an attributed definition? Leadership, like so many other concepts in this field, has wide social meaning but questionable scientific, shared meaning. We hear that leadership and management are different, but how and why? We have argued that this differentiation is often very unhelpful. In Part 1 we distinguished between two types of relationship: between one person and another person or persons, and between a person and an object or objects. The distinction between leadership and management sometimes implies this difference: that, somehow, leaders are concerned with people whilst managers look after resources such as plant, equipment, stores, budgets and so on. In contrast, we associate both leaders' and managers' relationships with specific sets of authorities. Thus all managers are leaders but not all leaders are managers.

So what do we mean by leadership? Most people will associate leadership not only with people but with influencing these people to act in a particular way (see Box 9.1).

The work of a leader is clearly a social process. The key element for us is the term 'over time'. We are not referring to a short-term process which, whilst effective, does not necessarily last. To take an extreme example, a person may go into a bank with the objective of getting the staff to give him the bank's money. He points a gun at them and they do so. Is this good leadership? A CEO visits a site. Employees rush around for a few days beforehand, picking up litter, painting or removing obvious eyesores so the place looks good. Is this good leadership?

Leadership is certainly about influence, as we discussed in Chapter 7. But how is it made possible? We have taken away many of the traditional tools; fear, coercion and intimidation. Yet we still want the leader to influence others to behave constructively, productively and creatively, and all of this for the most part willingly. This is not an easy task in any social setting whether at home, in the office, in a religious organisation, a political party or a voluntary organisation (see Box 9.2).

If leaders are to be effective, they must be skilled in the management of *social processes*. The ability to read a social process and intervene to produce a productive outcome is at the heart of leadership. The leader must genuinely like people and be committed to using social process as the main tool and not simply as a carrot before bringing out the stick. One of the

---

Box 9.1 The Work of a Leader

The work of a leader is to create, maintain and improve a group of people so that they achieve objectives and continue to do so over time.

---

worst leaders we came across used to explain his 'process': 'First, I give them the chance to agree with me. If they don't, I sack them'.

Thus the leader's first and foremost tool of leadership is social process. But how is this used effectively? We have identified some work for the leader to do. The leader must be able to answer the following questions to test the understanding of social process:

1. How do team members (that is, those whom the leader is leading) perceive each other?
2. How do they perceive the organisation?
3. How do they perceive the leader?
4. Can the leader predict how they will perceive particular changes, for example, of working practices, organisation, benefits, and so on?

This is not a superficial process that can be solved by simply saying, 'Well, if the change is positive, they will view it positively.' People often perceive situations in quite different ways. The key to understanding this perception is to understand their mythologies; to see through their mythological lenses. This is not a question of right or wrong. Their mythologies may be based on stories and experiences from years ago.

One of the authors asked a group of people if they trusted the leadership of their organisation. One of the group answered, 'No, not after what they have done in the past.' On exploration, the examples he came up with were more than 15 years old and from a time when none of the current management were even at the organisation! Such stories echo down the years and may still influence people today. We have found that some organisations are better than others at telling and relating to stories, and building and sustaining mythologies. Union leaders are often good at this, and excel at reminding people of the past, relying particularly on tales of untrustworthy or dishonest management. Some organisational leaders may find this frustrating. Frustrating or not, it is part of today's reality and must be addressed.

This is where the values continua: trust, love, honesty, courage, respect for dignity and fairness are applied. The leader can use the core values to help answer the questions above. Do people trust each other and the leader? Do they think the organisation is fair? Is the leadership courageous? If the answer to some or all of these questions is no, the leader must ask why and try to explore the underlying mythologies. This is often best done by listening, a very simple technique, but one which is frequently underused by leaders. Leadership, especially of the charismatic kind, is often characterised by the inspiring speaker, the person who 'leads from the front', someone with apparently boundless energy and determination. Yet good leadership is more often the result of good and careful observation and listening followed by considered action.

This is not to imply that good leadership is doing what is most popular. It may be the case that what needs to be done will initially be seen negatively, for example cost reductions, changes in organisation or location or new work methods. The understanding of mythologies

---

Box 9.2 What Makes a Good Leader?

In our view good leadership involves influencing the behaviour of others without the primary use of force, manipulation or power.

---

can be the basis for more effective explanation, setting better context and directly addressing concerns.

One organisation we worked with eventually faced closure. The economic argument was compelling. Employees were, not surprisingly, unhappy at the prospect. However, the leadership used their understanding of mythologies to design information systems, relocation options and retraining to make this process as positive as possible. This was well received and employees left with views that placed their own experience and the leadership as positive on the values continua. They felt they had been treated with respect for their dignity, told the truth and that the leadership had openly confronted the difficult issues (see Box 9.3).

If the purpose is unclear, ambiguous or suspected to be covert, the social process will be fragmented. Others will articulate alternative purposes, and energy will be dissipated. The exercise of power will result and an alternative, subversive, purpose may be promoted. Clarity of purpose is an essential part of the social process. Articulating a clear purpose does not guarantee agreement, however. The leader must also understand why people disagree. Using the values continua, concerns or objections must be examined to understand the mythologies. We once worked with an organisation whose workforce went on strike because the company increased sick leave benefits! The leadership had overlooked the negative placement of the action. It was as seen through the lens of suspicious and negative mythologies about the purpose of the change and the workforce feared that increased sick leave benefits would be linked to a loss of benefits elsewhere (which had happened in the past). It is tempting in these often tense circumstances to dismiss these sorts of objections as irrational. Do not dismiss them. The mythology which explains their rationale must be found (see Box 9.4).

People often resort to three simple explanations for behaviour they do not understand and often turn to one of three simple answers: they must be *bad*, *mad* or *stupid*.

Why did they damage that vehicle by running it without checking the oil? Why was he not wearing the proper safety harness, causing him to fall from the scaffold? Why does she keep complaining about lack of information when she has access to our new intranet?

Frustration can offer quick explanations: They are bad, he is mad and she is stupid. We ask leaders to explain a range of behaviours that they see as negative in the workforce without resorting to any one of these simple explanations or excuses. It can be a tough task. It is even more poignant to see politicians and world leaders resort to such simplicity to explain others' behaviour. Like the values it always seems easier to see *other* people whose behaviour we do not like as negative rather than reflect on ourselves.

Leadership is obviously not merely a matter of responding. While the development of an understanding of the current situation is critical, creating a new, different situation is essential (see Box 9.5).

All leaders must change behaviour, their own and their team members'. Even if the current situation is quite satisfactory, the context will always be challenging and so demands will change (see Box 9.6).

We have defined culture as a group of people who share mythologies. The leader's work is to create a single, productive, culture. Leaders must have a clear idea of the desired behaviour they need for constructive and productive results. This is no abstract matter. The core values of

---

Box 9.3   Overcoming Negative Mythologies

A leader must have, and be able to articulate, a clear purpose.

Box 9.4   Avoiding Emotional Arguments

When understanding other people who are behaving, to our eyes, in an irrational way, it is often easy to enter into an emotional argument. When two Macdonald Associates consultants presented a report to a managing director that revealed some strong negative mythologies about some changes he had made, he became upset. He had worked hard at these changes, which he genuinely believed would, over time, benefit employees and the organisation. He eventually became exasperated and just kept saying, 'Well they are wrong, just plain wrong.' It took considerable time and discussion to move away from an absolute position to consider the questions 'Why, if you have made these changes in good faith, would someone also genuinely, not trust they are beneficial?'.

---

trust, love, honesty, fairness, dignity and courage only have meaning in relation to behaviour. Exactly what behaviour is fair?

A client of ours came across one of his crew fishing in a nearby river. 'I thought you were on shift today?' said the client. 'Yes, I am' said the crew member, pleasantly. 'Then why are you here fishing?' said the client. The reply came, 'Oh, I'm on a sickie'. He then sensed that he might be in serious trouble and quickly said, 'Oh, it's OK. I phoned in before the shift so they could arrange cover'.

To this crew member, 'taking a sickie' was not unfair. Letting his crew down by not giving notice was. His calmness in the face of the manager suggested this was common practice (which it was). The leader had to change this behaviour. He needed to create a culture where taking a day off sick when you are well was not perceived as fair or honest.

What was he to do next? What do you think would have been the reaction, in a highly unionised mining operation, if he had disciplined the crew member there and then? Instead he said he would see him back at work and then thought carefully through the mythologies and what influenced them. He created new mythologies and, by the time he left that mine, the behaviours had changed.

So far we have highlighted the need for:

* clarity of purpose;
* understanding mythologies as part of social process and
* the need to create culture.

The three tools of leadership

Creating a culture builds on clarity of purpose and is achieved through three main leadership tools (see Box 9.7). Since we first articulated this set of leadership tools in the mid-1980s, they have been used to great effect in a wide range of circumstances. Indeed they have proved so

---

Box 9.5   The Purpose of Leadership

The purpose of leadership is to change behaviour.

Box 9.6   The Leader's Work

The leader must create a single, productive culture.

> **Box 9.7   The Three Tools of Leadership**
>
> The three tools of leadership are:
>
> *   behaviour
> *   systems and
> *   symbols.

useful there is at least one book based entirely on this small but significant element of systems leadership theory. We see it as an integral part of the system leadership framework.

BEHAVIOUR

The leader's own behaviour is highly significant. Phrases like 'walk the talk' or 'practice what you preach' are typical. A saying used in child development also underlines its importance: 'Do not worry if your children don't listen to you. They're watching you all the time.'

The consistency of a leader's own behaviour will be scrutinised by team members. It is not helpful if, in trying to improve timekeeping or housekeeping, the leader is a poor timekeeper or walks past litter at work. Role modelling is essential in challenging behaviour. People really do notice and either take heart or are discouraged according to what the leader actually does. Some people use the term 'attitude'. We hardly, if ever, use this term, as behaviour is so much more important. We can see behaviour; we can only infer an attitude. It is a change in behaviour that will produce results.

SYSTEMS

Stewart, one of the authors, coined a phrase while he was managing director of Comalco Smelting: 'systems drive behaviour'. This was because much potentially helpful structural change had occurred in his business but the business did not seem to be benefiting as it should. By concentrating on changing the systems, he was able to accelerate that change and the results he wanted.

Systems are important because they operate all the time, all day every day. Unlike the behaviour of a leader, the systems are ever-present. The alignment of systems and behaviour is very influential. It is difficult for a leader to counter bad systems and behaviour by behaviour alone. Leadership dependent upon role modelling alone will not last. Behaviour will revert unless reinforced by systems. Macdonald found many instances in health service institutions, mental hospitals and hostels, where excellent staff who were struggling against countervailing systems of depersonalisation ended up in burn-out (see Macdonald, B., 2001).

SYMBOLS

Symbols can be used by all leaders but become more significant as the organisational distance increases between the leader and the employees or team members. Behaviour itself is highly symbolic but there are other examples of symbols: uniforms, staff facilities, flags, logos, car parking or housekeeping. How people perceive symbols offers very clear examples of mythologies (see Box 9.8).

If the systems and behaviour are aligned, symbols can be very positive and helpful. If they are not, they can be counterproductive and symbolic of the negative mythologies, for

---

Box 9.8   An Example of How Symbols Are Perceived

A coal mine in Australia was taken over by new owners. It had a history of poor industrial relations. The new owners wanted to make a fresh start and appointed a new general manager for the mine. He issued good-quality baseball caps on the first day printed with the new company colours and logo. Every employee was given one free. At the end of the shift, each side of the road leading to and from the mine was littered with discarded caps. This behaviour demonstrated the depth of negative mythologies. As one miner commented, 'They are not going to buy us with a bloody cap!!'

---

example, lack of trust prevalent in the organisation. The workforce can become even more cynical.

Symbols become more important as we move up through levels of work: presentations, awards, letters of recognition, visits, commemorative plaques, office space, furniture, decoration and cars/vehicles can all have significant meaning.

The next chapters explore these concepts in more depth and guide leaders as to how they can be practically applied.

10 *Leadership, Policy and Systems*

The role of policy and systems

We have discussed the importance of creating a culture using the tools of behaviour, systems and symbols. This chapter explores the role of policy and systems in more depth.

The purpose of the organisation can only be achieved through work. Purpose reveals intent; the policy and systems provide the boundaries for the enactment of the how of turning intention into reality. For our definitions of policy and system, see Boxes 10.1 and 10.2.

LEADERSHIP AND POLICY

In the previous discussions of work, we saw that all work is necessarily carried out in the context of constraints. For example, we never have unlimited resources or time. We also saw that some of the constraints were imposed by an external authority, for example, by law. Others were chosen – for example, the make or type of equipment to be used.

If an organisation, as an association, employs people to help achieve its purpose (in the form of an employment hierarchy), it cannot act as if it has no constraints. There are legal constraints and resource constraints – the capital available, the nature and size of the market, the availability of people and materials, social customs and practices. In addition, we argue that the board and the executive leadership must go beyond legal compliance. *The purpose of any activity implies ethical principles*. If the organisation acts amorally, the result will be fragmentation not only of the association, but of the employed group.

What we mean by this is simply that in all human endeavours the end does *not* justify the means, if this implies that any means will be acceptable providing the end is achieved. We have discussed how human beings are social creatures and thus also moral creatures, as evidenced by the values continua. There will always be opinions and differences of opinion as to the nature of the process to achieve the purpose. Our view is that while it is necessary to discuss the technical aspect of this (that is, will the process actually work?), it is also essential to consider the ethical principles of the social process.

The association and leadership must determine the constraints around how the purpose is to be achieved. These constraints are articulated in the form of policies as we have defined them, 'standards of practice'. Policies are critical, especially if the organisation works in different states or countries with different laws. For example, if the law in one country with regard to employment conditions, health and safety, or the environment (pollution) is different from the laws in another, does the organisation merely comply with such laws, or does it have a policy on safety that requires a particular standard even if the law does not? Answering these questions is part of work of the board and the CEO's team.

The policies of an organisation have a strong bearing on its identity and reputation. The policies of a company will have a significant bearing on who associates with it and

---

Box 10.1   Definition of Policy

Our definition of policy is 'a statement that expresses the intended standards of practice and behaviour of an organisation, including behaviour'.

Box 10.2   Definition of System

Our definition of a system is 'a specific methodology for organising activities in order to achieve a purpose'. This involves directing flows of work, information, money, people, materials and equipment. The system provides the framework within which these flows take place.

---

who supplies it or buys from it. Some investment companies have policies not to invest in armaments or military companies, or companies with poor environmental or human rights records irrespective of the return to shareholders of such companies.

Rio Tinto (a London-based mining corporation) has a community policy that requires all its global operations to develop a positive programme of engagement with the local communities whether local laws require, encourage or ignore such issues. Rio Tinto also has a policy that explicitly requires the settlement of land rights and access to lands without relying on the pure technical, legal rights tested to the full in courts where laws are often ambiguous and the legal process lengthy.

Collins and Porras (1994) provide numerous examples of ethical behaviour in the companies that are 'built to last'. For example, Merck states, 'We are in the business of preserving and improving human life. All of our actions must be measured by our success in achieving that goal' (Collins and Porras, 1994: 89). Johnson & Johnson says, 'The company exists to alleviate pain and disease' (Collins and Porras, 1994: 89).

Merck chose to provide streptomycin to Japan immediately after World War II to eliminate the tuberculosis that was rampant and severely eroding that society. They did not make any money, but the CEO Roy Vagelos said, 'the long-term consequences of such actions are not always clear, but somehow I think they always pay off'. It's no accident that Merck is the largest American pharmaceutical company in Japan today (Collins and Porras, 1994: 47).

Policy sets the standards or the intended standards for the organisation. The chief executive is most directly involved with policy, and the CEO and their team will have endeavoured to create a strategic plan that will achieve the purpose of the organisation while operating within the policy standards. This is one of the reasons why work at this level is both abstract and complex. It also has the potential to develop and improve the organisation or, when done badly, to endanger the very existence of the organisation. Problems in this area are well documented as the collapse of Enron, Worldcom, Global Crossing and other corporations has demonstrated.

LEADERSHIP AND SYSTEMS

The leadership of any organisation must work to ensure that employees act in such a way that they contribute to the purpose of the organisation while at the same time working within the law and the organisation's policies. Leadership is about behaviour and changing behaviour.

If we consider ordinary human interaction, it is well accepted that non-verbal behaviour is more important in conveying meaning than verbal behaviour. If we are talking to someone whose eyes are half-closed and who is yawning, we are not going to be convinced that they are paying attention to what the other person is saying (see Box 10.3).

Box 10.3   The Importance of Systems and Behaviour

In organisations, systems are the equivalent of non-verbal behaviour in human interaction.

Systems become embedded. Like habits, they require a specific repertoire of behaviour and eventually people just get used to them and act according to their dictates. 'It's the way we do things round here', 'Oh you can't do that', 'We don't do it like that round here', 'We've always done it like that'. The major problem is that systems, like all habits, can be good or bad. Even good systems over time can become outdated and counterproductive.

Systems need to be designed so that all activities help in achieving the organisation's purpose. This is a very difficult task. Many systems actually run counter to the organisation's purpose both actively and symbolically. Take a very simple example. If you run a service business that is intended to be 'customer focused', you may have a system that receives customer phone calls for inquiries, orders and so on. Now, such a system may be technically very advanced. The system may be automated and start with a variety of options: 'To place an order press 1, for overseas sales press 2, for technical support press 3 ...' and so on. Having negotiated the system thus far, the customer may eventually work out an option that seems relevant and then get a message stating that 'All representatives are currently busy. Your call is important to us. Please stay on the line. A representative will be with you shortly.' Then (the crowning glory), the customer listens to some form of music or sales spiel for 15 minutes while intermittently being told, 'Your call is very important to us. Please hold.'

After this experience, will the customer feel that their call is really important to the organisation and that they are receiving good service? Is the company customer focused? Here we return to the values continua. All systems can be rated on the continua in a similar way that behaviour is rated. Do the systems demonstrate fairness or honesty, courage, respect for human dignity, love or trust? Clearly, in many cases, they do not. Reflect for a moment on your experience either as part of an organisation or relating to an organisation as a customer or supplier. Clearly some systems are actually frustrating the purpose of the organisation, undermining its strategy and even contradicting stated policy.

Systems should enact policy. They should be the means by which policy becomes reality. They might not, however, accomplish this in practice. Intentions to have good relations with the local community are undermined if no one is familiar with the local culture, or speaks the language or is properly trained in the field of local community relations.

Equal employment opportunities can be frustrated by unfair recruitment systems, poor communication or advertising, or opportunities or requirements that effectively exclude certain groups. However well intentioned the leader, however hard they try, the systems may be frustrating the leader's purpose.

An organisation may claim to be performance based – a meritocracy – but the reward systems may actually not allow any significant differentiation. Poor performers may be protected by highly convoluted procedures that effectively mean it is impossible (or at least extremely difficult) to remove poor performers from their roles. Proper exercise of authority may be hindered by too many levels of organisation that slow decision making and cause inefficiency.

Overtime systems may become so complex that the supervisor spends an inordinate amount of time calculating time and rates. There may be bureaucratic rules about who can be asked to work overtime so that, even if you find someone to do it, because of seniority it may not be the appropriate person.

Such inefficient systems are extremely costly, not just in time and money but even more so in terms of affecting people's willingness to use their capabilities to the full in their work.

Tools for analysing systems

TWO TYPES OF SYSTEM: 'WE ARE' AND 'I AM'

As mentioned above, Stewart coined the phrase 'systems drive behaviour'. This has become a very popular phrase, taken up by Jaques (2002) and others. It recognises the significant influence that systems have on behaviour but it can be too simplistic unless followed up by a clear analysis.

We have found it useful to distinguish between types of systems and so understand their influence. The first distinction that we make is between *systems of equalisation* and *systems of differentiation*.

All organisations are social entities. They are in existence to achieve a purpose. To maintain social cohesion and shared purpose there must be a sense of belonging, a sense that 'we are'. People in organisations are chosen and appointed, however, because of their particular, perhaps unique, skills and abilities. This too needs recognition: 'I am'.

Systems of equalisation treat people the same way. A system of equalisation does not distinguish between an operator or a manager, a supervisor or a CEO. The most obvious example of this is safety. It does not matter who you are; if you enter a certain area you must wear a hard hat and boots, ear protection and so on.

Systems of differentiation treat people differently. That is, they distinguish people in roles. The most widely used system of differentiation is remuneration or compensation. Some roles are explicitly paid more than others. Within a group of people in similar roles there may be further differentiation on the basis of individual performance.

It is important here to be careful not to be confused by a system that applies to everyone and then assume it is one of equalisation. Remuneration applies to all paid employees. A disciplinary system may be available to all. In fact, all systems that flow from policy should apply across the whole organisation. The way to understand if a system is one of equalisation or differentiation is to consider its *intent*. Is the intent to differentiate or to equalise? We may all be subject to disciplinary systems but they should only be applied on the rare occasion when someone breaches the code or rules; in such cases not everyone in the organisation is to be disciplined.

GOOD OR BAD?

Sometimes, particularly in organisations based in democratic countries, it is easy to slip into the general view that equalisation is good and differentiation bad. This is certainly not the case. Whilst, as mentioned, it is very important to reinforce a sense of belonging, this involves the proper use of both types of systems (see Box 10.4).

We might think of a range of systems that could fall into either category, for example, car parking, clothing/uniforms, health care, cafeterias, facilities, transport, leisure facilities, cars or office size.

Our argument is that, if you are going to differentiate, there should be a clear work-related reason. Why should some roles have a set number of days for sick leave and others have no

---

Box 10.4   Basic Principle of Systems of Differentiation

All systems of differentiation should be based on the work (to be) done.

---

set maximum? Why should a certain group park within the site boundary and others not? The answer to these questions depends upon whether there is a good work-related reason. So, for example, most sites have disabled parking bays near entrances or lifts/elevators. We understand the reason for this, but why should a manager have a reserved parking space? Differentiation can be justified, for example, if the company has a health insurance scheme – it may be enhanced for some roles where the people in such roles travel to countries where health care is less available or more expensive.

Conversely it is demoralising if systems that are supposed to equalise really differentiate. One of the authors, Macdonald, was running a workshop in a remote Australian mine site. He asked a group of tradespeople what they saw as the most unfair system in the company. They were all members of a union and from a generally very egalitarian culture. The answer came back: 'hourly rates are the same'. What they meant was that pay for electricians was the same rate no matter how well, hard, poorly or carefully a person worked. Further, they all knew who the good performers were and who were the poor performers but there was little anyone could do about it, especially with regard to pay. This, in turn, did not encourage good performers or recognise their particular contributions.

In our own work in the United States, Australia and Great Britain, we have found that in employment roles, differentiation based on the work of the role is acceptable; even necessary. Different pay based on different work and differing levels of performance is seen as fair.

Equalisation is more likely to be perceived as fair in instances that are not directly related to the work, for example, if everyone in the plant wears the same uniforms. Other examples where equalisation is perceived as fair and differentiation unfair are in health benefits, safety systems, cafeterias and company services.

Another example comes from General Roderick Macdonald based on his experience as the leader of a British Royal Engineer Commando Regiment. He took over the regiment at a time it was experiencing severe leadership problems. There were a number of elements he had to change, but one in particular illustrates the importance of systems.

At the time he took over the regiment, officers were allowed to wear any boot they preferred as long as it was black. The soldiers were required to wear the military issue boots only. This was a source of dissatisfaction among the troops. Macdonald was aware of this, so one of his first acts was to allow soldiers the same freedom as the officers. While this may appear trivial, it was widely appreciated by the soldiers who recognised that this commanding officer was different. Commandos operate on a basis of greater equality between officers and soldiers, so the change was not disturbing to the officers. The mythologies supported equality as fairness. This was, of course, one of many changes, but its symbolic importance began the change process.

A company in New Zealand was considering a major change in employment systems as the finale to a period of significant leadership change by offering staff contracts to all employees. This had the effect of equalising all benefits except pay. Prior to this offer, the general manager and his team met with one of the authors, Macdonald, under a task set by the managing director (another author – Stewart). The team examined every system in the company in detail over several days. If there was no work reason for the system to differentiate, the system was equalised. This included not only the obvious systems: transport to work, uniforms, car parking, canteen facilities and benefits such as holiday and sick leave, but also the highly symbolic systems such as biscuits provided with coffee and tea (previously only a 'staff' perk) and the 'staff' Christmas party, now open to all. It was interesting that for most employees, previously employed under a collective arrangement, these smaller, symbolic changes were seen as the 'real' demonstration that the company was serious. Within a matter of weeks well over 95 per cent had chosen the new arrangement. The results were dramatic rises in productivity at the plant. (For a fuller and detailed account of this significant process and its elements, see the case study New Zealand Aluminium Smelters Limited.)

All systems should be designed deliberately according to their respective purpose taking into account the mythologies of the people who must work within them. To be a good leader you must understand your own mythologies and the mythologies of the workforce. When you implement a system, you must know whether it will be perceived as fair or unfair, honest or dishonest, as demonstrating respect for human dignity or lack of respect. Understanding how people perceive systems is as important as understanding how people perceive behaviour.

Systems should be designed to be productive; to achieve a purpose and in doing so encourage positive behaviour. If people see the system as unfair to them or showing the company does not trust them, they are unlikely to behave in a constructive or enthusiastic way.

AUTHORISED AND PRODUCTIVE?

Another tool that we have developed to analyse systems and their impact on behaviour is one which asks how authorised and productive systems are. This model has been of significant practical value to many organisations we have worked with over the years.

You will note that we use the terms 'authorised' and 'unauthorised'. That is, they are either approved or ratified by the organisation, or not. This distinction reinforces the distinction we made earlier between authority and power. We do not use the terms 'formal' or 'informal' because some so-called 'informal' systems are enforced by intimidation and significant pressure and are not informal at all.

Obviously we are trying to design and implement systems so that they fit into box A: authorised by the organisation, and productive because they contribute to achieving the purpose of the organisation. We are all familiar, however, with systems that, while authorised, are actually

	Productive	Counter-Productive
Authorised	A – Well designed and implemented	B – Restrictive practices that have been adopted by the organisation
Unauthorised	C – People 'cutting corners' or breaking rules in order to get their work done	D – Alternative leadership based on power e.g. intimidation, racism, sexism, stealing, work quotas, etc.

A All right

B Area for change

C Positive opportunities for change or education

D Must be addressed, challenged and ultimately, done away with

Figure 10.1   Matrix for the Analysis of Systems

a hindrance to working effectively (box B). We often describe such systems as bureaucracy, red tape or irritating. They are obstructive and often people will 'get around the system' in order to do their job. They cut corners to be more efficient or effective. Thus we get box C.

Box C behaviours and systems can be very creative and productive, but they can also be dangerous, especially if any safety rules and behaviours are compromised. In some organisations, box C may be the only way to get the job done, but there is a danger of denial of due process, inequities, as well as safety issues. Box C may provide ideas for positive change and innovation, but the ideas must be examined carefully to ensure other problems are not being created through the box C behaviours.

Box D behaviours and systems are not acceptable. Very simply, box D behaviour results in personal gain at the expense of the organisation. It may involve theft, racism, sexism and may be maintained by covert methods of intimidation. Behaviours and systems in box D must be eradicated. Their existence is evidence of poor and weak leadership. As one worker said, '[the boss] either has no guts or no brains.'

Thus, while box C and D both involve the use of power they are predicated upon very different motives and intent. It is essential to differentiate between them. A leader who disciplines someone who is well intentioned but who 'bent' the rules, yet turns a blind eye to racism or sexism has effectively destroyed their own credibility in the workforce.

We will examine the model and how to use it in more depth in Part 4. We have found its application to be one of the most useful of all our models in practice. It is important to see it as a dynamic model.

Summary

We have argued that organisations, as social entities, not only have purpose but also have standards by which purpose can be acceptably achieved. These standards are effectively the ethics of the organisation and help inform and create its culture. These ethical standards are

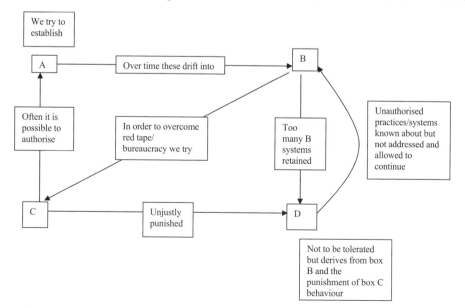

Figure 10.2   Possible Processes Driven by Different Categories of Systems

most clearly expressed by the leadership in policy. Policy is not merely compliance with the host society's laws; it must go beyond this to express the nature and culture of the organisation itself.

The leadership of the organisation, the board, CEO and senior executives may be able to articulate policy but to employees, customers, suppliers, the local community and other shareholders it is the systems and behaviour that demonstrate the reality of the policy. In this way systems frame the work (turning intention into reality) and are critical to the actual achievement of purpose.

We have looked at ways of understanding systems: equalisation/differentiation, authorised/unauthorised, productive/counter-productive and will use these and other models later to look in more depth at the design and implementation of systems. This chapter has highlighted their significance in the enactment of policy and the identity of the organisation.

11 *Task Formulation and Assignment*

What are tasks?

We have put forward concepts and a framework for understanding work, leadership, authority and systems. An essential part of leadership work and achieving success in general is the proper assignment of tasks.

Like many other concepts, assigning tasks may appear deceptively simple, but we have seen and experienced a significant amount of wasted time and effort because of poor task assignment. When one person is not clear and another has misunderstood, the result is waste, inappropriate blame, poor performance review and the creation of negative mythologies.

As in the case of work, the term task has many meanings if you look in a dictionary. Webster's International Dictionary defines 'task' as 'To rate, appraise, estimate; labor or study imposed on another, often in a definite quantity; broadly, anything imposed upon one by duty or necessity; undertaking; work; the amount of work required of a worker or group of workers in order to earn an established wage; censure as in taking one to task.'

Again, these various social meanings are useful, but for the purpose of improving our understanding of management and organisations a sharper definition is needed.

If work is 'turning intention into reality', a 'task' is a statement of intention with *context purpose*, *quality/quantity*, *resources* and *time* (CPQ/QRT), defined explicitly to provide boundaries within which the work is to be done (see Box 11.1).

Human work, tasks and the exercise of discretion

Given the large body of literature on 'delegation', and our experiences in a variety of organisations, it appears that many managers have considerable difficulty in the task assignment process. Some do not trust others to do a good job and, therefore, spend a great deal of time checking and re-checking their work. Others assume their subordinates know what to do and give little direction or advice. Many never explain why a task is to be done – its purpose or its context remain a mystery to those who are supposed to carry it out.

For the purpose of this section we will assume that the manager is assigning a task, although there may be circumstances where people assign tasks to others outside a managerial relationship. The manager must provide certain information to the person and also leave room for the person to create a pathway (exercise discretion) to achieve the objective. There is considerable research to suggest that when people speak about work, and when they place value on their own work, what they value is their use of judgment and choice as they turn intention into reality.

As we have noted, the ability to use judgment and make decisions to achieve a goal is a distinctly human characteristic. By allowing and encouraging the application of the full

---

Box 11.1   Definition of Task

Task: An assignment to carry out work within limits that include the context, purpose, quantity and quality of output expected, the resources available and the time by which the objective is to be reached (CPQ/QRT). See also Jaques' definition of task in *A General Theory of Bureaucracy* (1976).

---

capacity of employees in using this judgment, managers demonstrate their recognition that employees are people with minds and ideas.

Inhibiting or preventing the use of judgment treats people as if they were machines (objects). It is not unusual in these circumstances for a person to breach a limit just to prove they exist. The result is inefficiency, work-to-rule, non-adherence to standard operating practices or even industrial action (slow-downs or strikes). See Table 11.1 for some essential differences between humans and machines.

For a machine (be it an automated machine tool, an automated production line, a cruise missile or a computer) to carry out a task, all three task components – output (quantity and quality), time to completion and resources – must be specified with tolerances where applicable. Purpose is set by the machine designer, who also specifies the environment (context) in which the machine is expected to operate.

In addition, the task methodology (pathway) must be completely specified. If the environment or limits change in any way, the specifications of the task must also change or the machine will fail the task. This task assignment constraint for a machine may be depicted as shown in the Figure 11.1.

Table 11.1   Differences Between Humans and Machines

Humans	Can think
	Adapt to changing conditions
	Create – find a better way
	Make mistakes
	Learn from experience and improve
	Lack consistency because of the need to experiment and improve
	Have minds of their own and can be difficult to control
Machines	Are consistent and reliable in an unchanging environment
	Do not demand humane conditions
	Do not go on strike
	Cannot think
	Cannot adapt to change beyond that for which they are programmed (by a human who must reprogramme the machine to adapt to changed conditions)

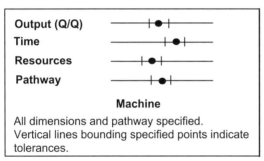

Figure 11.1 Task Assignment Constraint for a Machine

This task methodology can be easily observed with machines that are programmed to follow a particular path in a warehouse to select parts. If a board is left in that path, the robot will run into it, and, if properly designed, send a signal to call for human help. If certain materials are moved to an adjacent bin, the robot will not find them.

Most of us have experienced something similar when we began learning about computers and discovered that they do precisely what they are programmed to do, nothing more or less. This can be frustrating to humans who are accustomed to giving less than complete instructions to other humans who have the ability to fill in the gaps (or think they can).

It is also important to consider the environment in which machines produce output. Great care is taken to ensure that as far as possible, the machine environment is stable within known limits and that allowance for environmental variation is built into the methodology. A machine tool, for example, may be programmed to allow for cutting tool wear.

A cruise missile has a degree of redundancy built into the landmarks that its sensors must recognise so it can miss a few and not lose its way. By doing this, the humans who devised the machine methodologies attempted to predict the future for the machine. In most instances, if the future is not as predicted, the machine stops and signals for help or fails.

People and task assignment

People, on the other hand, are able to understand overall objectives and purpose, take note of changes in their environment and adjust their work accordingly by exercising judgment and coping with uncertainty. It is therefore absolutely essential that the pathway be left open for the exercise of judgment, so that variations in the environment which might be expected but which cannot be predicted can be managed.

This is the value of people. They can take into account purpose (which machines cannot), and they can adapt and change in furtherance of that purpose as conditions change. Such abilities are essential in an environment which is changing and where the rate of change and the volatility of change are increasing. People can and do live with uncertainty; machines have great problems with this. Of course the tolerable level of uncertainty may differ among people; this is actually the basis of level of work.

If people are to use judgment effectively, they must not only understand the purpose of what they are doing, they must also have at least one component of the task left open so they know what the manager wants maximised (or minimised) as the task doer carries out their work. Thus two components of a task may be specified, but one component must be scoped, given a range between two specified values where one point in the range is worth more than all other points. (The specified limits of the scoped component may also have tolerances.) See Figure 11.2.

It would, of course, be possible when dealing with people to leave all three components open. As will be shown further on, leaving more than one component open makes it very difficult to build a system of merit and accountability. Specifying all three components makes it impossible to build a system of merit and accountability and has the additional disadvantage of attempting to turn a person into a machine. This will be resented and resisted, and the attempt to specify all three components will lead to failure due either to 'malicious compliance' (working to rule even when it is obvious the purpose of the work will be negated) or through arbitrary decisions where the individual will scope one or more components of the task and then be angry when the manager says that is not what the individual should have done.

TASK ASSIGNMENT PROCESSES

The purpose of these processes is to ensure the persons assigned the tasks (task doers):

- have a clear understanding of the task they are to do;
- are able to commit themselves to doing it and
- are in a position to accept their manager's judgment of their performance as fair.

Clear understanding requires that the task be formulated and assigned correctly. To gain commitment it is usually helpful to provide the people (task doers) with the opportunity to involve themselves in the task formulation process. To place employees in a position where they are able to accept their manager's authority to judge their performance as fair, task doers must know what the manager wants them to do, and they must know the basis on which the manager will judge their performance. They must have an opportunity to have their task performance reviewed and recognised in the context of the conditions under which the task occurs in reality.

The task formulation and task assignment processes provide a methodology and logic for good management practice. As such, they are *guidelines* for managerial judgment. It must be emphasised, however, that guidelines can never take the place of managerial judgment.

The guidelines are not a statement of absolute requirements to be articulated and recorded at every step. As the relationship between a manager and team members develops, clarity in task assignment may be achieved without a complete articulation as provided for in the guidelines. Attempting to articulate everything at all times and under all circumstances is likely to become mechanistic and unproductive.

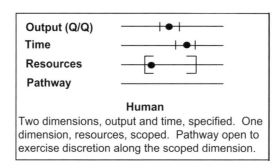

Human

Two dimensions, output and time, specified. One dimension, resources, scoped. Pathway open to exercise discretion along the scoped dimension.

Figure 11.2   Task Assignment Constraint for a Human

IMPORTANCE OF CLEAR TASK ASSIGNMENT AND ACCOUNTABILITY

There have been endless discussions of 'delegation' and how best to do it, but there is little consistency regarding what is to be done or how to do it. Delegation can mean passing on a notion from someone higher in the organisation. It can mean abdication of responsibility on the part of the person who is delegating. It can mean giving orders or suggesting something might be a good idea.

We use the term 'task assignment' to make very clear what is to be done and then to provide guidelines on better ways to assign the task. Businesses are created to produce goods and services by employing people to do work. Therefore it makes sense to assign that work in such a way that people accept accountability for ensuring it gets done properly.

It is important to realise that accountability only exists if it is accepted by people in the organisation. No matter what managers may believe, accountability cannot be imposed on people. To gain the acceptance of accountability requires an understanding of the conditions that are necessary for such acceptance.

If work is to be done effectively and efficiently, it is also crucial that people be recognised and rewarded based on merit: better performance should be more highly rewarded than poor performance.

Again, a system of merit (meritocracy) exists only when the organisation's members accept differential reward and recognition as being a measure of merit applicable to themselves. Saying we have a system of merit does not make it so. Statements about how we reward for merit when it is patently obvious that we do not, lead to cynicism on the part of the workforce and contempt for managers who are seen to be dishonest. As with accountability, we must understand the necessary conditions for the acceptance of differential reward as a measure of merit before we can create acceptance of a system of merit.

If, however, those carrying out the tasks are to accept accountability for their work and accept differential recognition and reward as a measure of their merit, they must know the criteria against which their manager will assign accountability and assess their work performance. Only when there is no doubt in the task doers' minds regarding these criteria will they accept the manager's decision. Therefore the manager must assign tasks correctly, that is, in a manner that does not produce doubt in the mind of the task doer. There is enough uncertainty involved in working out how to do something without confusion and uncertainty as to what needs to be done.

TASK FORMULATION

All tasks that are to be assigned to another person begin in the mind of the person assigning the task (usually the manager in employment hierarchies). This might be in response to needs the manager perceives or suggestions from the team member or other member of the organisation.

Task formulation is a process whereby the manager assesses the situation, determines what is to be done, why it is to be done, the deadline for its completion, the resources available to perform the task and the limits within which it must be accomplished. As will be shown further on, it is usually good practice for managers to seek guidance from the task doers as to some, or all, of these elements of task formulation.

Such a formulation always contains an assumption about the environment in which the task will be carried out. This assumption is rarely called to attention because it serves as background to our very existence. It is like the water in which the fish swims: present, but not consciously considered unless subject to drastic change. Our usual practice as managers is to assume the environment will not change all that much during the time in which the task is to be executed – often a good assumption. Nonetheless, we must bear in mind that tasks are always assigned in the present for performance in the future, and no one is able to predict the future with complete accuracy.

It is interesting to note there is one environment – that of war – where the assumption about the future being similar to the past is not made. Whenever a task is assigned for a military assault, there is enormous effort put into trying to predict all the aspects of possible variations of the future. Great effort (sometimes at the cost of human life) is put into gathering intelligence to do this.

Despite this effort, all military commanders know they cannot predict the variations that will take place in battle. Therefore, throughout history great military commanders have gone to great pains to explain the purpose of the mission and the wider context in which the mission fits. They know the time spent in this process is essential in order to place the officers and soldiers going into battle in the best possible position to cope with the unexpected changes and contingencies of combat.

It is probably natural that in everyday life managers rarely go to such pains. It may be that we should give more consideration to possible environmental changes and future contingencies, especially with the rate of change that is occurring in the world today.

STATING PURPOSE/SETTING CONTEXT

The most vital element in the task assignment process is the statement of the *purpose* you hope will be achieved by the accomplishment of the task (for a definition of *purpose*, see Box 11.2). Too often the purpose is assumed or ignored when telling someone to 'do this'. This is particularly true at the lower levels of the organisation where employees may be treated more as objects (machines) than as people.

Setting the *context* involves answering questions about the circumstances in which the task is to be performed, the background as to why the task needs to be done (for a definition of *context*, see Box 11.3). Is there an ongoing problem or an emergency? Other key points:

• Why the task is important?
• How does it relate to other tasks?
• Who is doing related tasks?

You may have had the experience of being assigned a task and had your manager say, 'You will need to be a bit careful with Fred for a few days. His daughter is quite ill, and he is not his normal self.' This is a manager assigning a task to be performed in an environment that is different from what the task doer might expect.

Box 11.2   Definition of Purpose

Purpose: What is to be achieved by accomplishing this task.

Box 11.3   Definition of Context

Context: The situation in which the task will likely be performed, including the background, relationship to other tasks and any unusual factors to be taken into account.

Knowing the purpose of the task and its context will enable the task doer to use judgment more effectively. A task doer with high capability may, perhaps, develop an innovative solution – achieving task results that are better, faster or less costly than the manager had envisaged. It will allow the task doer to recognise if the context changes and make it more likely that the unforeseen change will be overcome. Most importantly, knowledge of context and purpose will allow the task doer to come back to the manager quickly to advise him or her of the unforeseen change in context or if the task does not appear to be achieving its intended purpose. In this way errors, injury, damage or waste may be avoided.

Knowledge of context and purpose has other benefits as well (see Box 11.4).

Task definition extended

We have stated our definition of a task as an assignment to carry out work within limits that include the context, purpose, quantity and quality of output expected, the resources available and the time by which the objective is to be reached. We have also noted that all work is carried out within boundary conditions that include all the prescribed limits of law, social custom and practice, corporate and department policies. These boundary conditions are the 'givens' that the person assigning the task cannot change in the task assignment process.

Many of these limits should be known to the task doer, but we highlight them here as a reminder that people who are new to role, or people who may not be able to keep up with all the changes in laws and regulatory policies, may have to be reminded of the boundary conditions if they are to be clear regarding the area for discretion in the task assignment. When things go wrong, it is sometimes a good idea to review whether or not the boundary conditions were known and not applied or if the boundary conditions were not clear.

TASK COMPONENTS

These must be set by the manager and include output, time and resources:

Output	Stated in terms of quality and quantity.
Time	The targeted completion time – a deadline indicating when the task is to be completed.
Resources	Defined in terms of cost or resource use. Resource use is required in circumstances where the task doer has no control over the component cost but may influence the number of components used. Other resources include people, authorities, access to information, facilities and assets assigned to facilitate completion of the task.

Box 11.4   Context and Purpose

There is an old story about two medieval stone masons, one bent and drained from a day's work, one singing. When asked what they had been doing, the first said, 'I have been lifting heavy stones all day.' The second, 'I have been building a cathedral.'

Issues in task assignment

Before a task can be assigned, the manager must not only formulate the task, they must also consider the task doer's capability: mental processing ability, knowledge, skills and application. Is this the right person for this task? If the person does lack the capability to complete the task satisfactorily, resources will be wasted, the manager will not meet their own targets, and the person's sense of self-worth may well be adversely affected.

The manager must also consider how much of their own input will be required if the task is to be carried out effectively. Some complex tasks may be done by someone less capable if the manager is willing and able to break them into smaller tasks and provide considerable feedback and coaching as they are being carried out. This may be acceptable with an inexperienced person who needs to learn the elements of the role. The need to do this may, however, be an indication of someone who is not able to perform the work of the role. When a person is fully competent in role, the manager can assign an appropriately complex task knowing the person is capable of completing it.

The manager must also consider the person's workload. In the case of overload, the manager may choose to extend the deadlines on other tasks, provide more resources, or modify the output required, that is, change the tasks. It is a part of everyone's work to advise the manager at any time they believe a task will not be completed within its limits. Judging a person's workload cannot always be done with precision, so the establishment of this information flow is crucial to both the task doer and the manager.

Finally, the manager must allow for the appropriate judgment and remove doubt from the mind of the task doer as to what is to be done. This requires that tasks be assigned with statements of purpose, context and using all three components of the task – output in terms of quantity and quality, targeted completion time and resources – with two of these components specified and one scoped.

INVOLVING THE TASK DOER IN TASK FORMULATION AND ASSIGNMENT

In most cases it is helpful to involve the task doer in the process unless the tasks are already familiar (as is the case in many roles at Level 1). Doing this allows the manager to gain information from the person to help the formulation of the assignment. It may also produce a better understanding of the task assignment and gain the commitment of the person to achieve the desired task result.

The manager may be aware that a particular person, for example, particularly one of considerable experience, would prefer to simply get the assignment straight out and get on with it. There may be other people, depending upon the task, the individual, as well as that individual's experience in the role, who need more involvement to feel they understand the task correctly. Managers must use fine judgment in deciding when or when not to involve people in task formulation and to what extent. Involving a person in the task formulation process may also expose any preconceived ideas which are held by either manager or the task doer and which often inhibit clear communication, leading to errors and waste.

For example, the manager assigns a task with a six-month deadline. The person says, 'That's no problem. I can have it for you next week.' Clearly the manager and person have different ideas about what the task is and what it will take to complete it. Further discussion is necessary to find out what each is thinking and what, in fact, is the nature of the task.

In other cases, the person may be a technical expert on the task in question. The manager may be clear on what is needed (the purpose or the output) but does not know exactly how long the task is likely to take or what resources will be required. Discussing with the person what you are trying to achieve and getting their input is essential. Such involvement does *not* mean the expert determines what is to be done. The final decision on the output required, the targeted completion time and the resources to be used *must* be made by the manager. The manager may decide to do exactly what the expert proposes but it is still the manager's decision, and one for which the manager is accountable.

In practice, the person may already clearly understand some or all of these matters, in which case there is no need to discuss them. The point is, however, that the manager must be sure that this is the case, not just assume that it is (see Box 11.5).

THE USE OF INITIATIVE

Does clear task assignment as we have described here mean a person never does anything on their own initiative? Of course not. The intelligent exercise of initiative is essential if any organisation is to survive and thrive over time. It is precisely when a person has a clear understanding of the (manager's) purpose and objectives that the task doer is free to use initiative, and where necessary, to deal with conditions which change unexpectedly in order to achieve the purpose.

It is also good practice for the task doer to check with the manager ideas on other tasks to be done, in order to ensure his/her actions are in agreement with the manager.

In our experience over many years we have found clear task assignment to be liberating, not constraining. Clear limits and boundaries provide external reference points that allow the task doer to assess and control the exercise of discretion based on objective outside standards. When properly formulated and stated, the reference points provide a clear space for the use of judgment. Unclear task assignment or the lack of assignments are the real constraints that leave people confused, sap energy and make it less likely initiative can be exercised effectively.

SCOPING AND SPECIFYING

In assigning a task it is possible to prescribe exactly what output is required in terms of the quality and quantity, precisely what resources should be used and on what day and at what hour you want the task completed. If this is done continually, it will be very difficult for the leader to make any judgment about the team member's work performance. There is no space for discretion for the task doer to demonstrate the quality of decisions and judgments they have made.

When a leader gives a team member an exact definition of a dimension of a task, they are allowing no variation from that target. This we call *specifying* the dimension. It is, however,

---

Box 11.5   When to Involve People in Task Formulation

Involving people in task formulation may not always be useful or appropriate. There is not much point if the work is routine and the person has experience of this type of task. In an emergency there may be no time to even explain the purpose, let alone involve the person in the task formulation process; in this case the person should understand that the task will be assigned clearly but without even discussion of purpose or context as in the example of a safety incident.

possible to allow the task doer a range in the quantity, quality, resources or time dimensions. This allows the task doer to express their capability in finding ways to get, for example, the fastest, the cheapest or the best quality they can within the given range. This we call *scoping*.

Generally we find that, if three dimensions are specified and one scoped, the task doer has a clear idea of where their leader is looking for them to use their discretion in thinking up a more creative solution. If most or all of the four dimensions are scoped, it may be impossible for the task doer to understand where their leader's priorities lie. As a consequence they will have to hazard a guess which might be completely wrong – frustrating for all concerned.

A leader will need to take a range of factors into account when deciding on the scoping and specifying of the dimensions of a task. Some of these will arise from the context and purpose – what is it that is crucial and non-crucial about the task, for example. The capability of the team member will play a big part. You are likely to specify more and give tighter scoping for someone who is new in the role or who has never done the task before.

TYPES OF TASKS

Although the examples given assume the manager will make a specific task assignment to a specific employee, not all tasks are so assigned. There are many variations in the process, and direct assignment may not be the one most frequently used.

Direct assignment

The manager assigns the task directly to the task doer: 'Give me the monthly budget report by the end of next week.' (This assumes the subordinate knows what the budget report is and the quality standards that apply. It also assumes the person has the information, staffing and budget resources to do the task.)

Task with inset trigger

The manager assigns the task to a person with the statement that when a 'trigger' event occurs, the person will carry out the task. These are the most common type of tasks: 'Sam, Jane and John are authorised to request equipment for their units. When an order comes in to you from one of them, make sure it is processed within 48 hours, though 24 hours would be preferable. If this cannot be done due to other commitments, let them know and inform me. The processing of such orders should average no more than three errors per month and you should not have to use any staff overtime.'

An example of an implicit task, which may be overlooked when performance is reviewed, follows: 'Discuss and resolve with your peers any human relations problems affecting your work.'

This task is triggered anytime the person encounters a problem in their relationships with their peers. It is therefore valid at the time of performance review to note whether or not this task was carried out effectively as problems arose in the conduct of other tasks.

Sequential tasks

The manager assigns a short-term task as prelude to a much longer-term task. This may be used to ensure a person understands what is to be done. It may also be used when the subordinate will have to formulate the larger task based on information he gathers as to achievable goals, required resources or alternative solutions to a problem. For example, 'We need to develop a new security system for the central office complex which takes into account the total number of facilities and the increasing levels of threat. I want the new system ready for use within 18 months, though you may find it takes as much as two years to be fully operational.' Or 'I'd like a report in three months on what might be feasible in this time frame, what the costs are likely to be, whether or not we can purchase such a system from a vendor, whether a vendor's system could be purchased but would require modification, or whether we are better off doing it ourselves. You should also consider if there are some better systems that might take longer to create or some stopgap solutions we can implement immediately. Come back to me with a proposal as to what we should do. When we agree on what is to be done, you will complete the project.'

Multiple tasks

This situation occurs when several tasks are created in the context of what appears to be a single task. It is important to clarify your priorities as manager if the person discovers that not all the tasks are feasible within your given limits. 'Create a project team of yourself and three team members to do an analysis of requirements for a Local Area Network (LAN) in the power supply department. Joe, Harry and Gail have been told you will be calling on them to negotiate for the temporary assignment of one or more of their staff to the project. I want at least two members of the team to be new to LAN technology, so that you can train them to use it on future projects. The analysis needs to be done within six months and at that time I would like to see your team fully developed with all members trained in LAN technology and capable of carrying out additional LAN projects on their own.'

Note the potential for confusion here. If the person cannot get both tasks done, which is more important: the analysis for power supply or having team members trained in LAN technology? The task doer must first carry out that analysis and report the possible conflict back to the manager for discussion.

TIME–BOUNDARY CONDITION AND RESOURCE

Often there is confusion and difficulty with the idea of time in the task assignment process since it is both boundary condition – one of the key components of a task assignment – and also quite clearly a resource. Both are measured in the same units – minutes, hours, days, years, but there is a crucial difference when thinking about good management practice. The boundary condition is a deadline (target completion time); the amount of time available prior to the deadline is a resource. Often this resource is expressed in staff hours available or overtime hours available, but it is clearly different from a deadline.

The 'how' – specifying the pathway

One of the things we have learned both as managers and as employees, no one likes to be told *how* to carry out a task unless the person is new to role and has no idea how to tackle a new assignment. People who know their job say, 'Tell me what to do, but don't tell me how to do it.' Think about how you have reacted to the 'helpful' advice offered to you on your driving, cooking or how you treat your children.

The 'how' is the creation of a methodology (pathway) to achieve the goal and that must remain within the task doer's area of discretion. There may be some limits on the methodology or pathway that needs to be created. For example, hiring temporary employees may not be allowed, or developing a new computer program may not be allowed. These are simply additional limits on the task, but within those limits the 'how' of the task is within the discretionary area of the task doer. They are, in effect, resource constraints.

When employees claim they are being micro-managed, more often than not, the manager is telling them not only what to do, but how to do it. That is why we said earlier that the pathway must not be specified for people in task assignment. Work for people is turning intention into reality by exercising their discretion. Correct task assignment for humans must concentrate upon our abilities to learn, to create and to innovate.

The clear exception to this is training where the purpose of the relationship is to learn *how* to do something.

The 'how' as a task assignment

As one moves up an organisational hierarchy, the objective of the task may be to articulate a methodology or pathway. If you start with a problem, then as a manager you must formulate and articulate potential tasks for a person or people to carry out. Depending upon the available technology, that task may or may not contain a complex pathway.

For example, take a problem from the management of diabetes – how to stabilise blood sugar levels, which fluctuate on a 24-hour basis. One task might simply be to give the patient with diabetes a pamphlet on diet and exercise. On the other hand, it might be that diet and exercise have been tried and failed. Then one must create a more complex pathway to try and solve the problem when easy technologies have failed.

The task, at the higher level, is not just to stabilise the blood sugar. The task is to create a *method* or a system which when followed will, in some cases, stabilise the blood sugar level. The output is actually the pathway itself – which then can be articulated in order to assign tasks to others. The formulation and articulation of a task is, in itself, a task.

At a much higher level, the creation of a strategic plan by a CEO is the creation of a pathway – the methods the business will use to achieve certain objectives. Creating the strategy is the task. Out of this strategy will come numerous tasks, which must then be carried out by others.

The decision to write or not to write a task assignment is a managerial judgment. It should not be made a requirement in all cases because it will then become a mechanistic and non-productive process. As a manager–subordinate relationship progresses, each will develop a clear understanding of what is expected, and a few words 'on the fly' may be all that is necessary to make clear what is to be done and how performance will be judged. In other cases, a manager may decide a written assignment would be a more productive means to communicate his or her intentions, and therefore decide to put it down in that form.

In some societies, for example in Russia, we have found that most tasks are written down. However, they are called orders and rarely contain context and purpose. While being clear, they do not encourage discussion.

Notes on 'empowerment' and 'self-organisation'

When boundaries and the area for discretion are clear, people feel truly 'empowered' to get on with their work. They are able to organise their work processes and carry on to achieve the goals of the organisation. Too often the terms 'empowerment' or 'self-organisation' are used as if employees can do anything they want; that there are no longer any boundaries or controls. This is nonsense – as virtually all employees recognise. Imprecise language and the ensuing misunderstandings lead to cynicism and the view that 'empowerment' is just another fad, and a fraudulent one at that. It appeared to mean one thing, while the reality was quite different.

In some cases where organisations claimed to be empowering their workers, nothing changed: excessive controls were maintained even though management denied they were there. In other cases, managers were taught these concepts in a way which lead them to believe they should not tell their employees what to do – just let them get on with the work. The managers, in effect, abdicated their accountability to give a clear statement of purpose and to assign tasks, saying employees were now 'empowered' to figure things out for themselves. Of course, if they did not figure out what the boss really wanted, penalties could be severe.

True personal empowerment comes from a clear task assignment that states purpose and sets clear boundaries, but leaves appropriate space for the exercise of discretion. It is in this area, as in many others in the field of organisation and management, that the problem may not be so much the idea as the way it is presented and discussed. For example, in an article in the *Wall Street Journal* on self-organisation, the headline states, 'Self-Organization Will Free Employees to Act Like Bosses'. (Petzinger, Jr., 1997) The article then goes on to quote various managers regarding what they are doing:

> *Strategic planning is considered futile at [Company X], which instead relies on its 12 employees to act on ever-changing customer cues. 'We function like an amoeba that flows with the environment and constantly reshapes its body,' says the owner.*

> *On a larger scale, [Company Y, Fortune 500 size] is hatching a bold new R&D initiative from the self-coordinated effort of several employee groups. 'If an institution wants to be adaptive,' [says the Chairman] ... 'it has to let go of some control, and trust that people will work on the right things in the right way.'*

In the first case, where 'self-organisation' or 'empowerment' seems to be successful, we would bet the purpose is clear to the employees, and they are simply being allowed to get on with their work with a clear (and perhaps larger than usual) area for discretion.

In the case of Company Y, use of judgment appears to be something new. We can predict that unless the company's purpose as well as the boundaries and area for discretion are clear, there will be some floundering as the employees test their situation and try to figure out what they are to do, within what time frame and with what resources.

The Chairman of Company Y did say, 'let go of *some* control', but how much is the right amount? How does a lower level manager discern the correct amount of freedom and the correct setting of limits? Where is it noted that an understanding of purpose is *essential* if discretion is to be exercised effectively? If questions such as these are not clarified, one can also predict that in a year or two, the organisation will have moved on from self-organisation into something new which will again purport to improve its organisational effectiveness.

Of course, there may be other interpretations of what is going on. It may be that some managers have been controlling the 'how' of task performance rather than the 'what', the 'when' and the resources. In this case, providing an area for discretion by loosening control over the 'how' should improve the situation. Whatever the facts behind the headline and the statements we have quoted, it is obvious such commentary is open to a variety of interpretations.

The task assignment methodology described in this chapter provides a clear statement of what is required for true empowerment of employees; it also answers the questions that were raised above. The examples in this chapter used simple tasks with short times to completion in order to make the principles clear. We recognise that at higher levels of the organisation the tasks may be significantly more complex, and the term 'task' (which often implies something small) may not even appear to be the correct term. However the need for good task assignment applies at all levels of the organisation.

Obviously tasks will be assigned very differently at different levels of the organisation. As you move up the organisation, the area for discretion grows, and often the limits have much broader tolerances. Many of the prescribed limits are assumed to be understood (though we still recommend a conversation to make sure there is full agreement even at the highest levels of the organisation).

An example of a high-level task is provided by the experience of one of the authors. Stewart was given the dual assignments to form an organisational development (OD) team to restructure a large corporate business unit and to develop an understanding of systems that would allow their effective design across the organisation. It was recognised that the first task would take somewhere between three and five years. It was hoped that the second task could be completed within one year, or at most two years.

He was given the authority to hire as many people as he needed from within the corporation – taking some from the business unit under study and others from other business units. He would have to get the permission of their managing directors, but it was made clear to the managing directors that unless there was a very good reason, people were to be released for at least one year to carry out this work.

The cost was estimated to be $4 to $6 million, and if it exceeded this, Stewart should get back to his manager and the CEO of the corporation to discuss the reasons and perhaps revise what needed to be done.

Although it was not specifically articulated, he understood that his work performance would be judged on the quality of recommendations made (in the judgment of his manager and the CEO) and also the quality of the systems developed. Some of the indicators of performance would be a reduction in industrial action, productivity gains, reduction in costs. There was a variety of other limits, including that no one would lose their employment as a result of the restructuring. Individuals' jobs might change, and they might be transferred to other sites, but employment within the corporation was guaranteed (at that time).

Stewart began to carry out these tasks, which were partially completed in two years. Another manager then took over the first task, which was completed two years later, while Stewart went on to develop, articulate and demonstrate the methodology in another role. As can be seen, there was considerable area for discretion and the limits were in some cases quite tight (no one is to lose their job) and in others had large tolerances (three to five years to complete the task). There would have been no reward for completing the task more quickly if the recommendations were of poor quality. There would have been no reward for spending less than $4 million if again, the recommendations had not been judged as being effective. In fact, approximately $6 million was spent, including all training, and this was considered by the CEO to be money well spent.

A few years later this was demonstrated under the pressure of a severe global economic recession and downturn in demand and revenue. Twenty-five per cent of the workforce had to be cut. The managing director who had to carry out this unpleasant task stated it would have been impossible without the understandings and structures developed in the OD process.

When the recession passed, the reduced workforce was able to produce more than had ever been produced before. With the implementation of new systems and changed managers to support the structural changes, working conditions and trust in management improved to the extent that, a few years after that, the workforce chose to work under staff conditions rather than keeping their union conditions and restraints. This was in an organisation that had had very difficult labour–management relations with more than 1000 work stoppages in a single year prior to the changes in structure, systems and key managers.

12 *Authorities and Role Relationships*

We have discussed the organisation as an authority structure and the difference between authority and power. One common mistake made by critics of hierarchy is that of assuming that authority is 'top down'. In fact authority is distributed throughout the organisation. *Every* role must have authority, for without it no decisions can be made and no work can be done. If people in roles have no discretion, they are in effect no more than machines. Apart from the ethical problem this poses (see Part 1), it is a waste of resources because people do not make good machines.

Authority is not, therefore, the prerogative of leaders alone but a necessary component of every role, if real work is to be done. There is authority in peer relationships. There is authority from team members towards team leaders. Our proposition is two-fold:

1. Every role should have clear, explicit authority.
2. This authority should be distributed on the basis of the work to be done in each role.

The terms authority and accountability are often vague and only used in their social meanings. Authority is thus wrongly seen as a vertical concept and at times absolute. Accountability often equates to blame at one extreme or mere words at the other. We are looking at a situation where:

* there is some clearly defined work to be done by someone;
* they need authority to do it – and this should be explicit and
* there should be someone else whose work includes determining whether and how well that work has been done and what consequences follow.

All too often we have found that the above conditions do not exist. People are unclear what they are really meant to be doing; they are unclear about what authority they have and are even unclear about who they report to. This is sometimes praised as 'flexible' or 'democratic' or even allowing for 'creativity'. In our experience such organisations are riddled with power and have a hidden rigidity. Personal agendas and implicit rules cause damage to all but the brightest or strongest. It is interesting to hear some critics of hierarchy and authority implicitly supporting and encouraging the law of the jungle – survival of the fittest. We do not regard this as a just or effective way of achieving purpose and releasing potential.

Jaques often used to ask people quite deliberately and provocatively, 'Can you give me the definition of a manager?' Almost invariably there was disagreement, debate or even stunned silence. Compare this with a chemistry class where a teacher asked for the formula for hydrochloric acid.

We argue that to be effective not only should all roles have authority but as some roles appear in many organisations or many times in one organisation they can be categorised generally. One such role is described by the term *manager*.

What is a manager?

There are almost as many definitions of a manager as there are managers. Unfortunately, most of them do not clearly distinguish between those who have leadership accountability and those who do not. In many cases it is difficult to determine who in the organisation is a manager and who is not, using the many common definitions.

If one wants to build an *accountability* hierarchy, a very precise definition is required. It is essential that everyone know who is accountable for what (see Box 12.1).

This definition excludes all persons in an organisation who do not have people reporting to them. A managerial role is pre-eminently a leadership role. As we have said, the distinctions made by some scholars between 'leaders', who are visionary and charismatic, and 'managers', who are rather dull drones, is both insulting to managers and seriously destructive of improved management practice and hence leadership.

If you are a manager, you are a leader of people. You have no choice in this matter. Your only choice is whether to become a good leader or a bad leader. To be fully effective a manager must work at one level above their direct reports and thus be able to articulate and fully encompass the work of the next level down.

For managers to accept accountability for the work performance of others, they must have certain minimum authorities. These authorities must always be exercised within company policy and the laws of the land. By definition authority is never without limits. There are constraints on the authority an organisation can grant to its managers, and there are constraints based upon the acceptance of a manager's authority by their team members.

Managers should behave within and act through authority systems, within limits that are subject to review. Their ability to act derives from a clear grant of authority from the organisation that holds role incumbents accountable for the proper exercise of that authority. It must be recognised, however, that authority is not only limited by organisation policies, but also has limits that are beyond the ability of the organisation to readily control. Failure to recognise this leads to abuse by power and creates the need for unions and regulatory legislation.

CONSTRAINTS ON AUTHORITY IN A WORK HIERARCHY

Many constraints on authority have been discussed in terms of laws, ethics, policies and systems. The necessity for those reporting to a manager to accept the manager's authority is less widely acknowledged as a constraint except, perhaps, in the cases of demarcation rules and other restrictive practices found in some industries. For example, the grip, who carries the light but cannot plug it in because this is the job of the electrician, is well known in the film industry.

The acceptance of authority depends upon social process and mythology. This in turn will depend upon how well the organisation is structured and how well its systems are designed. However, if leaders have no training or expertise in social process, their own poor leadership behaviour will undermine their authority.

Box 12.1   Definition of Manager

Manager: A person held accountable for their own work and for the work performance of people reporting to them over time.

The work of a manager is critically concerned with people. Accountability is a social relationship, that is, part of the social process. The manager's work involves reviewing, recognising and rewarding work performance of team members, which only makes sense if the manager can actually assign tasks. Further, it makes sense that, if managers are to be held accountable for the team's work performance, they must have some say in who is a member of the team and who stays in or leaves the team. The proposition is simple. If a person does *not* have these authorities, they will not feel it is fair to be held accountable for the work performance of their team(s). The converse is also likely to be true, providing they have the appropriate capability. Jaques, Rowbottom and Billis and others at BIOSS (Brunel) have articulated this need and the authorities were refined in work with CRA (now Rio Tinto) under Sir Roderick Carnegie in the 1980s.

Manager–subordinate relationships

The authorities represented in Figure 12.1 are the minimum required by managers if they are to accept accountability for the work performance of team members. The VAR^{3}I authorities are the foundation underlying the definition of the term 'manager'.

V: *Veto selection*. A manager may veto the selection of a new team member. In practice this means that the manager who is exercising the veto cannot be forced to accept an employee whom the manager believes, would be unwilling or unable to contribute positively to the work of the output team.

It is important to note the difference between the authority to veto and the authority to select. Even when a manager is authorised to select a person for a role, that selection is subject to veto by their manager, manager-once-removed, manager-twice-removed, and so on. Veto means you do not have to have anyone you do not want. It does not mean you can always have your first choice.

It is also important to note that the veto is an authority and must be exercised within policy limits that include no unfair discrimination.

A: *Assign tasks*. This is the authority to assign tasks to direct reports. No one else in the organisation may assign tasks to a manager's reports unless they first gain the approval of the person's manager. (See Chapter 11 for tasks with an inset trigger where it may appear others are assigning tasks, but in fact the person is responding as his or her manager has authorised.)

R^3: *Recognise, review and reward work performance differentially.* The manager recognises and reviews the overall work performance of direct reports in order to improve their work performance and the manager's own work performance. They evaluate work performance and, within limits set by organisation policy, recognise and reward people differentially based on the manager's judgment of their work performance. No one else in the organisation may

V - Veto selection

A - Assign Tasks

R^3- Recognise, review and reward work performance differentially

I - Initiate removal from role

Figure 12.1   Authorities of a Manager

differentially reward a manager's direct reports without their approval. We do not just rely on reward such as money but note how significant review, feedback and non-monetary recognition are in influencing behaviour.

In the application of differential recognition, it is important to acknowledge the strength and necessity of psychological rewards – public recognition, special assignments and so on. The focus should not be entirely on monetary rewards, though obviously these are very important. It is important to note that recognition of poor work performance is also the work of the manager.

I: *Initiate removal from role.* This authority means a manager should not be required to keep a non-performing member of their team after the requirements of organisational policy have been met. The manager will be expected to give valid and fair reasons for initiating removal from role, and the person to be removed must have been given proper warning and adequate help and opportunity to improve and has not responded.

The process is iterative as the manager's manager (M + 1) may ask the manager (M) to take specific actions to coach and counsel a person whose performance is not satisfactory. This is done to ensure fairness and, where necessary, to determine a case for dismissal. When all company policies regarding warnings and help have been given, M+1 may not require M to keep a person who is not satisfactory.

Once the person is removed from a particular role, the M+1 must decide if the person is to be transferred to another role within their organisation (subject to the veto of the manager who is to take this person into their team), or is to be removed from the organisation (see Box 12.2).

The same constraints determine the reality of the authority held by the manager-once-removed as those that determine the authority of the manager, namely: law of the land, corporate policy, social custom and work practices and acceptance by the team member(s). See Figure 12.2.

The authorities of the manager-once-removed are:

V: *Veto selection.* Authority to veto, in the same manner as the manager, above.

AP: *Assess potential.* This involves a judgment about an individual's capabilities to do higher levels of work and their potential for promotion. M will be expected to comment on potential or to recommend promotion, but the authority to decide lies with M+1. This must be the case since only M+1 is in a position to decide if P is ready to work at the level of M.

The individual whose potential is to be assessed must be informed that M+1 has this authority and is accountable for this process. M+1 needs to learn about the person's

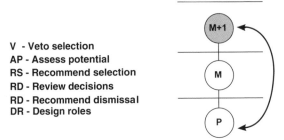

V - Veto selection
AP - Assess potential
RS - Recommend selection
RD - Review decisions
RD - Recommend dismissal
DR - Design roles

Figure 12.2　Authorities of the Manager-Once-Removed

> **Box 12.2 Managers' Additional Authorities**
>
> A manager may, in practice, have additional authorities – to spend money, allocate resources, sign contracts or select team members, subject to the veto of superiors – but the VAR^{3}I authorities are the minimum.
>
> If a manager lacks the VAR^{3}I authorities, they will not feel fully accountable for the work performance of their reports over time. If the realities of corporate policy or industrial practice limit these authorities of the manager, M+1 must make adjustments to match accountability with the reality of authority limits.
>
> Even though the organisation authorises a person to use the VAR^{3}I authorities, there are still limits on their right to veto appointment and initiate removal from role. There are limits on the tasks they may assign to their reports. There are limits on the rewards that may be earned.
>
> The authorities also carry with them an accountability to exercise them well. A key element in the judgment of managerial performance is how well they exercise these authorities. Decisions made in the exercise of these authorities by a manager are subject to appeal to M+1.

interests, knowledge fields, skills, ambitions and so on. They should discuss the assessment with the individual and learn more about the person's interests and ambitions in light of this assessment. M+1 may indicate possible career paths, educational or training opportunities and other steps which might be taken, and their timing, to allow P to undertake self-improvement more effectively. This should indicate when the organisation should be taking steps to provide developmental opportunities to P, taking into account M+1's assessment and P's career aspirations. The M+1 must also advise P if he or she is judged not to have any potential for promotion to a higher level. This is often found to be a liberating judgment.

RS: *Recommend Selection.* As part of M+1's accountability for the development of P they also have the authority to recommend selection to the manager of an individual to fill a role as one of M's reports. The manager's authority to veto selection still applies. M+1 may recommend an individual based on knowledge of the person's capability, the belief that a particular role or project assignment will be good for the individual's development, or any other reason which is within M+1's authority and the limits of law and policy. Managers need to understand the reasons for this authority and accept its validity as part of the process of the development of people for roles at the manager's own level.

RD: *Review decisions.* This includes the authority to hear appeals from their manager's reports. It is necessary that everyone in the organisation knows that the M+1 level has the authority of the organisation to review a manager's decisions. The manager must know this and factor it into the approach adopted when confronted with a problem. The person must know this, so neither the person nor the manager feel that the person is stabbing the manager in the back by going 'over their head'.

RD: *Recommend dismissal.* The authority to initiate removal from role will, after appropriate processes, remove a person from the manager's team, but not from the organisation. The decision to dismiss from the organisation should rest at a higher level to ensure fairness when someone's livelihood is to be removed.

Some organisations give M+1 the authority to dismiss; in others this lies with M+2. If it lies with M+2, then M+1 recommends dismissal. Where the authority to dismiss resides is a policy decision of the organisation.

DR: *Design roles.* The authority to design more roles (for more Ps) rests with M+1. (This includes the authority to re-design roles.) There are two main reasons for this: one positive and one negative.

M+1 is in the best position to understand the context of the specific work involved and to judge whether a new role is required to undertake that work. They have a good view of the wider business purpose and how the new role helps achieve that purpose. M+1 can ensure consistency of role design and fairness across the teams. The other reason is that M will generally have a self-interest in creating another role reporting to them (or resisting the idea that a role may no longer be required). Any change in numbers of direct reports or in the role descriptions of those reports will affect the ability of M to achieve performance objectives.

Of course, M will have an important input to the details of the role design work, as will others in the organisation like M's team and M+2. While the work of M+1 as a team leader is to be accountable for the work of their team members, and M's work will be affected by the role (re-)design, they are in the best role position to design or re-design new roles in the organisation.

NOTES ON SPONSORSHIP

The M+1 is sometimes called a sponsoring manager to emphasise the accountability for development.

While something like sponsorship goes on in many organisations, it is often done only for a favoured few, and it frequently carries implications of power. A manager knows they are in favour because 'their people' get promoted. In some organisations there is continuing gossip about the various power groups as higher level executives compete to get their people promoted into key positions. This drains productive energy from the work of the organisation, and it also means that many talented people may never get noticed because they are excluded from the power system.

A system of clear authority for the M+1 reduces these problems, and ensures that everyone in the organisation gets fair consideration from someone who should be able to discern developing capability from their position one step above the person's manager.

The authority to veto selection goes up through the entire hierarchy, though obviously it is rarely exercised by M+2 and above – see Figure 12.3. Nonetheless, the authority reflects a

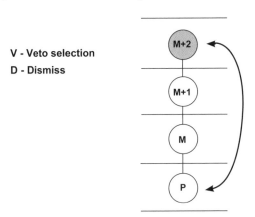

V - Veto selection

D - Dismiss

Figure 12.3   Authorities of the Manager-Twice-Removed

reality of organisation life, that someone high in the organisation may have knowledge and good reason for vetoing the selection of a person to the organisation.

NOTES ON THE AUTHORITY TO DISMISS

In many organisations, there is a policy that the decision to remove the economic livelihood of an employee is held at the M+2 level. This practice makes it known to all employees that dismissal is never taken lightly and the organisation is making every effort to ensure it is not done arbitrarily or for reasons of prejudice. This may provide significant legal protection from wrongful dismissal suits.

The decision to dismiss someone from an employment role is a very serious one. This has been recognised in law in many industrial societies as larger segments of the population rely on employment work for their livelihood, their well-being, their status in the community and their family's security. Setting up a fair and decent policy for handling this process is essential.

While we have suggested a policy where M+1 recommends dismissal and the authority to dismiss is held at M+2, there are a number of valid ways to handle this process. We will not discuss all of them here, but simply mention some patterns we have seen which appear to have worked for the organisations which use them.

As has been said, in some organisations, the authority to dismiss is kept at the M+1 level. Other variations are also possible. Where a remote site is headed by a person in a level IV role, the authority to dismiss from level I roles may be at the M+2 (level IV) level to assure consistency across the site. Dismissal from level II, III and IV roles is retained at the M+1 level.

There are valid reasons for a variety of policies regarding dismissal. The important thing is that no one may lose his or her job based solely on the authority of a single individual. This must be part of a known process, subject to higher level review, which complies with law and accepted standards of fairness.

Authorities of the supervisor

The role of the supervisor is often contentious. We have come across people who are deeply offended by Jaques' categorisation that they interpret as 'not real bosses' that is, not managers. However, in deeper discussion nearly all have actually agreed with the authorities described below. Our experience is that the main stumbling blocks are due to:

1. a confusion between 'boss', 'manager' and 'leader' and
2. a sense of lack of respect symbolised in representing the role 'out to the side' – see Figures 12.4 and 12.5.

Often the supervisor role is represented as follows:

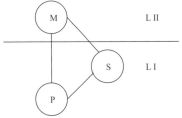

Figure 12.4   How the Supervisor Role is often Represented

This seems to run counter to the psychological experience of supervisors being much more direct and immediate leaders of people (especially at level I). Therefore we represent the role as follows:

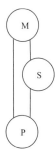

Figure 12.5 Our Representation of the Supervisor Role

This does not mean an intervening manager but someone in a leadership role with clear authorities as described below. All of this can of course be confused if the title supervisor is actually used for the first line manager. What is most important, as always, is:

1. What is the work?
2. What is the authority? (see Box 12.3)

In our experience, the term 'supervisor' is most often used to describe leadership work within level I. The supervisor role is most often created to provide leadership to other workers in level I roles in the following circumstances:

• the work load at level I is large;
• the manager in level II has too many direct reports to give them day-to-day attention and the feedback they may require and
• the work can be ordered into demonstrable procedures that do not require the frequent resolution of higher complexity problems.

Box 12.3 Authorities of the Supervisor

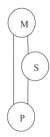

Figure 12.6 Authorities of the Supervisor

• RV: Recommend veto on selection
• A+/–: Assign tasks within limits set by M
• R²+/–: Review task performance and recognise differentially within limits set by M
• RI: recommend initiation of removal from role.

The supervisor role may also be needed when workers in level I roles must work at sites remote from their manager; when there is shift work; or when there is a heavy induction and training load. There is no need to create a supervisor role unless the total work burden is too large for a single manager at level II.

The principal function of the supervisor is to lead a crew that is part of an output team or service team. The output team manager is the manager of both the supervisor and the members of the crew, and this must remain clear at all times.

The same constraints on authorities that apply to managers also apply to supervisors. In addition, there are other limits on the authority of supervisor roles, which are determined by their managers in line with organisational policy – a manager may not pass all of his or her authority to a supervisor.

RV: The supervisor recommends the veto of someone being considered for selection to the manager's output team if they believe that the person would be either unwilling or unable to contribute positively to the work of the output team. While a supervisor has the authority from the organisation to recommend to their manager that a person not be selected to the output team, the decision rests with the manager.

A+/–: The supervisor may assign tasks as required as part of the work of the role. There are the usual limitations on this imposed by law, corporate policy, social custom, work practices and the acceptance of team members. In addition, the manager's authority to assign tasks requires that they specify, at his or her discretion, the range (indicated by A+/–) over which a supervisor may assign tasks within the manager's output team.

The authority of the manager allows each of their supervisors to have different limitations on their respective authorities to assign tasks. These limitations may be varied from time to time as the tasks or the experience of the people in the output team change. Tasks outside these limits remain the preserve of the manager (see Box 12.4).

R^2+/–: The supervisor will review task performance and recognise differentially within limits set by the manager. R^2+/– refers to the kinds of performance review and feedback the supervisor may give to members of their crews. It is rare and, we think, inappropriate, for a supervisor to have the authority to reward crew members financially for performance. The supervisor will inform the manager of decisions on R^2+/–.

It is important to note that the A+/– and R^2+/– must be kept in balance by the manager because the team members will have no reason to carry out the supervisor's assignments if the supervisor lacks commensurate authority to recognise good and bad performance.

RI: The supervisor may recommend initiation of removal from a role on the supervisor's crew, where justified, for those people to whom the supervisor has previously given proper help and opportunity to improve and who have not responded. This recommendation may or may not be accepted by the manager, who has the authority to decide on initiation of removal from role.

Supervisors may have budgets for recognition: a dinner, social occasion, gift voucher or presentation, but not cash. The supervisor does have the authority to recommend

---

Box 12.4   **Managers and Supervisors**

The practice of good leadership on the part of the manager requires that they make known to the crew where the limits of the supervisor's authority to assign work (and recognise differentially, see above) are. The manager must also make clear that they will not breach these limits from the outside without letting the supervisor know, unless it is an emergency.

to the manager who should receive pay increases, or not. However, like V and I, this is a recommendation. These authorities sometimes become confused because, if supervisors are good at their work, they may rarely, if ever, have their recommendations rejected. This does not change the authority.

It is important for managers at all levels to understand the sensitivity and subtlety of managerial and supervisory relationships. Where the organisation requires supervisory roles, the success of these relationships is crucial for the effective functioning of the organisation. It is also essential that the differences in authority and accountability be reflected in the systems of performance review, performance evaluation and differential reward.

For example, should the performance of the output team not be of acceptable standard because of the poor output of one of its members, the supervisor may be held accountable for the way tasks are assigned and recognised. They may be held accountable for recommending removal of the poor performer. However, it is the manager who has the authority to initiate removal from role, and therefore is held accountable for the poor performance and for the work associated with such removal, not the supervisor.

This differing accountability, because of differing authority, has important implications for the manager at level III of the manager at level II. The manager at level III needs to be very aware of the limitations set by the manager at level II on the authority of the supervisor. This is important when the work of the manager (at level II) is reviewed.

A project involves a group of people who are assigned to work on a special task instead of, or in addition to, their normal work load. A project is created to give concentrated attention to a task of limited and specific duration, which may require interdisciplinary skills and expertise, or expertise from various organisational units.

These authorities apply in the relationship between a project team leader and a project team member who is not a direct report of the project leader in the normal organisation structure but is specially assigned to the project team. Project team members remain direct reports of their regular managers. Project team members may work in the same work level as the project leader or they may work one or more levels below the project leader. On some occasions a technical expert who works at a higher level than the project leader may be assigned to the project to provide specific expertise.

A project team may operate on a full- or part-time basis without any need to modify the authority set as shown in Figure 12.7. The project team member must be informed of the limitations that apply to the project team leader's authority.

PL: *Project leader.*

PTM: *Project team member.*

VP: *Veto selection to project team.* The project leader carries the authority to veto the selection of people to the project team.

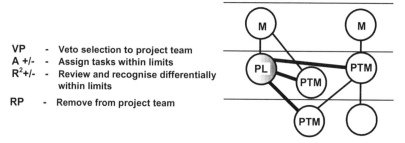

VP   - Veto selection to project team
A +/- - Assign tasks within limits
R^2+/- - Review and recognise differentially within limits

RP   - Remove from project team

Figure 12.7   Authorities of a Project Leader

A+/–: *Assign tasks within agreed limits.* This authority is similar to that held by the supervisor, but in this case the additional limits are imposed by the project team members' managers. The agreed limits apply for the duration of the assignment to the project team though they may be renegotiated if demands of the work or the work environment require changed limits.

R^2+/–: *Review and recognise differentially within agreed upon limits.* Again, the authority to assign work and the authority to recognise differentially must be commensurate. As with the authority to assign tasks, the limits to the authority of the project leader to recognise differentially are set by the project team member's manager.

RP: *Remove from the project team.* The project leader has the authority to remove a project member from the team. The project team member returns to their previous role and organisational unit upon the exercise of this authority by the project leader

It is essential that the project leader have people properly assigned to the project by their managers and that his or her authorities are clear. Too often we have seen people told to lead a project where they have to 'persuade' others to help them, where team members have to resolve conflicts between their project work and the work assigned by their manager, and where the project leader has no authority to review or recognise team members effectively.

We have been told in a few organisations that giving a person such a project without proper authorities is one way to find out if they have a future in management. One of us spoke with a highly talented person who would have made an excellent manager. He was so disgusted with what he had to do on the project that he said he never wanted to be a manager. Without adequate authorities and other resources, this person thought he had experienced 'management' and he wanted no part of it.

Role relationships

In addition to the vertical relationships, every organisation has many horizontal and diagonal relationships. Often they are left to chance, or are termed the 'informal' organisation. We believe this is the cause of much difficulty in organisations – the 'silo' effect; the miscommunications between individuals in different organisational units; or the unwillingness of some people at a higher level of work to speak with someone at a lower level.

Much is to be gained from clarification of these multiple role relationships. We have found that to be consistently productive it is useful to have a clear understanding of what a role relationship is and the authorities that may productively exist between roles (see Box 12.5).

Box 12.5   Principles

Our major point here is that to determine working relationships the following principles need to be applied:

- Determine the work required of the people involved; be clear about expectations.
- Allocate the appropriate authorities to the people concerned clearly and openly, so all know what they are and why.
- Ensure that these authorities do not conflict with other authorities but rather take them into account. For example, ensure that the managerial relationship and project leader relationship do not overlap.
- The level of authority should match what is necessary to achieve the work the person is being held accountable for.

Organisations would not function without cross-functional, peer, diagonal and a whole range of other non-managerial relationships. We emphasise the line relationships because they form the authority spine around which other relationships are connected. It is a fruitless task to argue if the spine is more important than the ribs, or less important than the skull. They are mutually interdependent. As Jaques always said, 'start with the work'. Then we can build relationships to get this work done accurately to the principles we outline above.

Jaques (1976) also outlines other types of relationships with different authorities including, coordinator and auditor. Such a list could be extended. Rather we again return to the principles and urge people to be as creative as possible within these. There is no need for the rigidity often wrongly associated with hierarchy. Authority and authoritarian are too easily and sometimes deliberately confused.

All role relationships are part of the social processes of the organisation. The nature of authority can be fundamentally affected by the way it is exercised. The exercise of authority is subject to the same principles described above in the work of leadership. It must take into account mythologies, current systems and capability. Whilst all managers have (or should have) the same minimum authorities, the way these authorities are exercised will be slightly different or even wildly different according to the person and context.

Finally, we emphasise that authority is not simply top down or even sideways but can be upwards as well. In the following chapters we will look, for example, at the authority of the team member with regard to the team leader.

We have come across many situations where team members have taught their leaders technology and skills. People are not just given authority to direct or instruct. We may have the authority to negotiate, consider, teach, recommend, give advice, inform. These are all significant authorities and can be distributed in many different ways according to the work to be done.

In our experience it is not authority that is the problem but rather the lack of clarity of authority, leading to the use of power. Lack of clarity is not resolved by 'being democratic' or 'flexible'; it is resolved by understanding what authority is needed either temporarily in project work or as part of a permanent role. It is then part of the work of anyone to exercise the authority accorded to them with skilful social process.

13 *Key Systems*

This chapter proposes some key organisational systems with regard to running a positive, successful organisation and looks specifically at people systems critical to effective leadership.

Leadership is fundamental in influencing behaviour. Further, influence should be based on authority not power. It would be naïve to think that the only source of influence is the leader. We have seen that mythologies are created in our early lives and continue to develop and grow. The mythologies created form the basis for how we interpret behaviour and systems, and how we construe meaning and intent. As employees or members of an organisation we are still open to a range of influences. For example, Macdonald, I. (1990) has shown the critical importance of feedback and recognition for psychological well-being. In this chapter we first look at some specific sources of influence and then how leaders in managerial roles can use their influence productively and to mutual benefit.

Sources of influence

Figure 13.1 describes the main sources of influence on behaviour. We then explain each source in more detail.

The first point is that this is not a passive model. The person is subject to the influences, some more direct and deliberate than others but is also an influencer. These are people–people relationships and, whilst not always equal, these relationships do have the potential at least for mutual influence. The following model concentrates on influences that have a bearing on work behaviour but could be used more generally.

1. *The person*: The person (each one of us) is influenced by all the relationships and may feel more or less able to reciprocate. Our identities are made up of the views and judgments that flow in these relationships. This in turn leads to behaviour and changes in behaviour. If we experience negative judgments (in terms of the values continua) we may choose to change our behaviour, to confront the judgment or over time to end the relationship. We also influence our own behaviour through reflection, consideration and learning.
2. *Family and friends* clearly influence us with comments about work, how we look (tired, happy), what our moods are, what material demands are made, whether we seem to be fairly paid or treated, and so on.
3. *Outside Commitments*: There are usually other influences that bear upon how we think and act at work. Our political or religious affiliation can be important, as can other organisations we belong to, for example, interest or pressure groups. The media can have a deliberate effect through advertising or news coverage. The reputation of the brand or nature of the organisation may be important. For example, being a firefighter or nurse may be different from being an arms salesperson, estate agent or nuclear power worker. This is the area of moral or ethical dilemmas.

Figure 13.1 Sources of Influence

4. *Interest groups associated with the organisation.* Similar to the above, this point involves membership of or association with, say, a trade union or professional associations. It may even be a social club or sports club.

5. *Significant others in the organisation.* This refers to people who influence us but not through a formal or even contrived direct working relationship. This might include a previous boss, a friend in another department, someone we listen to or what we might call opinion formers. Such people are sometimes referred to as mentors in a general sense. These are people who one might talk to in order to help make a decision or reflect on work-life.

6. *Peers.* These may be immediate team members or colleagues. Peers, especially fellow team members, have significant influence on each other. It is the daily comments and discussions that build mythologies, allow for comparisons and, in the absence of authorised leadership, set the norms and establish the box C and D systems (see Chapter 10). We have often heard people say that considerable pressure has been put on them to work slower, or not to get over-enthusiastic in order to maintain current standards. Perhaps the best book on peer influence is Ben Harper's *Rivethead* (1992), which demonstrates how a work culture grew in opposition to the leadership.

7. *Customers.* Many customers or clients might feel they do not have enough influence, but without satisfied customers or clients there is no need for the organisation. Any organisation, commercial or not, is providing goods and services to someone. It is highly appropriate, therefore, that customers have influence.

8. *Team members: direct reports and their reports.* People reporting to you and the people reporting to them clearly have influence, which we have covered in discussions on

authorities, role relationships and particularly teamwork.

If we look at all these relationships and suppose that the person is the head of a small business, then they will have to manage and balance all of these relationships themselves. The more usual case is that the person is part of an organisation with a manager and a manager +1. Therefore, when the manager assigns work, they must be aware of these other influences. There will be times when these other influences are counter productive. The manager needs to address this. We have seen organisations where third parties or peer groups determine the work culture. Leadership has evaporated; there is little discipline. An excellent portrayal of this can be found in the film *Patton* when the character General Patton arrives early at his new headquarters to find a series of examples of poor leadership and indiscipline. The leadership should determine the work culture. This is not to say that the other relationships are to be suppressed or ignored. The leaders must, through good social process, integrate these other relationships so that they are complementary to the work culture. If this cannot be done, it becomes a critical issue that needs to be addressed. For example, in one organisation suffering an illegal strike, there were a small but significant number of Seventh Day Adventists employed in the company. These people could not strike due to their belief that they must not knowingly break the law. When the court declared the strike illegal they were compelled to go to work. This involved crossing a very hostile picket line. Their managers were present at every shift change at the picket line to ensure their protection.

It is crucial that the leader has available good systems to help build a productive work culture. The next part of this chapter outlines some key systems that should be operating well if the culture is to be effective.

People systems

We, like Jaques, always start with considering the work to be done. Some organisations place too much emphasis on building structures and grades and salary for career development and career opportunity. This can result in confused or over-complicated structures which do not help to get the work done. The circle of people systems are represented in Figure 13.2.

ROLE DESCRIPTION

We start with the need to do work and the bundling of that work into roles. As we said earlier, a role contains a group of tasks and it is usually productive to have the core work of the role focused around a level of complexity. There will always be work of differing complexity in a role but it is important to be clear what is at the heart of the work of the role. Therefore, role descriptions should describe the work specifically.

Role descriptions should:

- *Have a clear and simple purpose statement*, that is, a positive description in one sentence, without using the word 'and'.
- *Have a simple title*. Role titles are one of the most significant symbols in an organisation. We have seen 'deputy, assistant co-ordinator' and 'assistant, vice principal, head of support services'. We recommend titles common to level and to role type, for example, the title manager, principal at level 3, specialist at 2, general manager at 4, and so on. The role title should tell you the nature of the work and what level it is.

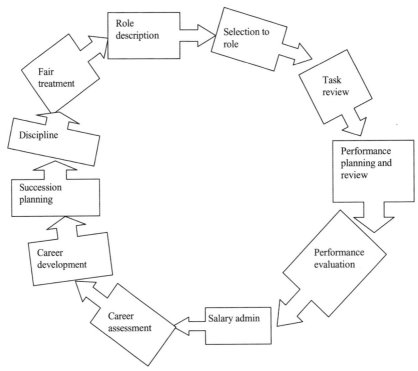

Figure 13.2   People Systems

- *Describe in simple terms the key work of the role in terms of type of work.* For example, is this primarily a leadership role, a support role or a service role? It should also include the *outputs* expected. These outputs are not the same as individual task outputs, but are more general. For example, there may be a general output: 'to make sure you and your team work safely'. It might include a task, which could be: 'to design and implement a new safety system in your department to reduce lost time injury frequency to zero'. It should not be necessary to list every task the person might do or could do.
- *Specify role relationships.* The main role relationships should be specified and should include the authorities in both directions. Too often we have seen the term 'accountabilities' used, which is actually a list of work. What is often missing is to whom the person is accountable and what consequences might result: positive or negative.
- *Include a statement of material resources.* Authorities in role-relationships are a resource but there should also be a statement of material resources, for example, a budget, spending limits, equipment and so on.
- *Provide for performance review.* Finally, the role description should be used and useful. It should be used in conjunction with the performance review and reworked by the manager and manager-once-removed (M+1) when it needs changing. The person who should authorise a role description is the M+1 even if the manager and the individual have put a draft together. It is the work of the M+1 to have an overview of the work of the team and to determine how that work is distributed.

SELECTION TO ROLE

Probably the single most important factor in selecting an individual to fill a role is a clear understanding of the work required in that role. The better the manager understands what is required, the more likely the manager will be able to identify a person who could successfully fill that role. Clear articulation of the principal function of the role, its accountability and tasks, its authorities and its role relationships is essential.

A current and complete role description becomes the basis for good selection of potential employees. It is necessary, however, to gather more information than simply knowledge about the role and the person being interviewed.

Preparation

From the role description it is important to use the capability model to create a specification for the role in terms of:

- mental processing ability
- knowledge
- technical skills
- social skills
- application.

The qualities with regard to social process skills may be determined by the required role-relationships. For example, what are the characteristics of the current team? What sort of customers might the person have to deal with? Are people in other areas, specialists and services easy or difficult to relate to? List other requirements that may be important. For example, is significant travel required?

The selection process

Do not just rely on interviews. Consider what other methods may be relevant. We have found that giving the person an actual problem to solve; an in-basket exercise, for example, is very helpful. A team problem-solving exercise or case study can also reveal useful information with regard to social process. We are not very impressed with psychometric tests, especially if they are done separately and standard reports not specific to the role. It is too easy to use psychometric tests as substitutes for judgment. If they are used, then be clear about their validity and reliability, exactly what quality or skill is being tested, and how this fits with the role.

It is very important to clarify the authorities of anyone who is part of the selection process. For example, we have seen people appropriately involved in the process but confused as to whether they have a veto or recommendation or advisory authority.

Mistakes

We have all made mistakes in selection and no judgment process is foolproof. It is important to reflect on past errors and successes. We are all susceptible to certain distractions. Some typical distractions include:

- *Energy and drive* (application) – it is easy to be over-impressed and mistakenly see it as a compensation for other areas.

- *Appearance* – looking good or not is a classic example. Remember appearances *can* be deceptive.
- *Assumed similarity* – the fact that a person has been to a particular college, has a certain qualification or worked for a particular company can invoke assumptions that are actually not warranted. One of the authors remembers a particular comment 'He must be good. He was in the first eight [rowing]'. Think of how many distractions have fooled or are likely to fool you.
- *References* – it is really worth checking these directly by talking to referees where possible. We have also learned a great deal from people who have worked for a candidate. Many people are good at managing upwards but treat their team members poorly.

Monitoring yourself (controls and audit)

When you select an individual, note in writing what you observed that led you to believe the person would be good in this role. Specifically record your interpretations of your observations and your thoughts as to why you picked this individual. Six months or a year later you can compare what was observed and how you interpreted those observations with the reality of the person selected.

If you do this every time you select an individual for a particular role, you will quickly learn your own strengths and weaknesses in the selection process. As we noted earlier, every human being has blind spots when it comes to selection. Some are fooled by a person who is very articulate; others rely too heavily on experience. Some prefer a person who appears very energetic or politically astute. All of these characteristics may be useful in some circumstances and may be just what is needed by the manager. On the other hand, they may also fool a manager into believing the person is capable of something they are not. You must be aware of the need for the mental processing ability of the person to match or exceed the complexity of the worth of the role.

Task feedback and review

We have already discussed tasks and task assignment. The task doer also needs to know how their work performance is judged by the manager. This is necessary if the manager's judgment of performance of the task is to be accepted as fair. The key elements of task feedback and review are:

- context
- purpose
- quantity
- quality
- resources
- time.

TASK FEEDBACK

Robert Ingersoll (1993) said 'In nature there are neither rewards nor punishments; there are consequences.'

Task feedback is information the employee receives regarding how well they carried out the task. Of all of the information associated with the task, this is the information that is most important to the employee. Some of it may come directly in response to their activities.

The reality is, that in most circumstances, the most trustworthy task feedback from the point of view of the task doer comes from nature or from the customer. Such feedback is effective because it is undeniable. For an electric utility, the power is either on or it is not. If not, some tasks have not been carried out successfully. For salespeople, they have either sold items or not.

Appropriate feedback, especially from customers, can be a powerful behavioural change or reinforcement agent. One weakness of such feedback is that it may reflect short-term satisfaction (or dissatisfaction) with task output without an understanding of overall work performance or longer-term consequences.

After nature and the customer, the next best feedback from the point of view of the task doer may come from peers. This applies more in poorly structured organisations where the manager is not at the right level of work to give effective feedback and where the real decision maker regarding an employee's rewards and compensation is someone other than the nominal manager. In this situation, peers provide psychological rewards that reinforce the individual's worth to the group – the sense that the work the individual is doing is of value (or without value).

It is important to note that task feedback from customers, nature or peers may, in fact, reinforce behaviour that is at odds with the desired direction of the manager who assigned the task.

The feedback from the manager comes last, not because it is unimportant, but because the manager always has a position of personal and organisational interest. The feedback from nature has no immediately apparent covert agenda.

This does not deny the importance of the manager's feedback, which can provide a longer-term perspective on work performance as well as significant psychological recognition.

In a properly structured organisation where the managerial authorities are real, people are aware that their manager's view of their performance will have direct impact on compensation and on whether or not they may remain in their role over time. This ensures that managerial feedback commands attention. It also increases its importance in relation to other sources of feedback.

TASK REVIEW

The purpose of task review is to learn lessons from both success and failure in order to improve work performance in the future. A task review is one form of task feedback, and is recognised in many organisations as the number-one system needed for improvement.

Task review is an informal process carried out on a regular but random basis by a manager as they comment (in a few words or at length) on task performance with their subordinates. Here the manager's role as trainer/coach is predominant. The emphasis is on a two-way, not a one-way process.

The employee may also initiate a task review when the employee thinks it is needed to improve their own work performance or the manager's work performance. It is valid and necessary to tell a manager from time to time, 'I could do my job better if ....'

Task review is intended to be an analytic process anchored in the concrete reality of specific tasks – where both the manager and subordinate look back at the task assignment, what was expected, and why – how well this was understood. Then they look at the execution of the task

– what was done, whether the task doer in fact met the specified components of the task and stayed within the range of the scoped component.

The manager and the task doer might discuss the various limits which applied to the task and whether they might have constrained efficient local performance. This can be a useful indicator for the manager to assess changes to their policy, departmental or corporate policy or systems, or perhaps even legislation.

They may discuss other tasks with inset triggers such as maintaining productive working relationships with fellow workers or servicing customers. If the task doer did not breach any limits, then task performance can be judged by how well they did on the scoped component of the task.

Task review is the time to look at whether the task achieved its intended purposes. It is the time to analyse the chosen pathway and perhaps discuss other pathways which might have been more effective or efficient. There should be discussion as to whether changes in the environment required changing the task assignment and how a similar task might be assigned and done better in the future.

Where things have not gone as well as they should, this is a chance to inquire as to what went wrong and what might correct the problem in the future. This is where, on a regular basis, the manager and the person talk about their work and where the manager can provide coaching to help the person improve their work. The person may also provide information as to what the manager could do which would help the subordinate to achieve task goals.

Coaching and counselling are the everyday processes of leadership and management and should be anchored in the concrete: what the person did; how they did it; how the task was assigned (clearly or not); and whether the performance was good, poor or failed entirely.

A general statement such as 'This is a mess!' or 'Great job!' conveys the manager's assessment but does not provide any information to change behaviour in the desired direction. Concrete cases not only provide more information to exemplify the issues and concerns regarding performance, they also make it more difficult to show prejudice on the basis of non-work related issues. Each task review is a teaching/learning opportunity.

The manager might ask the person, 'How do you think you might perform such a task more effectively?'; 'How will you do it next time?'; 'What can I do to help you improve your work performance?'.

The manager should ask him/herself, 'How should I assign a task like this to ensure it gets done to my standards of quantity, quality, timeliness and cost?'; 'Does this person have the capability to do tasks of this type?'; 'The capability to do other types of tasks?'; 'The capability to do more than is called for in this role?'.

It is of absolute importance that in the task review process the manager focuses on the work and on the task result, *not* on characteristics of the person. Treating an individual in a derogatory manner denies that person's human dignity. It will make the person angry, and even if it does not show, it will give them good cause to ignore the validity of everything else the manager might say.

Exceptionally good or bad performance should be noted in writing *at the time it occurs* and sent to M+1 as well as being reviewed with the person concerned.

Performance planning and performance review

PERFORMANCE PLANNING

The purpose of performance planning is to make clear what is to be accomplished this year (or in a time-frame appropriate to the role – one year, two years, three to five years, ten years, and so on). This process:

- links the work of each individual to the corporate strategic plan;
- clarifies what the manager is expected to do and where the person fits into the manager's plan and
- provides clear articulation of what constitutes excellent performance:
  - outputs can be measured and
  - work performance of the employee can be judged by the manager.

It is a good idea to discuss the manager's plan with the entire team to get their input and ideas. After the manager's plan is set, then individual plans can be made. It is also a good idea to have another team discussion, so that each knows what the other is doing and why (see Box 13.1).

Performance planning is the beginning of the performance management cycle, which includes task assignment, task review, performance review and performance evaluation. Task assignment and task review are ongoing throughout the year. Performance planning, performance review and performance evaluation form an annual cycle with performance review required at mid-point of the cycle. (More frequent performance reviews may be productive if managers or their reports wish to do them, but only one is required.) Performance evaluation is the end of the cycle and is immediately followed by performance planning for the next cycle.

Performance planning is a two-way discussion where the manager lays out their perspective on what the situation for the division or unit is likely to be, given what is known about corporate, business unit and department purpose and goals. The entire team discusses the feasibility of the goals, recommending changes where necessary. To be effective, planning must be both two-way and iterative. As people at any level bring issues to the attention of higher level management, purpose and goals may need to be adjusted.

In addition to the essential tasks, which the person must complete in order to meet the manager's requirements, the plan should indicate the resources allocated and the freedom of action available to the person at this time (areas where the person is encouraged to exercise initiative to improve the quality of work). This is also the time to discuss context, purpose, quantity and quality of output, resources, and planned time to completion for the significant activity planned.

Box 13.1   What Is a Good Plan?

A good plan reflects a thoughtful commitment to what can be foreseen with the information available when the plan is made. It must allow for variation to cope with changing conditions and unpredicted opportunities. Good management means responding to opportunities as they arise. A plan must not become a straitjacket.

There should also be a statement of what actions are planned by both the manager and the person to improve their work performance. These may include any training or on-the-job experiences that are planned for the person as well as special projects assigned by either the manager or the manager-once-removed (M+1) to develop the person's career potential.

We believe any such training must be needs-based, costed and budgeted for. We have seen many organisations wherein promises of development are made and ignored year after year.

PERFORMANCE REVIEW

The purpose of a performance review is to improve future work performance by examining how well *both* the manager and person are doing in carrying out their respective elements of the plan and their specific tasks. Performance review is a formal two-way analytic learning process for both manager and team member in order to:

- review what they planned to do – their purpose and plans – and what they actually have accomplished to date;
- review their work performance as individuals and as a team and
- make specific plans to improve their work effectiveness for the rest of the year (or next year).

Performance review must be carried out at least once a year, typically about six months into the performance plan. For persons new to a role, a performance review should be given after six months, or even quarterly, in addition to the annual performance review. We also recommend that it be done again, at the end of the year to inform the next year's performance plan.

A manager has the authority to decide that a formal performance review is needed at any time during the year due to particular issues or perceived problems. This is particularly important if someone is performing poorly. Such a discussion may uncover the source of the difficulties and provide a solution that will allow the manager and person to devise clear steps which need to be taken to improve performance.

In addition, a person may ask for a performance review whenever they feel this is needed. The requested performance review needs to be done within the time specified within the system given overall work commitments.

Note: As with all task and performance reviews in a work environment, the focus must be on the work, not on the person.

The performance review process involves an analysis of the work and tasks of both manager and team member to assess what has been accomplished over the six months or year, to evaluate the quality of what has been accomplished and to discover better ways of working together to achieve better results.

This is, in effect, a summing up of the task reviews that have taken place on a random basis during the year and provides a longer overview of performance – a look at the forest as opposed to the trees. It is a joint effort designed to reduce defensiveness by involving both manager and team member in an appraisal of what was accomplished and an analysis of what happened. Typical questions would include:

- What have we done? Results.
- How have we done? Have we achieved our purpose?
- How did we do it?

- Where are we in relation to the plan?
- Can we devise better methods for finding out how we are doing? Any measures?
- Where things have gone well, why has this occurred? How can we replicate this in the future?
- Where things have gone badly, what went wrong?
- Was the purpose unclear?
- Did the environment change in ways which were unanticipated when the task was assigned?
- Was there clarity on what was to be done – the manager's standards of quantity, quality, timeliness and cost?
- Can we think of alternative ways of doing this? Might one of these be better?
- Has the manager provided clear task assignments, adequate task feedback, appropriate resources – material, staff hours, budget, information, enough time to get the work accomplished?
- Does either person need additional training to perform their current role more effectively?
- Is there evidence of a deeper problem such as MPA not matching the work of the role?

At the end of this review both manager and person should agree as to what work will be done to improve performance in the future. For example, they may agree on steps to be taken by each of them to clarify task assignments. Any other steps agreed to for either party should be noted. This should be written down and signed by the manager and the team member.

Performance evaluation

UNDERSTANDING PERFORMANCE

We have found that the term 'performance' is used to mean two different things when organisations come to evaluate individual or team performance and when they wish to 'pay-for performance'.

Output and performance

1. *Output or results*: Hard measures of same, which may include:
   - relationship between targeted output and achieved output;
   - outputs such as tonnes produced, number of cheques processed;
   - results such as market share, industry rank, operating costs.

2. *Work performance*: How well or poorly a person has achieved the results, or output taking into consideration the quality of leadership, team membership behaviour and all relevant circumstances.
   - How has the person exercised discretion?

Output or results

Output or results can, and must, be *measured*. Valid measures are usually different at each level of work. Each employee's measures of performance must be relevant to his or her role purpose and task assignments. Measures are essential:

- to compare achieved outputs with target objectives;
- to allow a manager to make adjustments in quantity, quality, resources or time in task assignment to ensure objectives are reached;
- to provide employees with feedback about how they are doing and
- to provide a clear statement of what is important, what should be monitored.

The caveat with all measures is that systems drive behaviour. It is important that the measures be valid and that the manager knows both what behaviour the measure drives and what systems surround the measure. The measure must be explicitly linked to the individual's work and the linkage to behaviour must be understood. Choosing a measure or measurement system that drives counter-productive behaviour is a serious error. For example, a manufacturing company provides certain financial or psychological rewards for safety performance, which leads to non- or under-reporting of safety incidents; a social work agency decides to assess performance based on numbers of cases closed and, as a result, the most difficult cases are set aside and fester while the easiest cases are dealt with and closed.

Work performance

Work performance is how well or poorly a person has worked to achieve the results detailed above, and cannot be measured. It must be *judged* by a manager.

The question the manager is paid to answer is, 'How effectively has the person worked to achieve the assigned output or result in the situation in which the work was performed?'

Work performance versus output measures and results

Work performance is a judgment made by the manager of the use of all the elements of capability – knowledge, social process skills, technical skills, application and mental processing ability – by a subordinate, based on the tasks that make up the role. The manager must take into account:

- the output or results achieved as measured by various indicators;
- the complexity of the situation in which the work was performed;
- the person's effectiveness (or lack thereof) in light of that situation;
- how the person balanced competing long-term and short-term demands and
- how well the person responded to changing conditions (see Box 13.2).

While there may be many objective measures of output and results, when it comes to the work performance of the individual employee, there are always mitigating circumstances that can demonstrate the objective measures are incomplete.

Box 13.2 Output

Output, correctly measured, is very important. It must be taken into account as an indicator of work performance, but it is not, by itself, the measure of an individual's work performance.

The work of a manager in team leadership – to create, maintain and improve a group of people so that they achieve objectives and continue to do so over time – cannot be measured. There may be measures to use as indicators of the achievement of these tasks – productivity, costs, number of college graduates hired, number of labour disputes, absenteeism, number of employees successfully promoted and so on – but none of these taken separately or together can determine whether or not the manager has succeeded in this essential task. The employee's manager must *judge* the employee's performance of this task.

In making that judgment, the manager must consider for example, what impact equipment or weather might have had on productivity. What impact might raw material, energy or legislation have had on cost? What is the quality of college graduates hired? Should there have been more labour disputes because significant change was needed? What was the effect of the flu epidemic on absenteeism? Were employees promoted as a means of getting rid of trouble makers?

Work performance evaluation is often the task most dreaded by managers. Many attempt to avoid problems by rewarding people with the average salary increase. This not only leads to salary distortion but undermines the concept of meritocracy by creating a seniority system wherein a person's pay increases with length of service and is not related to work performance.

Properly done, a face-to-face evaluation of work performance is a healthy element in an honest work relationship (see Box 13.3).

The purpose of performance evaluation is to assess the work performance of employees in order to recognise and reward differentially.

Box 13.3   The Desire (and Need) for a Good Productive Relationship

Perhaps the primary reason for performance evaluation being so disliked is that managers are dependent upon their team members to carry out tasks that will have direct impact on the quality of the manager's work performance. This dependency often brings about a strong personal relationship. Making judgments about another's performance may feel like making judgments about the person – something that is likely to damage, or at least endanger, the relationship, with the consequent ill effects upon the organisation's performance and the manager's work performance.

This major problem is caused in part by the confusion between judging the person and judging the quality of work performance. Many people feel uncomfortable when called upon to judge another when there are specific consequences. Our evidence, from many different organisations, shows that managers do make judgments about their subordinates' work performance, but seek to avoid telling individuals what that judgment is. It is a requirement for a well led team that there be a close mutual bond between the team leader and the team members.

All of us learn the relationship rules for families and friendships early in our lives, and practise them throughout life. The rules for work relationships are learned only when we join the workforce, and they are very different. We make judgments about the behaviour of our family and friends, and in some circumstances may tell them, but the outcome of that judgment is very different from judgments in the workplace. We believe that much of the difficulty managers have with an open face-to-face work performance discussion stems from the unconscious confusion of these relationships.

Informing subordinates about one's evaluation of their work performance, however, is necessary in the employment setting if the organisation is to get fair value for the salaries it pays, if individuals are to know where they stand in the eyes of their manager, and if the work performance is to improve over time.

If done properly it:

- confirms to an employee the worth of his or her work;
- makes visible what the organisation and the manager desires by what they recognise and reward;
- recognises differences in the work performance of different employees;
- allows the demonstration of managerial capability, fairness, honesty and courage and
- provides an evaluation methodology that can apply to a variety of salary administration systems, for example, straight salary adjustment, at risk salary adjustment, bonuses and profit-sharing (see Box 13.4).

PERFORMANCE EVALUATION PROCESS

Performance evaluation is an exercise in the managerial judgment of the quality of the person's work performance against the expectations of the manager. When doing this, the manager needs to think back about a subordinate's work performance over the entire period under review. It is important that the manager does not base their rating solely on recent, possibly dramatic, incidents, although if there are any, they must obviously be taken into consideration.

The manager must do this for all of his or her subordinates and rank their work performance, an exercise that helps to discipline the process. There are many methods of ranking work performance. We have seen many in action and a few work well. All come down to some form of rating scale. The primary problem with these scales is that there is often an effort (or requirement) to make the numbers fit a bell curve, where in fact a good manager will try to select and develop his or her people to move to the right side of the curve. Forced ranking may require managers to have a certain number of people at the bottom of the scale and a certain number at the top. This punishes the best managers and best organisational units, while rewarding the poorest. As one manager in an organisation that used such a system said, 'What really pisses me off is that HR will have 15 per cent of their people in the top rank.'

Finally, however apparently scientific or numerical these scales are, in the end it is a matter of judgment by the manager, and no evaluation system should force this judgment into a pre-set result. The manager should have the most complete knowledge of tasks assigned, task results and the context in which tasks were carried out. We do not suggest that the judgment of any or all managers is infallible; it is not. This crucial task of performance evaluation must be carried out in the larger context of the organisation, where other managers are rating their subordinates' performance as well.

The judgment made by managers about the work performance of subordinates must be subject to scrutiny and review by their manager-once-removed (M+1). We have found a system wherein the M+1 meets at one time with all his or her direct subordinate managers and leads a review of ratings by these subordinate managers to be highly effective. They can learn from each other and comment on their perceptions from interactions with some individuals. This is

---

Box 13.4 Pay and Meritocracy

The intent is to create conditions where all employees are in a position to recognise that this organisation is a meritocracy – a place where people are paid on the basis of work performance merit, not seniority, technical skill or membership in a favoured group.

Over time, the people with consistent high work performance should get the highest pay.

not a negotiation to change ratings. Following the meetings, managers review their ratings in light of what they have learned and then discuss the ratings individually with their manager (the M+1 of their subordinates).

This type of review becomes more difficult if managers are forced into pre-set ranking standards. One of the underappreciated disadvantages of forced ranking systems is that they attenuate the manager's judgment and by so doing make good and poor judgment more difficult to identify.

In an endeavour to ensure fairness across an organisation, it is essential that the judgments of managers be compared so that individual employees are not penalised because their manager is tough, rewarded because their manager is lax or treated unfairly because a manager is incompetent or dishonest. This requires a cross-comparison of the manager's ratings by the M+1 to ensure that all managers are using comparable scales. Just as the initial rating is an exercise in managerial judgment, so is the process of cross-comparison that is carried out by the M+1 to provide an assessment of consistency and fairness.

Scales

The rating scale used should be broad enough to reflect the fact that this is a system of differentiation. In order to be statistically useful (that is, where a statistical analysis of the data will produce a result with a 95% confidence limit) there need to be at least 21 different scores possible. This is not an obviously convenient scale on which to rate the work performance of a manager's direct reports, and not one we would recommend. We have had most experience with a 10-point or 100-point scale; both have their advantages and disadvantages. We have found many excellent managers who will add a decimal to get a 6.5 or 8.2 rating, thus creating an effective 100-point scale.

Using a 100-point scale invokes memories of all people, causing those who use them to think of school grading systems where 70 points is a C, 80 a B, and below 60 a fail. Thus the scale can be biased toward the top end. This can be avoided in part by linking the scale to a salary band, where a rating of 50 equals the mid-point of the salary band.

This linking to a salary band obviates the need for descriptors that are often pseudo-scientific measures, for example, 'meets 75 per cent of objectives'. We recommend strongly that the scale not include relative and confusing descriptors. For example we often see 'meeting' or 'exceeding expectations'. What if expectations are low because the person is a poor performer? Even simple descriptors such as 'below acceptable standard' or 'significantly above standard' may appear better, but they still become topics for argument. The judgment must be against a standard of performance required by the manager for the work of the role to be completed successfully.

Without descriptors, the rating scale is a device that forces managers to make and express for scrutiny the relative judgments they make about the work performance of their subordinates. Narrow scales and descriptors provide poor managers with an escape route and are extremely annoying to good managers who know it is essential to make judgments of subordinates' work performance and to justify those judgments to the subordinate and to their manager.

Using numbers against a scale does not make it scientific. There are many types of scale, including equal interval and ordinal, that do not assume mathematical properties: it is a scale of judgment not scientific fact. This does not imply that such a scale is arbitrary or chance. The judgment must be justified; it must be founded upon good task review and regular performance review. The ultimate test is whether the evaluation is a surprise; it should not be, whether pleasant or unpleasant.

Objectivity

The main objection we have heard expressed to this system of performance evaluation is that it is not fully objective. It relies on managerial judgment. While many would like greater objectivity, extensive experience and research have not been able to develop purely objective criteria that are demonstrably valid. Every supposedly objective measure of work performance fails the test of being independent of how the measure was achieved.

The so-called objective systems, when examined, are found to be reliant on managerial judgment. The difference is that this system makes the judgment explicit and visible so it can be observed and evaluated by others. The problem with most performance evaluation systems is that they subvert managerial judgment by trying to lock it into allegedly objective criteria. These criteria can include:

- Profit – What if the market moves?
- Share price – Where in the economic cycle?
- Absenteeism – What about a flu epidemic?
- Labour turnover – What about a manager deliberately changing the staff to improve a non-performing department?
- Productivity – What if it is new equipment, not the manager's effort, which is the primary cause of the change?
- Work performance of others – What if the output team is being taught a new process by this person, which in the short run is disrupting the team?

For every allegedly objective criterion there are circumstances that demonstrate the alleged objectivity is not validly linked to the work performance of an individual and in some instances may be contra indicators. All of the criteria listed above, and many others, are important and over time will be indicators of good or poor work performance. The good manager should consider all of these, which are believed to be relevant to the person and role being evaluated. As noted earlier, objective measures and results may be good *indicators* of work performance; it is just that they are *not the same* as the work performance.

When making an evaluation of work performance, the manager draws a complex balance across a number of factors, a balance which is, of necessity, subjective because objective measures do not measure people's work performance. There are subtleties that can be difficult to articulate, but their articulation can be illuminated by a single rating if the manager's judgment is not constrained by a poor system. The numerical rating forces the discussion and review of the judgment.

If we return to a key theme of this book, subjectivity is not the same as idiosyncrasy or bias. It is based on a person–person relationship, not a person–object relationship. The core of this relationship lies in behaviour which is assessed as falling consistently on the positive end of the scales of shared values especially trust, honesty, respect for dignity, fairness, courage and love.

Halo effect

Rating on the basis of overall judgment has been criticised as being vulnerable to the 'halo effect'. A person may be rated higher or lower based on previous assessments of work performance rather than on the work performance of the prior year. In other instances, recent notable incidents, either positive or negative, have allegedly biased the manager and prevented a balanced judgment of a person's performance over the entire 12-month period which is to be assessed.

Halo effects are a well-known psychological phenomenon to which all human beings are vulnerable. They depend upon myths about a particular individual or group. Part of the training in the use of this system must be to alert managers to this problem and suggest means for overcoming it. The safeguard built into the system is the requirement that the manager rates all of his or her subordinates' work performance at the same time, which allows for relative comparison. In addition, the manager's judgment will be reviewed by the M+1 and M+2, up to the CEO if need be, which reduces the opportunity for a halo effect in rating to escape through the system.

Teamwork

One of the major concerns of many team members and their managers is that a system of individual rating of this type may lead to cutthroat competitive behaviour which will destroy effective teamwork. Such cutthroat competition will, of course, become a certainty if managers reward such behaviour.

On the other hand, managers may prefer to reward cooperative behaviour that has a positive impact upon the entire output team, unit or division. In this case ratings would be heavily influenced positively by the behaviour desired.

Using an effective performance evaluation method, managers make visible the work behaviour they really desire. Therefore they must take care to recognise and reward those behaviours that are productive for the organisation in both the long- and short-term, whether this be cooperative or competitive behaviour or any other behaviour the manager believes is productive – including teamwork.

Managers who have other managers as subordinates need to be on the lookout for any such subordinate who demonstrates behaviour upward, which is positively placed on the values scales and behaviour downward which is negatively valued by those subject to it. Rewarding such people is destructive for the organisation and is, unfortunately, not uncommon.

PERFORMANCE EVALUATION AND STRUCTURE

Poor implementation of work performance evaluation can be predicted where an organisation has too many layers of management. Under these circumstances it is often the case that a manager may be working at the same level as his or her subordinates. In other words, the complexity of work that the manager is able to understand is essentially the same as that of the team members, even if the manager has greater experience or more time in the role.

In this situation, the manager is unable to judge work performance effectively because he or she does not have a larger perspective from which to comprehend the real impact of the context upon the work as it was performed. Therefore the manager cannot pass effective judgment on its quality and contribution to the larger organisation. This results in performance evaluation at best being a judgment of the person, because that is all the manager is able to do.

In our experience, it is more usual for the manager to evade the work of making such a judgment. Both the manager and the reports offer excuses such as, 'We work as a team around here. We don't like to make judgments about each other's work.' It follows that the systems of salary review are based on seniority or some other mechanism that allows managers to avoid making the judgment that they are not capable of making regarding subordinates' work performance. One manager in this situation said, when asked about performance evaluation, 'I'm not about to cut my own throat. These people know more than I do about their work. I want to keep them happy, so why should I criticise what they are doing?'. Of course evaluation is not simply criticism, it is recognition of the quality of the work performance both good and not good.

This manager's team members felt there was no one to evaluate their work, to let them know how their work fitted into the larger picture or to give them feedback on how they were doing. Although they liked their manager well enough as a person, one team member said, with regard to leadership 'He's useless. When I need to know something I go to [the manager one up].' These people all said they felt they were drifting without anyone to guide their work, and several said they were worried about how they were perceived in the organisation. It was evident that they were not clear about how they were assessed by the organisation, and they expressed concern about careers or job loss if there were reductions in the workforce.

In a properly structured organisation, providing the selection role process is reasonably sound, this situation is less likely to occur, since the organisation is designed to have managers and direct reports separated by one work level, providing enough distance such that managers are in a position to judge the work performance effectively because they will have an understanding of the context in which the subordinates' work was performed. In this situation, the performance evaluation is more often perceived accurately as a judgment of the person's work performance.

Summary of performance evaluation systems

1. Why are many performance evaluation systems not effective?
   - Poor design causes the forms to be too time-consuming to fill out.
   - Reliance on allegedly objective measures rather than the combination of objective measures and the subjective judgment that is required.
   - Subjectivity disguised with so-called objective standards. As one manager put it, 'The system asks the manager to create an objective-looking document to explain what is really a subjective judgment.'
   - The system asks the manager to perform two psychologically contradictory processes simultaneously: The manager is expected to help the person improve his or her work performance – to act as a trainer/coach, while at the same time evaluating a person's work performance and making decisions that will have impact on salary – to act as a judge. These activities need to be in separate systems, operating at different times.
   - The evaluation process may even require a recommendation regarding the future potential of the subordinate, all of which must be done at the same time using the same system. This creates confusion between work performance evaluation, the work of the manager; and potential review, the work of the M+1. This creates deep psychological and practical problems. It also encourages defensiveness on the part of both participants.
   - These factors cause managers to fudge their thinking and their statements (in effect to tell lies), which is known to both manager and team member. This dishonesty puts the relationship at much greater risk than any honest evaluation of work performance.
   - If the system will have an impact on an individual's future career, there is a tendency to soften a negative evaluation for fear of doing long-term damage to the person's career or to escalate a positive evaluation to ensure future potential for advancement.
2. Some possible inadequacies which the manager may need to confront:
   - Were task assignments really clear?
   - Did I give recognition, task feedback and conduct task reviews?

- Did I let the person know I was dissatisfied with certain aspects of their performance at the time it occurred?

   If the answer to these questions is 'no', evaluating work performance will most probably be perceived as unfair by the subordinate: 'If that was what you wanted, why didn't you say so?'

3. Some managers have told us of concerns that their ratings will be different from other managers.
   - Some managers have said they are concerned they are being too hard on their people as compared to other managers.
   - Some managers say they are concerned about being too easy on their people as compared to other managers.
   - The real issue is equity – similar treatment across units, divisions, and business units.

4. Fear of legal challenge: The words written by managers on performance evaluation forms may come back to haunt them. There are enough cases of legal challenges regarding discrimination and unlawful dismissal that managers often are concerned about the legal consequences of what they say or write.

   This concern has been argued as a case for bland, innocuous statements, which are less likely to be used in court, but which, in turn, have little or no positive impact on individual performance. They are seen for what they are, an exercise that demonstrates a lack of courage: everyone knows performance evaluation is an exercise we must go through, a lot of sound and fury signifying nothing.

   The threat of court action has been put forward as a reason for managers to give everyone a good or adequate rating and an average salary increase. Later when it can no longer be denied that someone needs to be dismissed from role for poor performance, these 'good' ratings over the years make legal challenge of the dismissal easy for the plaintiff and often costly to the organisation and the individual manager.

   The courts openly recognise the requirement for managers to make judgments. They are concerned that the judgments be legal, consistent, fair and supported by clearly articulated and understood systems that do not differentiate on non-work-related grounds.

PERFORMANCE EVALUATION IS A HUMAN PROCESS

The discussion of performance evaluation here has been designed to provide insights and advice for managers as they work to create a set of systems that have a positive impact upon the work performance of individuals and the organisations of which they are part.

Following these principles does not, however, make it easy. Nonetheless, managers have the task of making hard decisions, including decisions regarding the relative input and worth of their employees to the organisation.

Managers need to do this in a way which is clear, provides for review to help ensure equity and which ask managers to do what they are employed to do: exercise their human judgment in this most human of processes.

Salary administration

One of the reasons that performance evaluation creates so much anxiety is that it is linked to pay. Task review and performance review leaves open the possibility for improvement prior to a judgment that affects what a person can earn.

There are almost as many salary administration systems as organisations. Rather than list them in this section, we outline some critical issues that are core to an effective system.

Initially we must distinguish between two fundamental components. First, fair pay for the work being done. Each role should have a salary that offers a fair monetary reward for the work. Jaques (Jaques, 1963) has been very specific about this in terms of amounts. We agree with Jaques' general statement that people have a sense of what is fair pay once they are clear about the work to be done (role description). Second, this sense is directly related to the work to be done in terms of level of work.

We have found exceptions to this; that is, in certain roles pay appears almost entirely linked, and fluctuates with, pure market pressures. These roles appear most obviously in professional sports, entertainment and trading in financial markets. These roles seem to be almost excessively based on a specialist technical skill that is (or is not) in particular demand. Employment of people in these roles is often represented by a very particular individual contract. Specific aspects are often involved in negotiating these contracts. People in these roles also rarely have career aspirations to move to other and different roles until that technical skill is no longer either valued or present (for example, the inevitable loss of skill over time for professional athletes).

We are referring primarily to a much larger category of employees who enter into a relationship with much broader opportunities and are not dependent upon a highly specialised technical ability. Most people in employment fall into this category and want a fair salary in return for their work. Most people can also differentiate between their own capabilities and the work required in a role. Many of us have been in roles, by choice or otherwise, which have not tested our capabilities. While we might feel we could earn more, we do realise that the pay fits the work required.

While, in general, salaries are affected by markets, it is important to take into account the related factors of fairness and level of work.

PAY FOR PERFORMANCE

The basic salary should reflect fair pay. However, there is also a need for a component that reflects the nature of individual contributions. The relative amount of performance pay in terms of percentage of salary may vary but we argue that:

- *It should be clearly understood.* The rules and triggers in some systems are almost impossible to understand.
- *It should be clearly linked to personal performance and contributions.* Whilst this is still a matter of judgment the evaluation should be fairly based on what a person has done. Deming has been very clear about poor systems that offer reward but where the control of the reward is out of the person's control or even the organisation's control. For example, neither a person nor an organisation can control international prices of commodities. An operator cannot operate if machinery and equipment is unavailable. Some so-called performance components are almost impossible to avoid. We have seen systems where simply turning up is almost enough to trigger the full performance component.
- *Do not confuse this system with bonus or profit share systems.* Many organisations pay a bonus for reaching targets that, as mentioned above, may be the result of many people and departments achieving objectives. Whilst these systems have the advantage of appearing to share wealth, they can also cause confusion or a sense of unfairness when 'I have done my best but because of X I have lost my bonus'.

Finally, with all payment systems the questions in the systems design chapter remain highly relevant. It is particularly relevant to ask:

- What is the purpose?
- Is it really a system of differentiation?
- What behaviour do you expect this to drive? Why?
- Does the person understand it?

We have seen many other components of salary given in other forms: cars, allowances, stock options and so on. We are very wary of such systems as they can create negative mythologies.

Our approach, consistent within this book, is to keep systems clear and simple with an unambiguous purpose. One operator at a plant in Australia commented 'I like working here, I have exactly the same contract as the General Manager except for the salary'; he paused and then said 'and I wouldn't want his job for love nor money'.

Identifying and developing potential

CAREER ASSESSMENT

While some people are content to stay in one role for almost all their employment career, most people do like change and do want a career. Even staying with 'one role' it is inevitable that that role will change and the person will need to learn new skills and knowledge.

Identifying potential and providing opportunities for people to develop and use their capability is essential. It is very important to distinguish between the work of the immediate manager and the manager's manager in this process (see Box 13.5).

In order to be effective, the M+1 should have a clear understanding of the various roles, career patterns and career opportunities in the organisation. It is helpful to know something about future corporate or departmental directions in order to guide people into new roles that are likely to be needed by the organisation. We use the term *mentoring* to describe the work of M+1 in preparing people for future roles. *Coaching* is the term to describe helping someone improve in his or her current role.

The manager once removed

The manager once removed:

1. Identifies people who are ready for promotion to the level of their immediate team and takes steps to see they are offered such a promotion either within their team or elsewhere. This ensures the business gets the best use of its most talented people by placing them in a role that matches their capabilities.
2. Makes a judgment of the likely career paths based on their abilities and interests.
3. Discusses career options on a regular but varying basis depending upon the stage of a person's career. For bright young people who are judged to have high-level potential and who, therefore, should move rapidly through the organisation, an annual or biennial review might be appropriate. A longer review period of three or even five years is appropriate for people who are comfortable at their current level. Toward the end of a person's career, one

---

Box 13.5   Management's Role in Developing Potential

In essence it is the *work of the immediate manager* to provide for the development of people who report to them directly in their current roles. That is, the manager should be working to develop their knowledge, technical and social process skills and encourage them to be more effective in doing their current work. It is the work of the M+1 to assess who, if anyone, has the potential to work at a higher level and who needs to change role in order to improve their contribution at the same level.

   This is not to say this is exclusively the domain of the managers and M+1s. The immediate manager may well identify people whom they think have potential and recommend them. Peers, colleagues and others may have an influence. The individual concerned has critical work to do. The person's own ambition, view of their own capability and valuing of the work is critical in this process. Understanding the difference between current performance and potential and who to discuss this with allows this process to succeed or fail.

---

assessment of potential may be enough for the person who will not advance further in the organisation and knows it.

Conducting assessments of potential too frequently is unnecessary and may cause difficulty especially if they imply promises of promotion.

Keep in mind that each person is responsible for his or her own career. The M+1 is in a position to advise people regarding many important aspects of their careers:

- the kind of organisation this is – its culture, what is valued in its employees;
- career patterns, how people advance in this organisation;
- M+1's assessment of the person's career potential;
- what types of roles and tasks the individual might undertake to gain needed knowledge or skills;
- education and training programmes the person might find useful;
- opportunities for special assignments;
- estimated timing of various elements of the person's career progression.

With the views of the M+1, the individual can put together a career development plan indicating interests and setting some target timetables to move into particular roles. Discussions with the M+1should also make clear if certain positions are essential if a person is to advance to higher levels of work. For example, in the US Army, few become a major general who have not had experience as a company commander and a battalion commander.

The M+1 is in no position to promise that the person will attain a particular role or a particular level of work in the future. This will depend upon the person's performance, when openings at a particular level or in a particular field come open, and who is available to fill those roles. The best person available at the time a role is open should get that position.

Career development as part of the M+1's work
In many organisations the manager of an individual is assumed to be accountable both for the person's work performance and for their career advancement. There are major problems with this assumption in regard to career advancement.

1. The manager is in the wrong position to make a decision about promotion of a direct report. They have neither the authority nor the perspective to make a decision regarding promotion.

Promotion moves the team member to the level of the manager. This requires a decision by the manager's manager (the M+1) to determine if the person is ready to fill a role at this level.

Only the M+1 is in a position to know and encompass the work of the manager and the manager's peers. Thus it is only the M+1 who can make an effective judgment if an individual is ready to work at a level immediately reporting to M+1. This does not mean that the manager cannot, or should not, make recommendations with regard to promotion. It is an important managerial task to bring capable people to the attention of their M+1, but the decision regarding promotion is made by M+1.

2. The M+1 will also have a better perspective on organisational needs and opportunities across the organisation, far beyond that available to the immediate manager.

3. Without an organised process of potential assessment, an organisation will draw from a small pool of talent (those who are noticed or are good at self-promotion). The people promoted may not be the best people, and the organisation accepts what happens rather than working to get the best use of talent to cope with the competitive challenges it will face over the years. Having able people to fill key roles is far too important to be left to chance and individual initiative.

Despite appearances to the contrary, business organisations do try to promote the best people, as the managers making the decision define 'best'. Yet without an ordered and known system based upon a correct understanding of managerial and M+1 authorities in the organisation, the process of promotion will be flawed to a greater or lesser extent.

4. Any given manager may have a team member who is more capable than them, one who carries much of the load for their manager. (In some cases incompetent managers may hide their shortcomings for a considerable period of time by having others do their work.)

Even with a competent manager, it is always tempting to keep an able team member beyond the time they should be promoted. Such talented people feel buried beneath a manager who has a vested interest in keeping them down, and they rightly feel resentment over this fact. Such people may leave the organisation, or if they stay, they may become resentful and work less effectively than they might if they had the opportunity to be noticed and promoted at the right time.

Finding and fostering the organisation's human talent

It is the work of the M+1 to identify the most able employees early in their careers and take steps to foster their development.

M+1s need to be held accountable for assessing the potential of *all* their people one level removed. This has the effect of opening up the talent pool by including people who usually go unnoticed in more informal systems.

Special training and job opportunities can be assigned to people who are judged to be most able – testing the M+1's judgment. This allows possible errors of judgment on the part of the M+1 to be corrected early in a person's career to avoid either too rapid or too slow advancement. It also increases the likelihood that the most able people will have challenges commensurate with capability talents, making them more productive for the organisation over their entire careers. The best people are more likely to stay in the organisation rather than seeking opportunities elsewhere. In this way the work of the M+1 helps to reduce (and eventually eliminate) the power games of informal mentoring systems.

The authorities of the M+1 to assess potential as well as the manager's authority to veto selection provide a system to inhibit such power games. Each is held accountable for exercising their authorities.

By giving all employees assessments as appropriate, the maximum benefit may be derived from the talent pool of the organisation. In doing this the M+1 can learn about the quality of managerial work exercised by their immediate reports. The insights gained from the M+1 relationships makes it possible to give their immediate reports better feedback and coaching to improve their managerial practices.

The M+1 authority leads to communications with people one level removed and these in turn may make it easier for these people to initiate discussions on other topics, including potential problems and opportunities which might otherwise remain hidden from higher level view (see Box 13.6).

In summary the M+1 is the appropriate person to assess potential, albeit with input and information from a variety of sources. The person being assessed will usually have a realistic view of their own ability if they really understand and have confirmed the nature of the work required. Once the assessment is made, career development can occur: finding opportunities inside and outside the workplace for the person to fulfil their potential.

Succession planning

The work on assessment and development with the associated information then should become part of succession planning. Succession planning is the proper ordering of all the information in career assessment and development to create an overall view of the organisation. The identification and development of a talent pool is necessary if the organisation is to survive

---

Box 13.6   How to Judge Potential

How does the M+1 judge whether a person is ready now or in the near future for promotion? This is done by first of all being clear about the work of the role and the capability required to be successful. As has been discussed in the chapters on capability, levels of work and selection to role, certain elements of a role are more amenable to training and improvement than others. One of the most critical issues is mental processing ability (MPA). This is a necessary but not sufficient condition. The M+1 must judge whether the person has the intellectual ability to handle work of the appropriate complexity. Sometimes this is obvious, at other times less so. There are always opportunities to test this by assigning tasks which require higher complexity processing to solve. Special assignments, projects and tasks can be given to see if a person can really work at a higher level. Then other elements of capability can be assessed to complement the MPA.

Some organisations have found that using an approach called career path appreciation (CPA) (Stamp, 1986) has been helpful in identifying potential. This approach can be of value because it is related to levels of work complexity. Our concern is simply that this should *not* be used as a substitute for the M+1's judgment. As with other psychometric and related instruments, this can assume the status of expert fact rather than opinion and allow the leadership to avoid accountability. Properly used, CPA can be a helpful second opinion. Finally the M+1 should not be trying to predict a person's entire career. The M+1 should be looking forward only one, two or at most three years. This avoids the negative mythologies associated with labelling and categorising people that can blight not only the person but the organisation.

and grow. If the systems of performance management, career assessment and development are in place these can form the basis of the succession planning system.

This system requires the M+2, with M+1s and input from HR specialists to review the organisational structure. The present structure and the proposed structure (based on the strategic plan) must be articulated. For every current and proposed role three names need to be identified as possible successors (unless the role is to go).

The identification should be made according to three categories:

1. *Ready now*: This is someone who could take the role today and perform well immediately.
2. *Ready within three months*: This is someone who could, within a short time, be ready for the role and only needs some knowledge or the addition of some technical skills that can be quickly learned.
3. *Ready within one year*: This is someone who may need some significant development in either knowledge, technical skills or social process skills. They may need to experience a leadership role or sales or financial/business work.

Names can then be discussed and the M+2 can decide on the final list and the category each is in. One rule is that no name can appear more than twice on the shadow chart. We now have a measure of how well prepared the organisation is for succession. Clearly fewer names or significant gaps give cause for concern. The context must be considered, however, and having three names in category 1 for every role might indicate an organisation where people are ready to leave. As one leader (M+2) explained to us, 'We only have one role at level 5. We recruit highly capable people. The trouble is the best leave if they see their chances diminish.'

Discipline and appeal

Throughout this book we have emphasised the importance of human judgment and human relationships. We are all subjects, and hence subjective. We have our own lenses through which we view the world and make those judgments. We do not want to be 'objects'. We are not simply at the mercy of scientific materialistic laws. The fact that judgment is subjective does not make it necessarily biased and idiosyncratic.

Human judgment can and should be informed by data and information. We can and must use evidence. Courts are a good example of the need for evidence, not merely speculation, but there is still a judge and a jury. Human judgment is informed but not replaced by facts and information.

At the heart of leadership is an attachment between people. People are not inspired solely by a sheet of objective facts or cash reward.

However, it is clear that judgment can be flawed, can be prejudiced, can be plain wrong. If someone has a manager and, in our model, accepts that the manager has the authority to judge performance, what can be done if the person believes the judgment to be wrong?

In this section we will look at different situations and how they can be addressed before recourse to third parties or the law. We will examine the importance of disciplinary processes.

We have noted that many managers find performance feedback, review and especially evaluation difficult. Very few people enjoy giving bad news whether that is concerned with performance or potential. Most people have been in this situation either as giver or receiver.

It is often characterised by a knotted stomach. Nonetheless, avoiding the issue of poor performance and disciplinary consequences is perhaps the most costly activity in a business. Avoiding difficult issues causes good workers to be demoralised. It gives rise to negative mythologies and a resort to power.

In this area, perhaps more than any other, the most important principle is that the systems and processes must be clear and accessible. Leaders, especially managers, must ask 'Do people know about and understand the limits?'. These limits include:

- policies
- systems
- code of conduct
- operating procedures
- safety regulations
- limits of a task
- limits of authority.

How easy is it to find out about the limits? If people are not aware of the limits, how can they be disciplined fairly for breaking them?

Do people know and understand the consequences? Again we would argue that all disciplinary systems should be clearly communicated and widely understood.

Do people know and understand disciplinary procedures? These procedures should include:

- verbal and written warnings
- authorised actions, for example suspension, stand down, dismissal
- legal rights.

We must start from the proposition that disciplinary systems should be known and/or easily knowable. These topics should be part of induction process and training. If that is the case, then we must start from a clear statement of the problem.

We offer two categories which are fundamentally psychologically different:

1. breaking limits
2. poor performance.

BREAKING LIMITS

This is the classic case study example. Here the issue is whether a rule has been broken, for example, drinking at work, fighting, polluting the environment, sleeping on the job, stealing, sexual harassment, racial abuse, and so on. In other words. 'box D' behaviour; that is, unauthorised and counter-productive. Here the investigation is more like a legal process: warning/arrest –> investigation –> judgment –> consequences. The focus is first upon gathering evidence to determine whether or not the limit was broken; second, whether the person should reasonably have known of the limit (for example, wearing a hard hat in that area of a plant) and third, whether the person acted with intent.

There must, of course, be due process, which again must be open to scrutiny. However, the consequences are severe if the rule breaking is proven and, unless there are mitigating circumstances, there is likely to be a dismissal. This whole process is similar to a legal process; it is subject to legal review and less common. Leaders and managers deal more usually with the second category: poor performance.

POOR PERFORMANCE

Judgments about performance are continuous; from completion of a small task ('Thanks, that's a great cup of coffee') to a major long-term effort ('Thanks for the completion of the harbour tunnel'). We are judging each others' performance all the time whether we are aware of it or not. If you ask a group of employees, in any organisation, to describe their leaders/peers, and so on, they will be able to do so instantly and those descriptions will always contain opinions and judgments about work performance. That is people do not simply say 'He is five foot seven, blue eyes and dark hair'. They will include statements like 'He is hard but fair', 'She never tells us what is really going on' or 'I don't trust him'. However, that is not to say those opinions will necessarily be accurate or fair.

It is the work of the manager to gather and synthesise all work performance behaviour into a judgment. It is rarely about breaking limits and more usually about how effectively the person has worked within these limits.

So what if the person being judged thinks either (a) the overall or (b) a particular judgment is unfair? These are the really difficult issues – the limit breaking ones are often more public and dramatic. In any organisation it is the daily operation that demonstrates its character; whether the underlying, ordinary operation functions well. If it does, there are not likely to be many limit-breaking cases. A classic example is that if people's daily behaviour is safe, there are obviously fewer or no accidents.

If managerial judgment is at the heart of the managerial hierarchy, then this is one of the most critical issues to address. All the advantages of a meritocratic, managerial authority structure are lost if the judgments made by the managers are unsound. What can we build in to try to ensure they are sound?

Below we outline the system which should operate on a daily basis and secondly the control to that system if there are still problems.

1. The work of a manager and leader involves the management of social process. So it is part of the role to establish a relationship where decisions can be discussed without appearing to be a direct challenge to authority. Therefore, in the first instance the two people involved should try resolve the issue. This may mean further explanation or a modification of the judgment or both.
2. If, however, it is not resolved the next step is to raise the matter with the M+1. Remember it is part of the M+1's work to establish a relationship with RoRs (reports one removed) such that these issues can be discussed without a formal complaint. It is also part of the M+1's work to review decisions of direct reports. Again this may result in a resolution, or it may not.

Thus the first option is to use the normal line of authority. While this should not be happening all the time, it should not produce undue concern unless the frequency increases. It can be minimised by good M+1 coaching of direct reports.

FAIR TREATMENT SYSTEMS (FTSs)

The person involved in procedures outlined above may not want or feel able to raise the matter with the manager or even M+1. The matter may be too personal, serious or demonstrate a fundamental breakdown in trust. This is such a critical area that we recommend all organisations have an internal fair treatment system (FTS). We have helped design many such systems and depending on the size and nature of the organisation they may vary in detail. However all FTSs have core principles in common. There is an example of an FTS designed at Hamersley Iron in Western Australia included here.

The system is enabled by the presence of advisers, called fair treatment advisers (FTAs). These are people who are chosen for their maturity (not necessarily age related), social process skills and reputation for keeping matters confidential. They are trained in the system details and their purpose is to advise on the process. Does the person (complainant) know how the system works? Is it serious? Is it another matter? They do not act as advocates.

FTSs are not a substitute for legal complaints. The system should not attempt to replace legal complaints. The FTS is designed to investigate unfair treatment, not illegal treatment. Thus the FTA may advise only on the existence of a case of sexual harassment, assault, fraud, negligence, and so on. This immediately suggests a limit may have been broken and therefore puts it in the first category (see above). If it is not (at least initially) a legal issue then the person can initiate the FTS process with the advice but not advocacy of the FTA.

The system requires the appointment of a fair treatment investigator (FTI) to carry out an inquiry. The FTI must be at least the peer, or, more usually, a level above the person against whom the complaint is directed. Thus, if I am complaining about my manager, then a person of at least his or her equivalent will investigate. We recommend one level above, but it depends upon the size of organisation. It must be remembered that this system now operates like an audit: it is a corporate policy and system owned and authorised by the board and CEO. The FTI has the delegated authority of the CEO. The FTI, who must be trained and also advised by the FTA, then has full authority to question, look at papers, e-mails, and so on, in order to investigate the complaint and make a recommendation.

The recommendation is then made to the manager of the person who has been accused of unfairness. In larger organisations it is the M+1 of the person unless these people have been a subject of the investigation (and perhaps involved in the complaint). The line manager then decides whether to implement the recommendation. Whatever the decision is it must be communicated to all involved including the FTA.

Appeal

If the complainant is not satisfied, they can then appeal to the CEO (if the complaint is not already at that level). The CEO then reconsiders the evidence, the recommendation and the decision and makes a final judgment.

We have also considered the involvement, during the FTI stage, of an outside party. While not ruling this out absolutely we recommend against this unless such a person is very knowledgeable about the organisation and is well respected in it for example, a recently retired executive. The FTS is an internal process and should be appreciated for this.

Using the FTS does not prejudice the person from using other avenues, such as an agreed process involving a union or industrial tribunal. However, if the complainant uses this first then they forfeit their right to use the FTS for the same complaint at a later date or if the outcome is unfavourable.

It should be emphasised that the FTS is not an HR system. Although FTAs may be from the HR stream, it is an executive system.

Audit and records

The results of the FTS case histories should be audited by the HR department as custodians of the system. The audit does not comment on the nature of the decisions but investigates:

- how many complaints;
- the role of the FTA;
- the acceptability of the decision from the complainant's perspective and
- most importantly, the complainant's view of the process.

The audit should produce recommendations as to the effectiveness of the system, if and how it should be modified and if training and communication are sufficient.

Any incidents of people either being intimidated into not using the FTS or punished after having used it need to be reported and, if proven, result in dismissal. This again is a question of breaking limits.

SUMMARY OF FAIR TREATMENT SYSTEMS

The FTS is not an alternative to other means of complaint. It is available as a control on managerial judgment, particularly with regard to task assignment and performance review. It is there to demonstrate that a person does not have to rely on third parties to achieve a fair treatment. Some may say it will only support 'the bosses'. If that is the perception, it already demonstrates low trust and poor leadership. Healthy relationships do still have problems, whether at work, in families or outside relationships. We regard it as important to first try and resolve these matters in house. The FTS is a system which is necessary if that is to be possible. For us it is one of the critical systems for a high-trust organisation.

Summary

All of these systems work together. They should be integrated and owned in the line not by HR. Failure to pay attention to careers and succession means the best people will leave and capability is wasted. While the processes need to be well designed, they still require and rest upon managerial judgment. There are no quick and easy short cuts. Although advice from a range of sources can be helpful, it can also be confusing unless authority is clear and the concepts compatible.

Most importantly, the one trap it is important to avoid is that of promising a future that cannot be delivered. It is easy at the time to either explicitly or implicitly give a person an impression that either their performance or their prospects are much brighter than they are in reality. This is often unintended, but dishonesty will cause disillusionment if not anger and plays back into power games.

Our experience is that people are quite realistic about themselves when given accurate information and feedback. They also do not need to have their entire careers mapped out, false ceilings or limitless sky.

Not everyone performs well; some break limits and this must be dealt with. As with all systems controls and audits are essential. The fair treatment system is itself a control on managerial judgment. Without it mythologies will grow that poor judgment rather than poor performance is the real problem and trust will diminish or evaporate.

14 *Teams and Teamwork*

In Part 3 we have looked at how a leader creates a culture and uses the tools of behaviour, systems and symbols to do so. We have emphasised the need for clarity in working relationships, especially with regard to authority and tasks. Here we look in more depth at another popular topic, teamwork. 'Teamwork' is another term used widely but often vaguely. It is simply not sufficient for leaders to exhort people to remember they are a team or just work as a team unless there is a deeper and shared understanding as to what this means: What am I expected to do?

In order to answer this question we need to return to the proposition that people are essentially social; that we form social groups in order to achieve together what we cannot achieve as individuals. There is, and always will be, a tension between what is advantageous for a particular individual and what is advantageous for the group. The key to a good organisation is managing the social process so that individuals are encouraged and allowed to use their capability to achieve the overall purpose of the group. The individual gains satisfaction and reward whilst achieving the common goal.

There has been, and continues to be, great emphasis placed on teams and teamwork in writing about organisations. It is clearly recognised that effective teams can be highly productive and satisfying to the members. The obvious example of the sports team demonstrates the need to blend individual talents into a complementary process.

The false duality

However, underlying this discussion is an implication that there is some sort of basic choice between two types of organisation. One is the traditional hierarchy. As we saw in previous chapters, hierarchy, authority and even bureaucracy have acquired negative connotations. They conjure up an image of command and control, top-down instruction, rigid structure and highly directive manager–subordinate relationships.

On the other hand we are invited to believe in the 'organic', 'empowered', non-hierarchical, creative organisation. People apparently work willingly and unencumbered; teams form and reform, often without leaders. This was the vision (or mirage) of the young dot com companies. In truth, neither of these options is viable. It is misleading to present them as a choice. Social organisations need both structure and authority to be effective. At the same time people need to work together in teams if organisational goals are to be achieved. So let us put aside this false duality and look at effective teamwork, what works and what doesn't.

We all need to balance our need for individual identity with the need to belong to a social group or team. It is both productive and comforting to belong. Just as with systems of differentiation and equalisation, an over-emphasis on one or the other can be detrimental. For example, *equalisation* does give a sense of belonging but if over-emphasised can blur identity into a homogenous collective. An example would be where all people in a particular role are paid the same no matter what their efforts. *Differentiation* gives a sense of individual identity reinforcing the self, but on its own can lead to feelings of isolation or extreme competitiveness at the expense of team members. An example would be basing all pay on assumed individual output with bonuses paid with no regard to others' input.

For us teamwork is not just about the collective. We reject the slogan 'There is no *i* in team'. Teamwork is about people collaborating for mutual benefit, clear about their mutual authority, their work and the relationship with the leader. The word 'team' is used very generally, as are many terms in management. We have chosen a more specific meaning:

Box 14.1   Definition of Team

Team: A team is a group of people, including a leader, with a common purpose who must interact with each other in order to complete their tasks.

There is nothing greatly contentious in this definition. However, the phrase 'who must interact' is crucial. It demonstrates the mutual interdependency of the team members. This distinguishes the work of a team from a *network* where some members of a network have no relationship with some others, even if they all have a common purpose. It also distinguishes the team from a group of people, say, passengers on a plane; all have a common purpose but do not need to interact to achieve it. We emphasise the need to interact. This is the difference between, for example, the members of a shift or project team from all the employees of an organisation as a whole.

This does not mean, however, that there is a blurring of accountability. The leader of the team holds team members accountable for their work as individuals – including that part of their work which requires establishing constructive and co-operative work relationships with other team members. If an organisation is serious about good teamwork this co-operation must be a part of the work of the role and reflected in review, reward and recognition systems. The leader is accountable for setting the context for such co-operation by creating the appropriate social processes. We outline such a process in this chapter.

In an employment organisation, people are employed as individuals and paid as individuals. A significant part of this employment role is to work constructively with others and the extent to which this is achieved should be recognised. Good teamwork is more likely where there is little role demarcation, that is, where team members are not artificially prohibited from helping each other provided each is properly trained and can work safely. This lack of demarcation does *not* mean everyone is the same or that there is no leadership.

If people are employed as individuals, then they need to be accountable to someone. It only makes sense if they are accountable to the person who assigns and reviews their tasks: the team leader.

'Team' tasks, goals and rewards

There is also some confusion in the use of language. Can a team have a task? Should a team be rewarded? Can a team be set goals?

In employment roles a *team* cannot be given a task. A task is given to an individual. That individual is usually in a team leadership role. If this is the case they may then say to the team members 'we' have to 'change all the beds on the ward by the end of this shift'; 'complete all your team's performance reviews by June 30th'; 'lay all the tables in the restaurant properly before opening time at 6.00pm'; 'produce X tonnes this shift' and so on. This is an appropriate way for the leader to define the *purpose* but he or she does not simply walk away at this point and say 'right, get on with it'. Even sports coaches who end their pre-match exhortations by extolling the whole team to 'go out there and win' are only able to summarise in this way if each person knows their role and the team tactics.

The fact that there are team leaders does not mean that the organisation has to be authoritarian. An observer may at times find it difficult to spot the leader once an activity is underway, especially if everything is going well. The 'empowerment' of team members is simply another way of expressing that the team leader is using all the capabilities of the team members. This can be more precisely described as encouraging the use of appropriate discretion, encouraging suggestions for improvement and only intervening to add value. If the organisation is working properly, people will be in roles that not only encourage but require good teamwork, sharing ideas and good or bad practice.

'Teams' are not an alternative to an 'accountability hierarchy'; they are *part* of an accountability hierarchy. An organisation which reduces discretion, inhibits creativity and does not encourage people to work together is not operating as a typical, authoritarian hierarchy. It is simply an organisation working badly.

There is quite some debate about team rewards. First, it is important to distinguish these from business bonuses, profit-sharing or gain-sharing. These are systems that apply to everyone and are in effect a regular component of income. However, should the team (a shift or project team for example) be rewarded collectively for their work? There is nothing in our principles that prevents a leader from recognising the efforts of all team members equally, for example, giving everyone a dinner, a day off or public statement of achievement and effort. This is not to be confused, however, with salary. The credibility of the leader rests upon their ability to recognise relative contributions. For example, the team may have achieved the output *despite* the poor contribution of one of two members. Giving *only* equal recognition will merely say that the leader is unaware of relative contributions. It is important that individual feedback is always given. It may be more appropriately done at the time of a performance review and later recognised in salary differentiation.

It is *not* divisive to recognise individual performance unless it does not reflect actual contribution. As such, poor leadership is extremely divisive especially if the leader insists on treating everyone the same whatever the circumstances or, attempts to abdicate, from the leadership role.

It is quite consistent with our principles, especially with regard to improved quality and measurement, to have run charts and output figures that reflect the combined output of team members. However, it must be clear what these are measuring. This is not *necessarily* a measure of team performance. They could refer to one of several processes, including the social processes of the team. As such, figures and charts may serve to enhance that process but only if there is complementary evidence that the leader knows in more detail what or who contributed to the result.

Team decisions

A rich area of confusion concerns the approach to decision making reflected in phrases like the 'team decided', or 'the team was against it'. These are examples of poor or muddled leadership. Individuals are paid to make decisions: it is at the core of our understanding of work. The workplace is not a democracy, unless the leader wants to share their pay amongst team members. Of course, good leaders are concerned and listen to ideas and suggestions. A good leader will know whether members are comfortable with or even understand a proposed course of action and will not ride roughshod over team members. If the leader does this, then an alternative leader will emerge over time or members will simply find ways to subvert the original leader. Good leadership and teamwork is not, however, based on a formal system of consensus or majority voting. A leadership role is far more than simply reflecting or representing members' views. Members must feel free to voice concerns without feeling that this is a 'vote' against a course of action. It is important to know what authority is operating, and not to muddle democracy, consensus or seniority with effective team leadership and teamwork.

Team processes

So far we have discussed team leadership and team membership in general terms. The team leader must also create the appropriate social processes. Team members need to establish constructive and co-operative work relationships with other team members. In our work with a diverse range of organisations around the world, we have developed some specific and practical steps to guide how this can be done. In particular we have developed a training course, 'Working Together', which helps people learn how to improve their understanding and practice of effective team processes. This experiential course uses exercises which are videotaped to help people see their own strengths and weaknesses and to observe and learn what behaviour makes a good team and what behaviour detracts from this. In 1992 Macdonald articulated this into a complementary process outlining the steps and traps that team leaders and members can use (and avoid) to improve their contribution and effectiveness. The following is an account of this process, which has been used and referenced by many organisations worldwide. It had its origins in work with CRA (the corporation that owned all the companies like Comalco where the modelling was largely developed) and is used in slightly different forms by organisations not only in the private sector but also in the public sector, including schools, indigenous organisations and even religious organisations.

LEADING A TEAM

There is a wealth of material on leadership and teamwork; theories and examples emphasise a range of qualities. There are debates about 'born leaders' versus learning to lead. While there are many concepts, we have found it useful simply to describe what good leaders do, and consequently what is expected of someone in a leadership role. In our experience it is at best pointless, and at worst dangerous to ask people to change their personalities, but you can ask someone to explain tasks clearly. The latter can be observed, recognised and improved.

We have observed good leaders in practice in a range of organisations over many years and analysed good practice in the experiential courses ('Working Together'). Leaders in employment roles do work in the context of an organisation; if the structure, role, authorities and accountability are unclear, good leadership is virtually impossible. Power replaces authority. Leaders' apparent effectiveness will be more determined by strength of personality, physical strength and the ability to influence personally or even coerce. This context can be improved in terms of structure, systems, capability, authority and clear tasks, using the models in this book.

The following set of steps and frequently observed traps are set out in order but are not a rigid, linear process. It may be necessary to return to earlier steps to review and reassess a plan or a particular step.

TEAM LEADER AND TEAM MEMBER STEPS

Explain the context and purpose

In setting the context the leader needs to explain the situation: an order may be overdue, production may be behind. There may be environmental issues, there may be a concern with the market or even the weather. Safety may be a particular concern.

It is surprising how many team members are unsure why they have been brought into a team and what they are meant to achieve. It is not sufficient for the leader to assume they know. The leader must spell out a clear and overall purpose in a single statement. If the leader can't do this, they probably don't understand that purpose clearly themselves.

A significant part of the context will be the constraints within which the team is working. These are known limits and may include safety, reputation, budget, time limits, fixed resources or the law. It is important at this stage to understand and communicate clearly what these explicit boundaries are.

Identify the critical issues/problems

It is important to clearly point out, prior to action, what the major problems might be. This is not a case of listing everything that might go wrong (an infinite task) but selecting, in your judgment, what the key threats are and what you will do if they do arise. As such this is similar to a risk analysis, often done for safety reasons, but we apply it generally.

A critical issue is something that threatens the purpose. People have described them as 'show stoppers'. We describe them as 'what-ifs' or 'how-tos'. For example, what if a key team member phones in sick? How do we clean the train in the short time between its coming into the station and when it leaves? How are we going to cover all the classes in the school while we train some teachers in the new exam marking system? The point here is not only to identify the critical issues, but to work out what to do if they occur. This is often called contingency planning. In our experience there are usually only three or four critical issues, no matter what the task. They are the sort of events that are revealed in enquiries after disasters. They have often actually been mentioned or recognised but not acted upon. A classic and tragic example is the case of failed 'O' rings on the Challenger space shuttle where the fault had been identified but not acted upon. It is also important to distinguish between Critical Issues and Constraints. Constraints are known limitations. They would include the resources, laws, policies, time to completion, quality requirements, essentially the QQRT (Quantity, Quality, Resources, Time – the Task Assignment model from Chapter 11) of task assignment. One participant on a course in California explained it well by saying: 'I see, so constraints are what you know, critical issues are what you have to work out'.

Contributions

Most leaders need help in order to identify critical issues. Even if you don't think you need help, there is always a risk in going it alone, that is, not listening to others and therefore implying they have no contribution to make. Some ways of encouraging contributions:

a. After explaining the purpose, give the team members time to think.
b. Ensure that each person really has an opportunity to offer the result of the think time. A member must feel comfortable even if they do not have earth-shattering ideas. In this phase the leader must be *accessible*. The positioning of people is important. If the group is standing the leader must see and be seen by everyone, as shown in Figure 14.1.
c. Be careful not to talk only to those next to you or to the most vocal. If you are sitting, the same principles apply. Long tables are a disadvantage. Do not be afraid to sit at the head: you are the leader. Non-verbal clues are critical at this time. People will give clues if they are bored; obvious ones are yawning, wandering off or sitting/ standing back. They give clues if they wish to contribute (leaning forward, increased body movement, hand gestures, raised eyebrows). The leader must be sensitive to these actions. Ignoring them leads to a feeling of not being 'listened to', even if words were actually spoken.

Make a decision about the planned action

Leadership is not a matter of democracy or consensus. If you are in a leadership role, it is likely that you are getting paid more than the members. Your position in the role is based upon your authority to make decisions. It is important to end the discussion stage in a timely fashion to avoid 'paralysis by analysis'. The leader is accountable for making sure all the critical issues and contributions have been considered carefully in constructing the plan. When they have decided on the plan, the leader needs to articulate the plan to the team. If some team members' suggestions have not been used they will need to know why. The leader should clearly indicate to the group what the intended actions are and what the critical issues are, including how they will be dealt with.

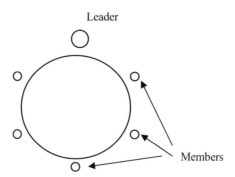

Figure 14.1   Accessibility of the Leader

Assign tasks

The decision or plan will be broken up into a number of tasks. These will be assigned to team members based on the leader's judgment of ability. People should know what they are meant to do. Using the task assignment model (CPQQRT) team members must know:

a. what their tasks are – and what to do next;
b. if and how their tasks complement other people's tasks and
c. how their tasks will help to achieve the purpose and overcome problems – *why* they are doing these tasks.

   If they cannot answer the questions above, the leader has failed and the team members will not know how and when to use their initiative when the situation changes (as it inevitably will!).

Monitor progress

The leader is held accountable for progress. If the leader does this, then team members are free to get on with their work. Progress is monitored along several dimensions (at once):

a. *Technical* (the most obvious): Are the solutions working? Do they need to be modified? Will the methodology/plan actually solve the problem?
b. *Social*: Is the team cohesive? Are people involved, using initiative, interacting or are they forming sub-groups, fragmenting, only doing 'what is necessary'? Do they look interested? Engaged?
c. *Temporal*: Is there a programme, a timetable/schedule? Is it being achieved?
d. *Environmental*: The *leader* is accountable for monitoring the environment, allowing team members to concentrate on the task at hand. What is happening around the team to help or hinder progress?

   Finally if any or all of the above are going wrong, what contingency plan do you have? Can you answer this *before* a problem arises, even if only in outline? Here you may have to revisit critical issues, stop the process and re-evaluate.

Coaching

As team members work they may need help to complete their tasks or improve their methods. Leaders are helpers. This is a very sensitive area because the *way* in which you coach will affect whether people will accept your help. First, make sure it is clear whether you are:

a. *Giving an instruction* – telling someone to do something differently and expecting them to do it.
b. *Giving advice* – suggesting a person think about using your ideas but leaving it up to them.
c. *Teaching* – showing/telling someone how to do something because they recognise that they don't know how. This area is critical to a leader as few people like being told how to do something while they are in the middle of work unless they think they are having problems. Consequently do not be afraid to ask.

d. *Asking* – gain information from members: for example Why do you do that? Do you want any help?

Although an important part of the leader's work is coaching, do not forget the leader may well learn from the team.

Review

At the end of the activity, whether the purpose has been achieved or not, the leader should review the process. Give recognition to others and comment on leadership behaviour positively and negatively. How would you do it differently? It is always important to debrief and hear team members' views. It is important to recognise people's work and to encourage individuals and the team to learn from what they have done – what they can build on and what they need to change. We all benefit from knowing if we have achieved our purpose (see Box 14.2).

Traps

A leader can make many mistakes and will make some. In our experience these are the most common:

Not seeing the problem from the member's viewpoint
This involves making assumptions that people know what you know and see what you see. You should be able, mentally, to step into someone else's shoes. What does the problem look like from their point of view. How anxious or confident are they?

Getting over-involved in the action
There is a temptation, especially if there are problems, to dive in and take over. This not only interferes with team members' work and shows that you have assigned tasks badly, but also prevents the monitoring work and good coaching. Some people rationalise this as 'leading from the front'. Instead, it shows a lack of confidence and produces dependency and/or resentment.

Feeling you have to have the answer
It is the leader's work to make sure the best solution is implemented. This may come from another member. This is not a failure – you are being paid for your judgment, not infinite knowledge. Often a leader fails to hear an excellent suggestion because they are anxious that an answer has not come to mind or is too busy trying to make the present solution work.

Being the technical expert
Like the trap above, this one also assumes you have to know more than anyone else, especially in the technical area. Superior technical knowledge and expertise is often mistaken for leadership. We argue that the leader does not have to be the best at any or all sub-tasks. The

---

Box 14.2   Individual Perspectives

The leader must be able to see the world from each team member's viewpoint.

leader must, however, be able to understand and question the logic of technical proposals. 'Explain to me, in simple language, how that is going to resolve the critical issue'.

Ignoring social and programming issues

Part of the culture that emphasises technical issues also downgrades the importance of or difficulty in the other areas of social process and programming. In most cases the technical solutions can be found within the team. However, it is critical that people put forward their ideas and that there are time lines associated with the plan. Programming is not simply recording or telling the time but checking progress against plan. At the same time, the team leader should be monitoring how the team members are relating to each other.

Issue fixation

Often one problem area will gain enormous attention. It may be a critical issue but it gets blown up, out of proportion. All resources are directed to this area failing to see how this affects other areas and what impact a new solution has on the rest of the problem. This also leads to a blindness to outside issues; there's not much point if, while changing a tyre, you get run over by a truck.

Not willing to stand out in a crowd

This is one of the most common and damaging traps – when a leader is reluctant to appear to be a leader. It is often perceived as against the grain to stand out, especially in a 'superior' position. Consequently there is an over-dependence on consensus, a collective accountability, a merging with the group resulting in a conservative, slow approach. Be reassured that groups/ teams *do* like the leader to be *decisive*. Consult, certainly, but team members may get very frustrated with a leader who will not be decisive.

TEAM MEMBERSHIP

If there is a library of material on leadership, there is much less on team membership. 'You're now the team' may be the only introduction some team members get. This section describes some of the constructive behaviours that all team members can demonstrate in order to achieve their common purpose.

The point about teams described here is that, from the viewpoint of the team member, in order for me to contribute effectively as a team member I am dependent upon others with whom I need to have direct working contact, perhaps not all at once but in the process of achieving the purpose.

Like the leadership section, this section draws on general observation of people in organisations and of specific behaviours by team members in activities on courses. One preliminary point before discussing behaviour: team members in employment roles clearly do not work in isolation. They operate within the organisation. If the structure, roles, authorities and accountability are unclear, then team members will have difficulty working with each other and the 'leader'. Teams may then be run on power, the power of personality or vocal, even physical strength. This is not the context that will create an organisation that will continue to be productive over time. We have described in earlier sections the need for clear authority and for accountability so that teams can work more effectively. However, even in this context there are ways of helping the process.

So how should team members behave and what are the traps? This section describes practical behaviour for all team members.

Context and purpose

Are you clear why you are here? If you are not, then ask. If you are not clear what the purpose is, the chances are that others will also be unclear. How many times have you failed to ask a 'stupid' question and found afterwards that other people were equally in the dark? If you don't ask, the leader will probably assume that you do understand.

Contribute to the 'how'

If you think of problems and ways of solving them, then you are accountable for putting these ideas forward. You may identify a 'trivial' point that is crucial. It is for the leader to decide in the end what is relevant. It is not only the leader who pays attention to the social process. Timing is critical if you want to be heard. Be available and accessible within the leader's sight. Don't give up if not heard initially. However, do not continue to press a point if it has been recognised.

Listen to others

It is important to make a contribution, but equally important to listen to other points of view. It is difficult for the leader if all members are switched to 'send' and none to 'receive'. You may find this difficult especially if you think others are making apparently 'silly' or 'trivial' suggestions or ideas you had already thought of and dismissed.

Accept decisions

In many types of organisations there are rarely appropriate times for voting. If you have had a 'fair go', you must commit to the chosen path even if your 'worst enemy' has had his/her suggestions accepted. You are there to achieve the common purpose not simply to prove that you are right. This is much more likely if the team process prior to this has been handled well.

Clarify your tasks

Are you sure:

a. What you are meant to be doing (CPQQRT)?
b. What you are meant to do next?
c. How your effort contributes to the purpose (why)?
d. How it fits with what others are doing?

If not, *ask*. Being a team member is an active process not a matter of blind faith. People working in parallel are not a team. You must be in a position to use your initiative especially if (or when!) something goes wrong (that is not to plan). In short, can you think into your leader's head? If in doubt, *ask*.

Concentrate on your tasks and co-operate

Try to complete your tasks while ensuring that you help and co-operate with others. Be prepared to give information and feedback on your progress and give encouragement to fellow team members. Do not hide information or use it as power.

Accept some coaching

No one is perfect and you can learn from others. It may be uncomfortable at times but try to listen to other people's ideas as to how you might improve your work.

Demand review

At the end of, or even during, the process it is important to check and review your performance. You must ask the leader what they thought and give your own view. It is also your work to suggest how it might be done better (next time). This does not mean proving *your* idea was right all along (see Box 14.3).

Traps

These are some of the most common traps we have observed over time.

Keeping quiet
This is where the team member does not ask questions or put forward ideas, often assuming that passive acceptance and blind obedience is what is required. It is not sufficient to assume that you will find out from others after the briefing.

Not listening
Allowing other people to speak does not equal listening. There is a difference between waiting for 'some idiot to finish' and actively listening. We have often seen some people repeat exactly the same point someone else has just made because they were not listening.

Getting on with my job
This involves ignoring the situation and the needs of others, with blinkers on, and continuing to do your own work whatever the circumstances. This is a situation where a person isolates themselves and has nothing to do with the rest of the team: 'it's not *my* problem'.

Getting on with other people's jobs
Some team members interfere with other people's tasks because they think they know better. This is often because they do not know what to do in their own tasks. It is also an attempt to use power and is different from co-operating.

Box 14.3   Teamwork

You are part of the whole. It is only by active co-operation, however, that the whole will be greater than the sum of the parts.

Wandering off

We have seen team members wander off either mentally or physically and often both, exploring possibilities without reporting back and in doing so missing vital information. Often it is with good intention, or due to boredom. However, it causes distraction.

Fragmenting the team

This is a variation of wandering off, and involves setting up ad hoc sub-groups to re-work the problems, changing the tasks and redefining the purpose, again without feedback. This can also be defined as power – setting up internal factions which polarise the team and undermine the leader.

'I knew I was right'

Going along smugly with a 'bad' plan, while actually undermining it in order to prove it was bad and having the dubious satisfaction of seeing it fall apart is especially common when the team member has had a 'better' solution turned down. It is essentially an ego problem.

Ignoring coaching

Being overly sensitive to questions from others (especially the leader) as to why you are doing something in a certain way. This may mean that you miss ways to improve. This is typical in 'we have always done it like that'. It is often an excuse when talking about safety: 'no-one's been hurt before'.

Fear of taking over

Holding back because you worry you might take over the leadership inhibits your potential and the team's resources. There are mechanisms the group will use as well as the leader that will tell you if you step out of line too much. While it is good not to dominate discussion it is unlikely that the leader will be undermined if you are constructive in your behaviour.

Summary

In this chapter we have taken a very practical approach to understanding team processes. We have stressed that 'hierarchy' and 'teamwork' are not alternatives. We do not believe there is such an entity as 'leaderless teams'. In all teams, leaders emerge. It is a question of whether they do so by authority or power. One of our most successful clients commented on his competitors, 'I do hope they adopt leaderless teams. It will give us a great competitive advantage.'

Teamwork is an overworked and often vague term. We have been specific in terms of both definition and process. Good teamwork is an essential component of an effective organisation. It is at the heart of an organisation's social process. Without good teamwork and co-operative membership an organisation will fail even if it has excellent technical and commercial processes.

Our unique approach has been and is to explain how the leadership role and membership role complement each other. This is a major reason why our model has been used so widely. The complementarity of the team leader and member steps can be seen clearly in Table 14.1.

Table 14.1   Complementary Roles of Leaders and Team Members

Leader	Member
Explain context and purpose	Clarify context and purpose
Identify critical issues	Contribute to the 'how'
Encourage contributions	Listen
Make a decision about the plan	Accept decisions concerning which plan
Assign tasks	Clarify tasks
Monitor progress	Co-operate
Coach	Accept coaching
Review	Demand review
Avoid traps	Avoid traps

AUTHORITY

Finally, we would argue that these steps in the process do not merely form some helpful practical advice. We recommend that they are actually confirmed as authorities of roles throughout the organisation. That is, team leaders should be held accountable for working through this process and team members held accountable for their part. Thus, it is not a luxury to review a task but a requirement. It is not just important or helpful for team members to ask questions and clarify but an essential part of their work. In organisations which have used this model as a set of authorities the improvement in the team process after the training has been very significant. As such it is an extension of the understanding of authority. It demonstrates that authorities are not just 'top-down'. The team member should be authorised to call the leader to account for following this process and to call other team members to account for their work in implementing this process. As with all behaviour, the way this is done, the social process, will influence the effectiveness of the process.

4 Making Change Happen – Putting Theory into Practice

So far we have explained the principles underlying behaviour: how and why people come together to achieve a shared purpose. We have examined the nature of work; how organisations have a purpose and how the formation and distribution of authority can help to achieve that purpose. In Part 3 we outlined the framework that leaders can use to be more effective including practical steps and key conceptual tools. Part 4 of the book explains in even more practical detail not only the content but the process of successful change, building upon the earlier material.

We begin by describing the change process and then examine the elements of that process in more depth. We then look at real examples and data to demonstrate the outcomes. There are many accounts of general processes but not always case studies with real results clearly connected to that change. We have also included a range of fuller case studies at the end of the book. They provide a unique account that crosses cultural and organisational boundaries and clearly shows the robustness of the conceptual material, while at the same time demonstrating its practical value.

15 *The Process of Successful Change: How is it Achieved?*

The authors and Macdonald Associates have been involved in many change programmes with many different organisations around the world. Associates have worked with schools, churches, international mining companies, financial organisations, voluntary organisations, indigenous communities, local authorities, manufacturing – in fact, a wide range across the private, public and voluntary sectors.

In all of this work we have provided advice and support to the leadership and members of such organisations. Such advice has been intended to encourage creativity by helping to create a set of conditions whereby people are able to express their potential through work. Much of this book has been concerned with describing these conditions and why they should lead to improvement.

Amongst the many projects and programmes in which we have been involved, not surprisingly some have been more successful than others. This chapter concentrates not so much on content but process. It draws on our experience to summarise the main elements in a successful change or transformation process. It is not a rigid prescription and depends upon specific circumstances, and so cannot always be followed exactly. However, it does provide a framework that is likely to lead to success. Where the process has been followed it has resulted in significant, positive change; in some cases exceeding expectations. Where the process has not been followed in this form, changes have been slower and have yielded less significant gains. The main argument is that there should be considerable attention paid to the process. A good idea can be ruined by poor implementation. Throughout this book we have emphasised the importance of understanding social process. This understanding applies no less to the social process of implementing change.

A change process or transformation can occur without specific outside consultancy. There is, however, always a need for specialist advice and reflection, from either an external or internal source. Our experience in such processes involves external consultancy. There are advantages to external advice, largely its independence and specific technical expertise. Also external advisers are not competitors for a potential career in the organisation. The advice can be considered and the relationship ended more easily, and the consultant never enters into a managerial authority relationship. In our work as consultants we endeavour to work in partnership with the leadership. Two phrases we do not allow a consultant to utter are 'if I were you' or 'you should'. We recognise executive authority; who has the authority to make the final decision over structure, systems or removal from role. Our advice tends to be analytical and predictive rather than coming in and 'doing the work'. If the partnership is not characterised by high trust between adviser (internal or external) and client, the process will fail or have at best a short-term impact. Applying a set of externally predetermined ideas will rarely, if ever, work unless the leadership has gained ownership of these ideas and helped to shape them in terms of the particular organisational application (see Box 15.1).

Box 15.1   Examples of Consultancy Relationships

There are many examples of these relationships. There was the relationship between Wilfred Brown (chairman of Glacier Metals) and Dr E. Jaques at Glacier Metals (1947–1977). In the 1980s a major restructuring of CRA (now Rio Tinto) in Australia was led by Sir Roderick Carnegie supported by Jaques and internal consultants including Leigh Clifford (who became CEO of Rio Tinto), Jack Brady, Terry Palmer and Karl Stewart. When Palmer and Stewart moved to managing director roles, they built similar relationships externally with Macdonald and others to bring about very significant change, as has David Murray at the Commonwealth Bank of Australia with Les Cupper as an internal adviser. There are many similar relationships involving both internal and external advisers to CEOs. These relationships are critical since it is helpful for a CEO to have someone with whom to test ideas, where that person is not a competitor. The function of the adviser is to give honest, direct feedback and evaluate these ideas against a set of principles and concepts.

The length and nature of this working relationship varies depending upon the circumstances. We do not favour two-, three- or six-month programmes with grand project titles. Such programmes or projects give the impression that there is a definitive start and finish time. We remember one surprised general manager who, when asked to work on some new systems, said; 'Isn't this what we pay you for?'. Our relationships tend to be longer term but may vary significantly in intensity and level of involvement. The fact that the relationship is one of active collaboration between consultant and manager does not mean it is purely pragmatic. The consultant must bring a depth of knowledge that can predict which modifications to principles will actually enhance the process and which will inhibit it.

The conceptual material in this book, as well as Jaques' theories, need to be seen as a discipline; that we must attempt to be rigorous in definition and analysis, not merely pragmatic or political. An impediment to such discipline is the adoption of a transformation process as a belief system. This is partly because all social processes are emotional and partly because belief can serve as a substitute for understanding. The concepts and models or principles then move from a set of predictive tools to be tested towards a dogmatic belief system with evangelists and sceptics. 'Failures' are perceived from both sides as proving their case. If a change 'fails' to produce the desired result for the sceptic, it proves the belief system is flawed; for the evangelist it has been deliberately undermined by the sceptic.

When the debate becomes suffused with intransigence and emotion the distinction between content and process becomes blurred. Similarly, with regard to systems, it is important to be clear whether the outcome (or lack of it) suggests inherent problems with content (the ideas and concepts) or problems with how it has been implemented: if the sound coming from my violin playing is alarming and tuneless, is it because the instrument is faulty or simply that I have never learnt to play?

Successful change process

The following section outlines the process, not as dogma but as a set of steps or criteria that can be used to examine where and why there might be problems. The process outlined below has, in our experience, been successful in terms of results over time. It is written assuming the positive relationship described above between a person (or persons) in executive roles (the leadership) and those in support roles (that is, consultants providing specialist advice).

STEP 1 – ESTABLISH A GOOD WORKING RELATIONSHIP BETWEEN THE CEO AND ADVISER(S)

These relationships can occur and develop in many ways and over different periods of time. However, our experience is that a direct, working relationship between adviser and the line executive is essential. This may not always be with the overall CEO. If not, then the scope of change will be limited to the area of discretion of that line manager. For example, it may occur in a division, a site or sector. If this is the case then at least those in the line roles above must be supportive if not driving the process.

Whilst this may be a very obvious point it is surprising how many so called change programmes do start and continue under a specialist banner, for example, HR or IT. They are doomed to failure or at best slow progress until the CEO (or equivalent) in a level IV role or above not only owns it but also is seen to own it. It is virtually impossible for someone in a level III role to drive significant change because the role does not carry the necessary integrative authority. This is not a negative representation for the person in a level III role and does not refer to that person's capability. If a highly capable person in a level III role does drive change without executive support, again by definition, they will have to use power, not authority. If we assume, however, that the relationship with the CEO has been established, then several critical issues need to be addressed.

What if other executives are not aligned?

Teamwork is critical and the CEO must lead a functional, productive team. Time and effort must be put into this alignment and, if particular team members cannot support the process, it is important that they leave. This need not be done punitively. In one particular instance an honest difference of opinion led to a very dignified exit with each party demonstrating mutual respect.

How best to create a productive relationship between external and internal consultants?

If external consultants are employed, their work must be complementary to internal consultants. A change programme must rest on common principles and language. Different models and conflicting advice will hinder the process. Essentially the problem is the same as that of alignment in the CEO's team and must be addressed.

What if other parties are not aligned?

Depending on the organisation there may be other parties to consider, for example trade unions. What is their view? How are their concerns addressed? This is a critical issue and must be addressed in the context specific to the organisation. We have worked in organisations where third-party response has been as diverse as literal, violent opposition or highly constructive engagement.

How best to engage the board?

If the change process is significant it is crucial that the board knows about it, knows what is trying to be achieved and at least in general terms how it is to be achieved. If this is not the case then early costs are difficult to accept. For example, during initial stages there may be a reduction in productivity, training costs may be high and there may even be some industrial unrest. This is critical work for the board, as explained in Chapter 6.

The process of addressing these critical issues is helped considerably by the next step.

STEP 2 – ARTICULATE WHAT THE CEO IS TRYING TO ACHIEVE

Often this articulation is called a 'vision' or 'mission statement'. These are often vague, even vapid, watered down truisms or platitudes. They are often hard either to agree or disagree with or to know specifically what to do as a result. Our experience has been that sometimes the CEO will have a clear picture in their mind but will be frustrated that it is not obvious to everyone else. We do not use terms as grandiose as 'mission' or 'vision' (except in the Church), but prefer 'purpose', 'goals' or 'objectives' because such terms are clearer and less abstract. Often it is useful to express this in very simple behavioural terms, for example, 'a place where people want to come to work', 'where people are listened to and their contributions valued'. It is important in this process to take into account the following critical issues.

How to make an integrated statement?

Any process should integrate the technical, commercial and social processes. As has been discussed, they must be related. It is not helpful to drive a technical change process such as six-sigma[1] unless the potential commercial benefits and social process impact are clear to everyone. A structural reorganisation (social process) is not helpful unless it is linked to a business case including how better to deliver the technical speciality of the business.

How much variation is there throughout the organisation?

Are some areas good/bad examples? Are some currently near or a long way from achieving these goals?

What is the overall business context?

Is obvious change needed or is it a case of 'if we aren't broke why fix us?'. Both of these last two will have significant impact on the timing and speed of the process (see step 5).

STEP 3 – HOW DO THE CONCEPTS OF SYSTEMS LEADERSHIP THEORY HELP?

It is critical that there is real and in-depth understanding by the executive leadership of how and why these concepts and tools can form a pathway to achieving the goals. As with the technical element, improvement is based upon process understanding.

Until this understanding exists, the change process cannot be owned by the executive and all technical questions will be passed to the 'specialist'. This can then lead to the 'belief system/dogma' approach discussed above. The critical issues are outlined below.

---

1   A disciplined methodology and approach which is widely used in industry for the reduction of defects in any process by examining and understanding statistical process data.

How to avoid the process being a 'black box'?

We have seen executives reluctant to understand the concepts by saying 'Oh well, that's HR' or 'That's why we pay consultants. Just fix it.'

There must be training and engagement at the highest levels. This is not just 'teaching' but interactive discussion which may result in changes in both content and presentation which relates to the critical issue:

How to integrate systems leadership theory with other models and concepts?

It is highly unlikely that a CEO or equivalent will have reached their position without having their own ideas based on their own experience. Others in the organisation will have their own concepts, especially to do with HR. It is important *not* to be overly precious, pedantic or dogmatic. It is the rigour and discipline itself that is important and some terms may be changed. These may be highly symbolic. One organisation did not like terms such as 'level' or 'stratum'. The concern was allayed by using general role titles and describing the type of work. Another leader insisted on no name for the process of change, which was highly successful because the organisation did not use technical or general terms. This ability to integrate without losing the integrity of the concepts is at the heart of the relationship and makes the difference between successful transition and imposed compliance.

Once there is an understanding and articulation of the change process, at least amongst the CEO's team and support staff/consultants, then it is important to take the next step.

STEP 4 – CARRY OUT A STRUCTURAL REVIEW

This is a paper exercise in that it requires the CEO team with advice to consider whether the current structural arrangements are appropriate and what needs to change to achieve the new purpose and goals. Using stratified systems theory and systems leadership theory an analysis can be made with regard to the critical issues:

- How to structure the required work?
- How to address the gap between what is required and what exists?
- What if there is not sufficient clarity of role relationships and appropriate authority?
- How to understand the use of power?

There should be shared understanding with the team of the change required and what the structure might look like in terms of levels of work, operations, services and support roles and other structural concepts discussed earlier.

At the same time or just after, it is useful to carry out the next step.

STEP 5 – CARRY OUT A SYSTEMS AND SYMBOLS AUDIT

This process is described in detail in the next chapter but is essentially an organisational health check. A review and interviews are carried out by an external consultant to determine, for example, how people view the leadership and systems. This is done using the values continua (love, trust, honesty, respect for dignity, courage, fairness). It identifies cultures and mythologies (stories about the organisation that underpin value judgments). Observations are made about internal consistency, for example, safety slogans visible around the site whilst extinguishers are missing and exits are blocked, or poor housekeeping, litter and waste during an apparent cost-cutting process.

Critical issues are:

- How to ensure that this process is explained and authorised by the leadership so that consultants are not seen as spies or the police. It may be better not to call it an audit but a review.
- How to avoid this being seen as if it is a survey based on statistical results. It is a process of interpretation where one person may have highly significant and insightful views and observations.

The structural review and systems and symbols audit thus provide the data to check out:

1. How far is organisational practice currently internally consistent? Is it doing what it says?
2. How far is organisational practice working for or against the purpose and goals?

As a consequence of this, the next step is for the CEO.

STEP 6 – THE CEO FORMULATES A PROGRAMME FOR CHANGE

Bearing in mind other business/organisational issues and the current context, what is the order of change and who will do what?

Critical issues here are:

- Alignment: how far is the diagnosis and the process shared? This may be influenced by the extent of information shared from the structural review and systems and symbols audit.
- How to ensure the proper choice of people who will engage in this process? This will be highly symbolic and indicate the seriousness of the process.
- What qualitative and quantitative measures are to be used to measure the progress and judge success against cost?
- How to review progress and change pace or direction if needed?

The next part(s) of the process depends, of course, on the nature and extent of the programme including what are priority areas. Certainly steps 7, 8 and 9 could well proceed in parallel.

STEP 7 – TRAIN

It is important that people understand what is expected and why. The Working Together course described in Chapter 18 is helpful as it combines context setting with knowledge and experiential learning. It is essential that courses are run top-down and are co-led, that is with internal course leaders and an external consultant/trainer. It provides an opportunity to discuss the strategy and produces important information about alignment and capability. As a result, people may choose not to be a part of this process and so will change roles or organisations.

It is critical to train internal co-presenters ('train the trainer'). Although the roles of the two co-presenters are different, the internal co-presenter should be able to demonstrate knowledge of the concepts and be able to present the business case.

STEP 8 – RESTRUCTURE

The extent of this process will obviously depend upon the gap between what is needed and what exists. However, it should be based on the nature of work (levels), understanding required authorities and a simple, effective role description system. The process again should be clearly led by the relevant executive head with support from internal and external experts.

*   It is critical that the process is not dogmatic or overly bureaucratic.
*   It is also critical that a differentiation is made between the work required in a new role and the capability of the current role incumbent. Do not refer to roles by people's names, for example, 'what about Jim's role?'. It is counter-productive for people to 'apply for their own job' – what is different about the role? Do not assume that because a person is currently in what appears to be a similar role that they are capable of the new role.

STEP 9 – SYSTEMS DESIGN

In Chapters 10 and 13 the significance of this work was explained. In Chapter 17, we will look at a very practical process for designing systems. Our experience suggests this work is both complex and iterative. It is so highly significant because of the influence that systems have on behaviour and their symbolic role.

Therefore, the critical issues in process are:

*   How to have small teams work on systems (four or five team members as a maximum), whilst taking input from others.
*   How to ensure that there is sufficient capability in the design team so that the systems are not bureaucratic and that they are designed quickly.

The key systems always to examine are:

*   safety
*   performance management
*   fair treatment.

These systems affect all employees and the latter two are fundamentally about managerial judgment, which is at the heart of a meritocracy.

The key to the analysis is to look first of all at the purpose of systems and to review *all* current systems in terms of differentiation or equalisation. Significant gains can quickly be made by changing systems that currently differentiate for no good reason to equalising systems, for example, car parking, uniforms, canteens or benefits. Similar gains can be made the other way (equalisation to differentiation), for example, performance pay from fixed hourly rates.

It is often helpful quickly to initiate some symbolic (but not cosmetic) system changes to demonstrate intent. Some systems may have irritated people for years and yet are relatively easy to change , for example, authorisation for stores, car parking, good safety equipment – even in one case decent work boots.

STEP 10 – REMOVAL FROM ROLE

This step is absolutely critical. We have seen many change programmes slowed, halted or fall into disrepute because, despite good structure and systems proposals, people are left in roles even when they cannot effectively carry out the work. This is especially true for those in leadership roles. This is perhaps the most difficult element of all. In successful change programmes we have often seen between a 30 and 40 per cent change in leadership roles within a year. Some of these may be by choice; others by requirement. It is rare that positive behaviour change will occur amongst those in level I or II roles if they see poor leaders left in the roles higher up. The symbolism of and dissonance produced by the removal from the organisation of a manager who has regularly and consistently used box D systems (that is, unauthorised and counter-productive systems as explained in Chapter 10) and behaviour can be highly advantageous to the overall change process.

The critical issue is, of course, how to manage this process in a fair and courageous way. It is important to differentiate between those who change roles (or leave) because they do not have the capability but are genuinely well regarded and those who leave because they are bullies or are operating in unauthorised or unproductive ways. The former should leave with dignity; the latter should be dismissed. Of course this distinction may not be so clear cut and there should be an opportunity for them with training and development to come up to speed. The critical issue here is not to use training as an excuse to avoid facing the hard truth.

There may well be a subculture of people who oppose the changes and are not aligned. The rest of the organisation will be watching this group carefully to see how they are treated. This is a key leadership issue and relates directly to performance management. Many initial 'opponents' have in time not only been won over but have also become enthusiasts. The critical issue is whether they are doing the work of the role. Removal from role of a poor performer who also opposes change can be very positively significant and symbolic. Retaining a 'critic' who is very productive may also be positive.

Despite the criticality of this step we have seen this avoided because it is 'too difficult', especially at higher levels. It is surprising how simple it seems to 'cut numbers', that is, objectify the loss of jobs lower down, whilst leaving a person in a level IV, V or VI role who is clearly *not* capable of the work of the role, or who uses power to obstruct the process.

STEP 11 – CONTINUE TRAINING THROUGH THE ORGANISATION

In our experience it is important to take the training through the organisation, not to stop at the top. Courses may differ in length or content but as mentioned above, these differences should have a work or business reason. The obvious similarity between courses for all employees helps in several ways:

1. It reinforces common language.
2. It helps build a shared culture (people at all levels can discuss their experiences).
3. It is a positive symbol of equalisation.

There are, however, two critical issues:

1. How to determine change?

There must be demonstrated change in behaviour by people who have been through training. The worst comment made on a course is 'I wish my boss had gone on this' – when the boss already has.

2. What if the course becomes ritualistic?

The course must not become a substitute for change. That is, we must avoid; 'we have nearly finished our change programme as 90 per cent have been through the course'. Such training can become ritualistic and detached from real change.

STEP 12 – SYSTEM TRAINING AND IMPLEMENTATION

There need to be measures of change that are clearly monitored. It is also important to train people in system design and implementation.

However good the system design is, it must involve training in the knowledge and skills needed in the new system and of implementation. This is an essential, but often overlooked part of the process. The critical issues here are:

How to ensure that systems are seen and experienced to be owned in the line?

If people systems are seen to be 'HR' or information systems 'IT', then long, protracted wars can break out between users and apparent owners.

How to build controls into systems that provide information for audits and reviews?

Too many systems are implemented with no or poor controls. They may start off well but drift over time and may become counter-productive without the leadership's realisation.

Further, it is important to identify priorities. Some systems are in urgent need of redesign; others can be left and others can be abolished. It is important to link the systems work with the training and structural work so that they are seen to be interdependent.

STEP 13 – REGULAR REVIEW

This is a critical step. The CEO, their team and relevant others must regularly review progress against expectation. This highlights the need:

1. to integrate the whole process;
2. to have good control and audit information;
3. to have good measures.

The review then will relate back to other stages as required, for example, restructuring, systems work, training, implementation and so on.

It is essential that this work is ongoing and remains actually and in people's perception the work of the executive leadership of the organisation.

The whole process can be summarised in terms of Figures 15.1 and 15.2. This process is not one which can always be followed exactly, nor can it be applied mechanistically. However, our experience is that missing out steps or failing to address the critical issues hinders the change process and can be counter-productive.

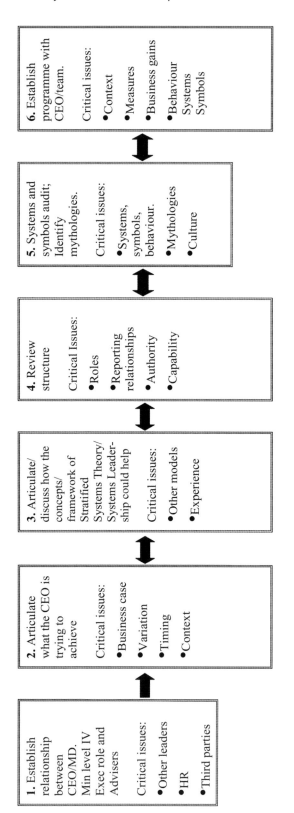

Figure 15.1 Successful Change Process (Part 1)

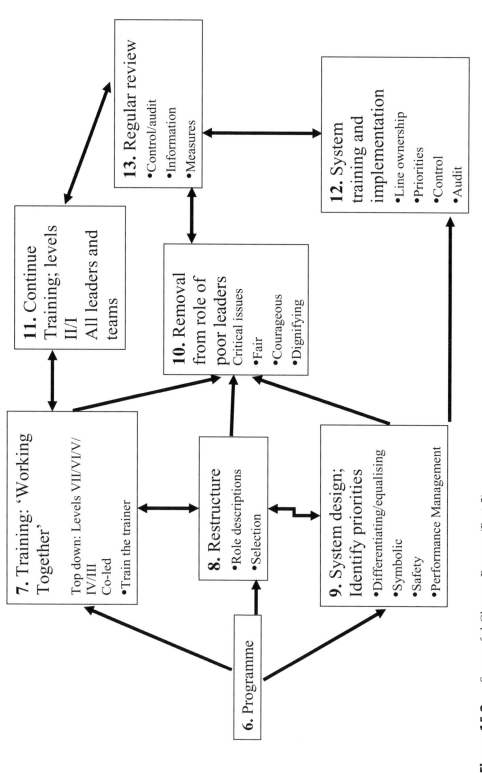

Figure 15.2 Successful Change Process (Part 2)

Summary

If productive transformation is to occur, then the social process must be managed as carefully as the technical content and the business case. Benefits to the organisation must be explicit and demonstrable. In summary the main lessons we have learned are:

- To ensure that the CEO or equivalent leads the process. Establishing a relationship between advisers and CEO is critical. It must also be clear that the relationship is advisory.
- During a change process a CEO (or the executive leading the change) may leave and be replaced. We do *not* assume that the process will simply continue. A new CEO may have different priorities. If the board understands and is supportive of the goals and process, it may well continue albeit with a different timescale, priority and certainly style. We have experience where the use of concepts and models has continued through a succession of CEOs (in one case four succeeding CEOs), and others where the new appointment has resulted in a different direction and the advice declined or put on the back burner. It is important to accept that an advisory relationship, which is based on mutual trust and respect, cannot be built overnight.
- The external consultants (and their team) must develop productive relationships with the CEO team. This is not likely if the consultants are perceived as 'zealots'.
- Although people in HR roles may seem to be the obvious allies of this process, this may not be the case. Indeed, people in the HR roles may see external consultants as rivals. Building a positive relationship and engaging with current concepts used by HR is important. At the other extreme the HR department may be seen as owners of the process and that the head of HR is the client. This must change over time or the whole process will be likely to be sidelined.
- It is important to understand the role of other external third parties, for example, union leadership. There may be vested interests in maintaining a distance between the organisation's leadership and its employees. It is important to discuss a clear strategy of if and how such organisations relate to or are involved in the change process.
- It is often a good idea not to name the process or the teams involved. Although this paper describes it as a particular transformation process, if it gets named, it is easy for the work to be seen as separate from the business. It is also easy for it to be seen as a 'project' (which will end or go away or fizzle out).
- All through the process it is important to keep in touch with mythologies within the organisation. These may be positive or negative to the changes and will affect both training and pace of change. Most successful transformations have been supported by the advice from 'wise counsel', that is, a few people in the organisation who do have good reliable networks and who have sound judgment and are prepared to give honest feedback.
- In relation to this point both internal and external members of the change process team must have a heightened awareness of their own behaviour. People will be actively testing for consistency and inconsistency and waiting for dissonant behaviour that might undermine confidence in the process.
- The pace of change will vary; timing is very important and clearly relates to resourcing. There is no fixed time for this process. However, it is likely to take more than a year even when conditions are favourable. Pacing will depend on many factors, resources as mentioned but also the current state of the organisation, capability of those involved and the perceived need and benefit of change.

- Finally, it is important to build internal resources to sustain and improve on the change process. Although some consultancies might regard this as bad for business, it is not helpful or productive if change is seen to be dependent upon outsiders.

There are several pitfalls we and the process can drop into, and some key overall lessons. From a consultant's perspective:

- It is essential to be disciplined but not dogmatic.
- Advise in such a way that avoids a class or even caste system developing over levels of work: 'she's just a level I', 'he can't do that; he's a level III' and so on. The concepts of capability and complexity must be distinguished.
- Spend a significant amount of time and effort on systems analysis and what behaviour results from it. Especially use the differentiation/equalisation and system matrix models.

From the executive/leadership:

- Demonstrate it is line owned.
- Link to clear results, qualitative and quantitative.
- Embed the work with systems.
- Remove poor performers from roles.

All involved must keep in touch with mythologies, help build positive new ones and be aware that the advisers and leaders will be constantly judged as to whether they are examples and role models of what is preached.

16 Systems and Symbols Audit – Organisational Health Check[1]

Analysis of systems, symbols and behaviour

This chapter provides a method that we have developed for reviewing the current state of an organisation in order to test the nature of the gap between the intention of the leadership and the reality of the situation.

The audit draws on the system leadership theory and in particular the analysis of systems, symbols and behaviour. We have used this approach in many organisations, the first of which was Hamersley Iron (now Pilbara Iron) in Australia, in 1992 (see Box 16.1).

These three questions underpin the audit process and act as general guidelines to the specific process described below. They can form a structure for reporting the audit results. Further, these three questions reinforce how important it is to design and implement good business systems, a topic examined in more detail in the next chapter.

The findings from this process can then contribute not only to decisions on what might be done but also, more particularly, on how this might be done. Prior to the audit it is important that there is some understanding of the concepts and models by, at least, the key leaders in the organisation. These should be discussed as part of the context setting for the work. This may result in some prior explanatory sessions, pre-reading and/or organising the feedback to take this into account.

It is important to state that no two audits are the same. The current state of the organisation, the purpose of the proposed change process, and the current industrial relations/employee relations context will all influence the actual design of the specific audit process. However, the underlying process and principles remain consistent and are outlined in this chapter.

Purpose of an audit

The purpose of the audit is to provide feedback to the leadership of the organisation on the effectiveness of systems in the organisation, as reflected in the workforce's interpretation of symbols and leadership behaviour. From these findings, the consultant provides recommendations for further action by the leadership team/general manager based on the insights gained during the process.

Audit steps

STEP 1 – INTRODUCE THE PROCESS

Careful consideration needs to be given as to how the process is introduced, explained and communicated. It is not always necessary or desirable to call it a systems and symbols audit.

---

[1]   This chapter is based on a paper written for Macdonald Associates by I. Macdonald and J. Grimmond, March 2000.

Box 16.1   The Three Questions

Underlying a successful organisation in our experience is a shared understanding of the nature and purpose of the organisation. We have found that the organisational health of an organisation can be gauged by whether people in, or associated with, the organisation can answer some basic, simple questions:

- What am I meant to be doing?
- How am I doing?
- What is my future?

If people have clear answers to these questions they are probably able to concentrate on their work. It is clear that these questions in turn are linked to the structure, systems and strategy of the business. Each question is directly related to elements in the business. If these elements are not in place, or are poorly in place, the person will not be able to answer and our prediction is they will simply spend time and energy trying to find the answers.

WHAT AM I MEANT TO BE DOING?

If a person can answer this question, then the organisation should have good systems of:

- Role descriptions: Outlining the *purpose* of the role and types of task a person can be asked to do.
- Clear task assignment: Including good *context setting* and again clarity of *purpose*, output, resources and time to completion.
- Clarity about role relationships: Including authority.
- Clarity about strategy: An understanding of how their work fits with others' and the wider business strategy.

HOW AM I DOING?

If a person can answer this question, then the organisation should have good systems of:

- Task review: Giving a person feedback on individual tasks.
- Recognition: Acknowledging the quality of performance (positively or negatively).
- Reward: Salary and pay linked to a person's performance over a period of time (annually).

WHAT IS MY FUTURE?

If a person can answer this question, then the organisation should have good systems of:

- Career review/assessment of potential: By the manager's manager (M+1) regarding career progression, including promotion.
- Development plans: Opportunities to develop skills and knowledge and enhance qualities, for example, leadership.
- Business information: Information systems detailing how well the organisation is progressing, its place in the market and comparison with competitors.
- Business strategy: Information linked to the above but specifically about where the organisation intends to go, how it will get there and what part the person might play in this.

These words may have negative connotations for some people, and many people may just regard such a title as jargon. Other terms can be used, so long as they honestly reflect the actual process, for example, employee relations review or employment systems review. It also depends upon what aspect the leadership would like to focus on.

This means, of course, that the specific purpose of the process for the organisation must be articulated beforehand. This work needs to be done by the consultant and the operations manager with his or her team. (The operations manager might be a site general manager, managing director or CEO, depending on the breadth of the review.) Then a communication needs to be made to the workforce from the manager. It may take the form of a letter or e-mail as well as briefings from managers and supervisors (see Box 16.2).

The actual letter should also contain more specific information about feedback from the audit. The nature and type may vary but should be clear so that the consultant can discuss this with people at the interview.

STEP 2 – SAMPLE

Talk to about 10 per cent of the workforce. This should give sufficient insight into the critical areas for attention. especially when coupled with other parts of the process (symbols audit, system documentation).

The employees may be interviewed individually or in small groups (maximum five). This should be determined beforehand. Some people may wish to be interviewed even if not

---

Box 16.2   Example Letter/E-Mail Informing of the Process

Letter to the workforce from the manager. Such a letter might read as follows:

For some time now I have had some concerns that our employment systems might be in need of a review and update. We have made significant changes and gains recently but we need to sustain and improve on them. I need to be sure that our systems can cope. By employment systems I mean, for example, how we recruit people, how we recognise and reward people, how people are promoted, how we communicate, how we train, how work is allocated, how safely we work and our employee benefits. I am not sure what system changes might result but I would like a greater understanding of how effective or otherwise our systems are now.

In order to gain a more objective view I have engaged a consultant (XX) to talk to people at all levels in the organisation about their views and in order to set some priorities. XX has many years' experience in this type of work and industry here and overseas.

All discussions will be confidential and no one will have to participate. About 10 per cent of the workforce will be chosen randomly and no individuals or work areas will be identified in the report back. Feel free to tell XX how you see things around here and what you would like to see changed.

You will receive feedback on the results of this work. If you have any questions about the process please ask your manager or me and XX if and when you meet.

Sincerely,

YYY

General Manager, Operations

chosen. This should be accommodated if practicable or, if not, a clear answer given as to why this is not possible. It should be noted that those who volunteer may have strong views and this needs to be taken into account.

STEP 3 – WORK TOP DOWN

Initial interviews should be with the general manager (or equivalent) and their team. If possible everyone in that team should be interviewed. Also, if possible, these should be one-to-one. Then a sample of about 20 to 30 per cent of the next level of management should be interviewed, again if possible one-to-one, but if needs be in groups no larger than three. Then about 20 per cent of supervisors (or equivalent), probably in groups of three or four. Then about 10 per cent of the workforce, again in small groups of three to five, but allowing for some one-to-one interviews especially if requested by the employee. Supervisor and workforce interviews can be interspersed but not integrated so that operators are not required to discuss issues with a person with (leadership) authority.

Each interview session should take no more than one hour but with a gap of between 15 and 30 minutes to allow for key issues to be distilled and captured. If notes are taken, then this should be done in an open manner. Our experience is that people in manager/superintendent roles in some low-trust organisations can occasionally be disturbed by a lot of note-taking, but operators and tradespeople are often pleased that notes are taken because it demonstrates listening and indicates the process is serious.

- The important thing is to ask for permission to take notes and not to start until you are sure that people are happy with what's going on. People should also be advised that notes are for the consultant's use only and will be destroyed at the end of the project.
- Names should not be recorded but interview groups can be by section, date and time for recall purposes when developing the client report/presentation.
- Under no circumstances should a tape recorder be used – no matter what the work culture.
- It may be desirable to also carry out interviews during the night shift and afternoon shifts. This can have a major symbolic impact as far as demonstration of the organisation's interest in obtaining widespread input into the process and greater openness can often result.
- It is always important to leave time between interviews to make notes or review notes taken.
- It is not productive to interview and write up for more than eight or nine hours per day if the interviews are done properly. It is also not productive to do more than five or six group interviews per day.

STEP 4 – THERE SHOULD NOT BE A RIGID INTERVIEW SCHEDULE

The interviews should be semi-structured and not programmed to a strict set of questions. A significant number of questions should be open ended with the opportunity to follow up leads in more depth. However, the interviewer does need a framework and prompts to ensure coverage and a similar experience for interviewees. Consultants should prepare a basic question list prior to the assignment commencing and continue to refine that list as organisational input is obtained (see Box 16.3).

The interview process at superintendent/ supervisor/ operator maintainer level should start with:

Box 16.3   A List of Possible Subject Headings

Consultants should prepare a basic question list prior to the assignment commencing and continue to refine that list as organisational input is obtained. Potential areas that might be explored:

- safety
- environmental performance
- communication
- task assignment (including demarcation, working hours, overtime, use of contractors, and so on)
- fair treatment or grievance procedures
- leadership practices
- training systems and skills development
- pay/benefits
- performance review
- reward and recognition
- recruitment/promotion
- discipline
- cultural diversity
- discrimination/harassment
- what people like about working for the company
- what they don't like
- what would they change if they could.

(Client input required plus client areas of particular interest to be included.)

- A personal introduction from the consultant.
- A check that people understand the purpose and ground rules. In many cases people will claim to have no idea what it is all about despite having been sent e-mails and other advice. The consultant should ensure that a copy of the advice or e-mail is available to refresh people's memories.
- It is a good idea, after the consultant has introduced themselves, to ask interviewees their first names and to ask people how long they have been in the organisation. People recently employed may have very different views from those held by 'long termers', and this can be used by the interviewer to good effect in discussing systems, mythologies and so on.
- The consultant should always clarify what the interviewees do. Sometimes a supervisor or a superintendent may have been inadvertently included in a group of operator/maintainers (that is, someone who missed an interview somewhere else and has been sent along to catch up). This can be difficult and can affect responses from others.
- After the formalities have been completed, the consultant will generally start with questions regarding the safety system, for example, 'I am really looking at systems. Can you tell me what safety is like around here?' 'Can you give me some examples where safety always comes first?' 'Are there examples of production coming first?' 'Why you think this is the safest place you've ever worked?'
- For every general answer a specific follow-up question should be asked both negative and positive, for example 'Could you give me an example of poor leadership?' 'Why do you like working nights?'

- Topics covered should be from a list of prompts, including the systems listed in the letter relating to employee systems. Not all topics need to be covered in depth at each level in the organisation but should be mentioned for consistency.
- The GM or equivalent may have circulated the general headings for questions, which will indicate the range of questions that will need to be covered.
- General questions need to be asked, especially with managers: 'What are the big issues at the moment?' 'What has been going on here the last three months, last six months, last twelve months?' These interviews will also be critical in determining what are the current critical issues on the site, and can assist in developing follow-up questions during the interview process.
- These sessions can also assist in determining managers' levels of understanding of the current mythologies like 'If I ask people what they think about safety, what will they say? If I ask whether they would use the fair treatment system, what will people say? Why would they say this?'

Care should be taken as to where interviews take place. They should be carried out in a setting where people cannot be interrupted and where they are comfortable. Operators are more likely to be at home in the lunch/crib-room rather than the boardroom. However, all interviews should take place on site.

STEP 5 – THIS IS NOT AN EMPLOYEE SURVEY

It is important to distinguish this process from the usual employee survey where people tick boxes on a prepared interview schedule. The purpose of such surveys is to gain an overall statistical analysis. This is more of a qualitative, judgmental process where the comments of one person or a very small number of people may be judged to be both highly significant and important evidence of a critical insight (obviously maintaining confidentiality). These interviews give much richer information but depend on the skill of the interviewer. The systems and symbols audit does not preclude the possibility of a survey. Survey data may be a good input or comparison.

STEP 6 – USE SOCIAL PROCESS SKILLS

The consultant (as interviewer) must have considerable social process skills. This is not a process that can be carried out by just anyone. The consultant needs to be able to establish rapport and build trust with the interviewees in a very short period of time. They must have some knowledge of the organisation, the sort of work done and ideally the general field of work (for example, refining, voluntary or social work, teaching, financial services, and so on).

The consultant must value contributions and seek to clarify them. They should never argue or correct unless it is to clarify purpose and ground rules. They must be at ease in virtually any setting, as mentioned above, the boardroom or the crib-room; a council chamber or a residential nursing home. The consultant must be able to modify style and language to fit the context without ever appearing false, insincere or patronising. The consultant should not try to 'fit in', for example, by swearing, colluding, overly dressing up or down, and so on. In essence the consultant must honestly be able to identify with the purpose of the process and be confident that results will be used constructively and for the improvement of the organisation. The consultant is neither the shareholders' representative nor the shop steward. The consultant is not there to 'take sides'.

> **Box 16.4**
>
> We have been asked whether it is possible to carry out a Systems and Symbols Audit (SSA) with internal interviewees. Our view is that it is not. The issues of confidentiality, judgment and authority are quite different. This is not to say that leaders or people in support roles do not listen to views and pick up information similar to this process. However, SSA is a particular process and its quality is based on the consultant's skills and independence.

The consultant must also value the work to a high degree to be able to demonstrate interest in the process and maintain this independent stance from the first question until the last during the interviews (see Box 16.4).

STEP 7 – USE SYSTEMS LEADERSHIP THEORY

The consultant must have considerable technical skills and knowledge in terms of systems leadership theory. The consultant must be fully knowledgeable about all aspects of the theory. This includes the values continua and system design criteria including the importance of symbols, steps and traps of team leadership and membership, as well as an understanding of levels of work, authority and accountability. The consultant must be able to interpret answers against these concepts, for example, the systems matrix, differentiation and equalisation, authority versus power and so on.

The consultant is essentially trying to articulate the mythologies of the workplace and link them to the systems. As such, in real time, they must be able to take a verbal statement ('management have no idea') and link it to one or more of the values ('they treat us unfairly and in an unloving way') through a reported behaviour ('the superintendent stays in his office most of the day, rarely enforces safety regulations and only makes negative comments about our work'). It can then be tested to see how general the myth is: Is this view shared by others in the organisation? How widespread is this view? Is it only about one superintendent?

Further, the consultant must then be able to link this with the relevant systems. From the above example, there are questions about the safety systems, work assignment review and recognition, as well as style. This would also raise questions about controls and audits especially with regard to the safety system. It may also reveal some unhelpful authorities and accountability, for example, that the safety system is the work of safety experts (officers) rather than the work of the line management.

The consultant must discern warning signals and emerging mythologies which, while only currently held by a small number, may be indicative of things to come. For example, 'I have noticed that the new bonus system related to safety encourages people to cover up injuries' or, of course, the converse.

STEP 8 – INTERVIEWS ARE NOT THE ONLY SOURCE OF INFORMATION

It is important that the consultant is not merely the conduit of opinion and comment. They must not only sift the information but also be alert to other data from the two other main sources of information reported below (steps 9 and 10).

STEP 9 – IDENTIFY SYMBOLS IN THE WORKPLACE

The consultant needs to take time walking about the workplace observing. He or she must look out for examples of good or bad practice. Some direct observations include housekeeping.

Box 16.5 Symbols

This is a very rich area and can give very strong clues as to what it is like to work in an organisation and what behaviour is encouraged, condoned or ignored.

In one organisation we observed that on the departmental notice board the graphs showing profit share payments were all turned upside down. There was considerable cynicism about this system. In another the departmental manager showing us round did not once speak to an operator or tradesperson but pointed out the state of the equipment.

In another a series of interviewees came in a very anxious state. It turned out they were told nothing about the context or purpose and we had to abandon the interviews. We have had people concerned that they have been chosen for interviews because they have been identified as troublemakers.

We look particularly at notice boards and intranets. On one intranet and information site we found the message: 'this site will be back on-line on X date'. This date had passed three weeks before. We saw one notice board with nearly every notice at least two years out of date. Housekeeping is quite revealing: how clean and how much litter is there? Are waste bins emptied or overflowing?

Behaviour can be highly symbolic, and in addition to interviews it is worth watching non-verbal behaviour – and just stopping to chat now and again.

Is the workplace tidy? Is there rubbish scrap, poor repair? What does the equipment look like? In particular, safety compliance can be observed and is a rich source of symbols. Are people wearing safety equipment? Are there locked fire doors? Are extinguishers in place? Another source is notice boards. What is on them? Are notices up to date? Are they in the language of the workforce? In one organisation the employees were largely non-English speaking but all the signs were in English. Who has put up notices? Are there union notice boards and what is on them? Are social events publicised? Is there a newsletter and what does it convey?

Behaviour can also be symbolic. While walking around, do people make eyecontact? Do they talk to you or each other? What do they say? What is the leadership behaviour? Do leaders talk to their teams? Are they in offices? How do they communicate? Less direct observations include – What is the atmosphere in the crib-room, staff-room, common areas, canteen and other places where employees gather? Do people personalise their workstations? Are there pictures? Of what kind? (see Box 16.5).

Clearly there cannot be an exhaustive list but essentially the aim is to gain an impression of what it is like to work in the organisation, noting variances between areas if they exist.

STEP 10 – REVIEW SYSTEM DOCUMENTATION

The other main data source is documentation. This includes actual system descriptions (if they exist), which can then be compared with reported practice. For example, if people have reported that they only get feedback once a year, is that consistent with the intent of the system? What are the policies of the organisation? Again, they can be compared with what people say.

It may well be difficult to find direct evidence of intimidation, racism or sexism – unauthorised, counter-productive (box D) systems (see Chapter 10) – because of their covert nature. However, indirect evidence may be available, such as a reluctance to speak or 'throwaway' comments such as 'I'd get the sack if I told you about that'. This needs to be considered carefully.

It may, however, occur that either by direct observation or in discussion, illegal or intimidatory examples come up. These incidents are probably the most difficult aspect of this work. The consultant must use their discretion in these cases. It is not simply a question of reporting or not reporting these incidents. While the person who raises the issue may be encouraged to use other channels to follow this up, the consultant must not become a conduit. This will be strongly influenced by the nature of the relationship between consultant and client. Hopefully it is such that it can be raised without specific reference but may well have a bearing on the continuation of the relationship. It is important never to betray a personal comment made in confidence.

STEP 11 – THE REPORT

The report is not a scientific or statistical paper. The report does not stand on its own as a written paper but should be presented to the management team as the basis for discussion leading to a plan of action. The report should contain an analysis of the numbers of people seen by level and general role title. It should identify cultures that may not be simply categorised by organisational level and role type. Essentially the report should reflect the sources of data, that is:

*   the interview/discussions
*   observations from the consultant (symbols)
*   systems commentary.

The extent of recommendation will depend on upon the original purpose and the nature of the relationship between client organisation and consultant. At the debrief it is useful to explain to the leadership 'that some of this will most certainly be factually incorrect. What I am talking about are mythologies and mythologies may be wrong in fact, but they are what people believe to be true'.

It can lead to considerable and unnecessary debate if people do not understand this basic concept.

When we reported to one managing director that several of his key systems were perceived to be unfair and disrespectful he first said, 'Well, they are wrong; that system is quite fair

---

Box 16.6 A Summary of Systems and Symbols Noted in One Audit Prior to Major Changes

*   monthly pay for staff, fortnightly pay for wages
*   monthly overtime sheet – daily time sheets
*   different sick leave
*   different leave forms
*   medical scheme only available to staff
*   superannuation
*   different coloured safety helmets based on craft/occupation/status
*   different practices with company uniforms
*   different employment application forms
*   shop floor employees not listed in company telephone directory
*   telephone barring system based on stratum not job requirement
*   authority limits based on stratum not job requirement
*   office size based on stratum not job requirement
*   different treatment of late arrival to work.

– I designed it. Are you saying I am unfair?'. It took a little while to revisit the concept of mythologies.

The report may be in the form of a presentation and/or a written document, depending upon need (see Box 16.6).

Conclusion

It is important to recognise that a systems and symbols audit is a general process that is highly interpretative and dependent upon the skills and experience of the consultant and the nature of the relationship with the client. It is not a rigid process or an employee survey but follows the principles as outlined above with emphasis directed by the original purpose. It is part of an approach (consistent with Macdonald Associates Consultancy work) that seeks to minimise the need to use power in organisations in order to get work done. It should lead to a programme of action, often centred around system design and redesign, directed to improve the quality of leadership and hence a more productive, effective and enjoyable workplace.

17 *How to Design Systems*

We have emphasised the importance of systems. The quote 'systems drive behaviour' underlines how important they are. How systems are designed and implemented has a significant effect on people's behaviour and consequently the productivity of the organisation. We have explained that leaders have three main tools: systems, symbols and behaviour. A leader may individually set a great example but, if the systems are counter-productive, it will seem like swimming upstream. If the systems are counter-productive, then it is likely that the organisational symbols will be perceived negatively. If you do not feel you are valued, then it is unlikely that you will take great care of company property, pick up litter, keep an area tidy, wear company clothing with any pride. It is not a very big step to see how this might affect the quality and commitment to work.

We argue that systems are the non-verbal behaviour of the organisation. If there is a contradiction between words and behaviour, people believe the behaviour. This applies to systems. 'Vision' and 'mission' statements are no match for the experience of actual systems. Putting 'safety first' is only tested in practice by the way systems operate or are tolerated. Missing fire extinguishers, blocked exits and out-of-date safety information tells the real truth. In this way slogans, visions and other vapid exhortations can be replaced by a single statement: 'This organisation tells lies' – unless the systems are authorised and productive.

We have introduced a simple definition of work: 'turning intention into reality'. Systems provide a framework within which flows of work activity take place. They help turn the intention of the organisation, as expressed in its purpose and policy, into the reality of day-to-day experience. The effectiveness of the organisation depends upon how well those systems are designed and implemented. Given the importance of systems it is surprising, in our experience, how many organisations do not properly resource their design and implementation. We believe this is largely for three reasons:

1. Their significance is underestimated or misunderstood.
2. The difficulty or complexity of the work of design is underestimated and/or assigned poorly.
3. There is not a simple set of criteria to guide the design and implementation work.

This chapter will address these three points.

Significance

We have already offered tools to understand systems; the systems of differentiation and equalisation and the systems matrix looking at authorised/unauthorised and productive/counter-productive activity. However, some organisations are still satisfied with policy statements, grand vision and mission statements, but are relatively careless as to how these are actually enacted. It is our experience that some organisations rely almost exclusively on behaviour. That is, the leadership assumes that people will make it happen despite the systems. Paradoxically we have found the most exploitative organisations are the most 'worthy'. Organisations with a true mission (religious, voluntary, health or educational), are more likely to exploit the goodwill of the staff than commercial organisations. For example, there is not a great deal of intrinsic enjoyment or satisfaction in standing over a furnace changing anodes in a smelter. Few see this as vocational work. Consequently if you want people to do this they will rightly require good systems: pay, protective clothing, facilities and so on. If, however, people are saving lives, souls or feeding the starving, it is tempting for the leadership not to treat its people very well; after all 'they will do it anyway'. It is surprising how many such organisations, including charities, are not run well nor are they anywhere near achieving what they could. This is often not a deliberate intent but a failure to understand the principles and influences underlying productive behaviour.

Complexity

The task of designing a system may appear easier than it is. Using the analysis of complexity it can be seen that this is work of *minimum* level III complexity. If the system is going to impact upon others it is almost certain to be at least level IV complexity. If it is organisation wide, it may well be higher depending upon the size of the organisation. Corporate-wide systems of international companies can easily require level VI complexity work. This does not always mean that only people in level VI roles should work on them, but that level VI-type mental processing ability needs to be applied. It does, however, mean that someone in a role at the required level (IV, V, VI) should be accountable for this work, its review and authorisation.

A common mistake is to underestimate the complexity of the work of systems design and to delegate it to a role too low down in the organisation where the incumbent might not have the authority, the mental processing ability or knowledge to be able to build a 'box A' system. The actual result is likely to be bureaucratic, add to red tape (box B) and not take into account possible variation. Instead of an enabling process we end up with a rigid set of rules which encourage people to find creative ways round the system (box C) or worse promote the development of covert box D systems (see Chapter 10).

A further and compounding error is to see system design as belonging to the technical experts. Thus, 'people' systems get designed by HR teams, just as commercial, technical or information technology systems are designed by teams strong in those disciplines. The result is often a system which, although it *may* be technically elegant, is seen by most users as difficult to understand, overly complicated, takes too long, does not take 'me' into account and, not surprisingly, needs constant 'help' from the technicians who probably designed it. We argue that all systems belong in the line. They are and should be executive driven. If not the systems can be avoided, criticised or changed. Tell-tale comments that this is happening include 'HR require us to do this', 'HR gave us little choice', 'The IT department doesn't realise we don't need this capacity' – and less polite alternatives.

Criteria: the 20 questions

It is easy to criticise, especially with hindsight. In response to leaders who were concerned with proper system design we wrote a paper outlining the criteria. These have proved extremely helpful. These criteria have been articulated into a series of questions the designer(s) should address:

1. WHY HAS THE SYSTEM BEEN CHOSEN?

This question is essentially about context. While we place a great deal of emphasis on systems, we are also aware of the time and resources required to design and implement good systems. So the first real question to ask is, 'If there is a problem, is the system needed in the first place?' It is often too easy to respond to a problem by saying 'It's the system', and then modify or bolt on amendments. An effective organisation is not one with a plethora of systems. The work of system design is to simplify. That is why it is high-level work. As Mark Twain commented, 'if I had more time, I would have written less'. So this question asks whether there is a need. If there is, then why this one and why now? In other words, how does this system (or potential system) fit with the business strategy? Does it relate to a current policy? How will improving this system integrate with what else is happening in the organisation? For example, it might be very useful to redesign performance review and assessment systems if the organisation is attempting to build a meritocratic, performance-based culture. We have found that sometimes systems are designed to avoid difficult issues. For example, rather than require managers to confront poor performance, which they are paid to do, a new system for discipline or training is designed.

2. WHO IS/SHOULD BE THE OWNER?

The owner of the system is someone with the authorised discretion to implement or significantly change a system (not merely propose changes). Too often the system owner either is or is perceived to be a 'specialist'. For example, the head of HR 'owns' the people systems. Our experience is that many organisations dilute leadership to their detriment by handing over authority for a core part of this work to such specialists. They confuse expertise with leadership. Our experiences suggest that system owners should usually be line managers (rarely, if ever, below level III and usually appropriately at level IV or above).

This does not mean that the owner has to do all the design work, This leads to the next question.

3. WHO IS/SHOULD BE THE CUSTODIAN/DESIGNER?

The designer is the person whose work it is to propose the design or redesign of a system. This can be complex, time-consuming and involve specialist knowledge. We have found that a small team (three of four members) with a range of knowledge and experience headed up by a highly capable person in at least a level IV role is an effective way to approach this issue. The team can call on people from all levels, especially users, for comment and advice. It should be clear to the organisation that, while the design team may work extensively on a system, it should be commissioned and authorised by the owner, that is, a line manager.

The custodian is simply the person who is accountable for monitoring the application of the system and advising the owner of the outcome of the monitoring. The owner, designer and custodian could be the same person (same role), but for company-wide systems this is usually not ideal due to the time needed for both design and monitoring of the system, once implemented.

4. WHAT IS THE PURPOSE OF THE SYSTEM?

Clarity of purpose is essential. We argue that the purpose of a system should be expressible in a single sentence without the conjunction 'and'. This is usually a difficult task involving significant debate, but without this clear purpose statement the rest of the design will not be coherent. The reason for excluding an 'and' in the statement is that it is almost inevitable that at some point in the design process these two purposes may come into conflict and may be resolved inconsistently. For example, the system may be called 'review and development'. Should the design emphasise one or the other? What if the review is highly critical? We have seen difficult issues avoided by simply moving quickly onto the 'positive' development aspects. Review and development should be two related systems. In system design it is not unusual to return to the purpose statement several times in the design process. This may seem tiresome but it is, in most cases, time well spent. Beware of hidden purposes. For example, is the design really intended to catch abusers (for example, of petty cash) or to promote good practice? Ask what behaviour you want the purpose to encourage and reinforce. It is usually helpful to have a positive purpose. For example, 'to provide security for company property', rather than ' to stop stealing'. The latter implies lack of trust, and may result in a design that treats everyone as a potential thief.

5. IS IT A SYSTEM OF EQUALISATION OR DIFFERENTIATION?

It is important to decide whether this is a system which is intended to apply to all employees or only to some, and if so, why? Should there be different benefits for health care, holiday or sick leave arrangements? The organising principle is that systems of differentiation should be justifiable because this helps to get the organisation's work done. If the reason for being treated differently is not explainable in this way, it may well be perceived by others as unfair or dishonest. If a person has improved insurance and health care benefits, it needs to be understood that it is because that person has to travel to countries which have poor public health services and not because they have become a vice president.

A system of equalisation is not simply one that applies to all. Remuneration and disciplinary systems may apply to everyone but the *intention* is to differentiate in both, that is, to pay different amounts according to the work (roles) or to distinguish between those who have performed poorly or broken policy requirements and those who have not.

6. WHAT IS THE UNDERLYING THEORY?

All systems and processes are essentially methods of changing an input (or inputs) into an output (or outputs). Do you know why these (should) work? Too often systems are designed and implemented in an apparently pragmatic way or simply because 'other organisations do it'. Interestingly this is more often the case in HR systems than technical processes, although IT comes pretty close to HR. For example, suppose a company that smelts aluminium decides to try a new technology with regard to reduction cells. It is unlikely that the new technical process will be introduced without examining the underlying metallurgical, chemical and electrical theories. Further, the company is likely to conduct trials and try to gain information from other sources as to the efficiency of the new technology. However, incentive pay systems are rarely examined with such rigour. What exact change of behaviour is expected as a result of such a scheme? Why should it produce a change? Will people work harder or more effectively? On what evidence? Or is the purpose really one of retention of staff? It is not that such questions will all be answered negatively. The point is that often such questions are not even asked. Most people have experience of expensive computer systems being introduced on the basis of claimed technical improvements in the hardware or software that are either not relevant to the needs of the users, or not actually realised in practice, leading to a 'need' for further upgrades. The articulation of the underlying theory or assumptions also helps with the consideration of relevant measures of success. This brings us to the next question.

7. HOW IS IT TO BE MEASURED?

Many systems do not have clear measures of success. Measurement should be directly related to the purpose: How do you know whether or not the purpose is being achieved? The issue need not be complicated by including a whole list of measures. What is the most important? How will it be displayed and communicated? Work in the quality area is very helpful here, such as statistical process control and run charts (see Deming, 1992).

Has the cost/value been fairly estimated? This may not always be easy but should be attempted and is part of the measurement of success. This costing includes the estimate of costs of design and implementation. In one business a good costing exercise resulted in the decision not to go ahead with the redesign since the cost of redesign, new equipment and training was greater than the reasonable expectation of gain.

8. WHAT ARE THE CURRENT 'BENEFITS' OF THE POOR SYSTEM?

It is important to know what you are up against. A new system may bring about cost savings and improvements, but some people may be gaining from the current inefficiency. For example, an overtime system may allow me to earn double time for four hours when I only have to be called out for half an hour. I may be able to use company vehicles for my own use and have come to assume this 'perk' as a right. I may enjoy my large office even if I don't really need it. I may gain extra pay for going on training courses, even when I don't need or use the skills learnt.

The question is whether there is an understanding that some people may feel they are losing out, as they may influence the way the system change is to be explained and communicated.

9. WHAT ARE THE BOUNDARIES OF THE SYSTEM?

There are no absolute rules for deciding where a system should begin or end. For example, we may have one system which is designed 'to fill roles in the organisation with the most appropriate people', or we could break this up into recruitment, appointment, induction, and promotion. Where the boundaries are depends upon the needs of the business at any time and is an executive decision (see also the discussion of system owner, question 2 above). All we are saying here is that the boundaries must be clear and logical. They must be known to people so that overlap and confusion do not occur. Smaller is usually better than bigger when it comes to system design.

10. WHAT ARE THE LINKAGES WITH OTHER SYSTEMS?

When designing a system, attention needs to be paid to existing and new systems that interact with the system under design. This affects decisions about the boundaries and structural issues. This part of system design involves work of at least level IV complexity. It is a common fault that systems are designed in isolation and the conflict with other systems is not appreciated until the system is implemented. A classic example is compatibility with technical equipment, especially in IT where software and hardware systems do not match. Another is where technological change is not considered in terms of its impact on social processes or current arrangements, for example the labour agreement, or even the availability of skilled labour. An incentive scheme may be introduced without proper reference to current appraisal systems or the general compensation system or grading system.

11. WHAT STRUCTURAL BOUNDARIES DOES IT CROSS?

Where a system flows across structural boundaries, for example, from one department to another, even from one organisation to another, there is potential for conflict and loss of efficiency. This is because the resolution of problems or misunderstandings may have to be at a relatively high level, where a crossover manager can be found. If crossing boundaries is needed, then it is even more important to have a detailed articulation of the system, including the authorities and accountabilities relating to the system. If management systems are crossing boundaries, it may be an indication of a need for a structural review. (This is often the outcome of business process re-engineering projects.) In general, it is useful to minimise these boundary issues, which may mean that a large system is better managed as several smaller ones.

12. IS THE SYSTEM ONE OF TRANSFER OR TRANSFORMATION?

A system is simply represented in Figure 17.1.

What occurs in the box is either a transfer or transformation. If it is a *transfer,* then the system is intended to deliver C in the same state as A. Obvious transfers are transportation systems like freight or postal deliveries. The system includes processes, which are intended to protect the object from unintended change, for example, packaging or refrigeration. Some business systems, however, are intentional transformations, that is, where C is significantly different from A. Typical examples here would be chemical processes, steel making, accounts or education (see Box 17.1).

Whatever the core business, transfer or transformation, it is critical in system design to minimise the other. The customer is usually reluctant to pay for the alternative. For example, I am unhappy if the products I ordered are delivered in a damaged (transformed) state, or if the main cost of steel includes the costs involved in warehousing and storage (hence the reluctance to maintain extensive inventory). Thus, complex systems that involve moving and storing transformed goods are wasteful and are likely to damage the goods in the process. Of course, I am also reluctant to pay for failed transformation; for example, when I send my team members to a training course and they return exactly as they were, having learned nothing.

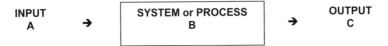

Figure 17.1   System of Transfer or Transformation

Box 17.1   Are Systems Magic?

Note: It is interesting to note that magic is essentially a clear transformation of something recognisable (as A) into a totally different entity (now it's C!) where the observer has no idea of the nature of the transformation (B). Too often systems appear more like magic than understandable processes.

Therefore part of clarification of the purpose of the system is to determine whether it is transfer or transformation and to minimise the other in the design.

13. ARE AUTHORITIES AND ACCOUNTABILITIES CONSISTENT WITH ROLE?

In the design of the system it is important that a person's work in the system is not at odds with their work generally. For example, imagine the situation where a manager may have the discretion to spend up to $20 000 but has to send a form to his manager's manager countersigned by someone in accounts to justify an overnight stay in a hotel on business. Conversely, think of what would happen if a specialist in HR (level II role) were required to check on the CEO's quality of interviewing and give feedback. There may be times when exceptions are required. For example, it is common that all overseas travel has to be approved by the CEO for a period of time because of tight business conditions. These should be exceptions that happen during a significant change process. We must be very careful in the design that systems do not replace discretion, that is, reduce the level of work and produce negative bureaucratic red tape limiting creativity and common sense. This is a common pitfall.

14. ARE THERE PROPER CONTROLS BUILT INTO THE SYSTEM?

A control in a system acts to provide information as to whether or not the system is being operated correctly, that it is working as intended. This is done by taking statistically valid samples of work to provide data to the operator, system custodian and owner. Controls are often useful around decision points. For example, if the 'assessment of potential' policy and system requires that only people who have been assessed as having potential to work higher should be promoted, is this the case? What information is there concerning recent promotions? It is our experience that while controls are required inclusions in financial systems, and common in technical systems, they are often poor or non-existent in HR and some IT systems. In HR systems a common problem is to apply controls only to quantitative elements and not qualitative. Thus 'I have done all my performance appraisals', does not say how well I have done them. Whilst it is important to build in controls, it is also important not to control every element or it may reduce discretion.

In addition to controls it is important to ask:

15. IS THERE AN EFFECTIVE AUDIT PROCESS?

Audit is different from control in that it first checks from time to time that the controls are in place and then reviews whether the system is achieving its purpose and is the best way to achieve that purpose. It is typical that auditors are independent of system operators but report findings to the system owner. In the event of exceptional circumstances such as financial impropriety or breaking of the law, the auditor may need the authority to have direct access to the board.

Auditors are not the most loved people in organisations but do essential work. They can appear less like police or spies if it is understood that they are reviewing whether the system is achieving its purpose or not. For example, a system may be operating according to its intent, and have effective controls in place but not achieving what it should effectively, such as a training programme which is no longer relevant. We find that one area which is often overlooked is the people aspect, or attention to social process. So it is important to ask:

16. HAS THE SOCIAL PROCESS ANALYSIS BEEN DONE?

This is partly covered by the prior question, but involves a much more specific use of the values model by incorporating the six values of love, trust, honesty, fairness, dignity and courage. How will the new system be viewed? What are the current mythologies of the users or potential users? What behaviour and mythologies do I want to encourage and create? Why will this system achieve what is required? This process involves discussion and imagination. It requires us to look through the lens of others and ask how would people view and respond to this change. It is not sufficient to extrapolate from your own views: 'Well, I think that is perfectly fair, so it is okay'.

To look at this properly we use the following set of sub-questions. It is strongly recommended that time is spent on this aspect as some very useful and sometimes surprising information is discovered. This can have a significant impact on the way the system is both designed and implemented.

a. How is the system currently seen?
  • What are the mythologies about it? (or lack of it)
  • How is it rated on the values continua?
  • Is it a system of differentiation or of equalisation?
  • Where is it on the systems matrix? (A, B, C or D)
  • What behaviour is it driving? (note that this may vary between groups)
  • What symbols are associated with the system (or lack of)?
b. Desired outcomes
  • What behaviours should it drive?
  • What mythologies do we want about the system?
  • What are the assumptions and theory on which the new design rests?
c. What are the recommended changes/design? How will these/it be viewed?
  • On the values continua?
  • Differentiation or equalisation?
  • Systems matrix?
  • Will any of these changes be symbolic? How?
  • What behaviour do we predict it will drive?

When these questions have been addressed, it is important to create a flowchart of how the system is meant to work since this creates a working model.

17. IS THERE A FULLY OUTLINED FLOWCHART?

There are many methods of flowcharting that are useful. Detailed flowcharting articulates the detail, whether it is a flow of materials, money, information, people, work or equipment. Our experience suggests that the flowchart should be understandable to an outsider and practical

---

Box 17.2   The 20 Systems Design Questions

1.   Why has the system been chosen?
2.   Who is/should be the owner?
3.   Who is/should be the custodian/designer?
4.   What is the purpose of the system?
5.   Is it a system of equalisation or differentiation?
6.   What is the underlying theory?
7.   How is it to be measured?
8.   What are the current 'benefits' of the poor system?
9.   What are the boundaries of the system?
10. What are the linkages with other systems?
11. What structural boundaries does it cross?
12. Is the system one of transfer or transformation?
13. Are authorities and accountabilities consistent with role?
14. Are there proper controls built into the system?
15. Is there an effective audit process?
16. Has the social process analysis been done?
17. Is there a fully outlined flowchart?
18. Is there full system documentation?
19. What is the implementation plan?
20. What is the final cost of design and implementation?

---

like a good set of instructions. For example, it is not sufficient to say 'at this point customer requirements go from sales to production'. What customer requirements? Who in sales is accountable for the work of sending them? Who in production is accountable for the work of receiving them? Then we can ask why should this be so. The flowchart should indicate decisions points, the steps prior to and post decisions and controls.

The flowchart is an essential part of documentation and so the next question is:

18. IS THERE FULL SYSTEM DOCUMENTATION?

Too often systems are in people's heads. This is why knowledge as well as experience may leave with a person. People need to know what they are meant to do, what authority they have and how they fit in to the whole picture. The need to know what they will be held accountable for. The process of system documentation in itself may reveal anomalies and errors. A note of caution here is that system documentation is a descriptive process. Be careful it does not become a bureaucratic rulebook limiting discretion. It should contain the flowchart and methods of recording the information flow of the system including control and audit information.

19. WHAT IS THE IMPLEMENTATION PLAN?

Sometimes systems fail because, although well designed, they are rolled out without proper training. Training in a new system can be a major undertaking especially if it is a corporate wide system. However, it is pointless to introduce a new system half-heartedly. Training and implementation programmes are not just about the technical details but should be informed by all these questions, especially the purpose, gains and social process and behaviour required for the new system to be a success.

20. WHAT IS THE FINAL COST OF DESIGN AND IMPLEMENTATION?

Finally, it is important to revisit the cost.

In designing the systems, its processes and implementation, critical issues will arise which need to be addressed. It is very rare to come up with an initial estimate that is accurate. This last step should estimate more realistically the overall cost and calculate it against the gains. It is not a failure if at this point the system is regarded as too expensive and rejected. Making that decision can save a commercial and social disaster but requires great courage.

Practical examples

This book contains several case studies on CD and in the back of the book; they are actual examples of where these concepts have been applied in a wide range of settings.

The Macdonald modelling falls into a number of areas:
* organisational change
* leadership
* system design
* team leadership and team membership

That work in CRA concerned work with particular business units. In the late 1980s and early 1990s, after the restructuring work was done, the managing directors of the new business units turned their attention to systems using the systems leadership model. Most notably Karl Stewart at Comalco Smelting and Terry Palmer at Hamersley (then as CEO of Comalco) specifically addressed a series of these.

The importance of controls is demonstrated from the Comalco New Zealand Aluminium Smelter (NZAS), which used the following work performance review control form (see Figure 17.2 on page 228).

The results of the control form, also included, demonstrated the positive relationship following the change of employment systems although there remains a problem with leaders following up on their commitments (see Figure 17.3 on page 229).

An example from Comalco's Bell Bay plant shows that system changes have some impact on behaviour. Figure 17.4 on page 230, a change to a 'staff system' of sick leave, implemented in March 1994, shows a significant change in behaviour.

In the case studies, there are also two examples from Hamersley Iron, which concentrated not only on design of systems, but how well people were trained and understood them. The first is a general understanding of work in the organisation. The second explains the fair treatment system to operators and trades people including the authorities of those involved.

This chapter has emphasised the importance of systems within an organisation.

We have seen that in many organisations systems work is done poorly because of one or more of the following: the significance of systems is underestimated, the complexity of the task is underestimated and there is no shared process for doing the work. This is why we have articulated the '20 questions' (see Box 17.2 on page 221).

We have worked with organisations who have used this model (and its earlier version) and those who have applied it thoroughly have benefited significantly. Systems are not well designed by a large committee but rather a small team led at the appropriate level (usually not below level IV) who then consult with others, especially users. As one of the fundamental tools of leadership, we argue that systems drive behaviour; it is a question of whether that behaviour is productive and ethical (see Box 17.3 below).

Box 17.3 'NOT TO GO' – Lessons In Systems Design

CONTEXT

Hamersley Iron transports the iron ore it mines in the ranges of the Pilbara region of North West Australia, by the way of the rail system it built and operates, to its port at Dampier. The distance varies, depending on the mine, and is between 300 and 400 kilometres. The rail system operates around the clock – at the time of this case study it was transporting between three and four million tons per month. It is now transporting five million. A train was made up of a rake of 210 100-ton capacity wagons, called a consist, and three locomotives. The wagons, steel boxes on wheels, are united in pairs by a solid draw bar so an individual unit is made up of a control car and a slave car. These units can be uncoupled from each other. They have two boxes, four cast steel suspension frames, two sets of brake mechanisms, eight axles, sixteen bearings and sixteen wheels. Each unit has an identification number. The fleet was made up of 2 500 wagons and 47 locomotives plus 300 other items of rolling stock. The operating schedule called for seven trains per day with one additional on Fridays.

The entire rail system was and is one of the biggest in the world in terms of tonne kilometres per day and is technologically very advanced.

The rail operations and maintenance group totalling 560 people had, immediately prior to this case study, been the first part of the Hamersley Iron Business Unit to go through the restructuring exercise based on the ideas of Elliot Jaques and the knowledge gained from previous exercises elsewhere in the CRA (now Rio Tinto) group.

DISCUSSION

One of the tasks assigned to the restructuring team leader by the CEO of CRA (Sir Roderick Carnegie) was to develop an understanding of systems in business which would inform their design and implementation across the corporation. Some work on this task had been done by the team leader and a few of the team members during the restructuring exercise over the previous six months. This small group chose the NOT TO GO system for its first trial of its ideas. It was a system vital to Rail, it was a system believed to be not working well and it depended upon the transfer of data and equipment across department boundaries.

The system was organised around the work of 30 traffic operations people, called car and wagon examiners (C&WEs), and 30 tradesmen from rolling stock maintenance, called wagon maintainers. The cycle of work was begun when one examiner walked up either side of the consist visually examining each wagon for structural faults and then standing, one on either side, while the consist was slowly pulled past them so they could listen for noise which would indicate a bearing or a wheel fault. The examiners each carried a gauge that they used to test the shape of any wagon wheel they thought might have worn undersize on the wheel flange or tread. The purpose of this work, which continued around the clock, was the identification of faults that had the potential to cause a derailment. As the general manager of Rail said, 'You start counting the cost of a derailment at a million dollars and it goes up by the hour from there.'

A wagon identified as having a fault had a card 250mm x 200mm marked up and placed in a pocket in one corner. The card had on it in large black print

NOT TO GO

hence the name of the system. The supervisor of the C&WEs also walked the consist noting marked cards, checking to verify faults and recording the cars to be cut out. This data was provided to the shunting locomotive crew who cut the NOT TO GO wagons from the consist and delivered them to a holding track outside the rail maintenance workshop. Codes on the NOT TO GO card indicated the fault identified by the examiner.

The relationship between the examiners and maintainers was not good. Recently, in response to criticism from the maintainers about the inspection quality, the examiners had placed NOT TO GO on 200 wagons over a weekend, all of which were waiting for the maintainers when they arrived for work on Monday morning. The maintainers worked three shifts per day, five days per week.

The myths each group held about each other may be gauged from the following quotes (from which expletives indicating the emotional state of the speaker have been deleted):

'The wagon maintainers do nothing to fix the wagons – they hit them a few times with a hammer, tear up the NOT TO GO card and put them back into service.' 'The wagon maintainers are too lazy to do any work, they sit around all day in the shade and read *Playboy*.' 'The maintainers are useless, they don't know one end of a wagon from the other and their bosses are worse.'

'Car and wagon examiners are all apes – they find them in the gutter outside the pub in Roebourne [a small, old, local town] and give them a job as C & W examiners.' 'The C & W examiners are so stupid they keep losing wheel gauges. How do you expect them to inspect wagons? We have got people doing nothing each day but make up wheel gauges.'

In fact, the work of the C & W examiners was difficult and unpleasant. It required intense concentration and at night; in spite of many powerful lights, shadows made examination more difficult. During the long summers the daytime temperature between the rows of wagons where the examiners worked was above 50 degrees C – every steel surface was too hot to touch with a bare hand.

The examiners and maintainers were members of different unions.

The systems team discussed the proposal to work on NOT TO GO with the GM of Rail and were given approval. They then ran an information session with the managers (level III), superintendents (level II) and supervisors (level I) who had a direct association with the system. These sessions produced some favourable commentary and a 'Best of luck'.

The information session with the maintainers was not so forthcoming. The union delegate for the maintainers informed the team that, 'The union leadership has informed us that it will give no support for the work and we will not talk to you,' to which the systems team leader replied, 'I grew up in the union. It is the members of a union who make the decisions in a union, not the leaders. We will talk to all those whom we please. You can tell us what you choose.'

This response was confrontational, and well removed from normal practice, but the meeting continued. The team members then went on to explain the process intended for data gathering and feedback on progress. The reception received from the examiners was almost as frosty.

The individual response the systems team got from these people over the subsequent weeks as they gathered data and discussed ideas for a new system was very straightforward and helpful. They spoke to people on all shifts. The union delegate for the maintainers was one of the most forthcoming on his work and his experience of the current system.

FINDINGS

The examiners were copying data seven times between the notebook they carried and placement of the NOT TO GO card on the wagon.

The maintainers received no information about a wagon fault other than what was marked on the NOT TO GO card as a set of codes which referred to a common type of fault.

There was no information provided to examiners on what maintainers had found or done. The maintainers expressed concern about standards of inspection. Sometimes they could not find a fault and sometimes they found a fault different from that marked on a card. The examiners had no idea what had been done to the wagons they marked. They were sure that on occasions a wagon they had marked was back in the consist a few days later with the same fault but they had no record unless they wrote the wagon number and fault down separately – which a few tried to do.

The leadership of both areas was satisfied with the system design and put the difficulties they were having with it down to poor quality employees and the fact they belonged to the union.

Both examiners and maintainers said their own leadership added no value to their work and the other group's leadership was condoning poor work practice. The examiners were not losing the gauges; they were throwing them into ore wagons in rage because they were so awkward to use and heavy in their shirt pocket where they needed to be carried.

The maintainers were making the gauges bigger from material much thicker than necessary so the examiners could not lose them so easily.

Data on wagon faults was collected for analysis by the operations department. Data on wagon maintenance was collected for analysis by the maintenance department. The systems team could find no evidence of any analysis in the previous 12 months and no consideration had been given to the analysis of both sets of data together.

The last derailment had occurred some 18 months previously and there was general concern that 'We are due for another one.'

NEW SYSTEM

The NOT TO GO card was redesigned. It now had a line drawing of the wagon on which the examiner could mark the position of the fault. The codes on the front of the old card were replaced by short descriptions of the fault with an 'other' category and columns for the examiner and the maintainer to mark. The card had sizeable boxes for comments from the examiner, who placed the card, and the maintainer, who worked on the wagon, both of whom were required to sign below their respective comment box.

Pocket-sized booklets with two-copy NCR paper were printed so the pages were a small replica of the NOT TO GO card. The examiners were to carry these and mark them up as the primary record of inspection. They kept one copy and the others were used as the data input for management and record keeping. The examiner transferred the data from his pocket book to the NOT TO GO card in the trackside work hut and then went out and inserted the card into the holder on the relevant wagon as in the old system.

The supervisor had a copy page from the examiner's book for each card placed.

As the design of the new system developed, proposals were taken out to the users for their comment. The management group advised that there would be trouble asking examiners and maintainers to sign the cards and that they would refuse. Very few examiners signed the present cards. The recognised 'leader' of the examiners was pungently critical of the system team's members and their work until he was shown the prototype of the pocket notebook, which he refused to give back to the team declaring it was 'A bloody good idea.' When it was explained that it had taken days to draw up each page by hand he laughed and told them it was about time they did some real work. From then on the team's work with the examiners was much more collaborative.

The new system required the NOT TO GO card to be completed and signed by the maintainer at the completion of maintenance work, checked by his supervisor, copied for maintenance records, sent to the examiner's supervisor for his reference and then given to the examiner who had initiated it.

IMPLEMENTATION

The systems team made a series of presentations explaining the new system to all users, answering questions fully and providing access to the new notebooks and cards. Immediately following the last training session the system was put into practice.

There was no objection raised to signing the cards.

OUTCOME

Two weeks after the implementation, a group of maintainers approached their superintendent with a proposal that they run a training course for the car and wagon examiners to teach them in detail about the parts of the wagons, the information which would most assist the maintainers, and special aspects of inspection which would improve and standardise inspection. Approval was given, the course developed and training began four weeks later. Training course attendance was 100 per cent and at the course each examiner was presented with a thin polished gauge on which his name was stamped. Three weeks after the courses had been run, one examiner identified an unusual fracture in a steel casting. It was in a location that made it visible only through a triangular opening about 50mm wide and, had it not been found, the fault would have caused a derailment. The maintainance comment written on the NOT TO GO card was 'A spectacular save.' The examiner carried his copy of the card in his crib tin (lunch box) for weeks to show it to people.

At a presentation to the upper-level management of the corporation which sought to explain the system, its design methodology and its outcome, the crew superintendents of both the maintainers and the examiners said, 'It (the new system) has succeeded beyond our wildest expectations.'

POST SCRIPTS

The original NOT TO GO cards were printed on dull red paper, which made them difficult to see against the brown of the wagon, particularly at night.

The new NOT TO GO cards were printed on fluorescent red paper so they could be seen easily by the locomotive crews who cut the wagons from the consist and took them to the workshop. The colour faded in the intense sunlight and the cards became difficult to identify. New paper was sourced by the systems team and replacement cards printed.

The systems team reviewed the operation of the system 12 weeks after it had been introduced and found it had been changed. The NOT TO GO cards were not being returned to examiners on a regular basis and maintainers and examiners were being required to transcribe data from the cards onto newly introduced forms. The examiners and maintainers were highly critical of the changes and said they had no idea of why they had been introduced by their respective managers. The working relationship between the examiners and maintainers remained excellent.

The systems team intervened, with the general manager of Rail, and the system was taken back to its original design. Eight months later the new system had collapsed completely. It had been changed back to its original form except for the design of the NOT TO GO card. The working relationship between the examiners and maintainers was still good but showing signs of strain, particularly with new members of the examiner team (which had always had a high turnover, in part because of the difficult working conditions). The working relationship between both crews and their supervisors and superintendents had deteriorated significantly.

WHY?

1. The new system was owned by the systems team and not by the general manager of Rail. He was very supportive but it was not his.
2. There was no clear articulation of the process of system change, nor of who had the authority

to institute change. Changes were introduced by people in level II and level III roles who simply believed they had the authority to do so.

3. The design process itself did not incorporate the person who should have been the system owner, or the users. They were presented with the output of design work done by the system team for their review and comment. Relevant managers in level II, III and IV roles were invited to join in the design team's work but they chose not to. Design work was slow and boring and they were busy.

4. Control and audit were not identified specifically as elements of the system. This activity was done by the systems team on an *ad hoc* basis. Only later was it fully appreciated that control and audit, carefully designed and formally authorised, are critical elements of all systems.

5. The system's purpose was confused: was it –

    a. To demonstrate the methodology of systems design?
    b. To improve the wagon inspection process?
    c. To reduce the likelihood of train derailments?
    d. To improve the relationship between the examiners and maintainers?
    e. To improve the data collection processes associated with wagon repair?
    f. To improve information flow across the boundary between two separate departments?

From the viewpoint of the system design team, the purpose was probably (a), but different groups or individuals associated with the system would have perceived it as one of the others.

The immediate impact of the new system was due primarily to the recognition of the work of the examiners and the maintainers. Neither group was receiving any recognition from their respective leaders; a common circumstance in a strongly unionised work environment.

This was, paradoxically, the primary reason for the new system collapsing. The old myths about the examiners or the maintainers being the 'enemy', depending upon the group to which you belonged, were not tenable with the behaviour generated by the new system and the management of both groups depended upon this set of myths to maintain what they perceived to be leadership authority.

The new behaviours openly challenged this authority, often on the basis of the information provided by the new system.

For the system design team, it was both an outstanding proof of concept and a salutary lesson showing them they had more work to do if they were to develop a full understanding of the complexity of system design.

It was, however, a spectacular demonstration that 'systems drive behaviour'.

Work Performance *Review* - System Control Form

Please ensure that you send this form to the:

- **Principal Personnel Adviser (if you are in a Stratum I or II role), or**
- **Chief Consultant Organisation (if you are in a Stratum III role)**

within five days of your review meeting.

Your answers will allow an assessment of the effectiveness of the Work Performance Review System and the use of the system by your leader.

The detail of the information you provide is confidential.

A summary of results will be given to you and your leader. If you are a member of a small team your input will be combined with input from the team members of other small teams to allow the organisation to meet its undertaking of confidentiality.

Please answer the following questions:

	Strongly agree	Mildly agree	Mildly disagree	Strongly disagree
1. My leader:				
(a) prepared adequately for the review	☐	☐	☐	☐
(b) allowed me time to prepare for the review	☐	☐	☐	☐
(c) devoted an appropriate amount of time for the meeting	☐	☐	☐	☐
(d) discussed all the key issues properly	☐	☐	☐	☐
(e) encouraged and supported my input.	☐	☐	☐	☐
2. My leader has given me due recognition of my work performance often enough during the period reviewed.	☐	☐	☐	☐
3. My leader honoured commitments made to me in my last review.	☐	☐	☐	☐
4. I was able to provide honest advice to my leader on his/her leadership.	☐	☐	☐	☐
5. The review was fair.	☐	☐	☐	☐

Comments:

_____

_____

_____

_____

_____

_____

_____

Confidentiality

_____
Signature

Access to this form is strictly controlled and restricted.

_____
Name

It is a Comalco Smelting policy that a leader is not permitted to access, or attempt to access, a control form completed by a member of his or her team. Failure to comply with this policy may result in the termination of the leader's employment.

_____
Date

_____
Your leader's name

Only people occupying the following roles have access to this form - team member; managers one and two removed; Principal Personnel Adviser and Chief Consultant Organisation.

Figure 17.2 Work Performance Review – System Control Form

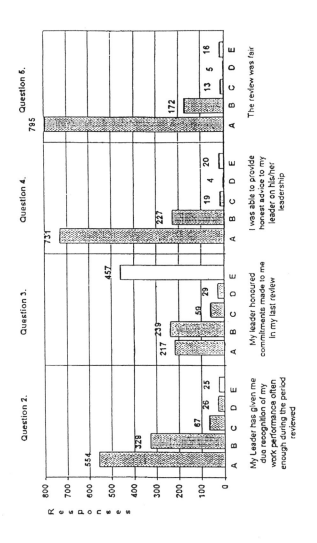

Work Performance Review –
Control Form Summary

NZAS

Comalco Smelting

A = Strongly Agree; B = Mildly Agree; C = Midly Disagree; D = Strongly Disagree; E = No Response

Figure 17.3   Work Performance Review – Control Form Summary

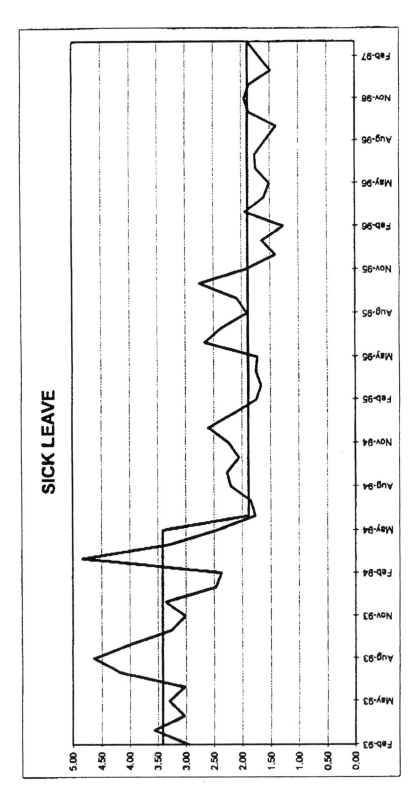

Figure 17.4   Sick Leave (% Time)

18 *Creating High Perfomance Teams*

Working Together

There is a mountain of literature about the importance of teamwork. The most obvious examples come from the world of sport where individuals interviewed in the media seem compelled to stress the importance of the team above individual achievement or success (except, perhaps, when negotiating their contracts). Similarly motivational posters inform us that 'There is no *i* in Team' or to be part of a 'star team rather than a team of stars'.

While the statements expressed are admirable, they are simplistic; exhortation does not replace explanation. We regard the apparent conflict between team and individual as a false dichotomy. Of course individuals have needs but, as we have argued throughout this book, life and achievement is a social process. We cannot succeed without others. It is not enough to emphasise good teamwork: we must also ask what it is and how to achieve it.

We have discussed in some depth the work of leadership and the steps and traps of team leadership and membership (Chapter 14). Putting this into practice is not easy and so we developed a specific training course, called Working Together, which has been designed to help people to develop their skills in both leadership and team membership.

The original course was designed as a result of an observation by Dr John Cliffe, who was head of HR at the engineering company Tube Investment in the early 1980s. Macdonald and Stamp, whilst working at BIOSS, Brunel University, had been involved in some consultancy work for him when one evening he explained to Macdonald that he had run organisational theory courses for the organisation. He thought they were good in content but people found them boring. On the other hand, he had sent people on what were called outward bound courses, involving challenging exercises in the wilderness, which they had found exciting but, he noted, he could see no change in people's behaviour or clear learning. He consequently asked Macdonald if he could design a training course that combined the excitement with the learning. Macdonald took this idea to his brother R. Macdonald, who at the time was a serving British army officer teaching at the Army staff college. Together they designed what was to become the course.

The key components of the course remain the same (see Box 18.1) although content and process have changed and developed considerably. Today there are a variety of forms of the course, of different lengths and with different emphases.

The original course, run by I. Macdonald and his brother R. Macdonald, brought in management theory, stratified system theory and systems leadership theory, exercises, presentations and case-study work. As far as we know this was the first course not only to use video, but to use it reflectively to compare actual behaviour with concepts taught on the course. The focus was, and is, the analysis of social process in leadership and teamwork.

On a visit to the UK in 1986 another of the authors, Stewart, attended the course and after redesign, implemented it in his business unit in Australia, Comalco Smelting then part of CRA. Terry Palmer attended in Australia and introduced the course into his business unit

---

Box 18.1 Essential Components of Working Together

- The courses are a collaboration between the company and Macdonald Associates, each providing a co-presenter.
- Each co-presenter has a clear role, and has been trained in that role.
- The course is a combination of presentation, experiential learning, indoor and outdoor tasks, role-plays, case studies and discussion.
- Exercises are videotaped and debriefed using the recorded material.
- Exercises are analysed in terms of safety and a course report written which includes a safety report.
- Each participant has an opportunity to experience a leadership role and team membership roles.

(Comalco Rolled Products) and then at Hamersley Iron. Both Stewart and Palmer used the courses as part of a much broader cultural change programme with highly significant results (see Chapter 19, What Difference Has This Made?).

There are now many types of organisations that have used the course around the world, each modifying the programme slightly and adapting the content but maintaining the essential components.

The course

Although the course varies the background, context and purpose usually remain the same. An example is shown below in Box 18.2.

Box 18.2 Working Together Course

BACKGROUND

The business environment is never still: changes occur in demand, technology and opportunity that require changes in the way work is organised and carried out. However, work will always involve people who determine the success or failure of a business. This success or failure is in turn strongly influenced by how people are led and whether they feel part of a team. Business is not simply a matter of understanding technology or finances; it is also critically about understanding people: how they feel about work and what they are asked and want to do.

This course assumes that people want to be constructive and creative and it is their environment and working relationships that influence how their energies are directed. An organisation that treats its people like machines, constrained by petty rules and regulations that contradict common sense and a sense of fairness, will fail. Building trust is not a simple matter; what one person regards as fair or honest may not exactly correspond with another person's view. Understanding how people see the world and acting on this understanding is a key element of leadership work and is central to this course.

PURPOSE

The purpose of this course is to help participants improve their understanding of leadership and teamwork so that they can apply this understanding at work and so become better managers, team leaders and members.

OUTCOMES

Participants should come away with an understanding of the core ideas and principles on

---

which the company bases its organisation and culture. In particular participants should be more aware of:

- their own behaviour and how this influences leadership and team membership;
- how to improve systems at work;
- the expectations of their role and their work;
- the rationale behind what the leadership of the company is trying to achieve;
- the importance of clarity in assigning, receiving and recognising work and tasks;
- the effects of leadership on organisation, structure and business culture.

METHODS

Most people are bored by sitting in classrooms listening to presentations/lectures hour after hour. This course is intended to be participative. While there are some presentations on the core material interaction is encouraged and the programme will be adjusted to meet the needs of the course participants. In addition there are syndicate tasks and practical exercises both in the teaching room and elsewhere.

Participants should wear casual/work clothing that they do not mind getting wet or dirty. Any person with a physical disability should make this known to the course leaders (this will not preclude involvement in the course). As you would expect, everything we'll do can and will be done safely.

Working Together Course
Timetable

DAY ONE

9.00am	Welcome and Introductions
	Context and Purpose of the Course
	Explanation of Course Process
10.45am	Morning Tea
11.00am	Activity: Jigsaw
12.00pm	Lunch
1.00pm	Theory Session: Team Leadership and Membership
2.15pm	Exercise 1: Blind Crossing
4.00pm	Afternoon Tea
4.15pm	Theory Session: Values Continua & Case Studies
6.30pm	Dinner
7.30pm	Crocodile Creek Briefing

DAY TWO

8.00am	Theory Session: Nature of Work and Task Assignment
9.00am	Exercise 2: Piranha Peril
10.00am	Morning Tea
11.00am	Theory Session: Work Complexity
12.00pm	Lunch
1.00pm	Theory Session: Authorities and Accountabilities
2.15pm	Exercise 3: Nuclear Waste
4.00pm	Afternoon Tea
4.45pm	Case Study Presentations

6.30pm	Dinner
7.30pm	Open Forum

DAY THREE

8.00am	Exercise 4: Kontiki
10.00am	Morning Tea
10.15am	Theory Session: Systems Leadership 1
12.00pm	Lunch
1.00pm	Theory Session: Systems Leadership 2
2.30pm	Exercise 5: Kubyashi Maru
4.00pm	Afternoon Tea
4.15pm	Theory Session: Systems Leadership 3
	Systems Review Assignment and Syndicate Work
6.30pm	Dinner
7.30pm	Crocodile Creek Plan Presentations

DAY FOUR

8.00am	Exercise 6: Crocodile Creek
10.30am	Morning Tea
11.00am	Systems Review Presentations
12.00pm	Lunch
2.00pm	Where do we go from here? – Applying the learning in the workplace
3.00pm	Finish

Courses are preferably residential and for 12 participants.

THEORY CONTENT

The 'theory' sessions cover systems leadership concepts and Jaques' levels of work. Depending upon the organisational needs and roles of participants, certain parts will be covered in more depth than others. What are always covered are the concepts of culture, values and mythologies and the team leadership and membership model.

EXERCISES

There is a range of outdoor and indoor team exercises. Two teams of six each rotate the leadership role and carry out exercises in parallel. We have developed a range of activities to be able to accommodate different abilities amongst participants and different physical settings and climates. No exercise requires above ordinary physical ability and no-one is forced to participate particularly if they have any reservations (for example, if they do not want to do any lifting). Safety is always paramount and all exercises have safety rules (with penalties for their breach).

CASE STUDIES

We also have a wide range of short case studies, which teams work on, analyse and present their answer(s). We write them for a particular organisation or industry to address topics relevant to the business at that time.

It is interesting to note how culture changes have been reflected in the answers given over time. In the late 1980s we used the case study *Dear John*, reproduced below in Box 18.3. This case study was developed because Comalco and CRA in general had identified safety as a key area for improvement. At first we had a range of answers but it was not unusual for 'John' to be moved, counselled (whatever that meant) or even sent on holiday to 'recover'. We were regarded as draconian for arguing for dismissal. Today there is very little point using this case study in Rio Tinto (formerly CRA) as the culture has changed so much it is 'too easy'. John's behaviour is not tolerated.

ROLE PLAYS

Either as part of the case studies or in addition to them, participants are asked to role play situations like interviews or dealing with difficult issues. This is to give an opportunity to put answers into practice and highlight the difference between answers in theory and answers in practice (see also core social process skills for leaders) (see Box 18.4).

FEEDBACK TO PARTICIPANTS ON EXERCISES

Box 18.3 Dear John – Working Together 'Case Study' Briefing Instructions

You are the Manager of John's section. One of your superintendents, John Davies, has been given a task by you.

You have asked him to install some new machinery (which he is used to) and train two new operators to use it. The successful installation of this machinery is critical to meet agreed orders from a regular client. You are in a very competitive market.

John Davies has taken longer than he agreed was needed to set up the machine (two weeks' delay) and, because it was installed badly, it is unreliable. Further, he has failed to train the operators properly. They constantly call on fitters and maintenance support (who have done more training of the operators than John). Your client, unhappily, has said he will not renew the contract.

John's time keeping is poor and the 'last straw' is that John has allowed the operators to use the machine without the safety guard in a bid to speed up work; no one has been injured and he did not instruct them to do so – they were being helpful. You are going to have to do something.

You have found out several facts about John:

1. He is 43, married with two children.
2. His wife left him one year ago, with the children.
3. One of his children has recently been in court.
4. John is reported to be drinking heavily.
5. However, even before these troubles he has been disciplined for bad time keeping.
6. Although 'bright', he has twice been passed over for promotion.
7. He has worked for the company for 12 years.

Assume you have already spoken to John who has verified that the facts relating to work are true as stated.

What are you going to do?

Box 18.4   Social Processes and Behaviour

We always concentrate absolutely on *behaviour* not 'attitude' or intent, and then consider the consequences of that behaviour.

Participants discuss the way they have approached activities and exercises. They are asked their views as to how well they have achieved the output *and* worked as team leader and team members. This view is then tested against the video record. Often the experience of dissonance is profound. People are regularly surprised at how quickly they have rewritten history either more positively or negatively. The point about the feedback is that it is made against the criteria of the models, especially the team leadership and membership steps and traps.

This feedback can be highly sensitive. Often it is enough for people to see on the video that they have not clearly assigned tasks, or asked for contributions or co-operated by helping each other. Under pressure people will often skip the thinking involved in identifying critical issues, preferring to relieve their anxiety by leaping straight into the action (see Box 18.5).

ROLES

The roles of the co-presenters are critical. We regard it as a principle that one be from the organisation (ideally in a leadership role) and one a consultant (from Macdonald Associates). The external presenter's work is:

* to manage the overall social process;
* to give primary feedback on exercises;
* to ensure technical accuracy of the concepts.

The internal presenter's work is:

* to act as a role model and symbol that the organisation is serious about this work;
* to provide examples from the workplace of good and poor practice;
* to produce technical knowledge of the organisation, for example, policies, systems, processes;
* to reinforce the business case for the training.

This is not a course that a managing director opens with a short introduction of how important the course is and then leaves it to external or internal consultants. The managing director must make very clear that this is the way business is going to be done and why they have made that decision.

Box 18.5   Different Learning Experiences

On one course we had two teams, one which was made up primarily of people involved in research and development work, the other made up primarily of operators. In one exercise the R+D team spent almost the entire time planning and constructing a prototype. They left almost no time to actually carry out the real task. In contrast the other team started building before the leader had even finished briefing the team. An exasperated leader asked what they were doing, as he was only halfway through explaining the task; 'don't worry' came the reply, 'tell us as we go along!' Neither team had a successful outcome on that task. With both teams present for the debrief it was an interesting learning experience.

We score each team's exercises in terms of output, social process and safety. The teams are left to themselves to determine how far they see the exercises as competitive. This also gives an insight into current culture.

The feedback at a personal level is mediated by the external presenter. If these courses were run entirely in house, even by trained co-presenters, the executive authority would become dominant and it would be very difficult, if not impossible, for people not to experience the course as formally part of a performance appraisal (see Box 18.6).

Box 18.6   Terry Palmer and the Working Together Course

In one instance the top executive team made up the course. The two teams were fiercely competitive and at times actively sought to sabotage the other team's activities. In the debrief, which pointed this out quite graphically, the defence was: 'Well, these are just games. Of course we are not like this in the workplace'. The managing director, who was co-presenting, quietly responded: 'You are exactly like this in the workplace and that is why you are on this course; to learn some teamwork'. This demonstrated the importance of the role of the internal co-presenter. Behaviour changed very quickly.

In another instance a course participant wrote of Terry Palmer's involvement in the Working Together courses:

'Terry attended each of these courses in full. I believe that there were at least ten sessions that year, meaning that Terry made a personal investment of ten weeks of his business and personal time. Looking back now I still find this level of personal investment astounding. There was no sense of rush and Terry's focus was on the job in hand and as a participant you felt you had his individual attention.

The courses were now being rolled out across the whole business to the entire workforce. Thus attendees included many people who had never been on a course, and certainly not a residential one paid for by 'the company'. Sadly for Terry he couldn't co-run them all, or even personally attend them all so he had made a videotape of him giving an introduction to explain why he wanted people to go through this training. Courses were starting at all sites and Terry was dropping in to demonstrate his commitment to the programme. He went into the training room and sat at the back while introductions went on.

At a suitable break he got up to introduce himself which meant walking round the horseshoe of participants shaking hands. As Terry did so, in his unusual relaxed yet confident way one of the participants was heard to whisper to another,

'Who's that?'

'I think it's Terry Palmer.'

'What the MD?'

'Yeah, I think so.'

Terry approached, held out his hand and said,

'How are you, I'm Terry Palmer.'

With a slightly cynical grin on his face the response came:

'Yeah, but who are you really mate?'

Quick as a flash, and with a smile as broad as the Nullarbor, Terry replied,

'I'm Terry Palmer alright and I've got a video to prove it!'

Terry had caused his usual dissonance and with his usual humour and good grace.'

PURPOSE

This last point raises the question as to the clarity of purpose. The course can be run as an assessment centre or an educational process. It should be clear to participants which is the case. We have run both types. Even when the purpose is educational it would be dishonest not to acknowledge that people will be making judgments. That is part of any endeavour where people work together. As Palmer put it:

> 'I am going to spend the next 3 days watching you solve problems and using leadership and team membership models. Do you think I can do that without forming some views?'

It is however important to emphasise that it is a learning process, where mistakes made do not have the same consequences as in the workplace. Failing to build a cardboard tower is not the same as failing to install equipment. The external consultant must mediate and point out, for example, that implementing models should improve with practice so that early leaders of activities have a tougher task than later.

CRITICAL ISSUES

Clarity of purpose, as with any activity is very important but there are also other critical issues that must be addressed if the Working Together process is to be really effective.

How to link the training with the work of the organisation?

This not only helps to set an organisational context but must show how this activity is to help the organisation and is part of a strategy for change. We have seen many instances where an organisation decides that 'we need some leadership and teamwork training' and embarks on a series of courses. These may be of some benefit but if they are not linked to an overall strategy and consistency in the use of theory and language, they can become a 'sheep-dip' process with little long-term impact.

In the CRA manual 'Working Together', the members of a team tasked with advising on leadership training wrote:

> Whilst an important aspect of implementing Systems Leadership is conducting the training Course, which is now being done in a number of Business Units, this will not, in itself, achieve any beneficial, lasting change. Only when the Business Unit's systems have been reviewed and the changes necessary to align them with the vision and strategy have been implemented will the potential benefits be realised. ... The work done in the Group (especially in Hamersley and Comalco Smelting) to provide training in Systems Leadership as part of an integrated process to change the culture of a Business Unit has provided considerable learnings. Most important is the requirement to undertake an integrated set of work for implementing Systems leadership throughout the Business. This will contribute to all employees perceiving that their management has "constancy of purpose". It would be simplistic and incorrect to focus solely on conducting the training course.

It also states:

> Leadership training is a topical issue in the corporate world. The current fad is to use outdoor, experiential learning which is loosely underpinned by behavioural theory. The linkage created

for the participants by the trainers and the leaders of the organisation's strategy is often tenuous. In contrast, the outdoor activities included in the Systems Leadership training Course are used to reinforce the theory; the theory which CRA has played a significant role in developing and on which CRA's organisation is predicated.

How to link the training with *individual change*?

Even if the organisational context is clear and this is seen as an integral part of the strategy individual participants need preparation and follow-up. Ideally participants should have a prior discussion with their manager to discuss the purpose of the course and what the individual needs to work on and improve. This might be social process in general or specific steps such as team member co-operation, better contributions, better task assignments or review.

After the course there should be a debrief. What has been learned? How can this be put into practice and monitored? Ideally tasks should be assigned and reported on. For example, people might be asked to apply that learning on the day-to-day social process of leading their own team, a system (re)design task, identifying mythologies or a cross-functional team project.

How to have consistency in presentation?

The course co-presenters must be trained and competent. As was mentioned, Macdonald Associates trains and accredits associates in the process. This competency is reviewed annually and new ideas and changes incorporated. There is also a 'train the trainer' course designed for internal co-presenters. This intensive experiential course is not easy and the leadership of the organisation must ensure the quality of delivery. There are many courses on leadership and teamwork but in our experience none is integrated as part of an overall coherent theory of organisation, none is a collaborative intervention requiring teaching partnership with the organisation's leaders.

We are not claiming that in all our practice these critical issues have always been completely addressed. What is evident, as our model of critical issues would predict, is that if they are not, the positive impact is significantly less than it could otherwise be and indeed the process may be detrimental.

Cultural relevance

Many courses and training are culturally biased and culturally limited. Because we have an underlying general model of culture these courses can be adapted to the type of organisation, industry and country. Courses have been run in the UK, Canada, Southern and Western Africa, Australia, New Zealand, China, USA, Indonesia, Russia, Ukraine and Thailand. Organisations have included, amongst others, schools, mining companies, banks and financial institutions, indigenous community organisations, non-governmental organisations, local government, health services, religious organisations and social services. Participants have included truck drivers, CEOs, miners, children as young as 14, aborigines in remote communities, priests and bishops, nurses, bank managers, traders, police, students and community leaders.

The courses have been adapted according to the context in which they are being carried out, for example, in the following two case studies (Box 18.7 and Box 18.8). However, the underlying process remains the same and in our experience the values continua have provided a valid cross-cultural link, especially when considering mythologies and behaviour. We find the same values but different behaviours that are seen to demonstrate those values.

There are differences that we have noted especially with regard to leadership and teamwork. These differences could themselves be the subject of a separate book and there is always a danger of stereotyping. In general terms, however, we have found that, for example, in Australia members of teams are often reluctant to stand out from the group because, culturally, this kind of behaviour is often considered 'showing off'. This is exemplified by the existence in Australia of the 'tall poppy' syndrome where those poppies which dare to grow too tall get their heads chopped off. In the USA, the opposite seems to be true and individuals are generally keen and encouraged to stick out from the group. We find that in Russia people are initially much more formal, more likely to make assertive statements, but reluctant to reveal emotion or inner thoughts until the formal parts of the course are over, that is, over dinner, in the bar or in the sauna.

Box 18.7 Constant Constance

Constance has been an active member of the Parish of St George's for the past seven years. Prior to the death of her mother, Constance attended church on special occasions but did not get involved in any church activities.

Her mother, Mary, spent a couple of years in a nursing home and was visited regularly by the Rector James Swallow. In fact James was 'called out' a couple of times and in the final weeks of Mary's life called by every day. He conducted the funeral, which was much appreciated by Constance.

Since that day Constance has been to church every day. She participates in virtually everything, remembering to apologise for the things she cannot attend. She has also been parish treasurer and now remains on parish council as well as chairs the social committee, helps at the Op Shop, with the banking and with morning teas on a Sunday.

Shortly after her mother's death, Constance was operated on for the removal of cancer of the breast. Since that time she has been in good health and remains so.

Recently James was told by Constance that the church was to benefit from her will. It is clear that Constance has dedicated almost her whole life to the church.

Constance has a rather 'snappy' approach to people and from time to time she has been very bossy and people have come to James to complain.

Last week two people came to see him:

Pamela the manager of the Op Shop (which raises $12 000 a year for parish funds) has had enough of her sharpness and bossy nature and has threatened to resign from her position if Constance does not remove herself from the volunteer helper list.

Annabel, a young parish council member and staunch helper each Sunday morning called James to complain about Constance and her abruptness and her off-putting approach to newcomers. 'I can't put up with it much longer!' she said. 'Something has got to be done, she is upsetting so many people.'

You are the Rector, what will you do?

Role play (10minutes) your meetings to resolve this problem, with Pamela, Annabel, and Constance.

Box 18.8   Bacon and Egg Sandwich

You are the manager of a team working in the field (bush). One of your team members, Frank, rolled a Toyota on a straight bit of sealed road this morning. The Toyota is wrecked (a write off). Frank told Peter, the person who helped him out of the vehicle, that because he was late for work he was eating his breakfast while driving. He dropped some of his food and when he looked up after trying to pick it up, he was off the road and it was too late to do anything. Peter said Frank smelled as though he had been drinking.

The accident investigation showed that there was no evidence of the brakes being used and the tyre tracks just veered gently off the road into the ditch. This would be consistent (agree) with Frank's explanation.

The police investigation showed Frank had a very high blood alcohol reading and he was charged.

Frank had been at a party last night. He wasn't sure what time he got home, but he had been to bed and felt okay when he got up in the morning. He said he certainly didn't feel drunk.

This is the second vehicle written off by your team and you know your boss will not be pleased. Last month Mark had a head-on collision on a blind corner. He was counselled and everyone was given a talking to about safe driving.

Frank is a really good worker and has had no other problems at work. He has only been with the team for three months and has a wife and two young children.

You have been told to report to your boss in one hour to explain what you are going to do about Frank.

What are you going to tell your boss?

We have endeavoured to remove a sexist bias, sometimes perceived because of outdoor, physical activities by including a wider range of activities. It is interesting to note that the early courses run in Comalco acquired the symbolic name 'Rambo courses'. This was partly due to the outdoor activities and partly because Brigadier R. Macdonald, commando trained, was a co-presenter. We tried to address this but failed. Eventually and paradoxically it became a help since the activities did not require great physical skills – but did require the application of appropriate mental processing ability and social process skills. The 'macho' approach, when taken, was exposed, inevitably failed, and then provided valuable material for discussing sexism. There were women on all courses.

There have been over 30 000 participants on various versions of the Working Together course worldwide. It is difficult to measure the impact in overall terms since the purpose is not always the same. It is our experience that the positive impact depends upon addressing the critical issues outlined above. When this is done, and particularly when the Working Together programme is part of an overall strategy for change, the impact is significant at both an organisational and individual level. The case studies at the end of this book examine this in more depth and refer to specific outcomes according to the type of organisation. It would not be valid to assess the Working Together courses on their own, since they are part of a process and part of an integrated theory and approach. Indeed this theory would predict that implementing the Working Together programme on its own would not have a major, positive effect and may indeed be negative. One recent analysis produced advice that made us wary of implementation because the organisation was not assessed to have the quality in leadership and systems to sustain what is taught. This is only one step in the process of change.

WHAT IT IS NOT

This Working Together process does not seek to change personality. It seeks to change behaviour. We do not confront people at a personal level, nor search for their inner thoughts and feelings. It is not a T. Group[1] process or pseudo-psychotherapy course. We believe a person's thoughts are their own business. Many people have fought wars and died over freedom of thought. While such personality-based courses often produce deep feelings, these do not last and do not result in behaviour change. The Working Together course clarifies what behaviour is required to help the organisation to be successful. It tries to help people improve their skills and practice in that behaviour.

It does require skilled and trained co-presenters. Its requires people with a knowledge of stratified systems theory and systems leadership theory. It also requires people who enjoy the creativity of others. The course helps to embed a shared language to underpin the culture and provides a common experience that a CEO can enjoy sharing with an operator, an archbishop with a vicar or a teacher with a student.

We leave the last words on Working Together to Terry Palmer who, as MD, could not physically co-present on every course at Hamersley Iron and so he made an introductory video. This was the script:

Welcome to this four-day course on team leadership and team membership.

Please excuse this video introduction, but I am unable to be with you today. Nevertheless, I do want to welcome you and make some comments on why you are here.

Every Hamersley employee participates in these courses. This takes a lot of time and consumes a lot of resources but I am sure it is worth it. Once you have finished the four days I think you will agree it's an investment in our future.

Just a few words about the PURPOSE of this course and what we want each of you to get from it. Firstly, we want each of you to learn a lot more about what TEAM LEADERSHIP is all about.

Secondly, for you to learn a lot more about what TEAMWORK and TEAM MEMBERSHIP is all about.

However, that is not where it ends!

We want you to go away from this course and change the way you behave as leaders and change the way you behave as members of a team.

All of us, including everyone in leadership roles, are in teams as members of those teams. So we must learn about both aspects ... and then we must make a concerted effort to change our behaviour.

For almost every one of us, the effort in changing behaviour will be great, the change required is large.

---

1   Facilitated experiential learning, focused on the here and now, in an unstructured small group setting.

It is not easy to change your behaviour. But change we must. The task for each of you is this:

To learn as much as you can about leadership and team membership and then, immediately after this course, to apply that learning to the way you go about your day-to-day job. The resources you have to do this are quite considerable.

There are the course materials and leaders while you are here, plus your fellow course members.

Back on the job you will have your manager and the other people around you who will also be working to change their behaviour. They should also be a resource. What about timing? When are you required to make this change in behaviour?

I want you to change your behaviour as soon as you start back in your regular work roles. Immediately!

Why so quickly?

Because the evidence is very clear. If you do not make a really big effort to change in the first few days after you return to your job then there will be no change in behaviour at all.

So that is a task that team working demands from each one of you. It is the most important task that will be assigned to you for a long time. It is not the only task that will come out of this course but the presenters will tell you about these other tasks.

We are doing all this work on teams because we need to continue building a better Hamersley. That is possible only if each of you is heavily involved.

Over the last couple of years Hamersley has changed a lot. It must change a lot more. This will only be possible if we have your help and commitment.

Let me describe the sort of Hamersley we are looking to build. It is best described by how the average shop floor employee would feel about their leaders, their managers and their employer. The average employee would feel like this:

'My manager really cares for my safety and well being.'

'My manager trusts me because:

* *confidential information is shared with me.*

* *I am allowed to get on with my job.'*

Remember, you cannot expect the people who work for you to trust you if you show that you don't trust them. Continuing with how the average shop floor employee would feel:

'My manager involves me in planning the work that has to be done. My suggestions are valued. All in all I am involved in the decision making.'

'Tasks are assigned to me clearly and the priorities made clear – I am trained well and given interesting work to do.'

'Although my manger is not forever checking on me s/he keeps an eye on how I am going. If I get into real difficulties I am not left to flounder because my manager steps in with help and advice.'

I am sure almost all of you would agree that if the average shop floor employee is really going to feel like this then Hamersley will have to change a lot more yet.

Core social process skills for leaders

We have seen that just knowing what to do is not usually enough. People need examples, role models and practice. We have attempted to address this with the Working Together courses but it was evident that a short course, even if intense and residential, is not enough to expect all people not only to change their behaviour but also to be good at new skills. One of the principals of Macdonald Associates, Tony Dunlop, a clinical psychologist, developed the next step: core social process skills training (Dunlop, 2000).

This grew out of the need for skills, not only in teamwork, but those required if systems are to be implemented effectively. The need became clear from performance reviews and Working Together courses. These core social skills can be taught in a whole course, as a smaller set or directly in relation to systems implementation (see Box 18.9).

Further details of this programme can be found on the Macdonald Associates website: www.maconsultancy.com.

Box 18.9   Core Process Skills Training

Like the Working Together course, core process skills training courses require a fully trained, social process consultant who cannot only teach but demonstrate the skills in role play and in real time. Like the Working Together course, variations of this programme have been run in many different countries, cultures and climates. And like the Working Together courses, the material can be dangerous if not delivered properly and professionally and with a clear purpose. There is no single template but again certain elements are necessary:

- collaboration between client and consultant especially as to context, purpose and delivery;
- fully trained leaders with a clear role;
- the 'course' in at least two parts, with learning followed by a period for practice with follow-up reflection and practice and
- use of video and observation to reflect and learn from a structured model.

---

19 *So What? What Difference Has This Made?*

There are many books about principles and modes of leadership, change management and organisational design. Very few attempt to link the ideas with actual, specific outcomes. Some may make general claims of significant increases in productivity or efficiency but do not provide data. Perhaps the exceptions here are in specialist areas: the internationally recognised Dupont Workplace Safety Training programmes and modular training materials for the support and further development of safety professionals, line and operations managers and line supervisors , or in technical processes such as six sigma.

This is understandable at two levels. First and most important, cause is actually difficult to attribute accurately. For example, a system change or behavioural change in one area may affect another area positively or negatively. An improvement in productive behaviour or better teamwork may coincide with improvements in technical processes or an upturn in the market. How do we separate these strands fairly? Second, change is made by people putting ideas into practice. That practice may vary – even unintentionally – or the ideas may be misunderstood, or both.

Organisations are not easily made into laboratories with experimental and control groups. People will vary in their opinions as to what caused what. In the words of an old saying, 'success has many fathers, but failure is an orphan'. Despite these difficulties it is worth trying to ascertain what effect has occurred and whether it is attributable to the implementation of particular ideas. For this purpose we have included several case studies at the end of this book and in the enclosed CD that discuss systems leadership in action across a wide range of organisations. We look at implementation in diverse situations such as the Anglican Church, schools and a variety of industries. They demonstrate that the concepts are not limited culturally nor to a sector or type of organisation, since the proposition is that they are based on fundamental principles of purposeful, human behaviour.

We also have to bear in mind that not all change is measured in output alone. Qualitative measures such as personal job satisfaction, a sense of achievement and pride in work are also relevant and meaningful to members of an organisation.

In this chapter we take a look at some changes and results from several examples where the introduction of systems leadership concepts was careful and deliberate and did not coincide with technological change, where the impact was recognised not only in the organisation but also in the wider society.

Before examining these cases we would like to reinforce the argument that consultants do not bring about change. The leadership of the organisation brings about change. Overall a change process is a partnership between the leadership, advisers (internal and external) and the members/employees of the organisation. This is reflected in the authorship of this book. Consultants who claim to 'change the culture' do no such thing. If changes occur, it positively involves many people working hard over a long time. Leave the silver bullets for the vampires. The most important platform for change is a coherent, integrated set of concepts that is available to and understood by people involved in the process. This is what we have attempted to provide in this book. This will not be the product of one mind but the product of working relationships. It is imperative that the concepts are internally consistent and make sense. The first test of any articulation of process is whether it can logically be justified or falsified. It must predict its own failures.

For example, in one organisation we worked in the change process that was almost entirely based on the Working Together course (the dangerous 'sheep-dip' – the idea that all you need to do is take your people through the course without any other support or systems work). Very little structural or systemic change occurred in parallel. Unsurprisingly, very little positive change occurred and the course itself became a negative symbol only serving to expose the gap between good practice in theory and the evident poor practice in reality. Systems remained that contradicted the teaching, and the leadership handed the process to HR which, as predicted, made things worse, despite some heroic efforts from the HR team.

Although this was a failure in terms of positive outcome, it actually reinforced the conceptual framework by producing the predicted poor results. It was not, however, our proudest moment and Macdonald Associates should have had the courage to withdraw sooner given the conditions.

In another example we worked with an organisation where there was a lack of capability in several key roles in the CEO team, as defined by our capability model. There was a lack of mental processing ability (according to the definitions) and an excess of energy and the use of power. Despite the CEO acknowledging this, it was not possible at the time to remove the individuals, and the change programme faltered because it was implemented in a patchy way. This is *not* to say the CEO was wrong. We must work in partnership, not to a set formula. All we can do is explain and predict that, if it is not judged appropriate to make certain changes, then this will affect the outcome. As was outlined at the beginning of Part 4, there is an ideal process but conditions for an ideal process cannot be created artificially. If the process is to be modified, so should expectations.

The remainder of this chapter takes a particular case (or series of related cases) that had a significant impact not only on the organisations concerned but the society itself. It has been the subject of television programmes, business magazine articles, newspaper columns and books. It could easily be a book or books in itself. We do not intend to explore all the potential issues. The industrial relations aspect has been well documented in Terry Ludeke's book *A Line in the Sand* (1996). The transcripts of the Australian Industrial Relations Commission (AIRC) case are available publicly. We concentrate here on the relationship between the systems changes and specific outcomes, with the intention of demonstrating a clear link between the two. We also do so because almost all of the material presented here was also presented to the AIRC and accepted as evidence. In other words, this data has literally been exposed to detailed, public examination and found to be valid.

The case studies concern a major change within two companies that were part of CRA in Australia during the 1990s. The companies, Comalco and Hamersley Iron, embarked on a major change programme which eventually led to almost the entire workforce choosing to change their terms of employment, a change that many said could not happen whether or not they were personally in agreement with it in principle. This was generally described as a move to 'all staff' conditions or 'individual contracts' for those in operator or tradesperson roles. Hamersley Iron was a major iron ore mining and rail operation in the Pilbara area of North Western Australia. Comalco was an aluminium mining and smelting operation with sites in Queensland, Tasmania and New Zealand. While much public attention has been paid to the eventual contractual change, the leadership of those organisations did not see the contractual change as the sole purpose. The contractual change was the outcome of a much more detailed strategy implemented in order to improve the leadership and systems of the organisation which used systems leadership concepts to bring about change. In direct terms, a person's behaviour does not change because they sign a piece of paper; it changes because the leadership and systems have changed.

Comalco

Comalco's smelting business unit consisted of three major aluminium smelters: one in New Zealand (New Zealand Aluminium Smelting or NZAS), one in Tasmania (Bell Bay) and one in Queensland (Boyne Island). The NZAS story is told in detail in the case study reproduced in the back of this book and on the enclosed CD. In more general terms Karl Stewart became managing director of Comalco Smelting in 1987. In his previous roles as head of an organisational development team and vice president – organisational effectiveness, he had been concerned about the quality of leadership and the negative effect of certain systems. He had not only identified the predominant 'them and us' division in employment but specifically linked this to the nature of employment systems. In effect, Comalco Smelting, like many other traditional industries, appeared to be two parallel organisations: one a 'staff' organisation largely attempting to function as a meritocracy with at least some systems of performance management and pay for performance; the other an 'award' organisation, of 'workers', hourly paid, with a range of role bands, negotiated systems of pay, attendance and overtime. Of course, this is the old 'white collar/blue collar' distinction, a distinction which was simply assumed by many in leadership and HR roles as if it was some sort of natural order. Essentially the staff were 'management' and primarily identified with the company while the 'hourly' employees were the 'workers' and primarily identified with the union. This was the case right across Comalco, Hamersley and most mining and heavy industry sites in Australia and many other countries. What was also apparent was that behaviour was very different between the two groups. Two very obvious and symbolic differences were sick leave and time management. In an article in the *Business Review Weekly* (BRW) (BRW, 31/1/1994) Stewart said, 'the difference between staff and award workers in terms of sick leave is a ratio of one to 10. In other words for every one day of sick leave taken by staff, award workers take 10'. With regard to time management staff generally did not watch the clock and had no punch-clocks (clocking in and out). Workers (under the award) left exactly on time and felt they were 'paid for time, not work'. This was also demonstrated by the very existence of overtime for one group but not the other.

This may seem obvious and is easy to describe; addressing it, however, is not merely a question of putting everyone on salary. How these systems are addressed, identified, redesigned and implemented is crucial. For example, the entire management team of the NZAS smelter met in Christchurch for several days of intense work. In two days every system was examined in terms of whether it was and should be a system of equalisation or differentiation. After the event it was interesting to find out (through confidential interview and audit) the comments made by operators and tradespeople. These concentrated upon the more symbolic systems to test whether the company was serious. As a result 'all staff' was tested not simply by the salary system and terms of employment being equalised, but by systems such as the 'staff Christmas party'. Would it now be open to all? The answer was 'yes' – with significant success. The availability of 'biscuits' with coffee and 'beer and cheese' staff briefings were seen as a much more crucial test than even equalising the sick leave system. Car parking, transport, uniforms, canteen facilities and bathroom facilities were others that were carefully watched by those deciding firstly whether to move to staff and whether it really meant they would be 'staff'.

Preparation was meticulous and detailed, using the systems leadership training concepts. Information about change was given to all on an individual basis by their manager-once-removed (M+1). Leaders were assessed as to their capability and removed from role if not up to the new role. As Stewart said in the BRW article, 'You can't expect the troops to take any notice of improved work performance if they have evidence of poor management.'

The Working Together courses were introduced to teach the new requirements of teamwork, rather than command and control. Eventually the entire workforce went through this programme. The Working Together courses helped in these specific ways:

- They clarified work expectations with regard to leadership and teamwork.
- They introduced a common language to help in work and communication.
- They built mythologies and a culture based on a shared experience as the course provided stories of success and disasters with rafts, ropes and planks.

So was all this preparation and planning worth it? First, there was a clear measure in simply the number of people who chose to remain with the organisation and to move to staff contracts: 98 per cent. The figures for all of the Comalco plants were not ends in themselves but indicative of a coherent approach, message and leadership. Indeed all the Comalco smelters and Hamersley Iron reached figures in excess of 97 per cent.

It is interesting when considering these figures that the AIRC found specifically that there had been no element of coercion. This can be compared with other organisations that thought they would 'do the same' and only offered the contract with some cash. These operations were fortunate if many more than 50 per cent signed. However signing a contract is *not* an end in itself. What benefits did it produce? The run charts (Figures 19.1 and 19.2) were submitted and accepted as evidence by the AIRC.

Box 19.1   Comalco Smelters

Tiwai Point (NZAS): 1991–1998

- 30 per cent reduction in hours worked per tonne of saleable material
- Permanent 20 per cent workforce reduction
- Controllable costs down 10 per cent
- High purity metal yield doubled
- Smelter expansion

Bell Bay: 1990–2000

- Absenteeism halved
- Current efficiency up 1.5 per cent
- Workforce 1500 to 500
- Tonnes per annum 122 000 to 150 000
- No technology change

Boyne Smelters Limited: 1995–2000

- Increase in production from 210 to 350 tonnes/employee at levels I and II
- Employment 1300 to 774

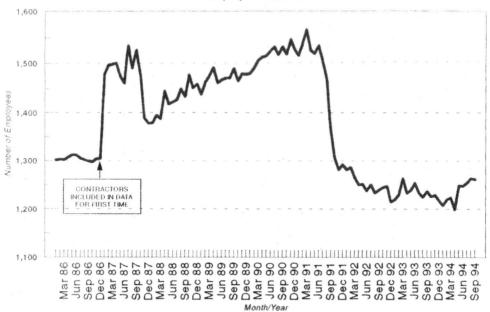

Figure 19.1   New Zealand Aluminium Smelters Employee Numbers

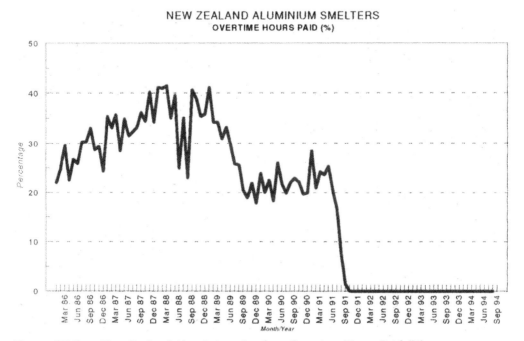

Figure 19.2   New Zealand Aluminium Smelters Overtime Hours Paid (%)

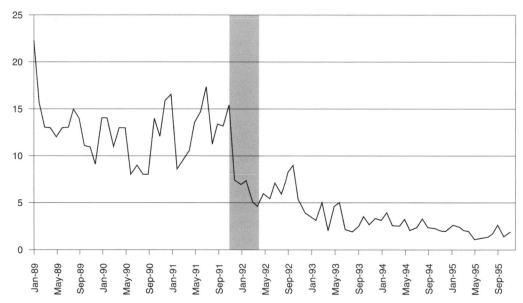

Figure 19.3   New Zealand Aluminium Smelters Off-Specification Metal (%)

These examples of output improvement are clearly linked to the change in leadership and systems. It should be clearly evident when that change occurred. All the graphs show significant change in September 1991 with preparation activity before that. It is interesting to note that the revenue to the smelter from the sale of the additional high purity metal (Figure 19.3) was greater than the cost reduction bought about by having fewer employees.

These changes caused a great deal of debate about the nature of the process, especially whether it was 'anti-union'. This is largely a distraction, even recognising the political significance. The approach was to improve leadership behaviour, appropriately re-design systems and manage symbols including understanding the symbolic significance of specific changes. *The purpose was to improve business performance by realising the capability of the workforce.* However, some months later, random interviews were conducted by external consultants about the effect of the changes on work experience. What was evident was the improvement of the work experience itself. Working around furnaces all day is not, for most, an intrinsically satisfying experience, but people reported a step change in the qualities of their working life. Examples included feedback that proved to the operators that they were listened to; they also appreciated that they could use their discretion more and understood the context better. In addition, many reported an improvement in their home life: 'I don't just go home and open the fridge for a beer, I'm spending more time with my children even helping them with homework' (cell-room operator) 'I can't wait to show my kids where I work, I never thought I'd say that, I have real pride in my work now' (tradesman electrician). These were not isolated examples.

The process was applied at the other two smelters with similar results, as shown in Figures 19.4 through 19.7.

Many of these run charts are not directly related to the 'people' systems. They are deliberately chosen to show the effect that changes in leadership and systems can have on operational technical processes.

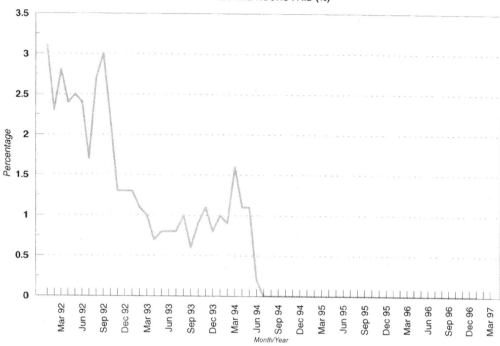

Figure 19.4   Comalco Aluminium (Bell Bay) Limited Overtime Hours Paid (%)

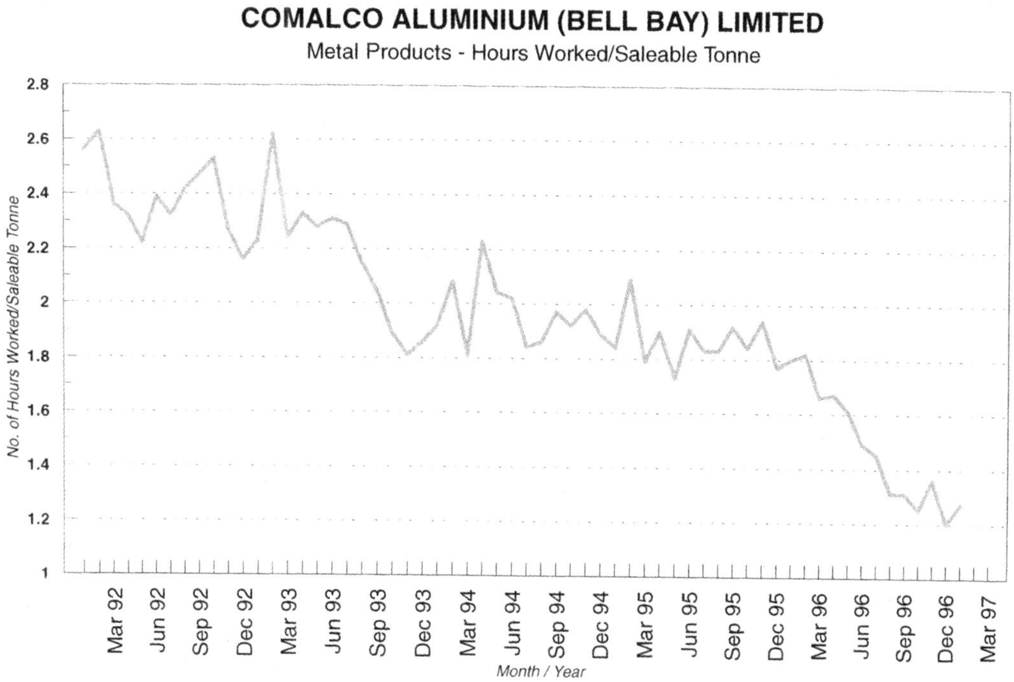

Figure 19.5   Comalco Aluminium (Bell Bay) Limited Metal Products – Hours Worked/ Saleable Tonne

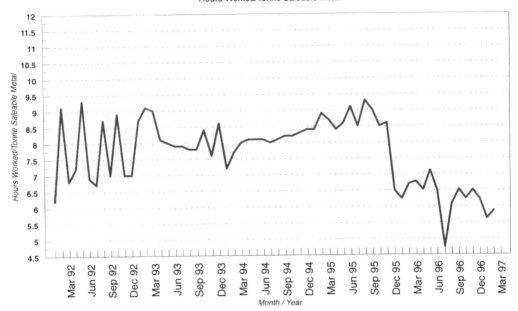

Figure 19.6   Boyne Smelters Limited Hours Worked/Saleable Tonne

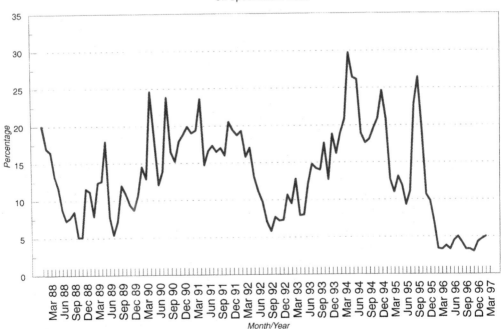

Figure 19.7   Boyne Smelters Limited Off-Specification Metal

The overall analysis of Comalco Smelters is summarised in the chart reproduced as Box 19.1, and which was prepared independently (see Box 19.1 on page 248).

Hamersley Iron

A full account of this process is contained in a paper by Joel Barolsky (1994) of the Graduate School of Management, University of Melbourne.

The Western Australian iron ore industry was characterised by industrial disputes in the 1980s – see Figure 19.8, which documents the dramatic effect after the change processes were implemented.

In June 1991 Terry Palmer was appointed managing director of Hamersley's operations. He saw the need for change and articulated it as follows:

> The 1980s had been a period of 'winning back the farm'. We wanted to restore management's right to manage and, to a large extent, we were very successful in realising this goal. Through this process, however, we in some ways encouraged the development of a very directive management style; we reinforced the 'us and them' and basically gave the unions a reason to exist. It became apparent that we had gone about as far as we should down that path. If Hamersley wanted to realise its full potential and become a truly great company, management had to effect a dramatic change in the culture of the organisation. We had to bring everyone on board; playing for the same team and by the same rules; all working together. The planning process was started so as to articulate and document this new vision for the company and to develop a coherent strategy around it. Once we had something on paper that managers could talk to, that people could relate to and get excited about, then we could really start leading the change towards a culture of commitment, continuous improvement and shared goals and values. (Barolsky, 1994)

This was not simply a matter of a general statement. Palmer then embarked on a detailed programme of change. This was largely on three fronts: systems (especially safety and HR

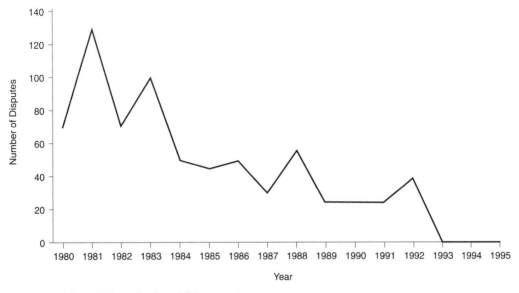

Figure 19.8   Pilbara Industrial Disputation

systems), capability and team leadership and membership. He and his team outlined key strategies:

- developing a 'customer-focused' culture;
- securing the company's resource base;
- restructuring the product mix;
- consolidating market leadership;
- improving the company's cost position;
- reorienting external affairs (Barolsky, 1994).

Joe Grimmond, who was at the time Hamersley's chief employee relations consultant, explained that:

> We recognised that many of these systems had been around for decades and were very much part of the Hamersley way of doing things. While we realised it would be difficult to fight against this momentum of the past, the senior management team had a strong resolve to succeed. This success wouldn't be measured by actual modifications to the systems themselves but rather by what behavioural change resulted from the changes to these systems.

The team identified several key systems that were in box B (authorised but counter-productive – see Chapter 10):

- active encouragement of new employees to join the union;
- seniority system of promotion;
- command and control task assignment;
- overtime system used as reward consequently encouraging inefficiency;
- pre-agreed leisure days off and personal days off, sick leave and stop work meetings;
- demarcation between unions and staff, for example, supervisors could not help in hands-on work;
- award pay increases on the basis of qualification not use of skill.

Palmer studied and learnt from the Comalco work, especially in New Zealand, and sent employees to the NZAS site. He started with key work around safety to build trust and implemented a new safety system. This initiative was led by managers in level III roles and the general managers.

He then initiated the Working Together programme and, with Macdonald, co-ran courses for his team (roles at level IV) and all people in level III roles – 13 courses in all. He used these to explain what he wanted to achieve and how he intended to achieve it. These courses (as mentioned in Chapter 18) covered all the topics of values, culture and mythologies; work complexity and capability; and the steps and traps of team leadership and membership. He and his team then reviewed the leadership roles and who was suitable.

Then the GMs in level IV roles presented the strategy in person to all employees. What was specifically emphasised was the need to be world competitive and 100 per cent reliable in supply, a target some thought was impossible. The use of the systems leadership theory in detail was complemented with business improvement projects including quality initiatives.

In June 1992 there was a major strike over refusal of an employee to join the union, which the company was no longer making compulsory. Despite the fact that enforced closed shop was illegal, the mythologies of the union leadership predicted that Palmer and the leadership at Hamersley Iron would give in. There was huge dissonance created when Palmer backed the individual's rights.

The details of this strike can be found elsewhere. However, the highly significant and symbolic battle to protect the right of people to work and to prevent harassment created many new mythologies – not least that the 'management' was prepared to be courageous and respectful of the law. The AIRC ordered a return to work on 19 June backed by the prime minister of Australia and the federal minister of industrial relations. The strike continued. On 29 June, workers voted to return to work.

In early 1993, the company was restructured. The workforce reduction of almost 20 per cent was unusual in that proportionally as many 'staff' roles went as roles covered by the 'award'. Voluntary separations were accepted by nearly all to whom they were offered. In fact a greater number left than was intended through the voluntary scheme.

This led to an opportunity to improve many systems, including a new recruitment system using input from shop floor team members. A fair treatment procedure was introduced and the Working Together course rolled out to all employees. Paul Piercy, a GM, commented:

Using these courses to introduce team concepts also provided us a chance to emphasise to supervisors the importance of their role in the new Hamersley. It was also a chance to start engendering a management style that was more participative and attuned to the needs of team members. For the shopfloor employees it was a way for us to communicate Hamersley's vision and strategies and to start building some trust and commitment to them. Most importantly, the courses were the beginning of creating more effective teams on the shopfloor. (Barolsky, 1994)

Piercy and all the GM operations co-ran these courses as did leaders in level III roles alongside Macdonald Associates' co-presenters.

Smaller symbolic changes were made, including no preferential parking for staff and supervisors eating with their crews.

Eventually staff offers of employment were made at the end of 1993. By 1 January 1994, 89 per cent had accepted. The results were similar to those at Comalco – production increased and costs fell (Figure 19.9).

In 1995, there was not as dramatic a change as was seen in the move to staff at the end of 1993 because the new systems had been introduced prior to this change. The staff employment was a consequence of change, not a cause. This demonstrates again that signing a piece of paper does not change behaviour, nor does simply leaving the union-negotiated employment conditions. It is the improved quality of leadership and the underlying work systems that provide real change.

It was the detailed, hard work of the leadership applied in a thoughtful, disciplined way that led to the change. In turn the new culture provided a platform for other important changes in work practices, quantity, safety and cost reduction. This is detailed in Rio Tinto annual reports from 1994 onwards. These later initiatives were more effective because of the work done in 1992/1993, in the same manner that the systems leadership work was more effective because of the earlier work of restructuring in the 1980s based on stratified systems theory.

The effect of the cultural change was highlighted by independent reports. In a March 1996 report in *Industrial Relations Magazine*, the following was written:

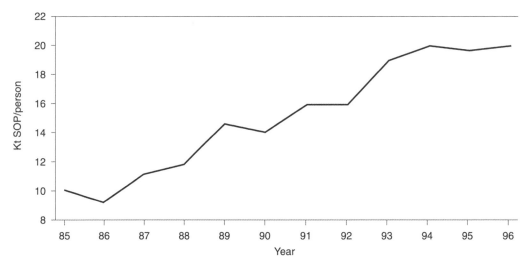

Figure 19.9 Hamersley Iron – Productivity

Without doubt, Hamersley Iron is the jewel in CRA's crown. In the six months to June 30, 1995, iron ore contributed $157.6 million to CRA's coffers. This was an 8% increase over the six months in 1994 and was due to increased sales tonnages and marginally higher prices.

First half shipments were at a record 26.4 million tonnes – a 9.5% increase over the previous record of 24.1 million tonnes set in the first half of 1993. Total production for 1995 was 52.2 million tonnes and total shipment 54.8 million tonnes. For '95, Hamersley's iron ore production and total shipments were the highest on record, despite the fourth quarter being adversely affected by a cyclone. Shipments to China and Europe were at record levels ...

... the change in company performance has been nothing short of incredible. Productivity has jumped from an average 15,000 tonnes of ore railed per employee per annum to 24,000 in 1995. The labour force has fallen from 3,000 to 2,500 and labour costs have gone from $186 million to $166 million.

Maintenance crews now work 12 hour shifts. There have been zero hours lost to industrial disputes and safety has improved markedly. For every million hours worked, there are now only seven injuries compared with 47 in the past. (IRM, March 1996)

The changes were highly public and the subject of press and media attention. Channel 9 in Australia ran a Business Sunday report (on 26 November 1995) on the changes, where in interview Paul Anderson explained that he was still a union member and stated: 'I have never had anybody even intimate that I had to give the union away ... production is through the roof and that's great.'

At no time in either Comalco or Hamersley were people asked, required or told to give up their union membership as part of the deal. They did have to change behaviour, but the biggest change was the behaviour of the leadership. As Geoff Neil, the manager of the rail division, said, 'the ball is in our court now, they have given us their trust, we must not let them down'.

People were not bribed. For many there was not much financial gain, given that there was no overtime and the removal of leisure days off and personal days off. Absenteeism dropped dramatically and people had, for the first time, a guaranteed income. The changes included the opportunity to do different work; one GM's personal assistant trained as a truck driver and many were able to use capabilities they had not been allowed to under old systems.

Finally, the worth to Hamersley was demonstrated when a comparison was made between Hamersley Iron and and a competitor organisation's operation. This is as close as like to like in industry and in fact the competitor's resource base is arguably slightly better than that of Hamersley Iron, as can be seen in Table 19.1.

Many commentators in Australia saw this as a CRA conspiracy. In fact, managing directors had significant discretion. In other businesses many of the concepts were introduced without an 'all staff' programme. Macdonald Associates have worked with the Rio Tinto, Anglesey Aluminium smelter in North Wales since 1993 where the leadership has implemented many new systems and gained improvements not only with a unionised workforce of operators and tradespeople – but also with a staff union!

Table 19.1   Comparison of Hamersley Iron and comparable iron ore company in Australia

	Hamersley Iron	**Comparable Iron Ore Company in Australia**
Tonnes railed (million tonnes)	65	65
Employees/contractors	2090	2485
Productivity (kilotonnes per employee)	31	26
		HI costs were 37 per cent lower and return on assets nearly three times more than the comparable iron ore company. Independent, external industrial comparison.

Les Cupper, the CRA vice president of organisational effectiveness, explained the changes at Comalco and Hamersley in the context of the business as a whole:

A key reason is that in all of our industries we don't control the exchange rate (a 1 cent movement in the Australian dollar against the US Dollar means a 22 million change to the bottom line). So what we had to do is concentrate on things we have control over – the work environment. (Way, Business Review Weekly, January 31, 1994, pp. 34–39).

The fear is that discipline can become dogma; that the purpose is lost in the process. This can happen in any initiative, be it organisational, implementing an IT strategy or merging companies. It is a concern that underlies the need for controls, audits and measures on any process. In these case studies our process and the companies output has probably been scrutinised more closely, at least in Australia, than any other. In the article 'The Art of War' in the *Sydney Morning Herald* (8 December, 1997), Helen Trinca wrote:

By the time Carnegie left in 1986 his impact had been profound. By then, as J.T. Ludeke says in his book The Line in the Sand, *Dr Ian Macdonald, a British consultant psychologist who had worked with Jaques at Brunel University in the United Kingdom, had begun working with CRA.*

He formed an alliance with Karl Stewart, the Managing Director of Comalco Smelting, developing training courses and preparing personnel strategies. Both men were crucial players in the ideas behind the push for contracts at operations in Bell Bay, Boyne Island and Weipa in the 1990s.

While this was the case, the article also links these processes with earlier work of Jaques and Hilmer, a consultant for McKinsey's. All of this work is connected – as Cupper pointed out in the BRW. It is long term, hard work and builds upon previous stages, just as new initiatives can build on this work further.

Rio Tinto is an example of a learning organisation. Many years ago Sir Roderick Carnegie expressed the view that gains would only become apparent when operators changed their behaviour. It was only when the systems work was integrated with the structural changes that such obvious changes could be expected and were found.

These case studies have both been from one corporation and a very particular one. This is not to imply that only mining or smelting industries can use these concepts. The breadth of organisations (and case studies in the back of this book and on the accompanying CD) that have used systems leadership theory demonstrates this clearly. The case studies in the body of this book were chosen because:

- They had a very high public profile at the time.
- Data is available that is already publicly accepted as evidence in law.
- There were no other major changes occurring at the same time (for example, technological process change).
- The case studies come close to meeting the ideal process outlined at the beginning of Part 4.
- The leadership of the companies were fully involved during the process.
- The leadership of these companies were actually developing the theory as part of the process.

When we started working in Comalco and Hamersley, people would ask why theories developed in health and social services at Brunel University were relevant in mining; when we worked in the financial sector people asked us why are we using theories from mining.

Our work in other countries in similar industries is questioned: 'Why do we use "Western" theories?' We hope to have demonstrated the general applicability of systems leadership theory. It is a theory about people in organised, purposeful activity – not 'just in mining', but in teaching, worshipping, healing, policing, learning, banking, running local councils, providing energy and many other activities. All are concerned with values, culture, mythologies, teamwork and systems that influence all of our behaviour and our willingness to use our capability to the full.

CHAPTER **20** *Implementation: Discipline or Dogma?*

The word 'guru' always rings alarm bells. Any theory or approach will have its champions, supporters and exponents. Successful change in any field, even the most scientific and technical, needs passion and commitment. It requires an emotional as well as a rational approach. This takes us back to Figure 20.1, the model we started with.

But passion can become prejudice; debate is replaced by dogma and what is essentially a set of propositions can become a set of beliefs. Many change processes are perceived as dogmatic. Some regard principles as a set of inflexible rules to be applied rigidly with little or no opportunity for discussion. Ideas, poorly explained, are experienced as being imposed. Whatever the authority, the experience is power.

Where ideas are imposed (or felt to be imposed) without a full explanation, then two results are common. First, there is a polarisation of 'believers' and 'sceptics' and second, the debate shifts from content to process and back again without distinction. Thus it is important to establish whether dissatisfaction with an outcome is due to content or process – or perhaps both. It is also possible to envisage excellent process, enabling the implementation of very poor content. This is often a criticism levelled at management consultants who have a great presentation style and a persuasive manner but no substantial or new ideas.

The model based on a dogmatic approach, Figure 20.2, explains how quite quickly the change process can degenerate into a power struggle between believers and sceptics.

The champions of change introduce a new but meaningless language, made up largely of jargon, which replaces simple language with much longer phrases. So the 'future' becomes 'moving forward in time'. We 'create new space' (as in 'we need to confront the lack in the motivational space'), which really means 'people lack application or energy'.

If 'guru' rings alarm bells, 'disciples', 'acolytes' or 'believers' signal meltdown. We must not invent a new religion. People's beliefs are their own business, not part of a process that must allow real testing of results. This is not to avoid a disciplined approach. People are so unused to discipline applied to social processes that it can appear to be dogmatic. As we said earlier in our discussion of social and scientific meaning, people find it hard work to be clear about definitions and meaning. Common language usage includes phrases such as 'like' as in 'it was like, really cool', or 'I was, like sacked'. Well, were you sacked or not? When it comes to our life's work, however apparently mundane to others, small, symbolic behaviours matter significantly. 'Yeah, this is sort of like your pay' is not acceptable unless it is my pay, properly calculated.

Being disciplined and precise is not the same as authoritarian. Being clear is not the same as pedantic. Those who are vague have an interesting time in the witness box of a court. Any process must be reviewed with discipline, as should the content.

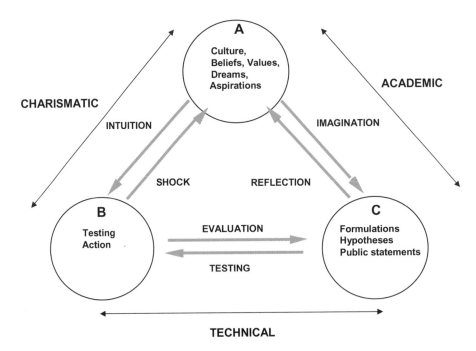

Figure 20.1   Human Decision-Making Model

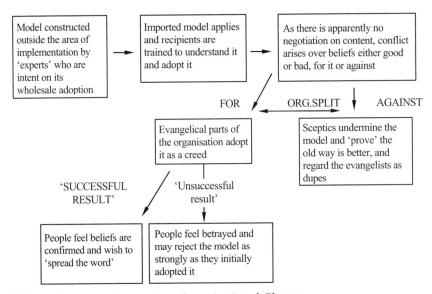

Figure 20.2   Dogmatic Approach to Organisational Change

Reviewing content and process

In reviewing the outcomes of implementation, it is critical to evaluate the process of implementation in detail. If we are to ask, as we should, whether the concepts of the principles proposed are valid (in other words, the content), we cannot test this just by examining outcomes (the bottom line). It depends how they were applied (the process). It is necessary to examine, in the cases of both failure and success, how projects were carried out. If, however, there is no base theory, only a belief system or set of slogans with no agreed content or process, then this becomes an impossible task. The theory must actually predict failure as well as success. Thus, if people are not capable of carrying out the work of the role, the structure should not work, that is, it should not produce more cost-effective results. If the leadership behaviour does not demonstrate trust, honesty, love, fairness, courage or respect for dignity, then people will not work to their potential, even though these words have been taught on a course. If tasks are not discussed and assigned clearly, we should not expect work to be carried out effectively. Therefore, in considering the effectiveness of the ideas, we must examine also the effectiveness of their implementation. People will find it difficult to assess another's performance fairly if they have received a poor or no assessment themselves. Thus, any evaluation must examine the rigour of lack of rigour in implementation. This will deliver a clearer comparison of outcomes.

Being precise about the implementation process is not a matter of dogma; it is essential for fair evaluation. Therefore, in discussing whether these ideas are or have been of value, it is important to evaluate the process. It may be found that the failure is quite predictable; that is, it tends to support the theory, not falsify it. Falsification occurs where conditions have not been met and yet the outcome is positive, for example, if increases in productivity have occurred and been sustained in situations of low feedback, random promotion, vague task assignment, low trust and so on. This would suggest no link between a particular process and outcome. The 'link' is the theory or content.

Nothing in the discussion above presupposes that there is only one theory or explanation. Many companies have been highly successful without explicitly adopting stratified systems theory or systems leadership theory. However, these theories are attempts to articulate good practice, and, like any valid process, have to meet the criterion of internal consistency. Theory is not a matter of welding bits of one model to another. For example, the fact that a car runs on petrol does not mean the driver is dogmatically or ideologically opposed to diesel. It is not reasonable to assume that, because one vehicle design can run on diesel, all can. Nor is it a matter of being pragmatic, of just trying it to see, or using diesel because there is no petrol. The results are predictable. It is also important to understand the skill needed in implementation. For example, the existence of a violin does not imply that anyone can use it. The fact that I cannot pick up a violin and play Tchaikovsky's violin concerto does not invalidate the instrument or prove that it doesn't work. Of course, it depends upon training, practice and probably some natural talent. The process is similar to leadership: some can play by ear, others only after a great deal of effort and practice – and some are quite tone deaf. However, we must also consider the purpose and what standard is required. We do not expect the same standard of musical ability from a school concert orchestra as we do from a professional national symphony orchestra. We do not require the same precision of language in social discussion as we do in a scientific debate. In friendships we do not require the same precise outcome of a product or service. We do not send the steak back at a friend's dinner party when we might send the same steak back at a restaurant. The purpose of a business relationship is to produce a required output, often with very rigorous criteria of quality. Thus, in terms of language, what in one setting is pedantic is essential precision in another.

Of course, we may have precise content and process but it may be too costly for our purposes. We could guarantee a particular outcome but the technical equipment and training required may be beyond our means or simply not cost-effective. This is not a question of whether precision is valued per se, merely a comparison of options. The point is that in comparing options we still need to have clear and common criteria of how to assess content and process in order to make a fair comparison. If another option is proposed, what specific advantages does it have? Does it explain in terms of content and process why these advantages should be expected? Is it internally consistent? What are the comparative data? What is the evidence from elsewhere?

Conclusion

All these principles do is articulate good process. They are not a belief system, nor are they dogma. They are not a fad. Fads are merely the replacement of one magic with another. Far from encouraging mystical processes social science should be in the business of demystifying processes. Power – as opposed to authority – often rests on mysticism because, when dependent on power, the process is kept in the inner circle and the results are dependency and fear. This does not encourage people willingly to give of their best. Of course, 'theory' is not sacrosanct. However, evidence for or against must be based not only on outcome data but also on an analysis of the process of implementation and a comparison of the implementation processes in relation to outcome. Further, it is important that any alternatives are also examined with equal rigour and evidence sought for their effectiveness, not only in apparent input–output measures, but in the predictive power of their articulated processes. In essence we must all be interested not only in what is done, but how it is done and why the result was achieved.

We are aware that we have raised the bar. We have seen new models adopted as they come into fashion, assuming that other models have an automatic sell-by date. We have invited disciplined critique but we also demand the same analysis of other approaches. When people discuss our 'failures', we need to know if it was a failure of theory or an unproductive business outcome. The former is much more important. If we have a success, was it because of the concepts or despite them?

In short, we ask you not to believe anything without putting it to the test. Test it in terms of internal consistency and predictive ability, and test it with rigour and discipline. Test any other approaches in the same way. It is only fair!

21 *Who Is There to Guard the Guards? Essentials of a Positive Organisation*

Checks and balances

We can create structures, systems and cultures but nothing absolutely guarantees that there will not be mistakes. Central to encouraging people to express their capability is the existence of safeguards in the event of error or arbitrary judgment. If we prescribe that judgment, we lose one of the major advantages of human organisation: human judgment. In attempting to prescribe judgment, we create authorised, counter-productive bureaucracy that stifles discretion and creativity. There must, however, be checks and balances.

These checks and balances can be provided in many different ways. First, there is the law. Paradoxically, in Western industrialised society, the union movement has been a victim of its own success. Many core, essential issues fought for over many years by the union movement are now actually part of the law. Laws about health and safety, equal opportunity, minimum pay and working conditions have improved workers' lives dramatically in the last century. This does not make unions redundant but means their focus must change. Nevertheless, the right to belong to a union must remain a fundamental right as a safeguard for employees if they choose to exercise it. Indeed, we regard union activity as a measure of trust and indicative of mythologies. The more activity and need for a union, in general terms, the more mistrust there is in the leadership and the state of the organisational structure and systems. This may be because of past behaviour, but an unhelpful mythology may live on if sources of the mythology are not addressed by the current leadership.

We do not regard it inherently necessary for an organisation to run well that it rely on third party intervention, actual or threatened. It does rely upon internal systems that monitor the use of managerial judgment. It is possible to implement systems in such a way that people choose to deal directly in an unmediated relationship. In evidence to the Australian Industrial Relations Commission, Macdonald's statement refers to the key elements of the relationship that have been explained in this book, viz:

The essential component of a staff relationship is individual judgement. That is, a person enters a working relationship where he or she is judged on the basis of his or her personal work contribution. This judgement is made by a manager. This relationship carries particular accountabilities for the manager and is personally very significant.

Thus, this is a relationship where another individual is accorded the authority (within the law and the policy of the company) to make judgements about another person's work performance and act on those judgements. These acts include a range of forms of recognition from individual feedback in words to salary changes. Work performance has a very specific meaning in this context. It is the pathway that a person builds in order to complete his or her tasks. It is the decision making along the way to achieving a goal. Measuring this by reference only to outputs is to miss what is essentially human, namely, the 'how' of achievement, or as will be described later, the equivalent of a person's signature. Thus work performance is different for each one of us even if our outputs appear the same. If the building of this pathway is ignored by the manager, the person will look elsewhere for recognition.

A staff relationship is central to a meritocracy. A meritocracy is based upon the assumption that any role in a company is filled by the person most capable of doing the work. It is commonly referred to but not very often enacted in its full sense, that is, in relation to all roles. It is the staff relationship in the context of a meritocracy which can allow younger people or new employees to be promoted ahead of longer serving colleagues, or people in apparently the same role to receive different amounts of pay because of judged differences in work performance in that role.

The continuation of a productive staff relationship is dependent on the quality of those judgements. The credibility of a meritocracy and staff relationships rests upon the demonstration of fairness by the manager in these judgements. And in addition, that promotion is based on demonstrated ability not favouritism or nepotism, and that discipline is based on actual negative behaviour not merely victimisation of a person who asks difficult questions.

Given that we are human, it is reasonable to suggest that sometimes mistakes will be made, so it is also essential that there is an avenue of appeal. This avenue must be internal to demonstrate that the company can be fair and just, even if individual managers at times are not. This does not preclude access to the law or external tribunals, but demonstrates that the company does not require that a person appeals outside of the company if they have a concern.

Thus, the staff relationship is founded four-square on trust. Trust in the leadership of the company and its ability to act fairly and with courage. The fear or anxiety aroused by such relationships is that this trust might be betrayed or is dependent on the goodwill or fairness of a particular manager/leader. Thus a person may be quite happy to enter into that relationship with the current manager, but is very concerned as to what might happen when he, or she leaves. In effect the person does not trust the company to replace the manager effectively.

Therefore, this relationship must be underpinned by well designed 'people' systems such as recruitment, selection, task setting and review, performance appraisal, salary review, career assessment, promotions and fair treatment systems. This range of systems must be open and public. It is important to note that such systems do not make the decisions but are the boundaries or limits within which decisions are made and, if necessary, appealed. These systems, and how they are implemented, have a fundamental importance in terms of their effect on employees' feelings of trust and fairness. If a person chooses to enter a staff relationship that person is making a statement of trust. People will make this decision on the basis of:

a. The personal behaviour of leaders/managers;

b. The quality of the people systems in operation.

Money alone does not buy trust.

Essentially if there is a relationship where one person has the authority to judge another whether that be at work or in any relationship, there is a universal concern as to what reviews, limits, appeals are there to that judgement. One of the features of democratic societies is the separation of the executive and legislature from the judiciary and further the opportunity of appeal within the judiciary. In contrast totalitarian states are characterised by a lack of distinction between the executive and judiciary and rarely offer the opportunity for appeal.

So we could caricature the organisation, especially large multinationals, as having so much more power (and authority) than the individual (employee) so as to be a totalitarian 'judge, jury and executioner'. Indeed, many third parties including trade unions and pressure groups would argue this way.

In our model there are explicit principles and safeguards. As mentioned previously, the controls on executive power are to be found inside the organisation in various forms:

1. There is the role of the M+1. This not only includes the opportunity for access from the person in a reporting role one removed but an active review of the managerial judgements of the intermediate manager.

2. There are also the policies of the company.

3. There are proper and effective 'people systems', as mentioned above, which should mitigate against capricious and arbitrary managerial judgement and decisions. That is a person's health and well-being should not be dependent on the character of any particular manager. Whilst some people will inevitably relate better or personally prefer one manager to another, this should not extend to an option of basic fair and reasonable treatment.

4. In addition as has also been discussed, every organisation should implement a fair treatment system which by its nature should expose decisions and behaviour to a wider examination and opportunity for appeal.

5. In addition it must be remembered that organisations exist within the context of the law. They are not free to outline policies and design systems which do not take into account the law of the land. What constitutes unfair dismissal is not solely for the organisation to determine, and the same applies to equal opportunities, racial or sexual discrimination.

Unions

Given all of this, is there a place for unions? If all these safeguards are in place, why would anyone need the protection of an outside organisation? The answer to these questions is quite simple: if the person feels the need for this extra safeguard it is their right to have it and not for anyone else to refuse it. A further feature of open, democratic societies is the right of association. People should be free to form unions and be members if they want to. Again it is a feature of totalitarian regimes that trade unions are banned or severely restricted in their operation ...

... Are the unions still needed? The answer depends upon the members and potential members. If they think so then unions are needed. The key element is co-ercive power. If people are not free to join or leave, the whole picture is distorted. The drop in the membership of unions over

the last 20–30 years has been influenced by union leadership and counter-productive systems such as 'closed shop', 'compulsory deduction of union dues' and a distancing of the leadership, in terms of full time officials, from the membership. In this way the union organisation and its effectiveness is no different from any other organisation we have discussed. Its continuance has been and will be significantly influenced by its structure, the quality of its leadership and the design and implementation of its systems. It is consequently as difficult to generalise about union organisations as it is with commercial organisations. We have worked in many organisations with active unions both well run and not so well run. We have also worked in situations where employees have either not felt the need for third party representation or have chosen to reject it. Whatever the situation, the key issue is that employees have the right to choose and it is recognised that unions have a potentially significant contribution to make in society. Thus, in a democratic society union membership is and should be another control operated according to the free choice of organisational members and not properly subject to external imposition or denial.

(Macdonald, 1995)

Given all these safeguards, is this now enough? Our answer would be not quite. It was argued earlier (Chapter 6) that the organisation as a social entity also expresses an ethic. That is, through its policies and work of the board, whether intentionally or not, it creates an environment which encourages certain behaviours and discourages others. We would argue that as part of that ethic and as a matter of policy there should be an 'employment charter', which states the mutual expectations of the leadership and membership of the organisation.

This is consistent with the continuing need for clarity in other areas such as role descriptions, task assignments, and review and authority. Clarity of expectation is a major control on power since most power is exercised in the context of ambiguity. When a situation is ambiguous it offers the opportunity for exploitation. For example, if your car is stopped by the police, is there a clear understanding of authority and rights? Are the parties clear about under what circumstances you can be legitimately stopped? What are you required to do and what can you refuse to do?

The employment charter

We spend a significant part of our lives in organisations. If we are not clear about expectations and what the boundaries are with regard to authority, then relationships are open to abuse and exploitation. Throughout this book we have argued for clarity in these areas. The final piece is a sample charter that describes what is expected (see Box 21.1).

Box 21.2 shows an example. It may be varied according to the nature of the business but the purpose remains constant.

The principles upon which this charter is based are founded on some basic assumptions:

- That people are essentially creative and constructive; that they want to work and achieve results.

Box 21.1 Charter Statement

'To clarify the conditions which each member of the organisation is entitled to expect in order to create a constructive, productive and safe environment which encourages people to work to their potential.'

Box 21.2 Employment Charter

For the organisation to achieve its objectives, improve and grow it depends upon the commitment of all employees to give their best. If they are to do so, there are mutual obligations that need to be met and, if in place, should result in mutual benefit. These are described below in the employment charter and explained in the attached statement of principles.

The leadership of the organisation will endeavour to provide for all employees:

- A safe and healthy work environment, free from harassment and discrimination in terms of race, ethnicity, gender or religious belief
- Behaviour towards all employees based on the core values of honesty, trust, fairness, love, dignity and courage consistent with the culture of the organisation
- Work that is challenging and appropriate to the capabilities of individuals

This means that all employees should have:

- Clear role authorities and accountability
- Clear expectation of what is required from each person by setting context, purpose, the quality and quantity of output providing specific resources within a completion time
- Feedback and appropriate recognition for work done without favouritism or arbitrary decisions
- Information about and opportunities for development

This involves the design and implementation of fair systems, specifically:

- Reward and recognition based on the quality of performance at work, disregarding other factors for example, favouritism
- Promotion based on merit with fair and open opportunity
- An opportunity internally to appeal against unfair treatment and/or unfair decisions

In so far as the leadership endeavours to provide such an environment employees are expected to:

- Behave safely and not harass others or act in an unfairly discriminatory way
- Behave towards each other based on the core values of honesty, trust, fairness, dignity, love and courage consistent with the culture of the organisation
- Respond to challenges using their capabilities to the full

This means that employees should:

- Seek to clarify expectations in role and tasks
- Ask for feedback and recognition
- Constructively give feedback to leaders
- Offer ideas for improvement
- Co-operate with other employees
- Seek information with regard to both the business and opportunities for development

This involves working with and offering ideas for the improvement of systems by:

- Using the process (steps) of team leadership and membership
- Working within systems according to their intent
- Using discretion productively
- Using the internal systems to appeal against any unfair treatment
- Contributing to performance review and career assessment by reflecting upon own performance and aspirations
- Accepting that if there is a continuing mismatch between the demonstrated behaviour of the person and the behaviour required by the organisation to meet its purpose the individual will be required to leave the organisation.

- That the creation of a productive relationship cannot be coerced but is experienced as a free choice.
- That productive working relationships are critical to a person's sense of self worth and identity.
- That there must be a demonstrable linkage between intention, action and results whether they are positive or negative.
- That people have a right to work in an environment that is safe and free from harassment and discrimination.

Foundations for this charter

MERITOCRACY

This first principle is that people are assigned to roles on the basis of merit, whether entering an organisation or moving within it. Appointments are made on the basis of the judgment made about suitability of the person to carry out the work of the role, that is, their capability in terms of knowledge, skills (both technical and social), intellectual ability and application. This is in contrast to other systems such as seniority, nepotism or favouritism.

CLARITY OF EXPECTATIONS

The second is that people understand clearly both what they are expected to do and what authorities they have to carry out the work. The accountability and authorities must balance. It is unfair to hold someone accountable for work when they do not have the authority, which includes resources, to carry it out. Each task must be properly assigned so that the context and purpose, the resources available to achieve a specified output in terms of quality and quantity and a time to completion are all clearly communicated and understood.

FAIRNESS OF JUDGMENT

Thirdly, people should receive timely feedback and assessment of their work performance. This, in turn, should be demonstrably linked to reward or pay. Such judgments should not simply concentrate on outcome but also the process by which the outcome was achieved (successful or not). The way in which a person approaches work, problem solving and the difficulty of decisions along the way is an essentially human process which must be central to any understanding and consequential judgment of work performance.

APPEALS

Since work performance is judged by human beings, mistakes may be made. Mistakes are not avoided by ever more specific and detailed output measures, which are time consuming and eventually still rest on someone's judgment. Rather, the person under review should have the opportunity to question such judgment within the organisation and have that appeal heard by someone other than the person who has made the original judgment. The employee should not feel that they have to take matters outside of the organisation in order to get a hearing, although they may exercise their right to do so.

CHALLENGING WORK

Work that is assigned should be challenging in that it demands work and engagement on the part of the employee. It should not be overly demanding, causing stress and anxiety; nor too easy, causing boredom and alienation. The level of challenge may and usually should change over time to maintain engagement as the person becomes more capable. Essential to the assignment of work is the fundamental requirement that it does not require unsafe behaviour.

DEVELOPMENT

There should be opportunities for an employee to develop their skills and abilities. This may be in the form of coaching, training or other role opportunities, but does not always involve promotion to another level.

SYSTEMS

All of the above require the proper design of 'people' systems. This is not an easy matter and such systems need to include in their design the opportunity for improvement as a result of feedback. Such systems include the structural design of the organisation in terms of level of work and role descriptions, recruitment, selection, task setting and review, performance appraisal, removal from role, salary review, career assessment, promotion and fair treatment systems. These systems, in the way they are designed and implemented, are fundamentally important in terms of their effect on employees' behaviour and feelings of trust and fairness. Whilst information about individuals should be confidential, these systems must be transparent.

BEHAVIOUR

Day-to-day behaviour is also of fundamental importance in whether an employee is likely to give his or her best. The way a person is treated according to a set of core values, honesty, trust, fairness, dignity, love and courage will profoundly affect their own behaviour. Of critical importance is the behaviour of those in leadership roles who by demonstration create a culture and set the standards of how employees' contributions are valued and given appropriate recognition.

THIRD PARTIES

If a productive work relationship based on trust can be achieved, there should not be a need for constant reference to third parties outside of the organisation. This includes lawyers, union officials and tribunals. However, an organisation cannot and should not compromise in any way the legal rights of an employee to have access to such third parties. It is a measure of trust in an organisation how far employees feel the need to actually engage third parties on their behalf. The attempt to build a high-trust organisation where people feel free to express their potential is no more anti-union or anti-lawyer than a community health programme is anti-doctor or crime prevention is anti-police. In this way it can be analogous to the felt need for insurance. If people feel insecure or in a dangerous situation, they are more likely to take out significant insurance policies than when they experience a safe environment.

The preparedness of people to give of their best and feel free to work to their potential depends on being in a particular environment. It is an environment where trust is possible because of good leadership and systems. It is one which, although safe and free from harassment and discrimination, is nevertheless challenging and, if those challenges are met, rewarding. It is an environment where appropriate and timely recognition is given. This is dependent upon good leadership behaviour, underpinned by well designed and implemented systems, so that the environment does not rely on a particular individual. Part of that environment is an explicit set of mutual expectations and obligations. The creation of productive relationships and a high-trust organisation not only offers the opportunity to improve the success of the business but also the fundamental quality of all employees' working lives, with resulting benefits for the wider society.

Any set of organisational expectations must not, however, compromise or detract from any individual's rights under law including the right to be a member of other organisations.

Thus, we recommend such a charter as the final piece in the jigsaw. We have said that systems run deeper than individual behaviour because the systems operate continuously and are analogous to non-verbal behaviour. Systems are a legacy but left without proper control and audit can atrophy and become counter-productive over time. A high-trust organisation will not automatically continue to be so. The charter is an overall reminder of the nature and conditions for a highly productive high-trust relationship.

We have been part of the process of building positive organisations in different countries and different sectors. Central to the issue of building a positive organisation is its maintenance over time. Just as systems, symbols and behaviour are used to build the positive organisation they are also potentially part of its dismantling and eventual destruction.

It is essential that (any change to) the core systems, symbols and leadership behaviour of the organisation are authorised at a level where the capability necessary for the task is available. We recognise this is not a guarantee of sound decision making if the necessary review processes are not in place because it is not unknown for people to be promoted beyond the limit of their capability. Unfortunately we have also seen good work undone because these principles are not understood or have been forgotten. We have found many instances of changes being made to systems, symbols and behaviour at relatively low levels and or by people without the capability needed to perform the analysis and synthesis necessary to have the change deliberately improve the organisation. We return to the work of a leader: to create improve and sustain over time.

Thus who is there to guard the guards? We have identified:

- capable people appointed in the first place;
- clarity of role expectation;
- manager-once-removed (M+1) review;
- controls and audits on all systems;
- fair treatment system;
- an employment charter.

All of this is set in the context of legal rights including the right to belong to a union.

22 *Complementary Theories and Practices*

As is true with any publication, we cannot cover all the issues that might be of interest to managers as they go about their work. In our own work we have found other theories and ideas that have helped us in our management and consulting practices. The many publications, which are listed in the bibliography, that are directly related to stratified systems theory have been important to us. In recent years Jaques chose the term 'requisite organisation', but the content is typically relevant to our work.

Even though they were written in past decades, the writings of Lord Wilfred Brown have been very helpful. His experience as a manager, CEO and intellectual partner of Elliott Jaques provides considerable insight into the realities of management processes. Jaques' many writings have, of course, been seminal in our thinking.

There are a multitude of writings on organisation and management. Many of these are difficult to apply in the 'real world', but many managers have told us that by using stratified theory as a base, they can then pull out and employ the many good ideas that appear confusing until you recognise they apply to a specific level of work.

For example, John Kotter (1999) shadowed managers to observe what they really do, not what they say they do. His article, *'What Effective General Managers Really Do'* is interesting, but it is hard to know what to make of all the different observations he makes. When you realise he is actually describing managers with the same title but who are working in roles at level IV, V and VI, the analysis and the ideas become far more interesting and useful.

Some writings refer to operational work in organisations; typically these include level I, II and III. General management typically refers to those who head a principal business function at level IV or to the chief executive of a national scale business or a corporate business unit, at level V. Executive management (corporate leadership) takes place at level VI and VII. Awareness of these levels can make general statements regarding organisations clearer: it becomes obvious when they apply to some parts of the organisation and not others.

Knowledge of the levels of work also helps one to understand high-level professional work where the direct output is produced at level II, III, IV or higher. These are the 'knowledge workers' described by Peter Drucker in *The Age of Discontinuity* (1969).

Our discussion of the need for an area of discretion for all workers echoes Drucker's ideas of knowledge workers – employees who are paid for their knowledge and for exercising judgment. Our theory applies this to the entire workforce, not just higher-level workers, but the ideas are entirely compatible.

This chapter is not a comprehensive review of all other theories, but a recognition that there are other practices which can, and do, result in benefit and which can be complementary to the concepts and practices we outline. Too often 'theorists,' 'experts,' or 'gurus' insist theirs is the only approach. This is disrespectful to most managers and practitioners. All good theory is derived from observation of good practice, and we do not claim a monopoly. We look at approaches from a variety of sources and show how they can be integrated with our work.

Theories we have used in our own practice

STATISTICAL PROCESS CONTROL AND SIX SIGMA

In our experience, one of the most valuable approaches toward improving organisation performance is statistical process control (SPC), made popular by W. Edwards Deming (1982) in his work on quality improvement. As Deming recognised, you cannot get consistent high quality production without changing the systems, management and structure of the organisation.

Because change is difficult, Stewart found that training his workforce in SPC not only gave them necessary knowledge to improve their work processes; it also brought pressure from below to make changes at higher levels of the organisation. Combined with his pressure from the top, change took place more rapidly and production quality improved.

Some writers on quality improvement like to create a quality 'manager' and a separate hierarchy to bring in the new systems. We have found this to be counter-productive. You may often need technical advisers who are expert in SPC to provide advice to managers, but the accountability for the work of improving quality must lie with the managerial hierarchy.

Although we have not personally used the material on six sigma (Eckes, 2000, 2002, 2005), it too works more effectively in a stratified organisation; it is an extension of SPC. Getting to six sigma requires changing systems, structure and behaviour, a difficult task made easier, we believe, using the approaches we suggest in this book. We have seen six sigma programmes become effective when adopted by line managers. The design of organisation systems we propose is consistent with the design of systems for statistical process control. The purpose of the system must be clear. The system design must provide a framework within which variation is acceptable, and must produce control data which is valid and must be subject to audit.

LEADERSHIP

Some of the best material we have found on leadership comes from the US Marine Corps. Don't let any stereotypes about the military turn you off; the Marines have some of the best leadership training in the world. Their lives depend on it. Although they don't use the term mythology, all Marines are required to study the history of the Corps: its great battles, the courage and the suffering. This teaches new Marines what it means to be part of the Corps. It teaches their mythologies. Most of their heroes are known only in the Corps, but their sacrifices in great battles at Guadalcanal, Iwo Jima, Tarawa, Chosin, Khe Sanh or perhaps in the future at Kirkuk or Fallujah, demonstrate what it is to be a Marine (Freedman, 2000; Carrison and Walsh, 1999).

We have found literature that tries to separate leadership from management to be more of an obstruction than a benefit to good management practices. As we stated in Chapter 12, all managers are leaders. Their only choice is to be a good leader or bad one. On the other hand, not all leaders are managers.

The writings of James Collins and Jerry Porras, *Built to Last* (1994), also make a fine contribution to the literature of leadership. Collins went on to make a further contribution with his book, *From Good to Great* (2001). Although neither of these books claims to be about leadership, it seems to us that both provide real insights into the practices of effective leaders.

SAFETY

One of the most important ways for a leader to demonstrate genuine care for their employees is by keeping them safe in the workplace. In 2004 in the USA, 5703 people died while at work (US Department of Labor, 2004); 4 257 300 had nonfatal injuries and illnesses in private industry alone (US Department of Labor Statistics, Bureau of Labor Statistics, Home Page, 2005). Clearly there is much room for improvement.

There is a great deal of literature supporting the use of behaviourally based safety systems to reduce the number of injuries and to eliminate fatalities. Several of our clients have used the Dupont STOP safety system with great success (www2.dupont.com/Consulting_Services/en_US/). Other firms use different safety systems, but all are easier to put into effect when there is clear accountability and the effective allocation of authority to undertake and to properly recognise safety tasks and practices.

Implementing safety systems and practices demonstrates the care and concern the leadership has for its workforce. Even under the extreme conditions of war, officers – commissioned and non-commissioned – are taught that their primary task is to take care of their troops: to demonstrate their love for the troops such that the troops can trust their officers not to waste their lives. The danger is real, and all know that some are likely to die, but the behaviour of their officers builds the trust necessary to face the rigours of combat. The effectiveness of this training and the resultant behaviour of the officers is the real determinant of the fighting ability of an armed force.

LEAN MANUFACTURING

In a manufacturing environment, the lean manufacturing ideas first developed at Toyota have proven to be highly compatible with systems leadership theory. A lean structure allows the development of lean manufacturing. Lean manufacturing refers to process changes that improve upon mass production techniques to reduce cost, reduce time to produce, reduce inventories and waste, improve quality and better respond to market demands. In a large part its successful application is dependent upon the rapid analysis and adoption of ideas from the lower levels of the organisation and a leadership that is able to induce the effective adoption of change (Dunning and Richert, 2003).

The ideas of 'pull' production based on customer demand, continuous flow, correct measures and waste elimination have revolutionised manufacturing production while reducing costs and cycle times dramatically. Waldo (1991) studied 48 US companies using just-in-time work teams and reported an average of:

- 35 per cent reduction in cycle time;
- 24 per cent reduction in late deliveries;
- 30 per cent reduction in hours per unit;
- 33 per cent reduction in work-in-progress inventories;
- 58 per cent reduction in scrap rates;
- 71 per cent reduction in customer complaints and
- 39 per cent reduction in floor space required.

Greenwood (1994) documented human effort in production and design was reduced by 50 per cent. Manufacturing throughput was improved from 20 per cent to 100 per cent. Time to market for a new product was reduced by 50 to 75 per cent.

THEORY OF CONSTRAINTS

Eliyahu M. Goldratt (1986; 2004) expanded upon the ideas of lean production, focusing on the constraints, or bottlenecks, that are present in every production system. He uses the accumulation of inventories as an indicator of problems in the manufacturing process. His ideas have been particularly helpful to practising managers because they are written in a clear and direct manner.

MYERS-BRIGGS TYPE INDICATOR

Although disparaged by many trained psychologists and psychiatrists, we have found the Myers-Briggs type indicator (Myers and Myers, 1980) to be useful in helping people sort out their different approaches to problem solving, communications and decision making. Dr Carlos Rigby of the Army Research Institute developed these ideas during the period when the authors worked with him on joint projects.

Rigby used the type indicator in somewhat different ways from those suggested by the original authors. He noted that one of the key differences was between the problem-solving and communications preferences along the I/E (introverts and extroverts) dimension. The introverts preferred to think about problems quietly, work out solutions and then communicate their ideas (or have the ideas pulled out of them by extroverts).

Extroverts, on the other hand, preferred to solve problems in discussion with others. They would demand answers from introverts who had not had time to think through the solutions, thus creating annoyance on both sides. The introverts thought the extroverts were just chattering without any thought behind it; while the extroverts thought the introverts were withholding ideas.

The J/P (judging/perceiving) dimension is another source of friction. People who are stronger along the J dimension like clear decisions and closure. Those who are stronger along the P dimension prefer to keep their options open. The J dimension tends to dominate higher-level executive positions in the US because decisiveness is an admired characteristic in that culture. When a person who prefers the P dimension achieves a high-level position, the J people below often become exasperated because they will not make a decision, at least not as quickly as they would prefer. The P person will also want to explore 'all' alternatives – again seen as delay rather than thoughtfulness by those who are more comfortable with the J dimension.

In our work and the work of Dr. Rigby, simply gaining an understanding of the existence of these eight preferences, allowed people to work together more effectively. One manager learned to let one of his 'I' subordinates know about a problem a few days ahead of a meeting, so she would have time to think about it and have a potential solution ready. A manager with a strong 'J' preference learned to accept the more open-ended approach of a subordinate, and even came to appreciate the benefit of hearing more alternatives.

Only one dimension N/S (iNtuitive/Sensing) seems to be related to mental processing ability (MPA). As noted by Myers and Myers (1980: 37–43), National Merit Scholarship finalists and Cal Tech science students seem to cluster in the N quadrants. Rigby also found that there were a disproportionate number of high-level officers with a preference for the N dimension. This would correspond with our findings regarding levels of work that using what is not there (negative information) begins with an MPA of level IV.

SYSTEMS AND OTHER APPROACHES TO ORGANISATION AND MANAGEMENT

The literature on systems thinking and the systems approach has been developed over the past 50 years. The work of C. West Churchman (1968), Russell Ackoff (1960; 1999) and Stafford Beer (1972) have all had an impact on our thinking. Perhaps most influential has been C. West Churchman's systems approach (*The Systems Approach and Its Enemies*, 1979).

With dozens of journals and thousands of books being published in this field, it is impossible to name all the fine thinkers whom we and our clients have found helpful. We name a few and apologise to those we should have named but were not able to include. Historian of business, Alfred Chandler, has provided us with insights into the development of organisations. Charles Handy's wide-ranging interests have also informed our thinking.

John Micklethwait and Adrian Wooldridge have provided both history (*The Company*, 2003) and insight into those who advise organisations (*The Witch Doctors: Making Sense of the Management Gurus*, 1996). Jerry Harvey has provided insight with wit into the behaviour and foibles of individuals in organisations. Harry Levinson's perceptive wisdom has helped us immeasurably along the way. Recent literature on complexity and chaos theory seems to us to be relevant to our understanding of both people and the organisations they create.

In looking at writings on public and non-profit organisations, the works of Gerald Caiden (1982, 2005). John Dewey (1927), H.H. Gerth and C. Wright Mills (1946), Luther Gulick (1937), Frederick Mosher (1982), Chester Newland (1984, 1997), Emmet Redford (1969, 1981), Herbert Simon (1997), Richard J. Stillman II (1998) and Dwight Waldo (1984) have all been influential. In addition the ideas of Karl Popper on the Open Society (1971, 1972, 1992), democracy and science have informed our work and our thinking.

Finally we must recognise the man who first discussed *The Practice of Management*, Peter Drucker (1954). Although not always appreciated by scholars, he was certainly appreciated by the many managers with whom he consulted and for whom he wrote. We have not always agreed with him, for example his statement, 'Management is doing things right; leadership is doing the right things,' as we have explained earlier.

Nonetheless, his ideas have permeated the field of management and systems. Management by objectives (MBO) has been around so long that we forget the idea originated with Drucker. The idea fell into disrepute because too many managers set one-year objectives for everyone rather than recognising that some objectives require many more months or even years. MBO also became excessively driven by data with financial rewards attached to measurable results. This was especially true in the US.

As we noted in Chapter 13, in performance management, measurable results are very important but they are only indicators of work performance. The work of a human being must be judged, taking into account the context within which the work was carried out, the actual work that had to be carried out to accomplish the results and the short- and long-term consequences of the way the work was accomplished.

Our ideas about an organisation as a social community and the flat networked structure are consistent with Drucker's writings. He felt that inefficient hierarchies had to be challenged. We hope that our ideas, following on those of Wilfred Brown and Elliott Jaques, regarding how hierarchies should be structured answer some of the challenges he raised.

In the end, we are all part of a learning community. No one has a monopoly on the best way to organise and manage the myriad of institutions that make up advanced industrial and post-industrial societies. Because our work has been applied in businesses, social service agencies, hospitals, city governments, national governments, armies, churches, public utilities and other unique organisations, we find a quote from Drucker particularly apt:

'The function of management in a church is to make the church more churchlike, not more businesslike.' (Byrne, 2005)

We heartily concur and endeavour to help managers to apply this dictum to the purpose of their own organisation, whether church, social service agency, hospital or army. We hope that whatever the purpose of a particular organisation that our work makes a contribution to help leaders create more humane and productive organisations that can both meet their objectives and improve the human condition.

Conclusion

This book is not just about leadership or systems but is primarily concerned with how people come together to achieve a productive purpose. Our survival has always depended upon our ability to form and sustain social organisations. People have a deep need to be creative and to belong. By creating positive organisations we can fulfil these needs and build a worthwhile society.

Such organisations do not happen by chance; a positive organisation must be based on sound, general principles of behaviour. We have tried to outline the work necessary to create such organisations and to give examples of these principles in action. It is hard work to understand the concepts, apply them with discipline (not dogma) and creativity, and sustain and modify them over time. However, such ideas should not be alien or completely counter-intuitive. We have observed and admired what good leaders and team members do and tried to distil the essence of productive, value-based relationships.

We do not claim to be totally original. Clearly we have been influenced by Jaques in particular, but also by numerous others. We do not believe that creativity is an individual activity. Ideas and efforts are the products of social relationships, which is why we are sceptical of 'gurus'. In the final analysis we are not creative only because of a contract, a job title or even pay; we are not, primarily, externally motivated. We believe people are inherently creative, energetic and positive – just observe small children. However, we also have a perverse way, from childhood, of inhibiting, stultifying and depressing that creativity by poor organisational design, inappropriate leadership, capability and the use of power to name but a few.

We have offered the principles and practices in this book to help build social organisations that allow the free expression of capability. We have had the privilege of working with people who have tried to do just that and if we, through this book, have contributed to that most worthwhile of endeavours, then we have realised our intention. It is for you to judge.

Bibliography

Ackoff, R.L. (1960) 'Systems, Organizations and Interdisciplinary Research', *General Systems Yearbook*, vol. 5, Society for General Systems Research, pp. 1–8.

Ackoff, R.L. (1999) *Ackoff's Best: His Classic Writings on Management*. New York: John Wiley & Sons.

Armstrong, M. (2000) *Rewarding Teams*. London: Chartered Institute of Personnel and Development.

Barnard, C. (1938) *The Functions of the Executive*. Cambridge, MA: Harvard University Press.

Barolsky, J. (1994) *A New Vision for the Company – Hamersley Iron Employee Relations and Change Management*. Perth: Hamersley Iron.

Becker, C. (1958) 'What Are Historical Facts?' in Snyder, P.L. (1958) *Detachment and the Writing of History: Essays and Letters of Carl L. Becker*. Ithaca, NY: Cornell University Press.

Beer, S. (1972) *The Brain of the Firm*. London: Allen Lane.

Belsky, J.K. (1990) *The Psychology of Aging Theory, Research, and Interventions*. Pacific Grove: Brooks/Cole Publishing Company.

Bennett, J. (1956–66) *The Dramatic Universe*. London: Hodder and Stoughton.

Bishop, W.S. (1989) *The Exercise of Discretion in the Work of Nursing: Nurses' Perceptions of Their Approach to Work*. D.P.A. Dissertation, University of Southern California, Los Angeles, CA.

Blanchard, K. (1985) *Leadership and the One Minute Manager*. Blanchard Management Corporation.

Blanchard, K. and Johnson, S. (1982) *The One Minute Manager*. New York: Morrow.

Blau, P.M. (1956) *Bureaucracy in modern society*. New York: Random House.

Bloom, B.S. and Krathwohl, D.R. (1956) *Taxonomy of Educational Objectives: The Classification of Educational Goals Handbook I: Cognitive Domain*. New York: Longmans, Green.

Boals, D.M. (1985) *Levels of Work and Responsibility in Public Libraries*. PhD Dissertation, University of Southern California, Los Angeles, CA.

Bolles, E.B., ed. (1997) *Galileo's Commandment: An Anthology of Great Science Writing*. New York: W.H. Freeman.

Boulding, K.E. (1989) *Three Faces of Power*. London: Sage.

Brown, W. (1960) *Exploration in Management*. London: Heinemann.

Brown, W. (1971) *Organization*. London: Heinemann.

Brown, W. and Jaques, E. (1965) *Glacier project papers, some essays on organisation and management from the Glacier project research*. London: Heinemann.

Burns, T. and Stalker, G.M. (1966, c1961) *The Management of Innovation*. London: Tavistock Publications.

Byrne, J.A. (2005) 'The Man Who Invented Management', *Business Week*, 28 November 2005, p. 104.

Caiden, G.E. (1982) *Public Administration* (2nd Ed), Pacific Palisades, CA: Palisades Publishers.

Caiden, G.E. (2004) 'A Cautionary Tale: Ten Major Flaws in Combating Corruption', *Southwestern Journal of Law and Trade in the Americas*, Volume X, No. 2, pp. 269–293.

Campbell, J. (1949) *The Hero With a Thousand Faces*. Princeton: Princeton University Press.

Carrison, D. and Walsh, R. (1999) *Semper Fi: Business Leadership the Marine Corps Way*. New York: AMACOM.

Cattell, R. (1971) *Abilities: Their Structure, Growth, and Action*. Boston: Houghton Mifflin.

Chandler, A.D., Jr. (1969, 1980) *Strategy and Structure: Chapters in the History of the Industrial Enterprise*. Cambridge, MA: MIT Press.

Chandler, A.D., Jr. (1990) *Scale and Scope*. Cambridge, MA: Belknap Press of Harvard University.

Chorover, S.L. (1979) *From Genesis to Genocide: The Meaning of Human Nature and the Power of Behavior Control*. Cambridge, MA: MIT Press.

Church, M. (1999) 'Organizing Simply for Complexity: Beyond Metaphor Towards Theory', *Long Range Planning*, Vol. 32, No. 4, pp. 425–440.

Churchman, C.W. (1968) *The Systems Approach*. New York: Delacorte Press.

Churchman, C.W. (1979) *The Systems Approach and Its Enemies*. New York: Basic Books.

Collins, J. (2001) *From Good to Great*. New York: Harper Collins.

Collins, J. and Porras, J. (1994) *Built to Last*. New York: Harper Collins.

Dahrendorf, R. (1985) 'Work and Life or the New Fear of Freedom', in Boekman (ed.) *Dignity at Work*. Stockholm: Streiffert.

Davenport, T. (1993) *Process Innovation*. Cambridge, MA: Harvard Business School Press.

Deming, W.E. (1982) *Out of the Crisis*. Boston: MIT Press.

Dewey, J. (1927) *The Public and Its Problems*. New York: Holt.

Drucker, P. (1954) *The Practice of Management*. New York: Harper.

Drucker, P. (1969) *The Age of Discontinuity*. New York: Harper and Row.

Dunlop, T. (1999) *Creating a Meritocracy*. Macdonald Associates Paper – unpublished.

Dunlop, T. (2000) *Core Social Process Skills for Leaders*. Macdonald Associates Paper – unpublished.

Dunning, R.A. and Richert, T.M. (2003) 'Applying Lessons from Lean Production Theory to Transit Planning', Advanced Transit Assocation. http://www.advancedtransit.org/doc.aspx?id=1129.

Eckes, G. (2000) *General Electric's Six Sigma Revolution: How General Electric and Others Turned Process Into Profits*. New York: Wiley.

Eckes, G. (2005) *Six Sigma Execution*. New York: McGraw-Hill.

Eckes, G. and Derickson, S. (2002) *Six Sigma Team Dynamics: The Elusive Key to Project Success*. New York: Wiley.

Emery, F.E., and Trist, E.L. (1960). 'Socio-technical systems', in C.W. Churchman and M. Verhulst (eds), *Management Science, Models and Techniques*. New York: Pergamon, pp. 83–97.

Fayol, H. (1930) *Industrial and General Administration*, translated from the French for the International Management Institute by J.A. Coubrough. London: Sir I. Pitman & Sons, Ltd.

Festinger, L. (1957) *A Theory of Cognitive Dissonance*. Palo Alto: Stanford University Press.

Frank, R.H. (1988) *Passions Within Reason: The Strategic Role of Emotions*. New York: W.W. Norton & Co.

Freedman, D.H. (2000) *Corps Business: The 30 Management Principles of the U.S. Marines*. New York: Harper Business Books.

Freud, S. (1923) *Das Ich und das Es*. Leipzig, Vienna, and Zurich: Internationaler Psycho-analytischer Verlag. English translation, Riviere, J. (trans.) (1927) *The Ego and the Id*. London: Hogarth Press and Institute of Psycho-analysis.

Friedman, T.L. (2000) *The Lexus and the Olive Tree* (updated and expanded edition). New York: Anchor Books.

Fuller, R. Buckminster (1969) *Operating Manual for Spaceship Earth*. New York: Simon and Schuster.

Gerth, H.H. and Mills, C.W. (1946) *From Max Weber: Essays in Sociology*. Translated, edited and with an introduction by H.H. Gerth and C. Wright Mills. New York: Oxford University Press.

Gladwell, M. (2005) *Blink: The Power of Thinking Without Thinking*. New York: Little Brown and Co.

Gleick, J. (1987) *Chaos – Making a New Science*. Harmondsworth: Penguin.

Goddard, H.H. (1919) *Psychology of the Normal and Subnormal*. New York: Dodd, Mead and Co.

Goldman, L.L. (1999) *Work Strata Selection as a Measurement of Law Enforcement Organizational Leadership*. D.P.A. Dissertation.

Goldratt, E. with Cox, J. (2004, First publication 1986) *The Goal: A Process of Ongoing Improvement*, 2nd rev. ed. Great Barrington, MA: North River Press.

Goleman, D. (1996) *Emotional Intelligence: And Why It Can Matter More Than IQ*. London: Bloomsbury.

Gould, D.P. (1984) *An Examination of Levels of Work in Academic Library Technical Services Departments Utilizing Stratified Systems Theory*. PhD Dissertation, University of Southern California, Los Angeles, CA.

Gould, S.J. (1996) *The Mismeasure of Man* (rev.edn). New York: W.W. Norton and Co.

Gray, J.L. (ed.) (1976) *The Glacier Project: Concepts and Critiques.* London: Heinemann.

Greenwood, T.G. (1994) *Lean Production Systems.* Alexandria, VA: APICS – The Performance Advantage.

Gulick, L. (1937) *Papers on the Science of Administration.* Edited by L. Gulick and L. Urwick. New York, Institute of Public Administration, Columbia University.

Hall, G., Rosenthal, J. and Wade, J. (1993) 'How to Make Re-engineering Really Work', in *Harvard Business Review*, November–December, pp. 119-131.

Hammer, M. (1990) 'Re-Engineering Work: Don't Automate – Obliterate', in *Harvard Business Review*, July–August, pp. 104–112.

Hammer. M. and Champy, J. (1993) *Reengineering the Corporation: A Manifesto for Business Revolution.* New York: Harper Business.

Handy, C. (1998) *The Hungry Spirit: Beyond Capitalism: A Quest for Purpose in the Modern World.* New York: Broadway Books.

Hargreaves, A. and Fink, D. (2005) *Sustainable Leadership.* San Francisco: Jossey-Bass.

Harper, B. (1992) *Rivethead.* New York: Warner Books.

Harvey, Jerry (1999) *How Come Every Time I Get Stabbed in the Back, My Fingerprints Are on the Knife?* San Francisco: Jossey-Bass.

Industrial Relations Magazine (1996) 'The Pilbara: A Mini Industrial Relations Laboratory'. March.

Ingersoll, R. (1993) *Some Reasons Why I Am a Freethinker.* Austin, TX: Amer Atheist Press.

Isaac, D.J. and O'Connor, B.M. (1978) '*A Discontinuity Theory of Psychological Development'* in Jaques E. et. al. (1978) *op. cit.*

Jaques, E. (1951) *The Changing Culture of a Factory.* London: Tavistock Publications.

Jaques, E. (1963) *Equitable Pay.* London: Heinemann Educational Books.

Jaques, E. (1976) *A General Theory of Bureaucracy.* London: Heinemann.

Jaques, E. (1982) *Free Enterprise, Fair Employment.* London: Heinemann.

Jaques, E. (1989) *Requisite Organization.* Falls Church: Cason Hall and Co.

Jaques, E. (1990) 'In Praise of Hierarchy', in *Harvard Business Review*, January, 127–133.

Jaques, E. (2002) *Life and Behaviour of Living Organisms: A General Theory.* Westport, CT: Preager.

Jaques, E. and Cason, K. (1994) Human Capability. London: Gower.

Jaques, E. (ed) with Gibson, R.O. and Isaac, D.J. (1978) *Levels of Abstraction in Logic and Human Action.* London: Heinemann.

Johnson, J. (1998) *Who Moved My Cheese?* New York: Putnam.

Jones, K. and Richert, T.M. (2000) *Training for Lean Construction I.* Chelmsford, MA: Linbeck Construction Corporation.

Kegan, R. (1982) *The Evolving Self.* Boston: Harvard University Press.

Kohlberg, L. in Mishcel, T. (1971) *Cognitive Development and Epistemology.* New York: Academic Press.

Kolbe, K. (1991) *Conative Connection: Acting on Intent.* Boston: Addison Wesley.

Kotter, J. (1999) 'What Effective General Managers Really Do', in *Harvard Business Reveiw*, March–April 1999.

Lavoisier, A-L. (1997) 'Preface to *The Elements of Chemistry'*, in Bolles, E.B., ed. (1997) *Galileo's Commandment: An Anthology of Great Science Writing.* New York: W.H. Freeman, pp. 379–388.

Lewin, K. (1951) *Field Theory in Social Science.* New York: Harper.

Ludeke, J.T. (1996) *A Line in the Sand.* Sydney: Allen and Unwin.

Macdonald, B. (2001) *Critical Incidents, Personality and Burn-out in Staff Working in an Intensive Care Unit.* Clinical Psychology Doctoral Thesis Cardiff University.

Macdonald, I. (1984) *Stratified Systems Theory: An Outline.* Individual and Organisational Capability Unit, BIOSS, Brunel University

Macdonald, I. (1990) *Identity Development of People with Learning Difficulties Through the Recognition of Work.* PhD, Brunel University.

Macdonald, I. (1995) *Statement to the Australian Industrial Relations Commission*. Evidence submitted to Commission.

Macdonald, I. and Couchman, T. (1980) *Chart of Initiative and Independence*. Slough: NFER.

Macdonald, I. and Grimmond, J. (2000) *Systems and Symbols Audit*. Unpublished paper for Macdonald Associates.

Macdonald, R. (1991) *Breaking the Frame: The Heart of Leadership*. MA Dissertation University of Southern California School of Policy, Planning and Development.

MacIver R.M. and Page, C.H. (1960) *Society*. London: Macmillan.

Marx, K. (1867; 1987 ed.) *Capital: A Critique of Political Economy*. Introduced by Ernest Mandel, trans. B. Fowkes. New York: Vintage Books.

Maslow, A.H. (1943) 'A Theory of Human Motivation', *Psychological Review*, 50, pp. 370–396.

Micklethwait, J. and Wooldridge, A. (1996) *The Witch Doctors: Making Sense of the Management Gurus*. New York: Times Books.

Micklethwait, J. and Wooldridge, A. (2003) *The Company*. London: Modern Library.

Mintzberg, H. (1989) *Mintzberg on Management: Inside Our Strange World of Organizations*. New York: Free Press.

Mosher, F. (1982) *Democracy and the Public Service*. New York: Oxford University Press.

Mu, D.P. (1993) *Managing Cross-Cultural Interchange: Interpreting Behavior for Mutual Understanding, the Case of China and the United States*. D.P.A. Dissertation, University of Southern California, School of Public Administration.

Mumford, E. and Hendricks, R. (1996) 'Business Process Re-engineering RIP', in *People Management*, Vol. 2, No. 9, pp. 22–26.

Munz, P. (1985) *Our Knowledge of the Growth of Knowledge: Popper or Wittgenstein?* London: Routledge and Kegan Paul.

Myers, I. Briggs and Myers, P.B. (1980) *Gifts Differing: Understanding Personality Type*. Palo Alto, CA: CPP Books, A Division of Consulting Psychologists Press, Inc.

Neustadt, R.E. and May, E.R. (1986) *Thinking in Time: The Uses of History for Decision Makers*. New York: The Free Press.

Newland, C. (1984) *Public Administration and Community: Realism in the Practice of Ideals*. McLean, VA: Public Administration Service.

Newland, C. 'Realism and Public Administration', *Public Administration Review*, Vol. 57, No. 2, M/A 1997, pp. ii–iii.

Orwell, G. (1945) *Animal Farm*. Harmondsworth, UK: Penguin Books.

Pateman, C. (1970) *Participation and Democratic Theory*. Cambridge, UK: Cambridge University Press.

Peters, T.J. and Waterman, R.H., Jr. (1982) *In Search of Excellence*. New York: Harper & Row Publishers.

Petzinger, T., Jr. (1997) 'Self-Organization Will Free Employees to Act Like Bosses', *Wall Street Journal*, 3 January, 1997, p. B1.

Piaget, J. (1971) *The Theory of Stages in Cognitive Development*. In Green, D.R., Ford, M.P. and Flamer, G.B. (eds.) *Measurement and Piaget*. Colombus: McGraw-Hill.

Popper, K.R. (1971) *The Open Society and Its Enemies*, 5th ed., rev., two Vols. Princeton, NJ: Princeton University Press.

Popper, K.R. (1972) *Objective Knowledge: An Evolutionary Approach*. Oxford: Clarendon Press.

Popper, K.R. (1992) *In Search of a Better World: Lectures and Essays from Thirty Years*. Trans. L.J. Bennett, with additional material by M. Mew. London; New York: Routledge.

Rappoport, C. (1994) 'Charles Handy Sees the Future', *Fortune*, Vol. 130, No. 9, 31 October, pp. 155–166.

Redford, E.S. (1969) *Democracy in the Administrative State*. New York: Oxford University Press.

Redford, E.S. and Blissett, M. (1981) *Organizing the Executive Branch: The Johnson Presidency*. Chicago: University of Chicago Press.

Ritzer, G. (1996) *The McDonaldization of Society*. California: Pine Forge Press.

Roethlisberger, F. and Dickson, W. (1939), with the assistance and collaboration of H.A. Wright. *Management and the Worker; An Account of a Research Program Conducted by the Western Electric Company, Hawthorne Works, Chicago*. Cambridge, MA: Harvard University Press.

Rousseau, Jean-Jacques (1762) *The Social Contract, or Principles of Political Right* (1968 trans.). London: Penguin Classics.

Rowbottom, R. and Billis, D. (1977) 'Stratification of Work and Organisational Design', in *Human Relations*, Vol. 30, No. 1, pp. 53–76.

Russell, B. (1938). *Power: A New Social Analysis*. London: Allen and Unwin.

Russell, B. (2004) *Power: A Radical View*. New York: Palgrave Macmillan.

Schutz, A. (1972) *The Phenomenology of the Social World*. London: Heinemann Educational Books Ltd.

Senge, Peter M. (1990) *The Fifth Discipline*. New York: Doubleday/Currency.

Shafritz, J., Ott, S. and Jang (2005) *Classics of Organisational Theory*. Belmont: Thomson/Wadsworth.

Simon, H. (1997) *Administrative Behavior: A Study of Decision-Making Processes in Administrative Organizations* (4th ed.). New York: The Free Press.

Sokal, A. and Bricmont, J. (1997) *Impostures Intellectuelles*. Paris: Editions Odile Jacob.

Stamp, G. (1978) 'Assessment of individual capacity' in Jaques, E. (ed) with Gibson, R.O. and Isaac, D.J. (1978) *Levels of Abstraction in Logic and Human Action*. London: Heinemann.

Stamp, G.P. (1986) 'Listening to My Story Has Been Really Interesting', A Guide to Career Path Appreciation. BIOSS Paper. Brunel University, Uxbridge, England.

Stewart (1994) 'CRA Pulls the Rug from Under Unions'. *Business Review Weekly*, 31 January, pp. 34–39.

Stillman, R.J. II (1998) *Creating the American State: The Moral Reformers and the Modern Administrative World They Made*. Tuscaloosa: University of Alabama Press.

Taylor, C. (2000) 'The Power of Culture: Turning the Soft Stuff Into Business Advantage', in *The Power of Culture: Driving Today's Organisation*. Sydney: McGraw-Hill Australia.

Taylor, C. (2005) *Walking the Talk: Building a Culture for Success*. London: Random House.

Taylor, F.W. (1972, c1947, orig. Harper, 1911) *Scientific Management; Comprising Shop Management, The Principles of Scientific Management [and] Testimony Before the Special House Committee*. With a foreword by Harlow S. Person. Westport, CT: Greenwood Press.

Trinca, H. (1997) 'The Art of War' in the *Sydney Morning Herald*. 8 December 1997, p. 11.

Tussman, J. (1960) *Obligation and the Body Politic*. New York: Oxford University Press.

US Department of Labor, Bureau of Labor Statistics (2004), Table A-1. Fatal Occupational Injuries by Industry and Event or Exposure, All United States, 2004, p. 1.

US Department of Labor, Bureau of Labor Statistics (1995), Home Page. http://www.bls.gov/iif/home.htm#tables.

Waldo, D. (1984) *The Administrative State: A Study of the Political Theory of American Public Administration*, 2nd ed. New York: Holmes & Meier.

Waldo, R. (1991) *Performance Improvements Through Just-In-Time (JIT) Work Teams*, AME Research Report.

Wall Street Journal, 'Disengaged at Work?', 13 March 2001, p. A1.

Watson, D. (2004) *Watson's Dictionary of Weasel Words, Contemporary Clichés, Cant and Management Jargon*. Milsons Point: Random House.

Way, N. (1994) *Business Review Weekly*. Fairfax. 31 January, pp. 34–39.

Weber, M. (1922) 'Bureaucracy' in Shafritz, J., Ott, S. and Jang (2005) *Classics of Organisational Theory*. Belmont: Thomson/Wadsworth.

Weber, M. (1947) *The Theory of Social and Economic Organization*. Trans. Henderson, A.M. and Parsons, T. New York: The Free Press.

Whyte, D. (2001) *Crossing the Unknown Sea*. New York: Riverhead Books.

Womack, J. and Jones, D. (1996) *Lean Thinking*. New York: Simon & Schuster.

Zimm, A.A. (2002) *Manifestations of Chaos in an Economic Theory of the Organization*. Doctoral Dissertation, University of Southern California, School of Policy Planning and Development.

Index